The Thunder
Of Justice

Picture courtesy of T. S. Bruchalski

St. John Bosco's Prophetic Dream. The "Twin Pillars of Victory" were the subject of a prophetic dream of John Bosco in 1862. It was revealed to him that peace in the world would come only after a fierce battle in which the Pope would triumph by anchoring Peter's barque, the Church, to the secure pillars of the Eucharist and a fervent true devotion to Mary.

The Thunder Of Justice

The Warning
The Miracle
The Chastisement
The Era Of Peace

God's Ultimate Acts Of Mercy

By Ted and Maureen Flynn

MaxKol Communications, Inc.

Written, compiled, and edited by Ted and Maureen Flynn
Library of Congress Catalog Card Number 92-073598
Published by MaxKol Communications, Inc. © Copyright 1993
ISBN: 0-9634307-0-X

Published in the United States of America
Picture of Planet Earth provided by NASA

Copies of this book may be obtained by contacting:
Maxkol Communications, 109 Executive Drive, Suite D, Sterling, VA 20166
Tel. (703) 709-0200; Fax (703) 709-1499

Dedicated To
Colleen and Danny

who have been a source of great joy
Ad Majorem Dei Gloriam

Declarations

Since the abolition of Canon 1399 and 2318 of the former Canonical Code, publications about new appearances, revelations, prophecies, miracles, etc., have been allowed to be distributed and read by the faithful without the express permission of the Church, providing they contain nothing which contravenes faith and morals. This means no imprimatur is necessary when distributing information on new apparitions not yet judged by the Church. The authors wish to manifest unconditional submission to the final and official judgement of the Magisterium of the Church regarding any events presently under investigation.

In *Lumen Gentium*, Vatican II, Chapter 12, the Council Fathers urged the faithful to be open and attentive to the ways in which the Holy Spirit continues to guide the Church, including private revelations. We hear: "Such gifts of grace, whether they are of special enlightenment or whether they are spread more simply and generally, must be accepted with gratefulness and consolation, as they are specially suited to and useful for, the needs of the Church.... Judgements as to their genuineness and their correct use lies with those who lead the Church and those whose special task is not to extinguish the Spirit but to examine everything and keep that which is good."

Table Of Contents

Acknowledgements

We thank Our Lord and His mother for the extraordinary gift of grace that we have received for reasons only Heaven can fathom. When we started compiling information, we never believed we would find such a rich vein of spiritual treasure. We have caught a glimpse of the profound mystery that is now unfolding for all the world to witness. Soon all will call Mary "Queen."

We thank our parents for all their support over the years in our adventurous endeavors, no matter the subject. We would never have done it without you.

A very warm and special thanks to Jim O'Rourke. In the late evenings while sifting through the massive amounts of material and trying to make sense of it all, a verse kept running through my mind regarding you, Jim: "Well done, good and faithful servant." Many thanks to the Gonzales family, Dr. and Mrs. Francis B. Hennessey, Stan Karminski, Bud MacFarlane, Bernie Marcotte, Malachi Martin, Rick Rotondi, Ron Stone, and friends who have had a hand in this effort—to you we are grateful.

To all of our friends at Signs of the Times—"the army of the faithful" spoken of in the messages—our magazine, *Signs of the Times*, and this book would never have seen the light of day if it were not for you. Tens of thousands of people world-wide for the last five years have been reading the result of your work. The Lord knows who you are.

Ted and Maureen Flynn
September 8, 1993

Foreword

Only a very distracted and unaware Christian of today could have avoided receiving at least a fleeting impression, by the "long hot summer" of 1993, that for a number of years now there has been a steady build-up of events—in the broadest sense of that word—all of which indicate that humanity as a whole and the Holy Roman Catholic Church in particular have reached a fateful threshold beyond which lies a new condition of human affairs.

Literally, every decade of this one century alone has piled one on the other, what Christ called "the signs of the times" (Matt:16 1-4).

In a general way of speaking, it is quasi-impossible to have totally escaped any awareness of these events, and the clamor of the claimant participants. Visions. Appearances. Messages. Predictions. Warnings. Interpretations. Weeping statues and bleeding icons. Miraculous spring waters. Spontaneous cures. Spinning dances of the sun, and eclipses of the moon. Little children telling the future. Uneducated men and women instructing popes and presidents. Nationwide publicity tours by bearers of special revelations. Throughout all of this, an obvious emphasis on the singular role of the Blessed Virgin Mary of Nazareth as the Queen of Heaven, Mother of All the Living, and—not surprisingly—as the Mediatrix of All Graces is pervasive.

It is as if the words of the prophet Joel were being fulfilled: "In those times, God said, I will pour out My Spirit upon all flesh. Your sons and your daughters shall prophesy. Your old men shall dream dreams. Your young men shall see visions" (Joel 3:1).

But such exultancy is soberly contrasted with the other side of this century's carnage. For this is a century that has witnessed and is still witnessing scenes of unmitigated horrors. The industrial slaughter of planned wars, of literally millions of men, women and children killed. The wiping out—sometimes as it were, overnight, of mighty empires. An ever-widening ripple of infanticide running to well over a billion in the last fifty years. An ever-climbing number of fratricidal wars—

245, at the date of this writing, are in progress. Waves of tortures and persecutions on all five continents. A continual stream of natural disasters without known parallel in human history as we know it. This world scene is overhung by a generalized economic depression, and the clear emergence of an as yet skeletal one-world government that is professionally secular, frighteningly dangerous for human liberty, and in dim outline resembles George Orwell's portrait of "Big Brother" in his *1984* scenario.

We are confronted today by an ocean of events, a deluge of details, a quickening kaleidoscope of happenings. It is a situation made to order to leave us confused and in disequilibrium. It is in such circumstances that men and women are prone to inaccurate judgements and therefore foolish counterproductive actions. Unhappy are those of us who, being largely self-convinced, rashly predict the actual dates and times and places and events of that new expected condition of our world. For, in ourselves and of ourselves, we can find no authentic consolation. And we need consoling. Tender consoling. For we are not a happy race.

Unfortunate and hopeless are those who, though at least vaguely aware, have for one reason or another, no source of enlightenment, no providential norm of right reason for calculating the likelihoods of our situation. For, without that precious light from on high, we can surely entertain no solid confidence beyond that of merely human hope—which can be a good companion, but is never more than a blind guide. The most pathetic among us are those who are especially skillful in analyzing material trends like the weather, the stock market, the latest political omens, and the most up-to-date vogue in fashions and sexual mores, but who cannot read what Christ emphasized as those telltale "signs of the times." The usually mild and loving Lord Jesus described such people as an "evil and adulterous generation" and dismissed them from His serious consideration.

Needed above all else, in this situation, are the bare facts, the truths as far as we can ascertain them of those happenings which emphasize the special role of the Blessed Virgin Mary, and which seem to have taken place for our instruction. For even the most prejudiced as well as the most lukewarm minds in regard to her must have willy-nilly remarked on the primacy of place accorded to her shining figure throughout the multifarious history of events many ascribe in all good faith to God's direct intervention into our world of the senses, as well to the preference of her Divine Son that this be recognized as the Age of Mary.

We need more than anything else a manual that, in an orderly fashion, gives us the most accurate history of those matters. It must be as complete as possible with the relevant details, but be an easy reference book. It must be non-partisan, yet clearly on the side of the angels. It must provide a solid basis for human credence, but not tempt to idle speculation or anticipate exaggeratedly the final judgement of the Church's teaching authority which alone can transform our human credence into divine faith. For that, and nothing short of that, is the only purpose worthy of a Christian's attention in these strange times at the end of the second millennium.

This volume by Ted and Maureen Flynn seems, in this writer's eyes, to embody all the characteristics listed above. It is much more than a mere computer read-out of bare facts, and much more helpful than a would-be "objective" account—the utopian ideal vaunted by most un-neutral observers.

For it has been put together in great reliance on the wisdom of her whom Catholics address as the mother of the Incarnate Wisdom, the holy bearer of Our Lord Jesus Christ.

It is being published for all God's children whoever they are; and it is being launched with that very ancient prayer of firm expectancy which Saint John expressed familiarly in words from his native Aramaic: "Maranatha!" Come Lord! Come Lord Jesus!

Malachi B. Martin
Feast of the Assumption
August 15, 1993

I Am Calling Them All

"The time has come when I will make myself more manifest in the Church, through increasingly greater signs. My tears are shed in many places to call everyone back to the sorrowful Heart of their mother. The tears of a mother succeed in moving the most hardened hearts. But now my tears, even tears of blood, leave many of my children completely indifferent. My messages...will become all the more frequent the more the voice of the ministers refuses to proclaim the truth."

Marian Movement of Priests
October 30, 1975

The Handwriting On The Wall

"You have defied the Lord of Heaven, you have had the vessels from His Temple brought to you, and you, your noblemen, your wives and your singing women have drunk your wine out of them. You have praised gods of gold and silver, of bronze and iron, of wood and stone, which cannot either see, hear or understand; but you have given no glory to the God Who holds your breath and all your fortunes in His hands. That is why He has sent the hand which, by itself, has written these words. The writing reads: MENE, MENE, TEKEL, and PARSIN. The meaning of the words is this: MENE, God has measured your sovereignty and put an end to it; TEKEL, you have been weighed in the balance and found wanting; PARSIN, your kingdom has been divided and given to the Medes and the Persians."

Daniel 5:23-28

Book I
A Call To Change

1

The Wake-Up Call: The Urgency Of Our Times

A chastisement worse than the flood is about to come upon this poor and perverted humanity. Fire will descend from Heaven and this will be the sign that the justice of God has as of now fixed the hour of His great manifestation. I am weeping because the Church is continuing along the road of division, of loss of the true faith, of apostasy and of errors which are being spread more and more without anyone offering opposition to them. Even now, that which I predicted at Fatima and that which I have revealed here in the third message confided to a little daughter of mine is in the process of being accomplished. And so, even for the Church the moment of its great trial has come, because the man of iniquity will establish himself within it and the abomination of desolation will enter into the holy temple of God.

Our Lady through Father Don Stefano Gobbi,
September 15, 1987 at Akita, Japan
The Feast of Our Lady of Sorrows

The Twentieth Century is witnessing a phenomenon that has simply grown too big for any reasonable person to ignore. The supernatural explodes in our midst on a near-daily basis. Because the manifestation of evil in this century is undeniably extreme, Heaven is pouring out great and unprecedented graces to provide us with the means necessary to rise above the moral decay that threatens to destroy us. Sin abounds, but grace abounds even more. Our Lady states the reasons for her warnings are to prepare us for the Second Coming of Jesus Christ. It is being stated in very clear and concise terms. The Holy Trinity has sent Mary, the Mother of God, Mother of the Church, our mother, to warn us.

The messages plead for our attention, but many refuse to listen. The hardness of men's hearts makes it difficult to hear the trumpets of Heaven. Statues weep human tears and blood, the young prophesy, religious communities sprout up, messengers receive warnings, Mary raises up an army of the devout, and reported apparitions of Mary appear at a frequency never seen before in all of recorded history.

People are being asked to turn back to God without delay. God is using apparitions (heavenly appearances) and locutions (interior messages) because other means have failed. He has warned us repeatedly that the times of His Mercy are about to come to an end, and the times of His Justice are commencing.

These apparitions have yielded a wealth of messages as well as remarkable fruits: millions of conversions world-wide; the reorientation of life towards the spiritual; and physical, mental, moral, and spiritual healings. An entire culture is arising spontaneously from the powerful shared experiences of those who have been touched by the unexpected and the supernatural. This culture is articulating itself through and by means of Marian centers, publishing houses, prayer groups, and alternative media networks. Many persons come away convinced that in the eyes of God, they are forgiven and loved, and infinitely important for the fulfillment of Heaven's plan.

Mary: Chosen Prophetess Of Our Age

Through this current deluge of apparitions and locutions, the Blessed Virgin Mary is issuing a wake-up call. She describes a huge battle now taking place. Satan has unleashed the full power of all his demons, for Heaven has granted him a century—this Twentieth Century—in which to do his very worst to try to destroy the Church. Satan's final goal is to extinguish the light of faith from the face of the earth, which Satan had boasted he could do. Pope Leo XIII had a vision of a confrontation between God and Satan. Pope Leo was made to understand that Satan would be allowed one hundred years to tempt and try to destroy the Church. In the vision, Satan chose for his one hundred years the Twentieth Century. He is full of furious activity, for he knows that his time is short.

The battle now being waged in the heavens will soon be played out in awesome fury before our eyes—in the very skies, in the seas, and on the ground. This battle cannot be understood or believed outside of the realm of faith. We are witnessing the intercession of the Blessed Virgin Mary, Queen of Heaven and true beacon for all Christians. It is now part of God's plan to have the "Woman Clothed with the Sun" (Revelation 12:1) appear throughout the world, to offer His people a safe haven in her Immaculate Heart.

The final battle is coming very soon. The remnant who will survive will be small in number. Yet there is one place of safety where all can be protected from the approaching storm: the ark of Our Lady's Immaculate Heart, full of maternal love for Jesus and for us. She is calling all of her children to enter, by acts of consecration to that Heart. The Chastisement is near. Our Lady invites us all to enter her refuge.

As the "purification" or the "chastisement" unfolds, we can expect the Church to be horribly persecuted—apparently almost destroyed. Mary warns that the earth will endure "three days of darkness" without the light of Christ, as Christ Himself spent three days in the earth. Yet at the end of this purification will come a resurrection in glory and the Era of Peace. Here is our source of hope as the Lord is the victor, and the scourge of sin is wiped away.

According to the prophecies of many Marian apparitions, the earth, the seas, and the skies will manifest destruction on a massive scale. Scripture states that when Jesus died the earth quaked, the skies produced lightning and thunder, darkness came over the whole land, and the veil in the Temple was torn asunder (Matthew 27:45-54). In today's world, with its materialistic philosophies and increasing sinfulness, it will not be long before the earth once more manifests its violent grief.

Before that happens, Mary declares there will be a warning and a great miracle. The warning will be a mysterious world-wide event, in which each individual will perceive the state of his or her own soul as God sees it. The warning is a call to change our ways. Within a year of the warning, a miracle—a great supernatural sign—will follow, which will be permanent, visible, and totally inexplicable by science. A short time after the miracle, terrible chastisement will follow, and only after a thorough "purification" will come an "Era of Peace." This will not be the end of the world as many may think, but the dawn of a new epoch, a new age in which God is adored.

The messages form a road map for our future. They speak of the sinful state of the world today and mention "secrets" that concern events to come. A series of cataclysmic events (both natural and supernatural) upon the earth will make mankind realize that God exists and that salvation should be our focus. We have forgotten that ultimately all of human life comes down to a simple choice of Heaven or hell; and Heaven apparently intends very soon to use powerful means of persuasion on a scale never before witnessed in the history of the world. Genesis shows us the extreme displeasure of Yahweh with His people; so great was His displeasure that God regretted making man, as Genesis 6:6 tells us. God cleansed the entire world by Flood; events of similar severity are prophesied by many reliable sources having Church approval.

Mary has the heart of a mother, one who lives for all her children. She is reaching out to those far away, the sinners, the atheists, those who reject God, those who fight against Him, and those who hate Him. She wants to help all men as their mother—for the hour is late.

The View Of The Theologians

The theologian Karl Rahner has pointed out that we are moved much more readily and effectively by those divine interventions that we call apparitions than by abstract teachings of knowledgeable theologians or the hierarchy of the Church.[1]

One of the greatest theologians in the history of Catholicism, Saint Thomas Aquinas, wrote in his *Summa*, "...In all ages, men have been divinely instructed in matters expedient for the salvation of the elect...and in all ages there have been persons possessed of the spirit of prophecy, not for the purpose of announcing new doctrines, but to direct human actions." It is apparent that what Saint Thomas is telling us is that private prophecy has a function, an important one. It is certainly a result of divine Providence, although no one is required to accept private revelations. According to Saint Thomas, most people seem to need the encouragement provided by private revelations as an aid to their salvation.[2]

Visionaries From Around The Globe

The messages given for the world originate with "visionaries" from every part of the globe, from enormously varied educational backgrounds and social classes. For example, Italian priest Father Stefano Gobbi currently receives detailed locutions that have resulted in the formation of an international 55,000-member Marian Movement of Priests. Father Gobbi once asked Our Lady, "Why do you not choose someone more suitable and capable than me?" Our Blessed Mother answered him, "My son I have chosen you because you are the least apt instrument; thus no one will say that this is your work." The movement began in 1972 and messages continue to this very day, each year becoming more specific.

Apparitions of the Blessed Mother are occurring in rural as well as urban and suburban areas, and on all continents of the globe. No place on earth is untouched by her presence. She seeks out the little-known places of the world, where the poor and the unfortunate live.

The current Marian times had their beginning in 1830, when Our Blessed Mother appeared to Catherine Laboure in the convent at Rue de Bac, in Paris, France, as the Mediatrix of all Graces, and gave the Miraculous Medal to the world. One side of the medal had an image of the two hearts: the Immaculate Heart of Mary and the Sacred Heart of Jesus. The other had an image of Our Lady with arms extended and rays of grace streaming from her hands.

Sixteen years after Rue de Bac, on September 19, 1846, Our Blessed Mother appeared to children at LaSalette in the French Alps. Mary spoke to the young children, Melanie Calvat and Maximin Giraud, about many things that upset her Son. She told them in 1864 that many demons would be unleashed from hell. LaSalette was approved by the Church in 1851. Pope Pius IX then proclaimed the dogma of the Immaculate Conception in 1854.

Four years later, in 1858, Our Blessed Mother appeared to a peasant girl, Bernadette Soubirous at Lourdes, France, announcing herself as the Immaculate Conception—confirming the dogma proclaimed by Pius IX. Bernadette had never heard the term until told by Our Blessed Mother.

Mary's next major apparition was at Fatima, Portugal, in 1917, to three children. She asked for all of the bishops of the world to unite and consecrate Russia to her Immaculate Heart. If this did not take place, she warned, Russia would spread her errors throughout the world. She warned that serious consequences would follow if Russia was not consecrated. This occurred prior to the Russian revolution in 1917.

In 1961, Mary appeared in Garabandal, Spain, where requests for the consecration of Russia again were not heeded. At Garabandal, she told the visionaries that the cup of God's justice was filling and that many sacrifices must be made, much penance done to avert divine punishment. In 1973, at Akita, Japan, Mary repeated that message, speaking of a chastisement worse than the flood that could converge on humanity if mankind does not convert.

In Medjugorje, in former Yugoslavia, six children (now young adults) in a rural village have been seeing Mary daily and receiving messages from the Blessed Mother since 1981. That remote village has been visited by an estimated 15 million pilgrims and 15,000 clergy. It has been the hub of Marian devotion in these times. Whereas Fatima was the most significant apparition for the early part of the Twentieth Century, Medjugorje is meeting the spiritual needs of this generation in the latter part of this century. His Eminence Joseph Cardinal Ratzinger has stated in *The Ratzinger Report*, "One of the signs of our times is that the announcements of 'Marian Apparitions' are multiplying all over the world."

With this frequency of events, we must not only focus so much on the phenomena as much as we should ask why. Why is Mary appearing? Here is a critical question we must honestly ponder in our hearts. Tears of water have been commonly observed and recently tears of blood on statues in many parts of the world. We have been told the significance of the statues with blood means the chastisement is near.

Scripture states that natural disasters such as famines, earthquakes, and signs in the sun, moon, and stars will provide warnings preceding the Second Coming of Jesus. Although "no man knows the day or the hour" (Matthew 24:36), Jesus has given us signs we should be watching for when this time approaches. Sixteen years ago, Pope Paul VI said he saw a definite pattern of events unfolding which gave him concern, that these may be the end times. Paul VI was a cautious man who spoke reservedly, yet still he made this observation. In 1977, one year before his death, he wrote: "There is a great uneasiness, at this time, in the world and in the Church, and that which is in question is the faith. It so happens now that I repeat to myself the obscure phrase of Jesus in the Gospel of Saint Luke: 'When the Son of Man returns, will He still find faith on the earth?' (Luke 18:8). It so happens that there are books coming out in which the faith is in retreat on some important points. The episcopates are remaining silent and these books are not looked upon as strange. This to me is strange.

" I sometimes read the Gospel passage of the end times and I attest that, at this time, some signs of this end are emerging. Are we close to the end? This we will never know. We must always hold ourselves in readiness, but everything could last a very long time yet. What strikes me when I think of the Catholic world is that within Catholicism there seems sometimes to predominate a non-Catholic way of thinking, and it can happen that this non-Catholic thought within Catholicism will tomorrow become the stronger. But it will never represent the thought of the Church. *It is necessary that a small flock subsist, no matter how small it might be.*"[3]

For all the dire warnings, we must not lose hope. Jesus is the victor, and He will not allow Satan to overcome His Church. Scripture has promised that evil will at last be purged from the earth. We must not lose hope during some dark nights ahead. The Bible says the very gates of hell will not prevail against the Church. Saint Augustine once said, "that which man builds man destroys, but the city of God is built by God and cannot be destroyed by man."

Mary indicates, in various apparitions, that her messages are meant for all peoples, and not for Catholics alone. Mary says the Catholic Church has the fullest expression of the many gifts which have been given to mankind for salvation and perseverance in battle against the devil's constant wiles; but she is the mother of everyone on earth.

The Blessed Mother asks each person of faith for a personal decision to strive for holiness. She stresses the necessity of making the commitment to "pray, pray, pray," not merely with the lips but from the heart. She tells us to fast, to be reconciled with God and neighbor, in order to attain peace for ourselves and peace for the world. The messages require change in our lives.

Mary has said of our age, "it is a time that is worse than the flood." Like ancient Nineveh, we are inches from destruction; but just as Nineveh averted catastrophe by accepting the warnings of Jonah and turning from its sins, we too can mitigate divine justice with prayer, penance, and fasting. God will never abandon His people if they respond. In Scripture, God warns the people of Israel on 177 different occasions for rejecting His infinite love and mercy. Seventy times, Israel responded favorably and was blessed. On 107 times, Israel did not heed the warnings and was greatly chastised for long periods of time. And here lies the deep mystery of our planet that hangs in the balance.[4]

God's Little Army

History and Scripture give us many examples of God communicating with His people and prophets. When King Nebuchadnezzar needed a dream interpreted he sought the advice of a young man named Daniel to whom "God gave knowledge and understanding of all kinds of literature and learning. Daniel could understand visions and dreams of all kinds" (Daniel 1:17).

The same was true for the Magi who looked for the birthplace of the Messiah. The story of salvation was in the stars and they knew the signs to follow (Matthew 2:2). They were warned in a dream that they should travel home by another route. The Magi were a learned group of men to whom God had given understanding. They were given a task and fulfilled it. Heaven was speaking and guiding them in a way they could understand. Scripture is filled with such events. *Those with knowledge and understanding of the ways of God are given glimpses of the future for the good of the general population. As the Nicene Creed says, "God has spoken through the prophets."* The prophets are a mouthpiece for the good of the people. It is an act of love when God warns us of impending danger or calls us back to follow His will.

Although God is extremely generous bestowing His graces, the number who respond is often small. Just like the army raised by Gideon in the Old Testament (Judges 7:4)—which God cut from 10,000 to 300 soldiers—people responding to Mary's messages are but a tiny fraction of the Church. But Mary promises victory to her cohorts. And, as was the case with Gideon, the very smallness of the movement will be a powerful witness that the victory is truly the Lord's.

Multiplicity Of Appearances

Currently, hundreds of Marian apparitions are being reported. A storm is approaching, and grace is telling us where our safety lies. In Medjugorje, Mary has said she will appear if necessary in every single household. Her love and concern for her children is that great in these troubled times.

The content of messages from even highly-regarded visionaries may not prove to be one hundred percent accurate. All messages must undergo the discernment process of ecclesiastical authorities. However, it remains true that a thorough and broad sampling of Our Lady's messages throughout the world yields a remarkable sense of consistency and logical development. The major issue we should be aware of is that the warnings are from Mary herself, the Queen of all Prophets, the Prophetess of our times. In addition, so many similar messages coming from such a pool of culturally disparate visionaries cannot be dismissed. Logically speaking, both the frequency and consistency of an event increasingly eliminate the probability of chance. Apparitions are happening at such a frequency we can no longer ignore the facts. The messages should be read with an open heart.

Just as apparitions are increasing, so too are locutions to specific souls increasing in frequency. An interior locution is not something strange or sensational. Rather, it is a mystical phenomenon present in the life of the Church and described in spiritual writings. In a locution, one does not see with the eyes, hear with the ears, touch with the body. Nor is a locution simply a good inspiration, that light which the Holy Spirit normally causes to pour down into the minds and hearts of those who pray and live by faith.

The interior locution is that gift by which God wishes to make something known and to help someone carry something out. The person becomes an instrument of communication while receiving the Word from Our Lord, or in the case of many of the locutions in this book, from Our Blessed Mother. The person receiving simply becomes a vessel of God to provide messages. In the history of the Catholic Church, this mystical phenomenon is not unusual.[5]

Our Blessed Mother told us through Father Gobbi in a message given September 18, 1988, that we have a period of ten years—ten decisive years: **"In this period of ten years there will come to completion the time of the great tribulation, which has been foretold to you in Holy Scripture, before the Second Coming of Jesus. In this period of ten years the mystery of iniquity, prepared for by the ever increasing spread of apostasy will become manifest. In this period of ten years all the secrets which I have revealed to some of my children will come to pass and all the events which have been foretold to you by me will take place."**

The foundation of our faith is Jesus Christ revealed to us both through Scripture and Tradition. Anything that detracts from this is heresy. The role of Mary does not detract but is meant to shine a light on Jesus. Her role is to glorify the Father, and at the same time be a messenger to His people.

As John the Baptist prepared the way for the first coming of Jesus, Mary prepares the way for His Second Coming. Mary proclaims that a new world and era is upon us, and the triumph of Her Immaculate Heart and the Second Pentecost (the outpouring of the Holy Spirit) will usher in the Reign of the Sacred Heart of Jesus. The Blessed Mother spoke through Father Gobbi On October 13, 1990, about the glorious reign of Jesus and His Second Coming: "The glorious reign of Christ, which will be established in your midst with the Second Coming of Jesus in the world is close at hand. This is His return in glory. This is His glorious return, to establish His reign in your midst and to bring all humanity, redeemed by His Most Precious Blood, back to the state of His new terrestrial paradise. **That which is being prepared is so great that its equal has never existed since the creation of the world."**

2

The Grand Finale: The Explosion Of The Supernatural Today

And afterward, I will pour out my spirit on all people. Your sons and your daughters will prophesy, your old men will dream dreams, and your young men will see visions. Even upon the servants, both men and women, I will pour out my Spirit in those days. I will show wonders in the heavens and on the earth, blood and fire and billows of smoke. The sun will be turned to darkness and the moon to blood before the coming of the great and dreadful day of the Lord. And everyone who calls on the name of the Lord will be saved; for on Mount Zion and in Jerusalem there will be deliverance, as the Lord has said, among the survivors whom the Lord calls.

Joel 3: 1-5

Mary's Plan

In a message dated November 9, 1984, Mary told Father Gobbi her plan for our times. Our Blessed Mother stated, "In these messages, I also reveal to you my plan in its silent preparation, in its painful realization, and in its victorious fulfillment.

"You are already about to reach the most painful and bloody conclusion of the purification which will take place in these years, before the great triumph of my Immaculate Heart in the coming to you of the glorious reign of Jesus. This is the plan which embraces this century: In 1917 at Fatima, I anticipated it, as in a prophetic announcement, at the moment when the great struggle between the Woman clothed with the sun and the Red Dragon became evident, a struggle which was to last throughout the whole century, as a proud challenge to God on the part of my Adversary, who was certain that he would succeed in destroying the Church and in bringing all humanity to a universal rejection of God.

"The Lord has granted him this space of time, because in the end the pride of the Red Dragon will be broken and conquered by the humility, the littleness, and the power of your heavenly Mother, the Woman clothed with the sun, who is now gathering all her little children into her army, drawn up for battle.

"Now that you are coming to the most painful and bloody years of this great struggle, I have intervened personally in order to form for myself my cohort through the Marian Movement of Priests, which is my work."

The Signs Of These Times

This chapter explores several signs of these times, both natural and supernatural. The pre-eminent sign of the present age is Mary. People from all parts of the planet are reporting strong messages of love and warnings from the Blessed Mother of Jesus Christ. She fits the description of the "great sign:" the "Woman clothed with the sun" of Revelation, Chapter 12, where Saint John prophesied her appearance as signifying "the end times."

These widespread reports of appearances of Mary, the "Woman clothed with the sun," are accompanied by many well-documented and scientifically inexplicable phenomena, which are also "signs." The appearance of the "great sign" is a fulfillment of Saint John's prophecy, indicating that we may indeed be in the "end times;" the special era immediately preceding the Second Coming of Jesus, for which Scripture solemnly warns us to be prepared.

Marian apparitions are not new. Throughout Church history, God has sent Mary, the Mother of the Church, to her children as a special sign of hope in troubled times. God sends "signs" not only to console His people with the assurance that He has not abandoned them, but also to warn them of how far they have gone astray and to help them get back on track. The multiplication of reports of Marian apparitions in our day and the "signs and wonders" being experienced by millions of ordinary people are indications both of deep spiritual crises and of very great hope. God's people may be losing sight of Him, but He has not lost sight of us. He is very much present and concerned over our deepening alienation from Him. His personal intervention is necessary and imminent. He is sending His very best messenger, His most treasured soul—His own mother—to warn us, to shelter us, to form us, to prepare us in every possible way so that we may be ready for the day of His coming in the very near future. We cannot fully grasp it all so we must open our hearts as little children. As the Scripture says, "Unless you become like one of these little children...."

Marian Times

In Scripture, Jesus speaks about "the signs of the times." For example: "The Pharisees and Sadducees to test him asked if he would show them a sign from Heaven. He replied, 'In the evening you say, it will be fine; there is a red sky'—and in the morning, 'Stormy weather today; the sky is red and overcast.' You know how to read the face of the sky, but how is it you cannot read the signs of the times?" (Matthew 16:1-3).

Signs of the times also can refer to Heaven's direct response to an epoch's spiritual status, with special supernatural graces sent from Heaven to correct the conscience of an age. Heaven has been flooding us with signs of the times, especially throughout our century, with a growing sense of urgency. As the events which characterize our age become more violent and openly demonic (abortion being the clearest sign of the times imaginable of this negative progression), Heaven's warnings are becoming more extravagant, more impassioned, and more ominous. In this sense, we feel we are beginning to see the signs of the times spoken of by the prophet Daniel and in the New Testament as including "wars, and rumors of wars." These signs increasingly point to a chastisement. Mary's messages tell us in simple terms that the era of God's mercy is ending, and the era of God's justice is about to begin. However, in our age of self-gratification and self-love, people do not want to hear about the justice of God.

These times can easily be recognized as the "Marian Times" prophesied long ago in the writings of various saints, who saw that as God chose to send Jesus to us the first time through a virgin, Mary, so He will choose the same for His Second Coming. This truth is not declared outright in Scripture, nor can it be deduced by logical necessity. It is rather a matter of private revelation and a developing understanding under the guidance of the Holy Spirit of Mary's role in salvation history. Vatican II affirms that the "reason" for Mary's role is simply God's good pleasure.

Although Marian theology has developed over the centuries, the underlying concepts were present in the very earliest practices of the Church and are seen in many writings of the Church Fathers that date from the Second Century, according to the famous Nineteenth Century theologian, John Cardinal Newman. Tenets of Marian theology have often excited controversy throughout Church history, yet they have passed the tests of discernment of the Church as a whole many times. A deep Marian perspective enriches rather than obscures our understanding of God's wisdom, and it is definitely presaged in Scripture. Mary as "a sign" is denoted in Scripture, always as the Mother of the great King—never in her own capacity. Similarly, Mary never appears on earth to glorify herself; **her mission is to lead us by the shortest possible route to her Son.** She is sent to us as a gift and should be perceived as such. The following Scriptures depict Mary, with her Son, as a sign.

"Therefore the Lord Himself shall give you a **sign**; Behold, a virgin shall conceive, and bear a son, and shall call his name Immanuel" (Isaiah 7:14).

"And this shall be a **sign** unto you; Ye shall find the babe wrapped in swaddling clothes and lying in a manger" (Luke 2:12). "And they came with haste, and found Mary, and Joseph, and the babe lying in a manger" (Luke 2:16).

"And Simeon blessed them, and said unto Mary, his mother, behold, this child is set for the fall and rising again of many in Israel; and for a **sign** which shall be spoken against; yea, a sword shall pierce through thine own soul also, that the thoughts of many hearts may be revealed" (Luke: 2: 34-35).

Messages From All Points On The Compass

Mary repeatedly chooses the innocent young to bring her messages to the world—messages of hope and the need for reparation to her divine Son. The innocent young have no agenda, and in their infectious idealism they have less concern for what others will think.

Mary has been chosen to intervene by the Holy Trinity to respond to this threat of Satan, also identified as the serpent, the dragon. On December 7, 1974, Mary revealed to Father Gobbi why she chooses the "little ones:" **"I, the Mother of the Church, am personally intervening and initiating my work of salvation. I am initiating it thus: with simplicity, with hiddenness, and in such a humble manner that most people will not even be aware of it. But this, my sons, has always been the way your Mother has acted."**

The frequency of the apparitions of Mary suggests some kind of closure, an explosion of the supernatural. We are presently experiencing the grand finale of this era.

Since Fatima more than three hundred apparitions have occurred significant enough to merit attention and investigation by Church officials. Allegedly, hundreds more are taking place, but the number will not be known until the great event in which Mary promises to validate all her authentic appearances by means of a permanent sign. Scholars and observers of Marian phenomena are sure that the number and frequency of reports have never before been on this scale. Even to the skeptics, these heavenly apparitions are events of undeniable sociological significance. It is impossible to give justice to more than a few of these apparitions. The messages are of peace, conversion, virtuous living, repentance, amendment of life, guidelines for following the Gospel, sacramental living, prayer, and purification. The apparitions are happening all over the world. There are simply too many to mention.

In our souls is an insatiable hunger for truth, for a real encounter with God. We are spiritual beings who long for the truth of God. Sometimes Heaven does not speak as clearly as we would like. The gospels tell us to judge a tree by its fruit, for a bad tree cannot bear good fruit. At Sabana Grande in Puerto Rico, Our Lady has stated that true apparitions will by marked by prayer, fasting, and mortification. This formula is a guide for us to follow because we must discern truth from falsehood. Spiritually speaking, we are in uncharted waters. We must be open to what the Spirit is doing in our midst today, for the events that Mary predicts are all mentioned in Scripture.

The messages are taking place on every continent throughout the world, all saying essentially the same thing. **The sheer numbers and** frequency of the messages is such that it is not possible to read, study, or know them all; nor is it necessary. Obedience to one is better than a knowledge of all. Mary appears to a particular region of the world for specific reasons, presenting a focus with regional benefits and admonitions. Why did she choose to appear in remote villages such as Lourdes, Fatima, Garabandal, and Medjugorje? As we see today, the area of Croatia and Bosnia-Herzegovina is a battleground near a region where World Wars have started. A wholesale slaughter is taking place in the name of ethnic cleansing; millions of refugees must flee their homes; and unknown thousands die of massacres and starvation. Only time will tell the exact reasons why Medjugorje in what used to be Yugoslavia is the focus of such extraordinary graces. The places in which Our Lady appears are as significant as the messages themselves. Heaven's plans need to be seen for their value in the present but usually are seen most accurately in hindsight.

In one place Mary plays the role of a gentle mother exhorting the family to a state of holiness. In another she is an advocate or counselor. At Garabandal, Spain, she gives a message of prophecy to the world that speaks of warnings. At Escorial, Spain, she speaks to those who are destitute and have been devastated by circumstances. While the messages are all different in their specifics, they are alike in their essentials: prayer, faith, conversion, peace, fasting, and love.

Mary's Master Plan

Pope John Paul II wrote in his 1987 encyclical *Redemptoris Mater* that Marian apparitions signify the Blessed Virgin's journey through time and space in a pilgrimage toward the Second Coming of Jesus and her final victory over Satan. This is her role now as it has been predestined from the beginning.

The Marian Movement of Priests message of October 30, 1975, spoke of Mary's tears being shed in many places to the point of blood. **We have been told the significance of tears of blood: they point to the fact that the chastisement is near.**

The more we study Mary's warnings, the more we are convinced of the accuracy of the valid apparitions. Inaccuracies do not exist when the apparition is approved by the Church—though problems with the interpretations of messages given through mystics over the ages have arisen on occasion and surely will continue.

Heaven's Mosaic

The participants in the Marian Movement must not hold too tightly to the apparition with which they are most familiar and disregard the rest as inferior or unworthy. People who closely follow Fatima, Garabandal, Medjugorje, and others must realize Heaven is weaving a beautiful mosaic to show the world Mary's presence. At San Nicolas, Argentina, on November 19, 1987, Jesus said: **"My mother must be accepted. My mother must be heard in the totality of her messages. Souls will come to Me through the means of her Immaculate Heart."** Trying to oppose one particular apparition with another indicates a narrow perspective on the larger role which the Trinity has appointed for Mary as the Mother of all mankind. All should try to grasp the truth and warnings, as Mary proclaims Heaven's messages for the benefit of all. We must be wise enough to discern that what Mary says in Rwanda may not apply to us in the United States but may be a special message for the people of Africa. We must not criticize other apparitions or messages, for we lack the larger perspective of God's magnificent plan. Much in the same way King David would not harm Saul because at one time he was the Lord's anointed, we should be careful before we pass judgment and leave this task to competent Church officials. If there is theological error, of course, the Church in due time through the guidance of the Holy Spirit will filter out those apparitions that are not authentic. In the Book of Acts, Gamaliel instructs the Church that if something is of God, it will last; if not, it will perish (Acts 5:38-39). Satan is no fool. Laced among true apparitions are surely false ones, inspired by the Father of Lies. It would be uncharacteristic of Satan if this were not the case. The design of the evil one is to create confusion and thus discredit them all. We would be surprised if this does not happen shortly. We should expect it.

The Times Ahead

Pope Pius XII warned about the "harsh and bitter sufferings" facing the human race. He said, "Mankind must prepare itself for suffering such as it has never before experienced." Pope Pius XII described our times as "the darkest since the deluge" and declared, "the hour has struck—the battle, the most widespread, bitter and ferocious the world has ever known, has been joined. It must be fought to the finish."[1]

In 1950, renowned Catholic churchman Archbishop Fulton J. Sheen wrote: "We are living in the Days of the Apocalypse—the last days of our era.... The two great forces of the Mystical Body of Christ and the Mystical Body of the Antichrist are beginning to draw up their battle lines for the catastrophic contest."[2] Mary's plan, plain and simple, is to prepare us for the times ahead.

The Growth Curve In Recent Years

As the number of Marian apparitions throughout the world have increased at an alarming rate, especially in the past ten years, we are reminded of the writings of Saint Louis de Montfort (1673-1716), in which he shared his conviction "that a Reign of the Blessed Virgin would precede a Reign of the Lord Jesus. Just as Mary preceded the first coming of Jesus on earth, so too the Trinity has ordained that she would precede Christ's Second Coming." Never before in history have we experienced the number of apparitions and supernatural phenomena as we have in this century, particularly the latter half. On December 8, 1990, Mary stated to Father Gobbi: "I was driven by the Most Holy Trinity to become the Mother of the Second Advent, and thus my motherly task of preparing the Church and all humanity to receive Jesus, who is returning to you in glory."

Michael Freze, SFO, in his book, *They Bore The Wounds Of Christ*, says there have been 321 authentic stigmatists in Church history. Sixty-two have been canonized. Some of those who have had the stigmata, the wounds of Christ, include: Saint Francis of Assisi; Saint Catherine of Siena (a Doctor of the Church); Teresa Neumann, the German stigmatist who lived only on the Eucharist for a period of several years; and Padre Pio, an Italian priest who died in 1968. These people had unique gifts and had a profound impact in their times. Today is no different. Christina Gallagher of Ireland; Amparo Cuevos of Spain; Mirna Nazzour of Damascus, Syria; Maria Esperanza of Venezuela; Patricia of England; Gladys Quiroga de Mota of Argentina; Father James Bruse of Virginia; Eileen George, Massachusetts; Sister Agnes Sasagawa of Akita, Japan—all currently have some form of the actual stigmata or a variation of visible or invisible suffering. Stigmatists are today becoming more numerous. These people are several among many saying severe events are coming our way in the very near future.

As one studies these apparitions in our century, one sees a slow but steadily developing divine plan, especially in the last two decades. This plan seems to be accelerating in the past five years as we can see the number of apparitions exploding. What does this all mean? Are we approaching something of monumental spiritual significance? Are we living in those times foretold in the Book of Revelation? Are we coming to a close of one era and entering into a new time? These are all fair and important questions to ask. Before we can really look into these questions, a review of important Marian apparitions is necessary. Many of the older ones are better known, so we have devoted more space to the recent. We have divided these apparitions into four periods.

Apparitions By Major Periods

We have adopted the historical framework suggested by Father Lambert Terstroet, SMM, a Montfortian Father living in Iceland, who divides the major apparitions into four distinct periods. The first period is that of Guadalupe, Mexico (1531), with its profound impact on the Americas. The second is the French period, commencing with the apparitions of Saint Catherine Laboure at the Rue de Bac, in 1830, and ending with Pontmain in 1871. The third is the "European" period, beginning with Our Lady's appearances at Fatima, Portugal (1917), and including Banneux/Beauraing, Belgium (1932/1933). It concludes with reported apparitions in Amsterdam (with messages spanning nearly forty years, from 1945 to 1984), where Mary appeared under the title of "The Lady of All Nations."

The fourth period begins in our times with the "Intercontinental" explosion, or world-wide grand finale of Marian apparitions, beginning with Garabandal, Spain, in the early 1960s. To give readers a sampling of the variety of Marian apparitions (this chapter is by no means inclusive of even a majority of seriously investigated reports), we will give a brief synopsis of several of these important "signs of our times."[3]

Our Lady of Guadalupe, 1531—Approved

Our Lady of Guadalupe means, "She Who Crushes the Serpent." The Indian word for She Who Crushes the Serpent sounds like the place name of Guadalupe, which the Spanish in error interpreted as referring to their famous shrine. Guadalupe as an apparition is linked closely in our day to the ending of abortion. Our Lady crushed the serpent in the Americas, ending the brutal Aztec practice of human sacrifice. The role of Our Lady of Guadalupe in this century is to crush the serpent and end our own era's resumption of human sacrifice—through approved abortion.

Rue de Bac, Paris, France, 1830—Approved

On November 27, 1830, Mary appeared in silence to Saint Catherine Laboure and showed her the image of a medal she wished to have struck. Our Lady appeared on the medal with streams of light pouring from rings on her fingers, signifying her function as "Mediatrix of All Graces." The graces are won by Christ but distributed by His Mother. Not all the rings gave off light, indicating that many graces God wished to bestow through Mary went unclaimed. Around the figure of Our Lady, these words were inscribed: "O Mary conceived without sin, pray for us who have recourse to thee." This medal came to be called "the Miraculous Medal," because of the many miracles associated with its wearing. **The back of this medal shows the Immaculate Heart of Mary and the Sacred Heart of Jesus together. This was the first occurrence in which the two hearts appeared together.** Twenty-four years after the apparition, Pope Saint Pius X, on December 8, 1854, defined the doctrine of "the Immaculate Conception." This dogma states, "the Blessed Virgin Mary, in the first instant of her conception, by a singular grace and privilege of Almighty God, in view of the foreseen merits of Jesus Christ, the Savior of the human race, was preserved from all stain of original sin."

LaSalette, France, 1846—Approved

In 1846, twelve years before Lourdes, France, two children, Melanie Calvat and Maximin Giraud, saw a shimmering apparition of a woman weeping. She spoke to them about many things that upset her Son. She warned of a coming famine, but that before the food shortage, many of the young children of the area would die of a serious disease. She said, "If you do not convert, I am unable to hold back the hand of God." Our Blessed Mother, in one famous version of the so-called "secret of LaSalette," revealed that "Lucifer was unleashed in 1864. The Church would be severely attacked and the monster [communism] would be unleashed at the end of the Nineteenth or beginning of the Twentieth Century. Rome will lose the faith and become the seat of Antichrist, and the Church will be in eclipse. Many chastisements are predicted, the Antichrist will be defeated, fire will purge the earth and consume all the work of men's pride, and all will be renewed." She called upon "the children of light, the few who can see, the true disciples of the living God, the true followers of Christ, the faithful of the last days to come out and fill the world with light, and to fight. For now is the time of all times, the end of all ends."

Lourdes, France, 1858—Approved

In 1858, four years after the dogma of the Immaculate Conception was proclaimed, Mary appeared to a very poor young girl, Bernadette Soubirous, eighteen times between February 11 and July 16, 1858. On March 25, 1858, on the feast of the Annunciation, Our Lady revealed to the uneducated Bernadette, "I am the Immaculate Conception." Because the dogma had been officially proclaimed less than four years earlier, and Bernadette could not even have known of its existence, great credibility was given to Bernadette by her repetition of the Blessed Mother's words. It was an affirmation from Heaven of the truth of the dogma. In addition, Bernadette was told by Mary to begin digging in the ground; she obediently did so, to the townspeople's scorn. Water immediately began flowing from the spot where Bernadette dug, a tiny stream that since has grown to the size of a small river. Thousands of healings have been reported as the result of bathing in or drinking this miraculous water. The walls of the grotto where the Blessed Mother appeared are lined with the crutches of the lame who have walked away from the waters, totally healed.

Pontmain, France, 1871—Approved

This apparition occurred during the Franco-Prussian War. The German troops were close to Pontmain. The people in the village prayed for protection. On the evening of January 17, for several minutes Mary appeared in Heaven wearing a dark blue dress with a crucifix in her hands. Below the apparition appeared the words, "Pray please. God will hear you soon. My Son lets Himself be touched." That same night an order from the German headquarters called the army back, and on January 28 the French-German armistice was signed. Pontmain remains a powerful example of the power of prayer to preserve us from disaster and war.

Fatima, Portugal, 1917—Approved

Fatima is perhaps the key apparition of the Twentieth Century. Many current messages from around the world are bringing our attention back to the Fatima events, most notably events in Russia. Mary, calling herself Queen of the Rosary, appeared to three shepherd children in the rural countryside of Portugal in 1917. This was the year of the Bolshevik revolution, and Mary entrusted vital messages for the people of the Twentieth Century to the three children, Lucia, Francesco, and Jacinta. Before the Bolshevik revolution, she prophesied that Russia would "spread her errors throughout the world." She gave secrets to the children concerning the future of the Church and of mankind. She told two of the children, Francesco and Jacinta, that they would soon be with her in Heaven (they died shortly thereafter) **but that Lucia would live to see the fulfillment of all of the messages**. It should be noted that at the time of this writing, Lucia is in her mid-eighties. At Fatima, Mary said Jesus wished to establish devotion to her Immaculate Heart. She desired the consecration of the world to her Immaculate Heart by all the world's bishops, and she especially desired the consecration of Russia. She also asked for First Saturday devotions to console her heart. In the end, she promised, if this were done, Russia would be converted, and an era of peace would be granted to the world. (For a more complete explanation, please refer to Chapter 9 on Fatima and the End Times.)

Beauraing, Belgium, 1932-1933—Approved

Fifteen years after the apparitions at Fatima, Mary appeared to children in Belgium, both at Banneux and Beauraing. These are the last Marian apparitions to receive the full approval of Rome, although many more recent apparition sites have the approval of the local bishops. The two apparitions in Belgium developed the Fatima message and prepared the way for the messages of Amsterdam. Our Lady appeared to five children at Beauraing: Fernande, Gilberte, Albert, Andrew, and Gilbert in thirty-two apparitions from November 19, 1932, until January 3, 1933. On December 21, 1932, Our Lady identified herself to the children, "I am the Immaculate Virgin." The children saw a golden heart in the center of Mary's chest. On January 3, 1933, she said to Andrew, "I am the Mother of God, the Queen of Heaven. Pray always!"

Banneux, Belgium, 1933—Approved

The eight apparitions in Banneux from January 15, 1933, to March 2, 1933, continued to develop the meaning of Mary's presence among us. Our Lady appeared to only one visionary, Mariette Bero, twelve years old, in a poor section of the country. Calling herself the "Virgin of the Poor," she said she had come to console the sick and the suffering. "I am the Mother of the Redeemer, the Mother of God," she stated.

A small detail, but a very important one in relation to the later apparitions at Amsterdam, is that on January 18 Our Lady told Mariette, "Put your hands into the water. This spring is reserved for me." (They were standing near a spring). The next day, Our Lady said, "This source is reserved for All the Nations."

Amsterdam, The Netherlands 1945-1984— Under Investigation

Our Lady reportedly appeared and spoke by inner locution over several decades under the title of "The Lady of All Nations" to a woman in Amsterdam named Ida Perleman. She had many messages of great importance for the future of the Church. She seemed to predict Vatican II and many of the specific issues addressed therein, more than ten years before the "surprise" council was called. She affirmed that many areas of modernization in the Church were necessary so Rome could take advantage of the special opportunities given it in our day to evangelize using modern means. She warned of a grave danger to the Church in the late Twentieth Century: a resurgence of the modernist heresy.

The Lady of All Nations predicted a "final Marian dogma" proclaiming Our Lady "Co-Redemptrix, Mediatrix, and Advocate," which would sum up and explain Marian theology, and would "crown" Our Lady. These apparitions are under investigation by the Church as of this writing. Cardinal Ratzinger reportedly has written the visionary that there are no theological barriers to the possible proclamation of the dogma. Some speculate it could be the proclamation of this dogma that will create the official schism in the Catholic Church, which is foretold by many visionaries to happen in the latter days.[4]

Seredne, Ukraine, 1953—Under Investigation

On December 20, 1953, in a vision during Mass, a woman named Hanya saw the hill of Seredne and a spot where there had been clear wells of water. She saw it clearly, even though she had never visited the hill. As the vision continued, she saw the Virgin Mary and heard her say, "My daughter, my daughter, you see what a fullness of grace I possess. But I have no one to give my graces to, for there are so many daughters and sons that have turned away from me, and no one asks of me in this jubilee year. I wanted to obtain a great forgiveness for poor sinners. **Disaster is upon you as in the times of Noah. Not by flood, but by fire will the destruction come. An immense flood of fire shall destroy nations for sinning before God.** Since the beginning of the world, there's never been such a fall as there is today. This is the kingdom of Satan. I shall dwell on this hill from which I see the entire universe and the many sinners, and I shall distribute many graces through this well. Who comes to repent of his sins and receives this water with faith, him shall I heal in soul and body."

Garabandal, Spain, 1961—Under Investigation

As the Cuban missile crisis threatened the world with nuclear annihilation, Our Lady was drawing thousands to a remote village in northern Spain, where she appeared to four young girls and displayed spectacular signs and wonders. Her messages were very detailed. Our Lady announced to the girls that the "cup [of divine Justice] is full, is overflowing, in fact." These apparitions seem to be tremendously significant: much of what they say dovetails with messages from other major reported apparitions, such as Medjugorje. This book devotes an entire chapter to the events at Garabandal, Spain. Mary speaks, in these apparitions, of the warning, the miracle, and the chastisement. After the warning takes place, many will travel to Garabandal to witness the miracle.

Akita, Japan, 1973—Approved By The Local Bishop

Sister Agnes Sasagawa still receives daily messages in these apparitions, which began when the then-deaf sister witnessed light flooding from inside the opened tabernacle. Sister Agnes was promised healing by Our Lady. That promise was fulfilled, though Sister suffers from the stigmata.

Her convent's statue, an exact replica of the image of The Lady of All Nations, has shed tears on 101 occasions. It was during the Lady of All Nations apparitions that Mary first spoke of herself as Co-Redemptrix. Sister's messages also refer to Our Lady as Co-Redemptrix. On October 13, 1973, Sister Agnes received a message of a chastisement with fire falling from Heaven wiping out the greater part of humanity and of the infiltration of the devil into the Church. (See Chapter 11 on Akita, which discusses these messages.)

Medjugorje, (former) Yugoslavia, 1981-Present

Since June 24, 1981, Mary has appeared as the "Queen Of Peace" to six peasant children in the village of Medjugorje. Since then, nearly all of the now young adults have received daily messages. The essence of Our Lady's messages is expressed in five key points: **she calls us to prayer from the heart, fasting, reconciliation with God and neighbor, conversion, and peace.** At the present time, these apparitions are the most influential of all the Marian apparitions. *Life* magazine estimates that over fifteen million pilgrims have traveled to Medjugorje over a ten-year period. Ten years to the day after the Blessed Mother began appearing to the children and begging the world to pray for peace, Croatia seceded from Yugoslavia, and the most brutal war in Europe since World War II began. Several current apparitions are "spin-offs" of Medjugorje, in the sense that the visionaries first experienced their reported visions after a pilgrimage there. (See chapter 12 on Medjugorje for greater details.)

Kibeho, Rwanda, 1981—Approved By Local Bishop

In November 1981, apparitions began in Kibeho, Rwanda, Africa, to seven visionaries: Alphonsine, Emmanuel, Anathalie, Marie-Claire, Stephanie, Agnes, and Vestine. Three of them were boarders in a college administered by nuns in a poor area, and three others live in the bush. Our Lord appeared independently to a young pagan, Sagstasha, who has since taken the Christian name Emmanuel. Our Lord taught him the Our Father and gave him instructions on the faith. Emmanuel was given the following message from the Blessed Mother:

"There isn't much time left in preparing for the Last Judgment. We must change our lives, renounce sin. Pray and prepare for our own death and for the end of the world. We must prepare while there is still time. Those who do well will go to Heaven. If they do evil, they will condemn themselves with no hope of appeal. Do not lose time in doing good and praying. There is not much time and Jesus will come."

Although the apparitions ended for six of the visionaries by 1983, Alphonsine continues to receive apparitions almost every year on November 28. Her last apparition was on November 28, 1989. In these apparitions, Our Lady calls herself the "Mother of the Word." She emphasizes the importance of the rosary and prayer and to love ourselves and others. Jesus told Emmanuel, **"Too many people treat their neighbors dishonestly. The world is full of hatred. You will know my Second Coming is at hand when you see the outbreak of religious wars. Then, know that I am on the way."** The Blessed Mother told them, "I have come to prepare the way to my Son for your good and you do not want to understand. The time remaining is short and you are absent-minded. You are distracted by the goods of this world which are passing. I have seen many of my children getting lost and I have come to show them the true way."

The apparitions in Kibeho, Africa, were approved in the first stage by the local bishop on August 15, 1988, thus allowing public devotion. The Church is continuing to review these events.

San Nicolas, Argentina, 1983—Under Investigation

In 1983, Our Lady began appearing to a woman named Gladys Quiroga de Motta in San Nicolas, Argentina. Gladys was given many messages by Our Lord and Our Lady. Since 1990, Our Lady has continued to appear to Gladys but without any messages for the world. Gladys received more than 1,800 messages from October 13, 1983, to February 11, 1990. Father Rene Laurentin, a leading Marian scholar, in his book *An Appeal From Mary in Argentina* writes that the message is a simple one: "God wants to renew the covenant with His people through Mary, His Ark of the Covenant."

The response of the people in Argentina to the apparition has been overwhelming. Thousands and thousands of pilgrims have visited San Nicolas, and many cures have taken place. Gladys has received the stigmata. The bishop, Monsignor Catagna, is very supportive. A special commission has been studying these apparitions, and official recognition seems to be near.[5]

England, 1985—Under Investigation

Patricia [surname withheld], an English housewife and mother of three children, started receiving interior visions and locutions from Our Lord and Our Lady regarding devotion to the Divine Innocence in February 1985. As a Protestant who married a Catholic, she had promised to raise her children Catholic and later converted to Catholicism. The messages, which are continuing, fall into two main categories: devotion to Crucified Innocence and devotion to the Mystical Wounds of Our Lady. Patricia's messages help to explain Mary's role as Co-Redemptrix, Mediatrix, and Advocate.

Christ is a victim soul, and Mary is a victim soul; both sorrowful Hearts suffer in reparation for sin. In these messages promoting devotion to the Crucified Innocence, Christ asks us to be victim souls also, united to His sufferings. In His cry of abandonment from the cross—"My God! My God! Why hast thou forsaken Me?"—He foresaw many victim souls throughout the ages who also were partakers in His victory. Christ has chosen the late Twentieth Century for the Devotion to Crucified Innocence to be revealed and propagated. It is intended primarily in reparation for the millions upon millions of infants now being aborted 2,000 years after Our Lord's death.

While Calvary was first and foremost the scene of Our Lord's Passion and death, it also caused Our Lady to suffer hidden and mystical wounds. No longer does God want the precious wounds of Our Lady to be hidden. Rather, His people are to understand the tremendous purification mankind received and will receive through devotion to Mary's Hidden and Mystical Wounds. Patricia has said, "When Divine Innocence triumphs in us, then Our Lady's Immaculate Heart will also triumph. This grace has been won by Our Lady's Mystical Wounds."[6]

Our Lady Of Lourdes Shrine In Melleray Grotto, County Waterford, Ireland, 1985—Under Investigation

In the Knockmealdown Mountains, Our Blessed Lady reportedly appeared at Melleray Grotto, where there is a shrine to Our Lady of Lourdes. She appeared first to a seventeen-year-old local girl, Ursula O'Rourke, in August 1985. During the following week she appeared and spoke to two young local boys, Tom Cliffe, twelve years old, and to Barry Buckley, eleven years old. Mary gave them messages of prayer and impending world catastrophes. Each evening Our Lady appeared to the boys shortly after their entry to the grotto and after some of the rosary had been recited. She always appeared on the statue's right hand side when delivering her messages and then receded back into the statue. The boys then would see her as the statue, but with flowing golden hair and a silver crown, her gown moving in the wind, and the fingers and lips of the statue moving to prayer or hymn.

Other local people, adults and children, saw visions of other saints and holy persons, such as Joan of Arc and Padre Pio. One evening, Our Lady appeared to a local farmer, Michael O'Donnell. She told him, "preserve Sunday for prayer."

On August 19, 1985, at Melleray Grotto, Tom Cliffe saw a vision: Our Lord and the apostles were sitting around a table in a big room. Outside in the streets were beggars and some people sweeping with brooms, and dogs were barking. There was a long table with Our Lord at the head. Our Lord had his finger up and seemed to be lecturing one of the apostles. This frightened Tom, as he thought Our Lord was directing his admonitions to him. That same evening, Our Blessed Lady said, "I have a message," and to the boys she said the following: "My message is peace and prayer—tell the people that the water is blessed." Our Blessed Lady was very close to the boys with her arms outstretched. Tom put out his hand to touch her, but she said, "No." She walked back up the steps again and turning at the top she said, "God is angry with the world. The people will have to improve and pray. My message is for all the people of God's Church. **The people have ten years to improve and pray, and if not, then this is what will happen.**" Mary then showed them a vision of future calamitous events.

Inchigeela, Ireland, 1985—Under Investigation

Since August 5, 1985, apparitions of Our Lady have been reported at two distant grottos near Inchigeela, Ireland. Three children, Rosemary O'Sullivan, Marie Vaughn, and Kelly Noonan have claimed to see the Blessed Mother. There have been no further reported apparitions to the children since March 1987. Some of the messages were as follows:

To Rose on June 16, 1986: "I am the Queen of Peace."

To Marie on November 2, 1986: "I wish that the Brown Scapular should be spread more."

To Kelly on February 22, 1987: "Sons and daughters of the world: I beg of you to recite and keep the Ten Commandments."

On July 25, 1986, Our Lady also appeared to Mary Casey, the mother of nine children. She has received several messages. To Mrs. Casey on August 20, 1986, Our Lady said: "Peace. Prayer is the best weapon you have. It is a key that opens God's heart. You must pray to Jesus from your heart. Let your prayer be of genuine gratitude to the Father. The devil is strong with those who fear him and weak with those who despise him. Satan can do nothing to people who have surrendered themselves to God. Go in Peace."

Bessbrook Grotto, Ireland (1987)—Under Investigation

Our Lady appeared in Bessbrook Grotto in the spring of 1987 to Beulah Lynch and Mark Treanor. On Saturday, May 30, 1987, Mark Treanor reported an instant inclination to go to the grotto. There he saw a lady dressed in white looking at him. She was wearing a golden crown. On June 2, Beulah Lynch saw Our Lady. She was unspeakably beautiful, young, motherly, and surrounded by light.

On June 11, Our Lady said to Beulah Lynch: "I am your Mother. I love you. **The world must behave. The world must change. A great catastrophe will happen to the world. Tell them to hurry. This is a command from God. The messages here are the messages in Medjugorje. The children in Medjugorje are the children here.**"

On July 10, Our Lady said to Beulah Lynch: "My child, the messages are not to be taken foolishly. They are serious. They are from God. The world is in great danger. God is not pleased. You have been given a gift from God. Tell the people to come and to pray. Pray and fast and do penance."

On August 20, Our Lady said to Beulah Lynch: "A great disaster will happen to the world. The world must improve. Satan is destroying the world."

On November 11, Our Lady told Beulah Lynch: "My child, I am your mother, Mother of God. You cannot know the wrath of God. God is very, very angry because of the sins of the world. I cannot hold back any longer. I cannot save the world. The people must save the world. The people must come to the grotto, to pray, fast, and do penance before the chastisements start."

Hrushiv, Ukraine (1914, 1986 to 1988)— Under Investigation

Much of what is known about the Ukraine has been provided by Josyp Terelya, former political prisoner of the former Soviet Union for twenty years. The Ukrainian apparition site, called Hrushiv, had long been a place of pilgrimage, with reported apparitions as long as two hundred years ago and up to the present day. Josyp Terelya states:

"In 1914 at the Hrushiv shrine, twenty-two peasants saw Our Lady and she predicted eighty or ninety years of hardship for the believers. As at Fatima, she also warned that Russia would become godless and bring mankind precariously close to destruction. It was a significant link to what Sister Lucia of Fatima was told years later—if Russia did not return to Christianity, there might well be another World War and whole nations would vanish."[7]

On April 26, 1987 (one year to the hour and the day after the Chernobyl nuclear accident), Our Lady appeared to twelve-year-old Maria Kyzyn in the small rural village of Hrushiv, Ukraine, close to a small Catholic church that has been for centuries a center of Marian devotion. This little church since has attracted large crowds of both Catholic and non-Catholic pilgrims. At one point 20,000 people gathered in a sweet potato field to get a glimpse of Mary. Some estimate that no less than 400,000 have had the great joy of seeing the image of Mary as she visited her children in that most Catholic part of the Ukrainian nation. These apparitions have yielded very powerful messages, as well as remarkable signs and wonders. We will quote a lengthy message from Our Lady, to indicate the powerful intensity of her words in the Ukraine.

Our Lady said: "Teach the children to pray. Teach children to live in truth and live yourselves in truth. **Chernobyl is a reminder and a sign for the whole world.** Constantly say the rosary. The rosary is the weapon against Satan. He fears the rosary. Say the rosary everyday, constantly at any gathering of people. I have come on purpose to thank the Ukrainian people because you have suffered most for the Church of Christ in the last seventy years. I have come to comfort you and to tell you that your suffering will soon come to an end. Ukraine will become an independent state. Repent and love one another. *The times are coming, which have been foretold, as being those in the end times.* See the desolation which surrounds the world; the sins, the sloth, the genocide. I come to you with tears in my eyes and I implore you, pray and work for good, and for the glory of God. Ukraine was the first country to acknowledge me as queen and I have received her under my care.

"Work for God, for without this, there is no happiness and no one will gain the Kingdom of God. You shall gain my heart and live in unity. Follow the leaders of the Church boldly and you will gain your own country and power and love amongst the nations of the world. I love the Ukraine and the Ukrainian people for their suffering and faithfulness...for Christ the King, and I shall protect the Ukraine for the glory and the future of the Kingdom of God on earth. Ukrainians must become Apostles of Christ among the Russian peoples for if there is not a return to Christianity in Russia, there will be a Third World War."

Ukraine is crucial for the conversion of Russia. Russia is the key to peace in the world. Finally, we are told Russia will be instrumental for the conversion of the West. The spark for this chain reaction is Ukraine.

It appears that the United States also has a critical role to play in the conversion of Russia that will bring about true peace. Josyp Terelya heard Our Blessed Mother say, "Pray for Russia. Russia will be converted only when all Christians pray for her restoration. Pray for the unification of the churches in Russia. All Christians should repent and through purification from sin stop the godlessness in Russia from continuing to spread through the world. Pray in brotherly love for the conversion of the Russian people. The believing Ukrainian Christians will save their own nation. Until the West acknowledges its own guilt before the East, Russia will not be able to receive Christ the King." [Note: In the year 1054, Christendom underwent a schism separating the Eastern and Western churches. The term 'conversion' implies the reunification of the disparate parts of the Church under the Pope.]

Mary also showed Josyp several more visions including one of the coup against Mikhail Gorbachev, former Premier of the USSR. Josyp Terelya had this vision in 1987; the incident of the attempted overthrow of Gorbachev occurred in August 1990, three years after it was predicted. We quote Josyp Terelya directly from *Witness*: "I saw a map of the Ukraine and the bloody river began to dry up. The earth in many places was scorched and took on a black-grey color. This was the color of death. But amid the black-gray ashes, I saw grass sprouting. It was very tall. I saw the people kneeling and crying but I knew these were the tears of joy and salvation. I saw the new Babylon, the red city, that was falling into the earth. In that city, under a Christian temple, was a secret hiding place. There were eight men there—eight rulers, all eight waxen yellow. They laughed horribly and bared their teeth. Gorbachev told me it wasn't he who was in charge of the state. I saw the real leader of the USSR behind a yellow screen: It was Lucifer himself, in the figure of Yeltsin, his eyes red and his face blushed. I looked and from the earth of that city, immense dull red rats, large as dogs, began running. These animals were awful. I know they were poisonous.

"I heard the voice of a woman full of love and goodness. She said, 'You have seen the godless East and West. The difference is that in the West godlessness is not officially recognized. But the goal of godlessness in the East and West is the same. In order to save Russia and the whole world from godless hell, you must convert Russia to Christ the King. The conversion of Russia will save Christian culture in the West and will be a push for Christianity throughout the world. But the Kingdom of Christ the King shall establish itself through the reign of the Mother of God."

[Note: Mary has said Russia must return to Christianity. Mary states in several other messages that the key for stability in the West is the conversion of Russia. Russia appears to have a more strategic role than the other republics in fostering Heaven's peace plan.]

Cuenca, Ecuador, 1988-1990—
Under Investigation

Patricia "Pachi" Talbott was a typical teenager, not very interested in religion. When her religion class showed a video of the apparitions at Medjugorje, her first response was, "that's ridiculous." Pachi was more interested in modeling, and she was very successful. However, over an eighteen-month period beginning in August 1988, the Blessed Mother has been appearing as "The Guardian of the Faith" to Pachi. Her messages advise remaining faithful to basic Catholic practice: Eucharist, penance, prayer, fasting, consecration to the Two Hearts, devotion to the scapular, visits to the Blessed Sacrament, and inner peace.

Pachi has also been given grave messages. For example, while visiting Tepeyac Hill in Guadalupe, Mexico, Patricia was told by the Blessed Virgin, "There are going to be bad things happening in the world, and what is asked for is conversion." Patricia was told not to reveal the actual secret, as "it would create panic." One month ahead of time Patricia will warn the world of the message through her spiritual advisors. The Virgin has told Patricia the secret has three parts and all three have to do with future chastisements for the world.

The Virgin reportedly told Patricia: "The war is near. It will be started with false peace treaties, treaties in which we should not place our trust. Many countries will be involved, among them, the United States, China, Russia, Rumania...this is why conversion now is so important."

Regarding the three days of darkness that many modern visionaries have predicted, Pachi stated: "The Holy Virgin spoke about them, saying that the earth would go out of its orbit for three days. At that time, the Second Coming of Christ will be near. The devil will take over the world. During those days, families should be in continuous prayer. Because of false prophets, who will falsify the words of Christ, we have to be in the state of grace so we can discern the good from the evil....

"We should not open the doors to our homes to anybody. We are simply to keep on praying. The Virgin said it would be better not even to look through the window because we will see the justice of God over the people. It will be so terrible, that we will not want to see it."

Pachi is not unlike many other youth of her age group. Before the apparitions, her parents had divorced, and in an act of rebellion she attempted suicide. Since 1990 her parents have reconciled. When she first received the apparitions, she was unfamiliar with the writings of Father Gobbi and other mystics around the world, many of whom claim they have received similar messages. Pachi emphasizes that time is short and there will be some point when conversion will no longer be possible.[8]

Litmanova, Slovakia, 1990—Under Investigation

Since August 1990, in a small town in Slovakia near the border of Poland, Mary has reportedly appeared to two twelve-year-old shepherd girls, Katarina and Svetka. Our Lady asked them to make sacrifices, attend church, and offer prayers for their sins and the sins of the world. The Blessed Virgin called herself the "All Pure Sinless One." She appears on the first Sunday of each month; in August 1991, over 500,000 people were present for the first anniversary of the apparitions. The people of Litmanova are Greek Catholic. Like Garabandal and Medjugorje, Litmanova is a poor village. A miraculous spring flows from the top of a mountain, and (as in so many other places) Mary has said that a sign will be left on the top of the mountain when the apparitions end.

The Vatican as well as the Greek Catholic Bishop of Presov and the Roman Catholic Bishop Jan Hirka are conducting investigations. Our Lady promised a new era of peace and joy. We feel it is important principally because Slovakia (part of the old Czechoslovakia) is a satellite of the former Soviet Union, and freedom of worship is so necessary to the struggling new democracies. The 500,000 participants at the first anniversary Mass shows that, as in Ukraine, the people of former communist lands have a great hunger for God and things spiritual.[9]

Apparition Sites

The following is a list of the better-known Marian apparition sites throughout the world. It is by no means exhaustive or conclusive.

1531—Guadalupe, Mexico, 1531: Juan Diego
1634—Quito, Ecuador, 1634: Mother Mariana de Jesus Torres
1830—Rue de Bac, Paris: Catherine Laboure
1846—LaSalette, France: Melanie Calvat and Maximin Guiraud
1858—Lourdes, France: Bernadette Soubirous
1871—Pontmain, France: Eugene and Joseph Barbadette
1879—Knock, Ireland: Fifteen People
1904—Poland: Father Maximilian Kolbe
1914—Hrushiv: Several People

1917—Fatima, Portugal: Lucia, Francesco, and Jacinta (children)
1932—Beuraing, Belgium: Voisin and Degeimbre (children)
Banneux, Belgium: Mariette Beco
1937—Poland: Sister Faustina
1938—Belgium: Bertha Petit
1940s–Hungary: Sister Marie Natalia
1945—Zagreb, Yugoslavia: Julka
1945—Holland, Amsterdam: Ida Perleman
1947—Marienfried, Germany: Barbara Reuss
1947—Montichiari, Italy: Pierina Gilli
1947—Tre Fontane, Italy: Bruno Cornacchiola
1951—Poland: Barbara Klosowna
1953—Sabana Grande, Puerto Rico: Three Children
1954—Seredne, Ukraine: Anna/Hanya
1954—Fostoria, Ohio: Sister Mildred Mary
1954—Calabria, Italy: Mother Elena Aiello
1954—Windy Gap, N. Ireland: Seamus Quail
1958—Turzovka, Czechoslovakia: Matous Losuta
1961—Garabandal, Spain: Four Children
1962—Skiemonys, Lithuania:
1963—Vietnam: Rosa Maria
1964—San Damiano, Italy: Mama Rosa Quattrini
1965—Belgium: Maguerite
1966—Porto San Stefano, Italy: Enzo Alocci
1968—Italy: Mama Carmela Carabelli
1968—Zeitoun, Egypt: Hundreds of thousands

Since 1970

1972—Milan, Italy: Father Stefano Gobbi
1972—Dozule, France: Madaleine
1973—Akita, Japan: Sister Agnes Sasagawa
1974—Binh Loi, Vietnam: Stephen Ho-Ngoc-Anh
1974—Canada: Brother Joseph Francis
1974—Rome, Italy: Mother Elena Patriarca Leonardi
1976—Betania, Venezuela: Maria Esperanza And Others

Since 1980

1980—Cuapa, Nicaragua: Bernardo Martinez
1980—El Escorial, Spain: Amparo Cuevas

1980—Taiwan: Five People
1981—Kibeho/ Rwanda, Africa: Seven Children
1981—Medjugorje, Yugoslavia: Six Children
1982—Eisenberg, Austria: Aloisa Lex
1982—Damascus, Syria: Mirna Nazzour
1983—Penablanca, Chile: Miguel Angel Poblete
1983—San Nicolas, Argentina: Gladys Quiroga de Motta
1985—Melleray Grotto, Ireland: Several People
1985—Ballinspittle, Ireland:
1985—Switzerland: Vassula Ryden
1985—Surrey, England: Patricia
1985—Oliveto Citra, Italy: Several Children
1985—Inchigeela, Ireland: Three Children
1985—Naju, Korea: Julia Kim
1986—Shoubra, Egypt: Thousands
1986—Manila, Phillipines: Soldiers
1987—Bessbrook, Northern Ireland: Beulah Lynch
        and Mark Treanor
1987—Hrushiv, Ukraine: Marina Kizyn
1987—Mayfield, Ireland: Sally Ann
        and Judy Considine
1987—Conyers, Georgia: Nancy Fowler
1987—Cuenca, Ecuador: Patricia Talbot
1987—Grushevo, Ukraine: Thousands
1988—Cortnadreha, Ireland: Christina Gallagher
1988—Scottsdale, Arizona: Several People
1988—Phoenix, Arizona: Estela Ruiz
1988—Lubbock, Texas: Three Adults
1989—Canada: Jim Singer
1989—Marlboro, New Jersey: Joseph Januszkiewicz
1989—Kettle River, Minnesota: Steve Marino
1990—Canada: Josyp Terelya
1990—Denver, Colorado: Theresa Lopez
1990—Litmanova, Czechoslovakia: Two Children
1990—Melbourne, Australia: Josefina-Maria
1991—Mozul, Iraq: Dina

And dozens and dozens more unmentioned...

3

Prophetess For Our Times

A great and wondrous sign appeared in Heaven: a woman clothed with the sun, with the moon under her feet and a crown of twelve stars on her head. She was pregnant and cried out in pain as she was about to give birth. Then another sign appeared in Heaven: an enormous red dragon with seven heads and ten horns and seven crowns on his heads. His tail swept a third of the stars out of the sky and flung them to the earth. The dragon stood in front of the woman who was about to give birth, so that he may devour her child the moment it was born. She gave birth to a son, a male child, who will rule all the nations with an iron scepter. And her child was snatched up to God and to His throne. The woman fled into the desert to a place prepared for her by God, where she might be taken care of for 1,260 days. And there was war in Heaven. Michael and his angels fought against the dragon, and the dragon and his angels fought back. But he [the dragon] was not strong enough, and they lost their place in Heaven. The great dragon was hurled down—that ancient serpent called the devil or Satan, who leads the whole world astray. He was hurled to the earth, and his angels with him.

Revelation 12:1-9

In our day, as issues of the faith are in crisis, Mary will make herself more known. In the message of July 3, 1987, through Father Gobbi, Mary specifically said, "These Are My Times."

"As of this year, in a strong and official way, the times of your heavenly mother will begin.... These are the times of the great chastisement. The cup of divine justice is full, is more than full, is flowing over. Iniquity covers the whole earth; the Church is darkened by the spread of apostasy and of sin. The Lord, for the triumph of His mercy, must as of now purify with His strong action of justice and of love. The most painful, most bloody hours are in preparation for you. These times are closer than you think. Already during this Marian Year, certain great events will take place, concerning what I predicted at Fatima and have told, under secrecy, to the children to whom I am appearing at Medjugorje. Jesus will restore His glorious reign. He will dwell with you and you will know the new times, the new era. You will at last see a new earth and new heavens....

"These are the times of the great mercy. The Father thrills with ardor and wills to pour out upon this poor humanity the torrents of His infinite love. The Father wants to mold with His hands a new creation where His divine imprint will be more visible, welcomed and received and His Fatherhood exalted and glorified by all.

"These are my times. 'These,' that is to say the days in which you are living, are 'mine,' because they are times marked by my great and strong presence. These times will become even more mine, the more my victory will broaden out and become stronger, surpassing the victory which at present is that of my Adversary. This presence of mine will become very strong and extraordinary, above all in the families consecrated to my Immaculate Heart. It will become apparent to all and will become for you a source of a special consolation."

Her intervening role has never ceased. God the Father has willed to use her. **She is the messenger and the prophetess.** Several of her titles are discussed in the following section.

Titles As Queen For Our Age

Throughout history, the Blessed Mother has actively interceded in the affairs of man.

Prophetess Of These Last Times

On November 22, 1992, Our Blessed Mother stated to Father Gobbi her role very clearly and succinctly. She said, "With the joy of a mother, who sees herself more and more heeded and followed by her little children, along the road which has been pointed out by me, as **Prophetess of these last times in which you are living,** with my Son, Jesus Christ...."

The Immaculate Conception

God prepared the one predestined to receive His Only Begotten Son into her womb, and into her life. Just as the instructions Yahweh gave for preparing the Ark of the Covenant in the Old Testament were detailed and precise, because God Himself would reside there, so too, the Church teaches, Mary was uniquely prepared in order to give flesh to her Creator, and to house His growing frame within her body. Because she contained Christ, she has been called the Ark of the New Covenant, and the Church teaches that God prepared her for this in a singular way. Christ did not receive His body from a sin-stained vessel; by the power of the foreseen merit of His death and Resurrection, He had already sanctified Mary by freeing her from original sin from the first moment of her conception within her mother's womb. Jesus created a vessel without sin and without any stain. Pope Pius IX proclaimed this dogma in 1854, and four years later Mary confirmed it when she identified herself at Lourdes as the Immaculate Conception.

Mother of the Church

Mary has always been seen as a model for the Church, and intimately connected to it as its mother. The Church sees the account in John's Gospel of Mary at the foot of the cross as denoting Christ giving Mary to the Church (as its new mother), and the Church to Mary (as her new children). This implies both maternal and filial commitment and responsibility. Mary mothered the Head of the Church—Jesus—so throughout time, she will also mother the Body of Christ. Pope Paul VI, in closing the Second Vatican Council in 1965, formally declared Mary to be "Mother of the Church."

Mary's unique role has been spoken about by others in the Church for centuries. Two such voices in the Seventeenth Century were Blessed Mary of Agreda, a Spanish nun, and Saint Louis de Montfort. Blessed Mary of Agreda said of the Blessed Mother, "It was revealed to me that through the intercession of the Mother of God all heresies will disappear. The victory over heresies has been reserved by Christ for His Blessed Mother. In the latter days, the Lord will in a special manner spread the renown of His Mother. Mary began salvation, and by her intercession it will be completed. Before the Second Coming of Christ, Mary, more than ever, must shine in mercy, might, and grace in order to bring unbelievers into the Catholic faith. The power of Mary in the latter days will be very conspicuous. Mary will extend the reign of Christ over the heathens and the Mohammedans, and it will be a time of great joy when Mary is enthroned as Mistress and Queen of Hearts. An unusual chastisement of the human race will take place towards the end of the world."[1]

Saint Louis de Montfort wrote, **"But the power of Mary over all the devils will especially shine forth in the latter times, when Satan will lay his snares against her heel: that is to say, her humble slaves and poor children, whom she will raise up to make war against him. They shall be little and poor in the world's esteem, and abased before all like the heel, trodden underfoot and persecuted as the heel is by other members of the body. But in return for this they shall be rich in the grace of God, which Mary shall distribute to them abundantly. They shall be great and exalted before God in sanctity, superior to all creatures by their lively zeal, and so well sustained with God's assistance that, with the humility of their heel, in union with Mary, they shall crush the head of the devil and cause Jesus Christ to triumph."**

Saint Louis de Montfort also wrote, "It is Mary alone who has found grace before God (Luke 1:30) without the aid of any other mere creature...she was full of grace when she was greeted by the Archangel Gabriel (Luke 1:28), and was superabundantly filled with grace by the Holy Ghost when He covered her with unspeakable shadow (Luke 1:35); and she has so augmented this double plenitude from day to day and from moment to moment that she has reached a point of grace immense and inconceivable."[2]

Mary as the New Eve

The idea of Mary as "the New Eve" was expressed beautifully in the writings of the famous Nineteenth Century convert from Anglicanism, John Cardinal Henry Newman. He wrote: "Though I hold, as you know, a process of development in Apostolic truth as time goes on, such development does not supersede the Fathers, but explains and completes them. And, in particular, as regards our teaching concerning the Blessed Virgin, with the Fathers I am content...the Fathers are enough for me."

Cardinal Newman insisted: "I fully grant that devotion towards the Blessed Virgin has increased among Catholics with the progress of centuries; I do not allow that the doctrine concerning her has undergone a growth, for I believe that it has been in substance one and the same from the beginning."[3]

On the ancient teaching of Mary as the Second Eve, Newman quoted from three sources: Saint Justin Martyr (A.D. 120-165), Saint Irenaeus (120-200), and Tertullian (160-240). Of these, Newman said: "Tertullian represents Africa and Rome; Saint Justin represents Palestine; and Saint Irenaeus Asia Minor and Gaul; or rather he represents Saint John the Evangelist, for he had been taught by the martyr Saint Polycarp, who was the intimate associate of Saint John, so of the other Apostles."

We quote from the earliest source, Saint Justin Martyr: "We know that He, before all creatures, proceeded from the Father by His power and will...and by means of the Virgin became man, that by what way the disobedience arising from the serpent had its beginning, by that way also it might have an undoing. For Eve, being a virgin and undefiled, conceiving the word that was from the serpent, brought forth disobedience and death; but the Virgin Mary, taking faith and joy, when the Angel told her the good tidings, that the Spirit of the Lord should come upon her and the power of the Most High overshadow her, and therefore the Holy One that was born of her was Son of God, answered, 'Be it done to me according to Thy word.'"

Cardinal Newman showed how the widespread territories represented by the three distinct witnesses indicated that this teaching on Mary as "the Second Eve" was firmly established before the year 200. From the earliest written records of the Church, there was general acceptance of Mary's role.[4]

Queen of Heaven and Earth/Queen of Peace

Mary's identity with the Church is nowhere more evident than in the scriptural passages of Revelation, Chapter 12. While some maintain that these passages refer not to Mary but to the Church, they refer to both. "The woman" cries out in the pain of childbirth and delivers a male-child, "the King who rules the nations with an iron rod," Christ the King. These passages strongly relate to the Marian apparitions of our times, which portray Mary as a Queen who will "crushing the serpent's head" in the final defeat of the enemy.

As with all her other titles, Mary's title as Queen of Heaven and Earth derives solely from her unique relationship to the King of Kings and Lord of Lords. The Assumption is the doctrine which prepares us to accept Mary's heavenly role as Queen of the Angels. For she is the first of the redeemed to attain the fullness of glory, both in body and in spirit. As she is first, she leads the rest of us to victory, by helping us to navigate through the deceptive snares laid down by Satan to distract and dilute the force of the Good News.

Mary leads us only to her Son, the Source of her life and joy. She teaches us basic, spiritual, common sense principles such as prayer, fasting, and reconciliation with God and neighbor.

The Assumption

Writings dating from the second century indicate that Mary was generally believed by Christians to have been assumed into Heaven: both her body and her soul were taken up to Heaven when her time on earth had come to an end. She has already attained the full glorification that all of the elect are destined to receive at the Final Judgment. Because of her sinlessness, her body did not have to undergo corruption in the grave.

There are many reasons for this belief in Mary's Assumption. Among them is the physical fact that the relics and tombs of the other early Christians were identified, venerated, and in a variety of ways, celebrated. There exists nothing pertaining to Mary, except the house at Loretto, where Jesus was supposedly reared. There is no record or celebration of her death, no tomb, no relics, yet she was perhaps the foremost member of the early Church, due to her closeness to its Founder. She was, after all, the Mother of the Redeemer.

The Church has always held the truth about Mary's Assumption, and in 1950 it was formally declared to be part of Catholic dogma by Pope Pius XII. Mary's Assumption helps bring other aspects of her role into sharper focus, such as her being the Queen of Heaven who has been given a royal part to play in the climax of the great spiritual war being waged in these reported "end times" (Revelation 12).

Devotion to Our Lady was a very strong aspect of the early Church and many church buildings were dedicated to her honor. For example, Clovis I, in the year 101, dedicated a church near Paris to "Our Lady of Argenteuil." "Our Lady Beyond the Tiber" was built in Rome by

Calixtus I in the year 224. Saint Helen built a chapel called "Our Lady of the Commencement," which was dedicated by Saint Sylvester in the year 320, and so on.

Legend has it that the first recorded chapel of Our Lady was dedicated by Saint Peter, one of the original Apostles, at Tripoli. The Assumption is not so difficult a doctrine to comprehend when we look at the honor Mary has been given throughout all of history.[5]

Queen of the Holy Rosary

As Queen of the Holy Rosary, Mary calls us to prayer as an antidote for our frenetic, late Twentieth Century lives. Previously, through the power of the holy rosary, Mary intervened to save Christianity from Islam at the Battle of Lepanto. The Holy Father called for all Europe to say the rosary when it looked as if Islam would overrun Europe. Many did pray the rosary , and Europe was not overthrown.

Our Queen leads us in a way of meditation that calms our racing minds, focusing our thoughts for an extended period of time on the mysteries of our Redemption. We are exhorted to pray, over and over again, for her powerful intercession on our behalf, both "now, and at the hour of our death," when we know the devil will be doing his utmost to snatch our souls. Mary has said repeatedly that the answer to our personal ills lies in "the frail cord of the rosary."

For example, on October 8, 1984, Our Lady appeared to the Medjugorje visionary Jacov Colo at his home. She said: "Dear children, all the prayers which you recite in the evening in your homes, dedicate them to the conversion of sinners, because the world is immersed in a great moral decay. Recite the rosary each evening." On January 9, 1989, Mary said to the visionaries in Medjugorje: "...during these days I invite you to renew the prayer in your families and to pray all the mysteries of the rosary every evening."

On June 1, 1984, she exhorted, "May the love of God be always in you, because without it, you cannot be fully converted. Let the rosary in your hands make you think of Jesus."

Moreover, on August 8, 1985, Mary instructed, "Dear children, today I call you especially now to advance against Satan by means of prayer. Satan wants to work still more now that you know he is at work. Dear children, put on the armor for battle and with the rosary in your hands, defeat him!"

Queen and Mother of Families

In the July 23, 1987, message to Father Gobbi, Our Blessed Mother stated her role in the family: "I am the Mother and the Queen of Families. I watch over their life, I take their problems to heart, I interest myself not only in their spiritual good but also in the material good of all their members. **When you consecrate a family to my Immaculate Heart it is as though you open the door of your house to your heavenly mother, invite her to come in and give her the opportunity to exercise her motherly function in an ever stronger way."**

On July 3, 1984, Mary said to the visionaries in Medjugorje: "Dear children, your mother asks you tonight, you who are present, when you get back to your house, renew prayer in your family. Take time for prayer, dear children. I, as your mother, especially want to tell you that the family has to pray together. The Holy Spirit wants to be present in the families. Allow the Holy Spirit to come. The Holy Spirit comes through prayer. That is why, pray, and allow the Holy Spirit to renew you, to renew today's families."

Mary as Co-Redemptrix, Mediatrix, Advocate

"The Spirit and the Bride say, 'Come'" (Revelation 22:17). These inspired words from the last sentences of Sacred Scripture should enkindle a hopeful confidence in the people of God concerning the ongoing salvific work of the Holy Spirit and Mary, His Immaculate Spouse, in their contemporary mission of advocacy for the Church today.

It is noteworthy that the scriptural use of the term, Advocate (Greek, "*parakletos*," literally "called in to help")[6] as used by Jesus at the Last Supper, refers to the coming aid of the Holy Spirit for the future Church (John 15:26). The later use of the same term for Mary's intercessory help for humanity by the Church Fathers further bespeaks the intimate association of the Spirit and the Advocate in the mission of heavenly intercession.[7] One scholar remarks that the title of Advocate "is used almost exclusively for Mary, and not for the saints. Because of its broad impact and because it is a name of Sacred Scriptures proper to the Holy Spirit, it contains also a special consecration. In this respect it is particularly appropriate to Mary, the more so since, by reason of her special relationship to Him, the Holy Spirit unites Himself to Mary's petitions with inutterable sighs.[8]

The intimate union of the Holy Spirit and Mary can be seen in terms of Mary's role as Advocate, interceding from humanity back to God, just as it was evidenced in Mary's role as Mediatrix, interceding from God to humanity.[9] The contribution of Saint Maximilian Kolbe provides a theological foundation for Mary's role as Advocate in interceding back to God on behalf of humanity in inseparable association with the Holy Spirit.

Saint Maximilian Kolbe explains Mary's role in this way: "Every action has a reaction in view. The reaction is the fruit of the action. God the Father is the primary Principle and the Last End. The Immaculata is full of grace; nothing in the way of grace is lacking to her. The path of grace is always the same; action: from the Father through the Son and by the Holy Spirit [and through] the Immaculata; and then the inverse reaction: from creatures through the Immaculata [by] the Holy Spirit and [to] Christ back to the Father."[10]

Mary, therefore, is at the end of the sanctifying action of God (as Mediatrix of all graces), and at the beginning of the reaction of the human family back to God (as Advocate for the People of God). Mary is neither the end nor the starting point of God's action to humanity, but has an instrumental presence at both points because of her intimate union with the Holy Spirit.[11] We see this unified mission of advocacy between the Spirit and the Bride of Pentecost. It is the task of Mary, Advocate for the People of God, to implore the descent of the Holy Spirit, the Paraclete, at times of particular need for the Church. She performs the task of aiding intercession in imploring the Spirit to descend upon the early disciples of the Lord, and will continue this advocating role with the Spirit for the Church. As John Paul II points out, quoting the words of the Second Vatican Council: "We see Mary (Acts 1:4) prayerfully imploring the gift of the Spirit, who had already overshadowed her in the Annunciation.' And so, in the redemptive economy of grace, brought about through the action of the Holy Spirit, there is a unique correspondence between the moment of the Incarnation of the Word and the moment of the birth of the Church. The person who links these two moments is Mary: Mary at Nazareth and Mary in the Upper Room at Jerusalem. In both cases her discreet yet essential presence indicates the path of 'birth from the Holy Spirit.' Thus she who is present in the mystery of Christ as Mother becomes—by the will of the Son and the power of the Holy Spirit—present in the mystery of the Church. In the Church too she continues to be a maternal presence, as is shown by the words spoken from the Cross: 'Woman, behold your son!'; 'Behold your mother'."[12]

Mary's role as Advocate, imploring the aid of the Holy Spirit for the Church in times of need, will continue for the Church until the Second Coming of Christ, the time of which "only the Father knows" (Mark 13:32). Saint Louis de Montfort, singled out by John Paul II among the many witnesses and teachers for his exceptional contribution to "authentic Marian spirituality,"[13] eloquently describes the ongoing fruit of the Holy Spirit and Mary in the members of the Body of Christ, an intercessory and sanctifying action that will only cease with the end of the world: "God the Holy Spirit...has become fruitful by Mary, whom He has espoused. It was with her, in her, and of her that He has produced His greatest masterpiece, which is God made man, and that He goes on producing daily, to the end of the world, the predestined and members of the Body of that adorable Head. This is the reason why He, the Holy Spirit, the more He finds Mary His dear and inseparable spouse in any soul, the more active and mighty He becomes in producing Jesus Christ in that soul and that soul in Jesus Christ.... Mary has produced, together with the Holy Spirit, the greatest thing which has been or ever will be—a God-man; and she will consequently produce the greatest saints that there will be in the end of time. The formation and the education of great saints who shall come at the end of the world are reserved for her."[14]

John Paul II confirms Mary's vital role in the preparation of the people of God for Christ's Second Coming through her special intercession, and as the "mediatrix of mercy:" "If as Virgin and Mother she was singularly united with Him in His first coming, so through her continued collaboration with Him she will also be united with Him in expectation of the second...she also has that specifically maternal role of mediatrix of mercy at His final coming, when all those who belong to Christ 'shall be made alive'" (1 Corinthians 15:26).[15] Since Mary's role as Advocate is inseparable from the divine action of the Spirit, it will be the Spirit and the Bride who will jointly prepare the world for the glorious return of Christ the King (Matthew 16:27; Mark 13:26; 1 Thessalonians 4:15-17) and again say, "Come" (Revelation 22:17).

But indeed not only at Christ's Second Coming, but whenever the Church faces difficult times, the Spirit and the Advocate are called in to help the People of God. Clearly in our own age, the Church and the world are not without their significant dangers and trials. John Paul II has repeatedly referred to the anxious times of the contemporary Church and world, and the new threats which face contemporary humanity.[16]

The present Holy Father specifies such grave concerns for the contemporary world in his encyclical On the Mercy of God: "Let us appeal to the love which has maternal characteristics and which, like a mother, follows each of her children, each lost sheep, even if they should number millions, even if in the world evil should prevail over goodness, even if contemporary humanity should deserve a new 'flood' on account of its sins....and if any of our contemporaries do not share the faith and hope which leads me, as servant of Christ and steward of the mysteries of God, to implore God's mercy for humanity in this hour of history, let them at least try to understand the reason for my concern. It is dictated by love for man, for all that is human and which, according to the intuitions of many of our contemporaries, is threatened by an immense danger."[17]

Our own age, therefore, is certainly not exempt from the need to recognize and call upon Mary as our Advocate today, so that she can once again implore the renewed descent of the Holy Spirit for the spiritual revitalization of the People of God in the modern world.

***

Church teaching warns us about exaggerating Mary's privileges. Mary must always be seen as subordinate to Christ.

Nowhere is this more evident than an incident in Medjugorje with Father Shamon of Rochester, New York, author of a recent book on the Apocalypse. While Father Shamon was visiting the apparition room in Saint James Church on three separate occasions, he brought the consecrated Host into the room. His intent was to "test the spirits." When Mary appeared to the visionaries, Father Shamon was unable to kneel as all do in her presence. His knees had locked! This happened all three times. Being greatly distressed, he then heard a woman's voice audibly say, "I will not have my Son kneel to me."

The texts of Vatican II explain, "We have but one Mediator, as we know from the words of the apostle, 'For there is one God, and one Mediator between God and men, Himself man, Christ Jesus, who gave Himself as a ransom for all' (1 Timothy 2:5-6). The maternal duty of Mary toward men in no way obscures or diminishes this unique mediation of Christ, but rather shows its power. For all the saving influences of the Blessed Virgin on men originate, not from some inner necessity, but from the divine pleasure. They flow forth from the superabundance of the merits of Christ, rest on His mediation, depend entirely on it, and draw all their power from it. In no way do they impede the immediate union of the faithful with Christ. Rather, they foster this union."[18]

"By her maternal charity, Mary cares for the brethren of her Son who still journey on earth surrounded by dangers and difficulties, until they are led to their happy fatherland. Therefore the Blessed Virgin is invoked by the Church under the titles of Advocate, Auxiliatrix, Adjutrix, and Mediatrix. These, however, are to be so understood that they neither take away from nor add anything to the dignity and efficacy of Christ the one Mediator."[19]

Writing in 1918, Pope Benedict XV spoke of Mary's role as Co-Redemptrix: "Mary suffered and nearly died with her suffering Son; for the salvation of mankind she renounced her mother's rights, and as far as it depended on her, offered her Son to placate divine justice; so we may well say that she, with Christ, redeemed mankind."[20]

Mary's message to Father Gobbi, on July 13, 1980, further elucidates her role as Co-Redemptrix. "Jesus is the only Redeemer because He alone is the mediator between God and men. He has however willed to take into partnership in his redemptive work all those who have been redeemed by Him, so that the merciful work of His love may shine forth in a greater and more wonderful way....

"I am for you the perfect model of your cooperation in the redemptive work accomplished by my Son. In fact, as Mother of Jesus, I have become intimately associated with Him in his work of redemption.

"My presence beneath the Cross tells you how my Son has willed to unite his Mother completely to all His great sufferings, at the time of his passion and His death for you.

"If the cross was his scaffold, the pain of my Immaculate Heart was like the altar on which my Son offered to the Father the Sacrifice of the new and eternal covenant.

"My task as a Mother is that of helping my children in every way to attain salvation; and today still, it is that of cooperating in a very special way in the redemption accomplished by my Son Jesus. **My role as true mother and Co-Redemptrix will become manifest to all.**"

On September 15, 1990, Our Blessed Mother reaffirmed her role as Co-Redemptrix through Father Gobbi. "You will see the greatest marvels everywhere, because the times of my maternal co-redemption have arrived." Saint Louis de Montfort called this role of Mary in the latter times a "great mystery, and let all tongues be mute."

Our Lady Of All Nations

Our Lady said at Fatima: **"In the end, my Immaculate Heart will triumph."** Has the time come for the Triumph of the Immaculate Heart to begin? Why was the statue of Our Lady of Akita designed from a picture of *Our Lady of All Nations*? Many Mariologists believe that the revelations of Our Lady of All Nations, also known as *Our Lady of All Peoples,* hold the key to these questions and foretell future events that the world will undergo before the year 2000.[21]

This doctrine brings forth the full truth about Mary and her participation in the work of man's salvation through faith and obedience. It was through her co-operation with the Redeemer, both at the Incarnation and at Calvary, that we give her the title of **Co-Redemptrix. The prefix "co" does not mean equal, but comes from the Latin word "cum" meaning "with." Mary does not participate as an equal, but as one who shared with her Son in the redemptive process. Co-Redemptrix literally means, "with the Redeemer."**

In her role as **Mediatrix of Graces**, Mary cooperates with the perfect mediation of Jesus Christ between God and man. She shares in distributing graces to the People of God, the "gifts of eternal salvation" obtained from the cross (John 19:26). As **Advocate,** Mary brings to God the petitions of the People of God.

The doctrine concerning Mary as Coredemptrix, Mediatrix, and Advocate does not present anything that is fundamentally new in Church teaching. These roles are firmly present in Sacred Scripture and Apostolic Tradition, as taught by the Church's Magisterium.

The apparitions of Amsterdam began on March 25, 1945, (the Feast of the Annunciation) and continued until May 31, 1959, during which time there were fifty-five visions. Our Lady appeared to a middle-aged woman named Ida Perleman and gave messages to Ida that foretold future events concerning many nations, especially changes that would take place in the Church. The most significant prophesy given by Our Lady concerns the last dogma in Marian history to be declared by the Pope. This dogma will declare that Mary is to be known as Co-Redemptrix, Mediatrix, and Advocate.

It is widely believed that the triumph of the Immaculate Heart can only begin after the Church declares this dogma. Let us look briefly at some of Our Lady's messages.

In her first vision of March 25, 1945, Ida was shown that World War II in Holland would end on May 5, 1945. In her message of May 13, 1955, she warned the clergy to be "on guard against false doctrines: especially in what concerns the Eucharist." She also warned of a great apostasy that would come from within the Church. Our Lady revealed to Ida the coming of the Second Vatican Council which was later opened on October 11, 1962, by Pope John XXIII.

During her fifty-fourth vision which occurred on February 19, 1958, Our Lady said to Ida, "I am going to tell you something you are not to mention to anyone, not even to the Sacristan or to your director. Once the event has occurred you will be allowed to mention to them that the Lady has told you this now. This is the communication: Listen, the present Holy Father, Pope Pius XII, will be taken up among our number at the beginning of October of this year. The Lady of All Nations, the Co-Redemptrix, Mediatrix, and Advocate, will lead him to eternal joy."

Since this frightened Ida, Our Lady told her to seal the message and give it to her spiritual director Father Frehe with instructions that it not be opened until October 1. Pope Pius XII died unexpectedly on October 9, 1958.

In her message of December 8, 1952, she said, "I come to unite nations, all nations in the Spirit, the true Holy Spirit." Our Lady said that the times foretold in the past have arrived and that a new era is opening. She frequently repeated, "these are our times."

On September 15, 1990, through Father Gobbi, Our Lady emphasized her role again: "You are the children of my motherly predilection. You have been chosen by me to form part of my victorious cohort. You are an important part of my plan as Mediatrix and Co-Redemptrix. My Son Jesus wanted me beneath the Cross, to associate my Immaculate suffering with his

divine suffering. He wanted to unite my human suffering to His and He associated me intimately in the mystery of His redemption. Thus He called me to be true Co-Redemptrix."

The Last Dogma In Marian History

One of the most significant revelations of Our Lady of All Nations was given on November 15, 1951, when Our Lady appeared on the Earth-globe, with a cross at her back, rays streaming from her outstretched hands, and a multitude of sheep gathered around the globe. She said: "The Lady of All Nations is here, standing before the cross of her Son; her feet are placed in the very midst of the world, and the flock of Jesus Christ surrounds her. It is as Co-Redemptrix and Mediatrix that I come at these times. I was Co-Redemptrix from the moment of the Annunciation. This is the meaning: the mother has been constituted Co-Redemptrix by the will of the Father. Tell this to your theologians. Tell them likewise that **this dogma will be the last in Marian history.**"

Our Lady revealed to Ida Perleman during her fiftieth vision on May 31, 1954, that on a future date of May 31, the Co-Redemptrix, Mediatrix, and Advocate would receive her official title of Our Lady of All Nations. In the course of the same message, the Lady also said: "When the dogma—the last dogma in Marian history—has been proclaimed, the Lady of All Nations would procure peace, genuine peace for the world. But the nations must say my prayer in union with the Church. Then they will experience that the Lady has come as Co-Redemptrix, Mediatrix, and Advocate. So be it."

On February 11, 1951, during her twenty-seventh vision, Our Lady taught Ida Perleman the following prayer:

LORD JESUS CHRIST, SON OF THE FATHER,
SEND FORTH NOW THY SPIRIT OVER ALL THE EARTH.
LET THE HOLY GHOST LIVE IN THE HEARTS OF ALL NATIONS,
THAT THEY MAY BE PRESERVED
FROM MORAL DECLINE, DISASTERS, AND WAR.
MAY THE LADY OF ALL NATIONS,
WHO ONCE WAS MARY,
BE OUR ADVOCATE.
AMEN.

When Our Lady gave this prayer, she said: "This prayer is short so that it could be said by everyone in this busy modern world. It is given to invoke the true Spirit on the world." The propagation of this prayer began after the ecclesiastical approbation in the Netherlands in 1951 and has been backed by the ecclesiastical approbation of more than thirty bishops abroad. The events are presently being investigated. We await the final judgment by the Catholic Church, which we expect in the next several years. For the fulfillment of all the events that were foretold, this dogma must be proclaimed. Cardinal Ratzinger as head of the Propagation of the Faith of the Catholic Church has prompted the re-investigation and has authorized Dr. Mark Miravelle of the Franciscan University to write and release information about this dogma. The information was released on May 27, 1993, in a book entitled, *Mary: Co-Redemptrix, Mediatrix, Advocate.*

Ark of the New Covenant

On that same night I will pass through Egypt and strike down every first-born—both men and animals—and I will bring judgement on all the gods of Egypt; I am the Lord. The blood will be a sign for you on the houses where you are; and when I see the blood, I will pass over you. No destructive plague will touch you when I strike Egypt (Exodus 12:12-13).

Just as the ancient Hebrews were warned to paint their doorposts with the blood of a lamb so the angel of death would pass over their houses, we too, are being warned about catastrophic events that lie ahead. The members of this invisible army, small in number and consecrated to the Immaculate Heart of Mary and the Most Sacred Heart of her Son, are being protected from the events that are to come.

After Israel was freed from slavery in Egypt, it was later protected by God's presence in the Ark of the Covenant. All were given the opportunity for refuge but only a few responded to the call of God's voice in Noah's time. Noah was a laughingstock—until the rains came. We are being told in graphic and specific detail where our safety and refuge should lie—in the Hearts of Jesus and Mary. Wrong has become right and right has become wrong (Isaiah 5:20). Pornography is not even questioned. The rock star Madonna has become a cultural heroine; she simultaneously wears a Lucifer ring on her finger and a rosary around her neck. The virtuous are scorned and ridiculed. "They are not enlightened, their approach has become simplistic, they are all so unsophisticated" is the common cry from those more worldly. In a world increasingly buffeted by forces seemingly beyond our ability to stem or stop—crime, war, abortion, famine, divorce—looking for strength in the simple Virgin of Bethlehem might seem a little naive. But God's plans often are directed to the meek and humble.

Consider what Our Lady said to Father Gobbi and the Marian Movement of Priests on October 29, 1977: **"Do not be surprised, beloved sons, that my Adversary does everything he can to obstruct this Work of mine. His favorite weapon is to sow doubts and perplexity about what I am doing in the Church. He tries to base these doubts on reasons which are seemingly solid and justifiable. Thus he instills a critical attitude toward whatever I tell you, even before you have received and understood my words.**

"You happen to hear of certain brothers of yours who are cultured men and often even experts and masters in theology, who reject those things I tell you, because they sift all my words with their minds, which have already been filled with the richness of their culture. And so they find insurmountable difficulties precisely in those phrases which are so clear to the simple and small. **My words can be understood and accepted only by one whose mind is humble and well-disposed, who has a simple heart, and whose eyes are clear and pure. When the Mother speaks to her children, they listen to her because they love her. They do whatever she tells them, and thus they grow in knowledge and life.**

"Those who criticize her even before they have listened to her, and those who reject what she says before putting it into practice cannot be her children. These people, even though they increase in learning, cannot grow in wisdom and life.

"I tell you this so you will not be troubled if you hear that even the learned and the teachers find difficulty in my words, while everything appears so clear and simple to whomever I call to be little. Look to your heavenly Mother who knows very well where and how to lead you so the plan of her Immaculate Heart may be fulfilled. Do not allow yourselves to be either discouraged or surprised by the doubts and the perplexities which can even increase, without however being prejudicial in any way to my great Work of Love."

On July 30, 1986, Our Blessed Mother explained another of her roles through Father Gobbi: **"This is the moment for all to take refuge in me, because I am the Ark of the New Covenant. At the time of Noah, immediately before the flood, those whom the Lord had destined to survive His terrible chastisement entered into the ark. In these your times, I am inviting all my beloved children to enter into the ark of the new covenant which I have built in my Immaculate Heart for you, that they may be assisted by me to carry the bloody burden of the great trial, which precedes the coming of the day of the Lord. Do not look anywhere else. There is happening today what happened in the days of the flood."**

Our Blessed Mother spoke through Gladys of Argentina on February 6, 1987, about her role as the Ark of the New Covenant. "My daughter, in this time, I am the Ark, for all your brethren! I am the Ark of peace, the Ark of salvation, the Ark where my children must enter, if they wish to live in the Kingdom of God."

Mother of the Second Advent

On January 1, 1990, through Father Gobbi, Mary further stated she is the Mother of the Second Advent. "...I want to take you by the hand and accompany you on the threshold of this decade, which you are beginning precisely on this day. It is a very important decade. It is a period of time particularly marked by a strong presence of the Lord among you. During the last decade of your century, the events which I have foretold to you will have reached their completion. Therefore it is necessary that you allow yourselves to be formed, one and all, by my motherly action.

"...During these years I am preparing you, by my Motherly action, to receive the Lord Who is coming. This is why I have asked you for the consecration to my Immaculate Heart: to form all of you in that interior docility which is necessary for me in order that I may be able to work in each one of you, bringing you to a profound transformation which should prepare you to receive the Lord worthily.

"I am the Mother of the Second Advent. I am preparing you for His new coming. I am opening the way to Jesus who is returning to you in glory. Make level the high hills of pride, of hatred, of violence. Fill in the valleys dug by vices, by passions, by impurity."

Mary as the Precursor of Christ's Coming

Pope John Paul II, in his recent papal encyclical *Redemptoris Mater*, speaks of Mary as the historical precursor of Christ: "The Church has constantly been aware that Mary appeared on the horizon of salvation history before Christ.... When the fullness of time was drawing near—the saving advent of Emmanuel—she who was from eternity destined to be His mother already existed on earth. The fact that she preceded the coming of Christ is reflected every year in the liturgy of Advent."[22]

Today's Marian messages are rooted in solid Church teaching about the Mother's role. They carry the basic historical themes into the peculiar atmosphere of our troubled times, when people of conscience know that things cannot continue to deteriorate as they are now doing. The following, rather startling message to Father Gobbi on July 30, 1986, seems to relate in an explicit way to the above quote from *Redemptoris Mater*.

"This is the moment for all to take refuge in me, because I am the Ark of the New Covenant. At the time of Noah, immediately before the flood, those whom the Lord had destined to survive His terrible chastisement entered into the Ark. In these your times, I am inviting all my beloved children to enter into the Ark of the New Covenant, which I have built in my Immaculate Heart for you, that they may be assisted by me to carry the bloody burden of the great trial, which precedes the coming of the Day of the Lord."

On January 1, 1987, Our Blessed Mother spoke to Father Gobbi about her mission: "I am the Mother of God.... The mission which has been entrusted to me by the Most Holy Trinity should now be acknowledged by the whole Church. I am the dawn which is arising to announce the great day of the Lord.

"During these years, the Church and all of humanity will be left stupefied before the great events of grace and salvation which the Immaculate Heart of your heavenly Mother will bring to you."

The Fragrance Of Roses

Mary's presence is manifested in many places. She often appears with the smell of perfume or roses. The people of the Marian movement are quite familiar with the scent of roses and it is her way of letting people know she is among them. On dozens of occasions we have been among people who will smell a beautiful fragrance and then someone will whisper, "Does anyone smell roses?" Usually several people will be in agreement. The Blessed Mother discussed this sign with Father Gobbi on January 24, 1984:

"A fragrant sign of my maternal presence is to be found in the apparitions I am still making in many regions of the world. Yes, in these times I am appearing in Europe, in Asia, in Africa, in America, and in distant Oceania. The whole world is wrapped in my mantle.... By the sign I give you with the fragrance I exude, sometimes of lesser, sometimes of greater strength, I wish to show you that I am always among you, but especially when you are more in need of me. If you do not recognize the perfume, or you notice it in a very faint way, it is not because I do not love you, or because you are wicked."

Uncharted Waters

Concerning the mystical phenomena around us, we are in uncharted waters. The apostasy, the tribulation, the purification, the imminent great chastisement, the second advent, and the new era of peace, have all been predicted in Scripture by Our Lord for the end times. Mary has been appointed to pilot us through these waters until the Second Coming of the Lord. As Saint Thomas Aquinas said after writing his *Summa*, and defending the faith for a lifetime, "All I have written is mere straw" as he encountered the living God at his death. The systematic theology for Aquinas was acceptable then, as it is today. Aquinas spoke and wrote about God with great inspiration from the Holy Spirit. However, when he met God in the supernatural realm of death, he realized his words had less value as they were no longer adequate to describe his emotions and what he was witnessing. As the mystery is manifested where Mary is appointed Co-Redemptrix, Mediatrix, Advocate, the Mother of the Second Advent, and the Ark of the New Covenant, and other names that baffle our thinking, we must remain open to the mysteries of Heaven.

The Blessed Mother is doing all that is necessary to assure the salvation of her children. Will a mother not do all that she can for the safety of her children if she is able? Because of the apostasy we are living through, the Blessed Virgin Mary told the world through the visionaries of Medjugorje she will do all she can in this span of time: "I wish to continue giving you messages like never before in history since the beginning of time." During the spring of 1982, the visionaries asked the Blessed Mother about other alleged apparitions. They asked, "People are surprised that you are appearing in so many places!" The Blessed Mother responded, "If it is necessary, I will appear in each home."[23]

Conclusion of Apparitions?

The October 25, 1992, message of Medjugorje states, **"Therefore, dear little children, listen and live what I tell you, because it is important for you, when I shall not be with you any longer, that you remember my words and all which I told you."**

This message is significant for us. Mary weaves a theme with her messages and often gives hints and directives on present or future events. It would appear her mission to provide warnings for the world may be nearing completion. Mary has told the visionaries of Medjugorje when her apparitions cease there, three warnings will come to the world. After the third warning, a visible sign will appear for all humanity to see at the place of the apparitions in Medjugorje. The sign will be a testimony of the authenticity of the apparitions. After the visible sign, those who are still alive will have little time for conversion. Recently, Mary is asking for weekly confession, frequent communion, and to remain in a constant state of grace.

4

Prophets In Our Midst

The eyes of Yahweh rove to and fro across the whole world to display His might on behalf of those whose hearts are wholly His.

2 Chronicles 16:9

Today, as never before, we have many special men, women, and children graced with gifts to help others prepare for the coming calamitous times. Just as in the Old Testament God raised up prophets to sound the alarm, today God has given to this era prophets and holy people.

Many of these messages are being heard in all the major faiths. Because the times are extremely urgent, Heaven has provided us with many signs and prophets to warn us. As the world becomes more chaotic and the apostasy, the loss of faith, in the Catholic Church increases, God has raised up these prophets in our times to point out the moral dangers, the heresies, the causes of our difficulties.

The majority of messages have been given since 1981, the year of the first apparition in Medjugorje. Many of the people presently receiving apparitions or messages have been to Medjugorje or have been profoundly affected by Our Lady's appearances there. Many prayer groups throughout countries today such as the United States are a fruit of experiences from trips to this remote village. These specially graced individuals are used as beacons of light to point out the hazardous obstacles on the way to a true faith in God. Today, we have no excuses for not reforming our lives, because Our Lady is appearing all over the world. If someone does not know of any apparitions or their messages, there simply is no interest on his part.

The messages and warnings speak foremost of the need for personal conversion. Our Lady in all authentic apparitions stresses the need for conversion, prayer, fasting, penance and personal consecration.

The messages from the mystics living today echo Our Lady's main messages and warnings. The Blessed Mother has spread her messages throughout the world, not only through her apparitions but also through her prophets' messages as well.

Discernment

One is not a sinner if he does not believe in locutions, heavenly messages, or visions. Belief in apparitions is not the cornerstone of our faith, nor should it be. Frequently, there have been instances of cross-cultural problems in interpretations. This is normal and sometimes is the cause of confusion. Heavenly appearances are more seasoning to what is already a sumptuous feast, and apparitions continue to feed our spirits. Mary's role is pointing to Jesus much in the same way John the Baptist said, "I must decrease, and He must increase" (John 3:30).

The last apparition to receive full recognition by Rome was Beauraing and Banneux, Belgium, in 1932/1933. Many more recent apparitions have the approval of the local bishop. To date, even Medjugorje has not received formal approval from Rome, although nearly 15 million persons have visited the site as well as an estimated 15,000 clergy. Because Marian apparitions are a stumbling block for so many of the faithful, formal Church approval for legitimate apparitions is desirable. On the other hand, the Church must move slowly to fully investigate and observe the long-term fruits and carefully discern exactly what is happening.

To allow more freedom of the Spirit for a particular age, Pope Paul VI allowed in 1966, "publications about new appearances, revelations, prophecies, and miracles to be distributed and read by the faithful without the express permission of the Church, providing that they contain nothing which contravenes faith and morals. This means no *imprimatur* is necessary."[1] This allows flexibility so the Spirit is not quenched.

However, this new freedom also opens the door for potential

abuse. The realm of the spirit means different things to different people, and Satan often appears as an angel of light. *The barometer must be the fruit it produces. Darkness cannot give light.* We often know God by what He is not. He is not envy, confusion, anger, or strife. God is virtue and integrity. He is peace, gentleness, love, kindness, meekness, and humility. The atmosphere surrounding an apparition can be a significant measuring rod for authenticity. Do the statements of the prophets stand the test of time? Are the visionaries obedient to the Magisterium of the Church and the local bishop? Are the messages creating peace or widespread confusion?

To understand more about these modern-day prophets, a short introduction will be given for several mystics. Keep in mind that these individuals are only a few, chosen by the authors of this book for their powerful messages. These people are under spiritual direction and many have gone through the scrutiny of an investigation by the Church. Like Medjugorje, the apparitions, visions, and locutions associated with each messenger are still continuing—for how much longer we are unsure.

The messages in their totality deliver more to us for our salvation than the messages that refer to the warnings of terror and tribulation for mankind. We have cited only excerpts from thousands of Marian messages to emphasize the seriousness of our age and the fervor with which Heaven is trying to get our attention. A complete anthology of Marian apparitions and prophets would be overwhelming. Some big events must be close at hand because Mary is speaking with a frequency and an urgency like never before in all history.[2]

Some Prophets Of Today

Father Don Stefano Gobbi. On May 8, 1972, a simple Italian priest named Father Don Stefano Gobbi was taking part in a pilgrimage to Fatima. An interior force began to assure him that "The Immaculate Heart of Mary" would provide a remedy for the problems the Church was facing among its own clergy. Our Lady, using him as a humble instrument, planned to raise up a cohort of priests throughout the world willing to consecrate themselves to her Immaculate Heart, make a strong commitment of fidelity to the Pope and the Church united with him, and lead the faithful into the secure refuge of her motherly heart. In July 1973, Father Gobbi began to write down some of the locutions Mary had been giving him. He gathered them into a book called, *Our Lady Speaks To Her Beloved Priests.* A later version, including more messages, was entitled *To The Priests: Our Lady's Beloved Sons.*

This truly remarkable book has been translated into many languages, and has been the main instrument used to form the Marian Movement of Priests (MMP). MMP is a true spiritual movement, not a man-made organization. To date, over 300 bishops and cardinals and over 55,000 priests world-wide have embraced its aims and made the suggested commitments. The messages themselves, which have come to Father Gobbi in the form of "interior locutions," deal with the end times, holiness, the coming of Christ in His glory, and a host of other topics pertinent to our day.

Christina Gallagher. Since 1981, a young Irish plumber's wife and mother of two teenagers has been receiving very urgent messages from Jesus, Mary, and various saints, with information about the sins of our day giving rise to calamities which are soon to come. No reputable visionary gives dates—the Blessed Mother warns us, as does Scripture, to be wary of those who speak of specific dates. Yet Christina's messages indicate that we can expect to see events unfold almost imminently. Christina is under the spiritual direction of Father Gerard McGinnity of Ireland, a noted Marian expert with a doctorate in patristics, who is convinced of the authenticity of Christina's experiences. Christina is one among an increasing number of visionaries who spontaneously receive, in their own flesh, wounds which are like those Christ had when He was crucified. Christina suffers from these wounds, called the stigmata, in the form of bloody welts around her forehead, like the crown of thorns.

Maria Esperanza. Maria Esperanza De Bianchini, a devoted wife and the mother of seven children, resides in Betania, Venezuela. Since the age of five, when a vision of Saint Therese (the Little Flower) threw her an actual rose which she caught and ran to give her mother, Maria has experienced a life filled with mystical phenomena. In fact, she was shown as a teenager a vision of a specific piece of land where Mary would later appear. Maria and her husband found the land that corresponded exactly to her earlier vision, and in March 1974 they purchased it. Since March 25, 1976, Mary has been appearing at Betania as "Mother of Reconciliation of All People." Before Our Blessed Mother appears to Maria, a large blue butterfly will often immediately precede her arrival.

Besides the apparitions with their beautiful messages, Mrs. Esperanza continues to be blessed with mystical phenomena: on Good Friday, she bleeds with the stigmata of Christ; at times the Eucharist miraculously appears on her tongue; the aroma of roses attends her presence. Many of the thousands of visitors to Betania also see the Blessed Mother. A Eucharistic host which spontaneously started to bleed in a priest's hands has been studied, found to be authentic, and is now enshrined in the bishop's residence. One particular apparition, when 108 people saw Our Lady in Betania, occurred on March 25, 1984, and has been approved by Bishop Pio Bello, head of the local diocese.

Maria has received many apocalyptic messages, including the following, which seems to refer to the warning: "**There is coming the great moment of a great day of light. The consciences of this beloved people must be violently shaken so that they may 'put their house in order' and offer to Jesus the just reparation for the daily infidelities that are committed on the part of sinners....**"[3]

Mirna of Damascus, Syria. Several yards from where Saint Paul reportedly was knocked off his horse, blinded, and commissioned as "Apostle to the Gentiles," a young housewife and mother of two toddlers has been receiving some of the most startling mystical phenomena being reported thus far. Mirna, a shy, beautiful young woman, a Melkite Greek Catholic, happily married to a Greek Orthodox man, receives words from Our Lord about His desire for unity, particularly between the Orthodox and the Roman Catholic Churches, which separated in 1054. The main unifying factor for the Orthodox and Roman Catholics will be the Blessed Virgin, as her proper role is understood in both faiths.

Mirna not only has the stigmata, which appear on Good Friday and have been captured on video footage, but icons around her pour forth oil—pure 100 percent olive oil. Mirna's body also exudes this pure olive oil, and sensational healings have been documented when people are exposed to the oil and Mirna's prayers. The local Orthodox bishop has posted his approval of Mirna's experiences above her door.[4]

Julia Kim. Mrs. Kim lives in Naju, Korea, and is a married convert to Catholicism and the mother of four children. She experienced a dramatic physical healing after doctors had sent her home from the hospital to die. Since June 30, 1985, a small statue owned by Julia has wept tears of water and of bright red blood—for over seven hundred days. Recently, the statue has been oozing fragrant oil. Jesus and Mary both appear to Julia, and their messages are profound. They have asked Julia to suffer as a "victim soul" to make reparation to Jesus for the sins of others, particularly the sin of abortion. She experiences intense agonies, signs of Heaven's distress at our wanton disregard for human life and God's will to create and bless it. Julia undergoes the agonies of a child as it is being aborted. Sometimes her sufferings last hours. When she receives the Eucharist, it has been photographed on her tongue as real flesh and blood. Julia has the visible stigmata, and the odor of roses is distinct (and remains so, often for months) on objects which she has handled. Julia is under the spiritual direction of Father Raymond Spies.[5]

Jim Singer. Jim Singer was born in Zagreb, the capital of Croatia, in 1952. He is married with two daughters and lives in Ontario, Canada. Until 1991, Jim was the plant manager of a well-known chemical company. In 1991, the firm restructured and made staff reductions affecting Jim. His wife Natalie works at the rectory of the Catholic church they attend. Jim and his wife are Croatian. In Jim's messages, Croatia is referred to as his "ancestral homeland." Long before the hideous war broke out in that part of the world, the Lord had predicted this to Jim and his family.

Jim received one hundred messages from May 1989 to September 1989; since then, they have been less frequent. Jim's messages contain originality, economy of language, and power. Much is said in a few words. Jim introduces us to a new title of Satan: the "Shining Darkness." On May 23, 1993, the Lord spoke to Jim about this "Shining Darkness."

"...so much of that which I admonished you is about to be fulfilled already. I speak to you again because so many of My beloved children of this world continue to wander through this perilous age apathetic to My admonishments, oblivious to the signs of this age, ignoring My calls. I entrusted much to you, I again say to each of you: use all My gifts; let My gifts be your only nourishment. The Shining Darkness lives among you; he is powerful and believe that he does exist. But I tell you again: do not live in fear of his evils. Instead, look at them, look at them well! Tear off the malefactor's numerous masks and firmly confront him. Let the gifts of My Spirit be your shield. Make your sincere, loving prayer your weapon. My children must know that they can only be saved through Me. Know that I alone am your true sanctuary. I want all My children with Me. I desire fidelity, I desire perseverance from each one of My children. I am the Truth, I am the Way, I am the Life. Never forget, it is I who fill with strength every step of each one of My children who walks through life in service to Me."[6]

Six Children of Medjugorje, (former) Yugoslavia. Because we have devoted a chapter to this apparition, we will only briefly mention here that since June 25, 1981, six children in a remote village in Bosnia-Herzegovina have been receiving daily visits with messages from the Blessed Virgin, calling herself the "Queen of Peace." She has been begging the people to amend their lives through prayer from the heart, fasting, reconciliation with God and neighbor, conversion, and peace. Ten years to the day after these visions began, neighboring Croatia seceded from the Yugoslav Federation, sparking the bloodiest war in Europe since World War II. Medjugorje is directly in the middle of this horror, yet all reports have described the people there as peaceful, calm, and loving. Medjugorje has had more impact on the world in the shortest period of time of any apparition—ever. Many other current visionaries report that their experiences with the Mother of God began only after returning from a pilgrimage to Medjugorje. *Life* magazine reported that over 15 million pilgrims have visited this tiny village. The reports of healings, conversions, signs, and wonders are truly astounding. Our Lady, Queen of Peace, has recently said that Medjugorje "is a sign" for the world. She warns about a coming chastisement which will make the war in Bosnia-Herzegovina look like mere child's play.

Luz Amparo Cuevas. Since June 14, 1981, Our Blessed Mother has been appearing to a poor, simple housewife and mother of seven children in Escorial, Spain. Our Lady has revealed herself as Our Lady of Sorrows and has pleaded with Luz Amparo to relay to more and more people the importance of prayer and fasting, of offering daily sacrifices to the Lord, of separating themselves more from the comforts and corrupting influences of the world, of cultivating devotion to the Sacred Heart of her Son, to His passion and death, and to His presence in the Holy Eucharist. By doing so, they can help to alleviate Our Lady's own sorrows and prepare themselves to confront the dangers of this age.

Luz Amparo has known continual pain and suffering since the

beginning of her life. Her mother died when she was six months old. Her father remarried, and her stepmother treated her cruelly. From the age of seven, she was expected to bring in money to the family by working at sidewalk sales. When the little child brought home little or no money, she was beaten, deprived of meals, and cast outdoors to sleep like a homeless waif.

When she was nine years old, she had to be hospitalized for prolonged exposure and for malnutrition. After that, her stepmother kept her at home, frequently locked up in a closet with only dry oatmeal and water for her nourishment. Her education was neglected, and she was rarely sent to church. The little martyr survived mainly on account of her great devotion to Mary, the Mother of God, whose protection she constantly implored.

At the age of sixteen, she married a man much older than herself who also treated her poorly. He suffered from alcoholism and frequent unemployment. Luz Amparo became employed in the homes of the wealthy to do housework and thus was able to raise and educate her children. One of her sons is now a doctor practicing medicine in Madrid.

In the late 1970s, she suffered from cancer and was diagnosed as terminally ill. Her wealthy employers took her to Lourdes in a wheelchair. At Lourdes she was miraculously healed, and two years later in 1981 the Blessed Mother began to appear to Amparo in Escorial. It was on October 16, 1980, that Luz Amparo began to receive her first favors from Heaven. That day she was doing housework for a family when she experienced an interior locution inviting her to "pray for the peace of the world; pray for the conversion of sinners." Almost immediately, she began to bleed from her forehead and from her hands. She asked in an audible tone, "What is this?" In answer to that question, she received a vision of Our Lord on the Cross and the following explanation: "My daughter, it is the passion of Christ. You are called to live it completely," to which Amparo replied, "But I cannot endure it!" Then she heard the voice of the Lord saying: "If you cannot endure these sufferings for a few seconds, how was I able to endure them for long hours on the Cross, dying for those who crucified Me? You will be able to help save many souls by bearing these sufferings." Amparo agreed to accept these sufferings for the salvation of souls.

From that day, the spiritual life of Amparo was deeply changed.

She began to receive invisible stigmata. These invisible signs of the Lord's sacrifice of His Body and Blood for our salvation, occasionally became externalized; her forehead, eyes, mouth, hands, knees, and feet were covered with blood. On all occasions, when the stigmata became externalized, a very pleasant and fragrant perfume surrounded her. Amparo has received many messages about the chastisement and the three days of darkness.

Estela Ruiz. A wife and mother of seven, who resides in Phoenix, Arizona, Estela has received apparitions and messages since December 3, 1988. Mary appears as "Our Lady of the Americas" with messages for all of us. These messages are read to the crowds of people that come to her home. Our Lady appeared to Estela almost daily in 1989, and all of her seven grown children were converted to lives of holiness.

Unlike her husband, Estela had been a skeptic of apparitions and messages until Our Lady began appearing to her. When her husband went to Medjugorje in September of 1988, she was more interested in beginning a career after raising seven children. While walking by a picture of Our Lady of Guadalupe that her husband had painted in their home, she heard the beautiful voice of a woman say, "Good morning, daughter." Her first response was to think that she was hearing things. Two days later, after forgetting about the incident, the same thing happened again. She began to think it might be real. After his return from Medjugorje, she looked into the eyes of her husband of thirty years, and he looked different. Something had changed him. Estela realized that Our Lady was changing her as well.

Several months later, in December of 1988, the Blessed Mother began to appear to Estela. During the first apparition, Our Lady told her, "I have come to ask you to be my messenger, and I want to know if you will do it? I'm going to help you and your children make many changes. There will be a period of time where I will prepare the family and I will send many messages to the family." Since then, the family has all experienced conversions resulting in great changes. A son who was addicted to drugs has been completely healed and is now a powerful witness for Our Lord.

A message received by Estela on January 19, 1991, is not unlike those in many other parts of the world. It referred to the basics of prayer, conversion, and fasting. Mary said, "For those who have listened to my call I now ask that you commit yourselves to my work.

Begin your life of prayer in earnest and let nothing keep you away from that commitment. I am now asking the Americas for fasting as a sacrifice of love. Begin your fasting immediately. I need your commitment of prayer and sacrifice. There is no more time to dwell on your small self concerns. Leave self-pity and anger with others. There is no more time for that behavior. If you have not yet learned to love those around you, how can you expect the world to learn the love of which I have been speaking about.... I ask that you offer two fasting days a week for peace in the world. We must not and cannot give up hope...."

On one occasion, Our Lady appeared to Estela Ruiz at the Immaculate Heart Church in Phoenix. Estela reported, "I asked Our Lady who she was, what she was doing, and who had sent her. Our Lady said, "I am the Immaculate Heart of Mary." She then said, 'This is my reign—this is the time of my reign. I am here to bring my children back to my Son. The one who sent me is God, Our Father.' I then asked her who she was and she said, 'I am the Immaculate Heart of Mary, but I am the same one that has appeared all over the world.' She told me, 'Look around this church and see all the different forms in which I have appeared.'"

Estela said that in this church they have statues of Our Lady of Sorrows, Our Lady of Guadalupe, and Our Lady of Fatima. Our Lady said: "Yes, I am the Mother of God, and I have appeared in different places. There is only one and that is I and I am all of these. But I come today, at this time, as the Immaculate Heart of Mary as this is the reign of my Immaculate Heart. And I've come to call my children back to God."

In another message given on March 2, 1991, Our Lady said, "I ask that you continue to pray for peace in the world. You need to understand that peace is not brought about by victory in a battle, but by change in men's hearts and lives.... Men need to understand that if hearts do not change, the devastation and destruction of each other will continue throughout the world...."

The diocese of Phoenix established a commission of inquiry under Bishop Thomas O'Brien to investigate the claimed apparitions. The bishop stated, after reviewing the findings of the commission: "It is our assessment that no harm is presently done to either the Church as an institution or to the faithful by the devotions...." As Our Lady of the Americas, Mary is inviting us to recognize the true meaning of our lives and to strengthen and intensify devotion to Our Lord Jesus Christ.[7]

Theresa Lopez. Theresa Lopez of Denver, Colorado, has been told she will be one of many sparks igniting the faith of the lukewarm in the West. Theresa grew up Catholic and like many others of her generation had lost interest in the faith so she could "go out into the world." Both she and her husband Jeff had not been married in the Church in previous marriages, with the problems of annulments, single parenthood, and divorce.

On April 3, 1990, Theresa awoke in the middle of the night hearing a voice telling her to "read the word." After realizing it was not a prank of her children, she opened the Bible to Ephesians 1:15-19. The words she read were: "For my part, from the time I first heard of your faith in the Lord Jesus and your love for all the members of the church, I have never stopped thanking God for you and recommending you in my prayers. May the God of Our Lord Jesus Christ, the Father of glory, grant you a spirit of wisdom and insight to know Him clearly. May He enlighten your innermost vision that you may know the great hope to which He has called you, the wealth of His glorious heritage to be distributed among the members of the church, and the immeasurable scope of His power in us who believe." After reading until dawn she conveyed her experience to Jeff, her husband. In amazement, Jeff produced a tattered piece of paper from his wallet written down ten years earlier during a low point in his life with the identical verse written on it. In March of 1991, Theresa felt called to go to Medjugorje, where she experienced several spiritual phenomena with the visionaries and with some of the pastoral team, including Father Slavko Barbaric, one of the Franciscan Fathers assigned to Saint James Church.

Upon returning to the United States, the spiritual phenomena continued. She heard a voice say, "Bring my children to the spring," and the only spring she could think of was at the Mother Cabrini Shrine in Golden, Colorado. Word began to spread and the crowds came much as at other apparition sites throughout the world. Another locution instructed, "I desire all of you to gather on the second Sabbath of the month." Phenomena such as the Blessed Mother's image on the tabernacle with two doves on each side, an image of Jesus as shepherd, bright lights shining from the tabernacle, and instances of people witnessing the visions of the Blessed Mother have occurred. On one occasion after a message, Theresa said, "Mother, I love you" to the Blessed Mother. She then came forward and kissed Theresa on the forehead.

The scene is similar to the one in Medjugorje and apparitions elsewhere in the world. There is no explanation in the natural realm. Only in the supernatural realm can such occurrences be explained. Self-described as a marginal Catholic, Jeff had never prayed a rosary until their infant daughter died of Sudden Infant Death Syndrome. Theresa would consider praying the rosary only at funerals. Josyp Terelya, who was imprisoned for over twenty years in the former Soviet Union because of his faith, has said that this site will be a place where many miracles will take place, and it will become a very great pilgrimage center just like Fatima and Medjugorje.[8]

Josefina-Maria. Josefina-Maria was born in Melbourne, Australia, of Italian parents. She is married, works as a schoolteacher, and lives a simple life centered on her work, her domestic duties, and prayer. Josefina began receiving messages from Our Lord and Our Lady on September 20, 1990; since then she has received over 1000.

Josefina's messages are meant for the world. They speak of peace, conversion, prayer, fasting, faith, simplicity, humility, and the limitless love and mercy of God. The messages have already borne much fruit in the Melbourne area, inspiring the formation of special prayer groups and renewed devotion to the Sacred and Immaculate Hearts.

As with others of today's visionaries, the Lord is using Josefina to warn the world that the times of God's Justice are at hand. More and greater chastisements loom on the horizon, says Jesus through Josefina. But He also tells us not to fear, for the punishments will serve for the salvation of souls and to renew a world that has been despoiled by greed and sin.

"Be not afraid, My people," Jesus said through Josefina on July 22, 1993. "I love you with My Most Sacred Heart. Everyone must pass through Me before they go to the Father."

"My people, many plagues and disasters are befalling the earth, and yet many do not recognize these as being those which are foretold in Scripture. But My people, do not be afraid, for My divine hand protects you like a blanket. Those of you who belong to Me have nothing to fear. You will not be harmed.

"The sufferings of the times we are in are for the salvation of souls,

My people, My little ones. Be not afraid, My humble ones; those of you who have given Me your lives, and given Me your all...My Father's plan [to renew the face of the earth] is unfolding. Remain in peace and be constant in love, leading My people in peace; but always reminding them of My love. Make sacrifices, My children, and be My co-redeemers in helping in My Father's plan."[9]

Joseph Januszkiewicz. The media also have extensively reported alleged Marian apparitions to Joseph Januszkiewicz of Marlboro, New Jersey, who was instantly cured of a serious, work-related back injury and a partial hearing loss after a visit to Medjugorje in 1988. He went there as a skeptic, but in 1989 he began receiving messages from Mary. The apparitions which began on a daily basis on March 17, 1989, now occur publicly on the first Sunday of each month and on a sporadic basis privately. There is a specific orientation of his messages for the clergy. This apparition is under examination by Church authorities in the Trenton, New Jersey, diocese.[10]

There are many more men and women of God that we want to mention briefly, such as Josyp Terelya, a Ukrainian Catholic dissident now living in Canada; Julka of Zagreb (former Yugoslavia); Sister Lucia of Fatima; Sister Agnes Sasagawa of Akita; the visionaries of Garabandal; Eileen George of Worcester, Massachusetts; Sister Anna Ali, Kenya; Father James Bruse of Lake Ridge, Virginia; Mariamante of the Apostolate of Holy Motherhood, Michigan; Sister Natalia of Hungary; Dozule, France; and others.

By no means is this list a definitive one. It is impossible to list all of the prophets in our age receiving messages from Jesus or the Blessed Mother. The Book of Kings tells the story of how Elisha would not leave the side of Elijah, as Elisha and "the company of prophets" knew in advance that Elijah was to be taken to Heaven. God had communicated this to the "company of prophets." The lineage of prophets from the earliest of time to the present day remains unbroken.

5

Our Lady's Role
In Salvation

...but the Blessed Virgin's salutary influence on men originates not in any inner necessity but in the disposition of God. It flows forth from the superabundance of the merits of Christ, rests on His Mediation, depends entirely on it and draws all power from it....

Lumen Gentium, Vatican II

Saint Louis de Montfort, in the Seventeenth Century, wrote about what it would be like for the Church in the latter days, and the role of Mary in that plan. He stated, **"In the Second Coming of the Lord, Mary will be made known in a special way by the Holy Spirit so that through her, Jesus may be better known and served.... Mary will shine forth higher than ever in these latter days to bring back poor sinners who have strayed from the Family of God....** However, souls hardened by impiety will provoke a terrible rebellion against God attempting to lead all souls astray (even those who oppose their revolt) and they will cause many to fall by their threats, snares and alluring promises.... Satan, knowing that he has little time left, will redouble his efforts and his combats. He will conjure up cruel persecutions and put terrible snares in the path of the faithful.... **Mary will raise up apostles of the latter times to make war against the evil one....** They shall be little and poor in the world's esteem and

will even be persecuted by other members of the Body of Christ. But
they shall be rich in grace and Mary will bless them abundantly....
**They will have recourse to Mary in all things and they will know
the shortest and most perfect way of going to Jesus and they will
belong entirely to Him....** They shall be the true apostles of the latter
times, to whom the Lord shall give the word and might to work
marvels and to carry off the spoils of His enemies.... They shall carry
the gold of love in their hearts, the incense of prayer in their spirit,
the myrrh of mortification and self-sacrifice in their bodies.... They
shall be true disciples of Jesus Christ, faithfully following in His
footsteps, teaching the narrow way to salvation according to the Holy
Gospels.... These are the great men who will come at the end of time
and Mary is the one who by order of the Most High will fashion them
to extend God's Kingdom and to manifest the Lord's victorious
triumph over the impious and over all His enemies."[1]

Given A Unique Role

The apparitions started as early as AD 41, with the arrival of Saint
James as a missionary on the Iberian Peninsula. One may hear and see
the story today in Santiago de Compostela in northern Spain, one of
the largest basilicas in all of Europe. It is dedicated to Saint James,
Apostle of Jesus Christ. It is interesting to note that Saint James was
the first apostle to be martyred in the Church, and the Blessed Mother
has said that her last apparitions for the public in this epoch will be
at Saint James Church in Medjugorje.

Mary has a unique relationship to the Holy Trinity: she is the
daughter of the Father, Mother of the Son, and spouse of the Holy
Spirit. It was solely from Mary that Jesus received His humanity, as
He had no earthly father. The Council of Ephesus in 431 declared that
Mary is "God-bearer" or Theotokos. No other creature had, or can
ever have, this unique relationship with the Creator of the Universe.
Through Mary's humility, obedience, and faith, the human and the
divine became blood relatives, in the Incarnation of the God-Man.
The Father chose one woman out of all the beings He created to
cooperate in giving a human nature to His only-begotten Son.

This is a profound mystery. No angel nor any man was chosen to
receive this honor of presenting the long awaited Messiah, the Light,
and the Redeemer of Mankind, into the darkness of the world.
Instead, a humble young Virgin was given the joy of assisting in

preparing a body for God (Hebrews 10:5), in order that He might manifest Himself as one of us. Mary was predestined from all eternity by God to carry out this role. She most perfectly represents the "highly favored daughter" of Zion, prefigured in Sacred Scripture, who cooperates in the deliverance of her people, Israel. She was the one whom the angel greeted with the words, "Hail Mary, full of grace. The Lord is with you," fulfilling to the letter Isaiah's prophecy made hundreds of years earlier that "Behold, a virgin shall conceive, and bear a son, and his name shall be called Emmanuel" (Isaiah 7:14), a name which means "God is with us."

Mary's role derives entirely from her relationship to Jesus Christ. She was enabled to receive God into her very being, because He had prepared her specifically for this role. By a singular privilege, she was totally pure, oriented only towards God, empty of all self-importance and self-will. Her humility and lowliness enabled the Light to be mirrored perfectly in her soul. Similarly, she was specially prepared by God so that she, like her Son, was never under the dominion of original sin. Like John the Baptist, Mary was a precursor to Eternal Light but was not that Light herself. However, she has an utterly unique relationship with that Light, and it symbolizes the new relationship we are all intended to have, when we finally attain the fullness of our heavenly reward.

As we explore the Church's understanding of Mary, we remember that she is a human being, and like each of us, has no glory whatsoever, apart from God. But because Our Lord became man through the Virgin Mary, we would be foolish not to seek out the fullness of the message the Lord wished to convey. For God's choices are not whimsical; rather, they are profound in wisdom. The Church's constant reflection and prayerful study over time have discerned great meaning in Mary's role, both in Heaven and on earth. Her preparation for her earthly role is "the Immaculate Conception," a doctrine stating that she was preserved at conception from the stain of original sin. This was proclaimed by Pius IX in 1854 and confirmed four years later to Saint Bernadette at Lourdes, when the Blessed Mother said, "I am the Immaculate Conception."

Nearly 2,000 years ago, God united a human nature to Himself, in the womb of a Virgin. The ancient Hebrew Scriptures had foretold this event, and the Jewish people patiently awaited the prophecies' fulfillment. An angel, Gabriel, appeared to Mary, as the angel Lucifer had once appeared to Eve. Unlike Eve, who succumbed to the devil's temptation to glory ("and ye shall be as gods"), Mary humbly consented to the Father's eternal plan, agreeing to conceive God's only-begotten Son within her womb. She said simply, "I am the handmaiden of the Lord, be it done to me according to thy word," and the promised redemption of all mankind began to unfold before the darkened eyes of the world.

Saints and Popes throughout much of Church history have spoken of Our Lady's intimate association with Christ in our redemption. They have also spoken of her mediation of grace to us and of her unceasing prayer to her Divine Son on our behalf. The Popes of the past have clearly taught the doctrines of Our Lady as Co-Redemptrix and Mediatrix of All Graces. These truths have not yet been solemnly defined as dogma, but they are a part of our Catholic heritage. Note that the dogma of the Assumption was not defined until 1950, even though the liturgical feast was established by the Church in the Sixth Century, and Christian writings testify to it as early as the Second Century.

Mary has revealed to many mystics that the Lord wishes us to accept and invoke her as Co-Redemptrix, Mediatrix, and Advocate to complete the Church's official recognition of what the Almighty has done for and through her (Luke 1:49). The visions of Ida Perleman of Amsterdam and "The Lady Of All Nations" confirm this role.

Jesus Christ, as Scripture and Tradition teach, is the Mediator between God and man, our Redeemer and Intercessor before the Father. From Christ, by the will of the Father and the power of the Holy Spirit, proceeds all grace and our salvation. But in His unceasing activity on our behalf, Jesus does not hesitate to share His own prerogatives with those whom He is not ashamed to call His brothers (Hebrews 2:11). For example, He is the only High Priest, yet He shares His priesthood with the ordained ministers of His Church. Jesus shares with His beloved Mother His divine privileges to the extent that she, as a created human being, is capable of possessing them. Vatican II teaches that Our Lady's mediation is a sharing in the unique source that is the mediation of Christ Himself.

The Greek Fathers understood the Incarnation to be a true redemptive act, not just the necessary prelude to the Cross. All of creation has been sanctified since the Son of God united a created nature to Himself. Thus Mary played an essential cooperative role in our redemption by giving flesh to the Word. Saint Augustine speaks of the womb of the Virgin Mary as the bridal chamber wherein divine nature united itself to human nature. Yet this is not the completion of her cooperation.

Our Lady said to the visionary Ida of Amsterdam: "The Lord and Master had predestined the Lady for sacrifice. For the sword had already been directed at the heart of the Mother"[2] (Luke 2:35). Mary was chosen by God to share interiorly in the sufferings of Jesus in a unique fashion—and this is not simply because she alone had a mother's love for Him. Jesus, the New Adam, chose to associate Mary, the New Eve, as a bridal partner in His work of redemption. Mary as the New Eve has been explicitly taught as early as the middle of the Second Century by Saint Justin.

The whole Church is the Bride of Christ. Mary, because she represented fully in herself the Church, not only suffered with Christ but also received from Him the fullness of the grace of redemption, for all people of all times. Because of this cooperation with our redemption, Our Lady has become the Mediatrix of Grace to all those whom Christ has made her children at Calvary.

Christ, as the God-man, accomplished the work of our redemption, yet He willed to associate Mary with this work. He grants His saving grace to the whole Church through the mediation of Mary, who stood by the Cross and took us all into her maternal suffering. Our Lady stands not only as Mediatrix of Grace from Christ to us; as Advocate, she brings our prayers and needs to Him. As Co-Redemptrix, Mediatrix, and Advocate, Mary lives in the glory of the Lord as His Mother and Handmaid.

Tradition

Catholic veneration of Mary is directly related to and derived from Catholic faith in Christ. If He is not the Eternal Son of God made flesh for our salvation, then Mary does not deserve any more honor than the mother of some famous person. Saint Louis de Montfort wrote that Mary is not worth an atom of importance compared to Jesus. Yet many of our beautiful writings about Mary come from Saint Louis. But if Jesus is all that the Bible and the Church say He is, then Our Lady is worthy of the honor due to the Mother of God. **Catholic teaching does not instruct anyone to worship Mary. Rather, Catholics venerate Mary because of the role that was given her.**

The Marian dogmas that were defined in the early Councils of the Church were done so to safeguard the truth of the Christological dogmas which were disputed. The Mother cannot be separated from the Son. Certain inescapable conclusions concerning Our Lady follow from what has been revealed about Christ. The Church has carefully defined and faithfully preached these truths throughout her history. Excluding Our Lady from the mystery of God and our salvation can only leave one with an impoverished form of Christianity bereft of the totality of Christ's redemptive mission.

Mary And Her Protestant Children: A Critical Explanation

The Catholic Faith and the other major denominations have been at odds since the Reformation on many issues. The definition of the Eucharist as a symbolic act or the Real Presence, the issue of faith and tradition, and the Blessed Mother are only a few of the issues that divide Catholics from Protestants. Due to the complex nature of this subject, it is impossible adequately to mention all of the issues which divide us, but, we hope some insight will be gained to shed more light than heat on the subject of Catholic devotion to Mary.

Devotion to Our Lady is a precious jewel in the crown of Catholicism, but it seems to be a thorn in the flesh for most Protestants. Practically all Catholic Marian doctrines are rejected by the vast majority of Protestants. This is an unfortunate heritage of the "Reformation," although the reformers themselves were much more Catholic in their thought and devotion than most of their spiritual descendants. The seemingly endless series of schisms which began with Luther have separated numerous Christians from their Mother the Church, and from their mother Mary, and yet Martin Luther himself had a deep devotion to the Mother of God.

Here we will briefly examine a few basic ideas characteristic of much of Protestantism, which constitute an obstacle to the acceptance of Marian doctrines as well as other truths taught by the Catholic Church. Admittedly, we cannot speak authoritatively for every Protestant church or sect, nor can we go into great detail. But we can gather some insights into a few common beliefs and ways of thinking among Protestants that unnecessarily limit access to the fullness of the truth of divine revelation and the means God has used to communicate it to us.

Holy Tradition is one of the chief areas of contention. The principle of "Scripture alone" (Sola Scriptura) as the sole source of divine revelation is a hallmark of Protestantism. Yet Scripture supports the concept of tradition (2 Thessalonians 2:15; 2 Timothy 2:2), and nowhere does Scripture state that Scripture alone is the whole of revelation. If the "Sola Scriptura" principle cannot be found in the Bible, how can it be upheld by those who believe only what the Bible says?

The Bible often refers to the preached Gospel, the oral tradition which preceded (and still accompanies) the written one. If the Bible is the only source of revelation, then the first generations of Christians had no revelation, for they had no Bible or rather, no New Testament. But in truth they did have the Word of God: it was preached to them by the Apostles and their successors.

There are doctrines concerning Our Lady which are not explicitly taught in Scripture, but which have been handed down through Holy Tradition, as faithful expressions of the beliefs and practices of the Church founded by Jesus Christ. Often Catholics speak of Scripture and Tradition as the sources of revelation. But perhaps it would be more accurate to speak of Scripture in Tradition, since every authentic teaching—whether oral or written—which has been handed down from the Apostles through their successors is part of Holy Tradition, the heritage of our Lord Jesus Christ

Teaching Authority Of The Church

Who determines that a particular teaching rightly expresses the apostolic faith? Here is another difficulty for non-Catholics: the authority of the Catholic Church. Jesus promised to set His Church on the rock of Peter, giving him the "power of the keys" to bind and loose, with the further promise that the gates of hell would never prevail against it (Matthew 16:18-19). He also promised that the Holy Spirit would be with His Church, leading His disciples into the whole truth (John 16:12-13). Therefore the Church, with the guaranteed guidance of the Holy Spirit, is empowered to judge the authenticity of any teaching which is proposed as expressing the apostolic faith.

The multiplication of Protestant sects is due in significant measure to the failure of their reliance on personal interpretation of Scripture (ostensibly led by the Holy Spirit) as a means of discerning the truth.

The Holy Spirit has not created the division and confusion resulting from contradictory personal interpretations.

A clear example of God's gift of the assistance of the Holy Spirit to His Church is that the Church was able to decide, among many writings attributed to the apostles, and other writings being read in the liturgical assemblies, which ones were divinely inspired and which ones were not. The canon of the New Testament was not completely set until the end of the Fourth Century (although most canonical books were accepted before then). If the Church can discern which writings constitute the word of God, then she can certainly discern which traditions and teachings constitute divine revelation.

The Ecumenical Councils are examples of the way the Church clarified the teachings of the Gospel and defended them against heretical misinterpretation. The history of the development of Marian doctrines is more evidence of the way the Holy Spirit has led the Church into the whole truth about the Christian faith. He did say that He would be with us always, that the Spirit would lead us, and that His Church would not be overcome by the power of hell. Jesus with us through His Spirit in the Church is the living Tradition which communicates with ever brighter clarity the Gospel of salvation to every age and culture. The very last paragraph in the gospel of Saint John (John 21:25) points implicitly to the existence of a tradition: "There are, however, many other things that Jesus did; but if every one of these should be written, not even the world itself, I think, could hold the books that would have to be written."

The Incarnation

The Incarnation of the Son of God is believed by all Christians. But Catholic theology rightly sees the Incarnation as much more than a necessary prerequisite for the atoning death of Jesus. Much Protestant theology focuses exclusively on the Cross, and this tends to restrict theological reflection on the Incarnation. Such reflection would naturally lead to the awareness of the indispensable role of Our Lady in the work of our salvation, and of her exalted dignity in the eyes of God.

Many Fathers of the Church, especially the great Patristic Fathers, understood the Incarnation to be itself a redemptive act, although not the completion of redemption. The astounding reality of God becoming man, uniting a created nature inseparably to His uncreated nature, is enough to sanctify all creation and to bring it into a new relationship to Himself. According to the wisdom of God, Mary's role in the divine Incarnation is essential: by her personal consent she gave flesh and blood to God. The Father saw Mary from all eternity as the Woman full of grace who alone would give His Son to the world as the God-man, our Savior.

But if Mary were just a devout Jewish girl who happened to be as good a choice as any to give birth to the Messiah (as well as to other children, many falsely claim), and who then could fade into obscurity, the ineffable mystery of the Incarnation is robbed of its richness. It is inconceivable that the only woman destined to give birth to God in the flesh would not have received extraordinary graces for this exalted vocation, or that God would not desire to glorify in a special way one so graced. Yet the great fear of giving the least bit of attention or honor to the Mother of Jesus keeps many from appreciating the fullness and depth of the wisdom and love of God, who "sent forth his Son, born of a woman..." (Galatians 4:4). The Incarnation also provides the rationale for the whole sacramental system as well as for the use of sacred images, all of which is generally rejected in Protestantism.[3]

Openness To The Holy Spirit

Mary's role is always one of "magnifying the Lord." In the first chapter of Luke, we see one of the most beautiful passages in Scripture. Zechariah, the High Priest, was married to Elizabeth, and both are on in years. Elizabeth is barren and childless and suffers from the humiliation of this state. Zechariah makes every attempt to please God and be a righteous man in his daily life. While in the sanctuary, the angel Gabriel visits Zechariah at the altar, and Gabriel says, "Elizabeth is to bear you a son and you must name him John. Even from his mother's womb he will be filled with the Holy Spirit...and be filled with the power of Elijah" (Luke 1:11-17). Zechariah the High Priest, the man of God, doubts the angel and says, "How can I be sure of this? For I am old and my wife is getting on in years." For doubting, the angel Gabriel immediately strikes him dumb until the birth of John. Gabriel did this "because you [Zechariah] did not believe my words (Luke 1:20). Elizabeth conceives, bears a son and names him John, as the angel had given her this prompting for his name. She no longer suffers humiliation as she is now with child.

Gabriel then visits Mary (Luke 1:26) and says, "Rejoice so highly favored! The Lord is with you." Like Zechariah, she is fearful at the beginning, and Gabriel says, "Do not be afraid, you are to bear a son and call him Jesus. He will be great and called Son of the Most High." Mary, being a virgin, does not understand how she can conceive. Gabriel responds, "The Holy Spirit will come upon you and the power of the Most High will cover you with its shadow" (Luke 1: 36). "And the child will be called the Son of God." Mary's response is in stark contrast to Zechariah the High Priest: "I am the handmaid of the Lord, let what you have said be done to me. And the angel left her" (Luke 1:38).

Mary believed with all her heart the angel's words; she just did not understand. Gabriel explained that God would miraculously allow her to be with child. She accepted everything, even without the benefit of complete understanding. She takes his words, on faith, to be true.

Mary visits Elizabeth her cousin and both are aware she is carrying the Son of God. Elizabeth, filled with the Holy Spirit, says, "Blessed is she who believes that the promise made her by the Lord would be fulfilled."

Mary's Response

Mary's response is the model for all Christians. She believed what Heaven ordained. She did not doubt, but in her littleness trusted. Nothing is more illogical than the Holy Spirit coming upon a virgin, the virgin conceiving, and then bearing the Son of God.

Since Mary was chosen from the very beginning for a very special and exalted role, is it not fitting that the role of Mary is to increase if Heaven ordains it? In contrast to Eve, she freely and willingly accepted the role, and thus allowed God's redemptive act to be accomplished through her. She, like Eve, could have rejected this, but she as the New Eve assumed the role destined for her.

Mary separated herself from all of humanity and accepted the Will of the Father in her life. She became the chosen vessel for Heaven to present the Redeemer of all mankind. The lowly woman of Nazareth had been created by God the Father for the purpose of bearing Jesus. God had chosen a way to come into the world defying all human reason, manifesting an unconventional birth to an unconventional death: the Redeemer, born of a poor and humble woman, in a stable.

Mary's journey from Nazareth to the Upper Room took thirty-three years in time, but it took far more in terms of her understanding of what it means to be a Christian. It was a most demanding journey: at times incredible, at times joyous, at times difficult, at times puzzling. It was a journey of many twists and turns, but at every bend she was open to God's Word, took it into her heart, and pondered its meanings and its implications.

And she trusted.

To listen to the Word of God, to ponder it, to accept it, not only with the intellect but with the heart and the will, and to be the source of its incarnation—this is what Mary tells us being a Christian means.

The Magnificat

And Mary said, "My soul proclaims the greatness of the Lord
and my spirit exults in God my savior;
because he has looked upon his lowly handmaid.
Yes, from this day forward, all generations will call me blessed,
for the Almighty has done great things for me.
Holy is His name,
and his mercy reaches from age to age for those who fear Him.
He has shown the power of His arm,
He has routed the proud of heart.
He has pulled down princes from their thrones
and exalted the lowly.
The hungry He has filled with good things,
the rich He sent away empty.
He has come to the help of Israel His servant,
mindful of His mercy—according to the promise he made
to our ancestors—of His mercy to Abraham and to his
descendants forever" (Luke 1:46-55).

Here is the Blessed Mother's gift and example to the world for all of us to imitate. The Blessed Mother magnified God's glory. Mary's will was God's will, and she was open to His gifts. Mary's role is that

of model and intercessor before the throne of God on behalf of all
mankind, as the words to this beautiful hymn proclaim:

Tota pulchra es Maria,   You are all beautiful, O Mary,
Et Macula Originalis   and the stain of original sin
Non, non, est in te.   is not in you.
Tu gloria Jerusalem,   You are the glory of Jerusalem,
Tu laetitia Israel,   You are the joy of Israel
Tu honorificentia   You are most honored
Populi Nostri.   by our people;
Intercede pro nobis   Intercede for us
Ad Dominum Jesum Christum   to the Lord, Jesus Christ.

Book II
A Mother's Warning

6

The Secrets Of
The Apocalypse

I am opening for you the sealed book, that the secrets contained in it may be revealed.

Our Lady to Father Don Stefano Gobbi
Marian Movement of Priests
October 13, 1988

For nearly 2,000 years, the Book of Revelation has been at best an enigma, a riddle, and a puzzle. Ask five people to interpret a verse and you will get five versions for a response. Maybe six.

Most of those who have tried to interpret this mysterious book of the Bible have failed. Some have speculated about the numerology of 666 and its applicability to several world leaders. Gorbachev and the port wine stain on his forehead were thought by some to be ingredients to the riddle; the beast with ten horns was the emergence of the ten nations of the Common Market with its one currency; the seat of Rome was the whore of Babylon. The list progresses from the entertaining to the absurd. Until now.

Revelation brings with it some unique promises: to all who read it, a special grace is given (Revelation 1:3); to all who add anything to the messages, "God will give to him the plagues contained in the book. For all who subtract, God will cut off his share of the tree of life" (Revelation 22:18).

In his book *Apocalypse: The Book for Our Times*, Father Albert Shamon suggests why this book is so hard to understand. He proposes it was written in such a symbolic manner as to keep hidden the secrets of God from the enemies of God. Enlightenment is needed. Until recently, Revelation has been a sealed book in which readers were given only rare glimpses of eternal truth.

Genesis And Revelation

The Book of Revelation cannot be understood rightly without going back to a passage in Genesis. Here, "the woman" (Eve) is forever cast out of the garden of paradise because of her cooperation with "the serpent," who is punished by being cast to the earth. "And the Lord God said to the serpent: Because thou hast done this thing, thou art cursed among all the cattle, and beasts of the earth: upon thy breast shalt thou go, and earth shalt thou eat all the days of thy life. I will put enmities between thee and the woman, and thy seed and her seed: she shall crush thy head, and thou shalt lie in wait for her heel" (Genesis 3:14-15).

Revelation promises that one day the head of the serpent will be crushed by "the woman" (the "New" Eve, as the Church Fathers would refer to Mary). "The woman" Eve had a decisive role in the fall of mankind, through her **disobedience** to God and desire to exalt herself. "The woman" Mary has a decisive role in the salvation of mankind, through her **obedience** to God, Who has "regarded the humility of His handmaid; for behold from henceforth all generations shall call me blessed." (Luke 1:48) The fulfillment of God's promise of salvation in Revelation 12 (the Woman clothed with the sun battles the serpent and crushes his head) complements the original promise made in Genesis 3.

The prophecy of Genesis 3 has been fulfilled with Revelation 12, where Mary is the great sign in Heaven: "And a great sign appeared in Heaven: a woman clothed with the sun, with the moon under her feet and on her head a crown of twelve stars." Pope Paul VI, in his 1967 encyclical, *Signum Magnum*, identified the Lady of Fatima as the biblical representation of the Woman clothed with the sun.

The Sealing Of The Scroll

"I saw in the right hand of the One sitting on the throne there was a *scroll that had writing on the back and on the front* and was sealed with seven seals. Then I saw a powerful angel who called out with a loud voice, 'Is there anyone worthy to open the seals of it?' But there was no one, in Heaven or on the earth or under the earth, who was able to open the scroll and read it. I wept bitterly because there was nobody fit to open the scroll and read it, but one of the elders said to me, 'There is no need to cry: *the Lion of the tribe of Judah, the Root of David,* has triumphed, and he will open the scroll and the seven seals of it' (Revelation 5:1-5).... Then I saw the Lamb break one of the seven seals" (Revelation 6:1-1).

In Chapters six, seven, and eight of Revelation, the seals are broken. The seventh seal in Chapter eight, "was broken and there was silence in Heaven for about half an hour. Next I saw the seven trumpets" (Revelation 8:6), which are various forms of disasters upon the earth. In Chapter eleven, the seventh angel blew his trumpet.

"The nations were seething with rage and now the time has come for your own anger, and for the dead to be judged, and for your servants the prophets, for the saints and for all who worship you, small or great, to be rewarded. The time has come to destroy those who are destroying the earth. The sanctuary of God in Heaven opened, and the ark of the covenant could be seen inside it. Then came flashes of lightning, peals of thunder and an earthquake, and violent hail" (Revelation 11:18-19). "Now a great sign appeared in Heaven, a woman clothed with the sun, standing on the moon, and with the twelve stars on her head for a crown" (Revelation 12:1).

Mary, the Woman clothed with the sun, appears as a sign and explains the secrets of the Book of Revelation. On April 12, 1947, at Tre Fontane (Three Fountains), in Rome, Italy, Our Blessed Mother announced, "I am the Virgin of Revelation."

The Virgin Of Revelation

Announcing herself as the Virgin of Revelation at Tre Fontane, Italy, Mary appeared to Bruno Cornacchiola, a hardened, extremist enemy of the Church, who was plotting to kill the Pope. She was carrying the Sacred Scriptures in her arms. Through this event Bruno experienced a profound conversion and was convinced of his false beliefs concerning Sacred Scripture and the error of his thinking on Our Lady's life. He was taught by Our Lady herself the history of her life, from its origin to her glorious assumption into Heaven. Bruno experienced a radical conversion and eventually presented to the Pope the knife that he was to use to kill him.

In recent years, Our Blessed Mother has been interpreting and explaining the Book of Revelation in messages given to the Marian Movement of Priests and to other reported visionaries. In these messages, she speaks of her reasons and mission in making these mysteries understood.

The Woman clothed with the sun explicitly stated her role through Father Gobbi on April 24, 1980: **"I am the Virgin of Revelation. In me, the masterpiece of the Father is realized in such a perfect manner, that He can shed on me the light of His predilection. The Word assumes His human nature in my virginal womb, and thus can come to you by means of my true function as Mother. The Holy Spirit draws me, like a magnet, into the depths of the life of love between the Father and the Son, and I become interiorly transformed and so assimilated to Him as to be His spouse....**

"I will bring you to the full understanding of Sacred Scripture. Above all, I will read to you the pages of its last book, which you are living. In it, everything is already predicted, even that which must still come to pass. The battle to which I am calling you is clearly described, and my great victory is foretold."

In 1846, Our Blessed Mother at LaSalette described the events foretold in the book of Revelation. In 1917 at Fatima she reiterated what she had said at LaSalette, adding certain details. The Blessed Mother foretold many major events that would take place in this century—events that did occur. These events included World War II, the spread of communism throughout the world and the persecution it would inflict upon the Church, ecclesiastical impurity, modernism, the apostasy, and the moral decline of our civilization.

On May 13, 1979, Mary spoke to Father Gobbi about the Woman clothed with the sun in Revelation 12. **"I have come from Heaven to reveal to you my plan in this struggle which involves everyone, marshalled together at the orders of two opposing leaders: the Woman clothed with the sun and the Red Dragon.**

"I have shown you the road you must take: that of prayer and penance.

"I am now announcing to you that this is the time of the decisive battle. During these years, I myself am intervening, as the Woman

clothed with the sun, in order to bring to fulfillment the Triumph of my Immaculate Heart which I have already begun through you, my beloved sons."

I Am Opening For You The Sealed Book

In words given to the Marian Movement of Priests and to other reported visionaries, Our Lady identifies entities, concepts, or institutions in the Apocalypse (the Book of Revelation) as beasts or animals. For instance, the Red Dragon is Marxist atheism, the Black Beast as swift as a leopard is Freemasonry, the beast like a lamb is ecclesiastical Masonry, and the number of the beast is 666. A full and satisfactory explanation is given in detail after centuries of speculation. In these messages, she also states in great detail the true nature of the Book of Revelation. For years the Blessed Mother had been preparing us; starting in the late 1980s, she began to reveal the specific meaning of the verses in the Apocalypse. Several of the more prominent interpretations are briefly given below.

In the October 13, 1988, message of Mary to Father Gobbi, Our Blessed Mother spoke of her role as a witness and a precursor to the secrets of Revelation. She stated, **"I announce to you that the time of the purification has now reached its culmination and that you are therefore called to live through the most painful moments which have been foretold to you. The Lord is sending me to you that I might bring to fulfillment the task which the Most Holy Trinity has entrusted to me in these times of yours.**

"I am opening for you the sealed book, that the secrets contained in it may be revealed. I have gathered you from all sides and you have been formed by me in order to be ready for the great events which are awaiting you. Only in this way are you able to carry out your important mission." [1]

The Red Dragon And The Black Beast: Communism And Freemasonry

On June 29, 1983, Our Blessed Mother through Father Gobbi exposed by name the two institutions that have made significant efforts to destroy the Church: "...The Red Dragon is Marxist atheism, which has now conquered the whole world, and which has induced humanity to build a new civilization of its own, without God. In consequence, the world has become a cold and barren desert, immersed in the ice of hatred and in the darkness of sin and impurity. The Black Beast is also Masonry which has infiltrated the Church and attacks it, wounds it, and seeks by its subtle tactics to demolish it."

The Huge Red Dragon

On May 14, 1989, the Woman clothed with the sun again spoke to Father Gobbi about the vast territory and conquests of the Red Dragon: "The huge Red Dragon is atheistic communism which has spread everywhere the error of the denial and of the obstinate rejection of God. The huge Red Dragon is Marxist atheism, which appears with ten horns, namely with the power of its means of communication, in order to lead humanity to disobey the ten commandments of God, and with seven heads, upon each of which there is a crown, signs of authority and royalty. The crowned heads indicate the nations in which atheistic communism is established and rules with the force of its ideological, political and military power.

"The hugeness of the dragon clearly manifests the vastness of the territory occupied by the uncontested reign of atheistic communism. Its color is red because it uses wars and blood as instruments of its numerous conquests.

"The huge Red Dragon has succeeded during these years in conquering humanity with the error of theoretical and practical atheism, which has now seduced all the nations of the earth. It has thus succeeded in building up for itself a new civilization without God, materialistic, egoistic, hedonistic, arid and cold, which carries within itself the seeds of corruption and of death."

Maximin Giraud, the visionary of LaSalette, spoke of the monster (communism) that would arise at the end of the Nineteenth or the beginning of the Twentieth Century. As mentioned in the Marian Movement of Priests message No. 267, the Black Beast is Freemasonry. The topic of Freemasonry is a large and complex subject; few people are aware how deep the roots of this sect actually reach. Freemasonry is perhaps the single greatest secular power on earth today and battles head to head with the things of God on a daily basis. It is a controlling power in the world, operating behind the scenes in banking and politics, and it has effectively infiltrated all religions. Masonry is an elite world-wide secret sect undermining the authority of the Catholic Church with a hidden agenda at the upper levels to destroy the papacy. The papacy remains a target because of the control and influence Rome exerts—something Freemasonry wants.

The messages Mary communicates are not idle talk. The Blessed Mother has stated clearly through Father Gobbi that the transition of power from communism to democratic freedom was a peaceful one in Eastern Europe and Russia because of her intervention. She also has stated that her next target to dismantle is Freemasonry.

The New World Order

Pat Robertson of the Christian Broadcasting Network has given an account of the secular and religious aspects of this movement toward a one-world government that is nearly unparalled in scope because of his understanding of both. What is the power that seems to thwart the things of God? Where is it? Who is in control of it now? Will a system of power and authority will be put into place without any groundwork being established? Does the enemy have a structure? Will it happen overnight or have foundations been laid? Remember the words of the Blessed Mother and the Scriptures on so many occasions. A frequently repeated message is that Satan is strong and wishes to destroy the work of God and uses many means to achieve that goal. According to Mr. Robertson in his book *The New World Order*, Freemasonry on both the secular and religious levels has had the greatest negative impact in society today in dismantling that which is of God. Its agenda is control. Mr. Robertson cited as a source the former prime minister of England, Benjamin Disraeli, who once wrote: "The world is governed by very different personages than what is imagined by those who are not behind the scenes."

Woodrow Wilson, whose principal adviser was a behind-the-scenes operator, said: "There is a power somewhere so organized, so subtle, so watchful, so interlocked, so complete, so pervasive that they better not speak above their breath when they speak in condemnation of it."[2]

The Beast Like A Leopard:
Secular/Political Freemasonry

In a message dated June 3, 1989, to the Marian Movement of Priests, Mary said how subtle and pervasive this force is in the world today: "If the Red Dragon is Marxist atheism, the black beast is Freemasonry. The Dragon manifests himself in the force of his power; the black beast on the other hand acts in the shadow, keeps out of sight and hides himself in such a way as to enter everywhere. He has the claws of a bear and the mouth of a lion, because he works everywhere with cunning and with the means of social communication, that is to say, through propaganda. The seven heads indicate the various Masonic lodges, which act everywhere in a subtle and dangerous way.

"This Black Beast has ten horns and, on the horns, ten crowns, which are signs of dominion and royalty. Masonry rules and governs throughout the whole world by means of the ten horns. The horn, in the biblical world, has always been an instrument of amplification, a way of making one's voice better heard, a strong means of communication. For this reason, God communicated His will to His people by means of ten horns which made His law known: the Ten Commandments. The one who accepts them and observes them walks in life along the road of the divine will, of joy and of peace.

"...The task of the Black Beast, namely of Masonry, is that of fighting, in a subtle way, but tenaciously, to obstruct souls from traveling along this way, pointed out by the Father and the Son and lit up by the gifts of the Spirit. In fact if the Red Dragon works to bring all humanity to do without God, to the denial of God, and therefore spreads the error of atheism, the aim of Masonry is not to deny God, but to blaspheme Him.... This is why in these times, behind the perverse action of Freemasonry, there are being spread everywhere black masses and the satanic cult. Moreover Masonry acts, by every means, to prevent souls from being saved and thus it endeavors to bring to nothing the redemption accomplished by Christ....

"The task of the Masonic lodges is that of working today, with great astuteness, to bring humanity everywhere to disdain the holy law of God, to work in open opposition to the Ten Commandments, and to take away the worship due to God alone in order to offer it to certain false idols which become extolled and adored by an ever-increasing number of people: reason, flesh, money, discord, domination, violence, pleasure....

"Now you understand how, in these times, against the terrible and insidious attack of the Black Beast, namely of Masonry, my Immaculate Heart becomes your refuge and the sure road which brings you to God. In my Immaculate Heart there is delineated the tactic made use of by your heavenly Mother, to fight back against and to defeat the subtle plot made use of by the Black Beast."

The Beast Like A Lamb: Ecclesiastical Masonry

On June 13, 1989, immediately after giving a tutorial on political Masonry, the Blessed Mother offered insight to the Marian Movement of Priests into ecclesiastical Masonry and its power on earth: "There comes out of the earth by way of aid to the black beast which arises out of the sea, a beast which has two horns like those of a lamb.... To the symbol of the sacrifice there is intimately connected that of the priesthood: the two horns. The high priest of the Old Testament wore a headpiece with two horns. The bishops of the Church wear the miter—with two horns—to indicate the fullness of their priesthood.

"The Black Beast like a leopard indicates Freemasonry; the beast with the two horns like a lamb indicates Freemasonry infiltrated into the interior of the Church, that is to say, Ecclesiastical Masonry, which has spread especially among the members of the hierarchy. This Masonic infiltration, in the interior of the Church, was already foretold to you by me at Fatima, when I announced to you that Satan would enter in even to the summit of the Church. If the task of Masonry is to lead souls to perdition, bringing them to the worship of false divinities, the task of Ecclesiastical Masonry on the other hand is that of destroying Christ and his Church, building a new idol, namely a false christ and a false church."

The writings and visions of Blessed Sister Anna-Katarina Emmerick, an Augustinian nun in the 1800s who bore the stigmata of Our Lord and spent a life of suffering, offer prophetic insight. Sister Emmerick wrote on May 13, 1820: "Once **more I saw that the Church of Peter was undermined by a plan evolved by the secret sect [Masonry], while storms were damaging it. But I saw also that help was coming when distress had reached its peak. I saw again the Blessed Virgin ascend on the Church and spread her mantle [over it]. I saw a Pope who was at once gentle, and very firm.... I saw a great renewal, and the Church rose high in the sky.**"

Sister Emmerick saw other visions between August and October

1820. She continued, "I see more martyrs, not now but in the future.... I saw the secret sect relentlessly undermining the great Church. Near them I saw a horrible beast coming up from the sea. All over the world, good and devout people, especially the clergy, were harassed, oppressed, and put into prison. I had the feeling that they would become martyrs one day."

"When the Church had been for the most part destroyed [by the secret sect], and when only the sanctuary and altar were still standing, I saw the wreckers enter the Church with the Beast. There, they met a Woman of noble carriage who seemed to be with child because she walked slowly. At this sight, the enemies were terrorized, and the Beast could not take but another step forward. It projected its neck towards the Woman as if to devour her, but the Woman turned about and bowed down [towards the Altar], her head touching the ground. Thereupon I saw the Beast taking to flight towards the sea again and the enemies were fleeing in the greatest confusion. Then, I saw in the distance great legions approaching. In the foreground I saw a man on a white horse. Prisoners were set free and joined them. All the enemies were pursued. Then, I saw that the Church was being promptly rebuilt, and she was more magnificent than ever before"

The Number Of The Beast: 666

In the following words from Our Blessed Mother through Father Gobbi, on June 17, 1989, she told how Satan has led mankind away from the true Church through numerous religious revolutions; revolutions that will continue until Satan finally appears in human form. Our Lady also explained why the Book of Revelation associates the Antichrist with the number 666. Below are insights into what may be the greatest historic riddle of them all:

"In the thirteenth chapter of the Apocalypse it is written, 'This calls for wisdom. Let him who has understanding reckon the number of the beast: it represents a human name. And the number in question is 666 (six hundred and sixty-six).' With intelligence, illumined by the light of divine Wisdom, one can succeed in deciphering from the number, 666, the name of a man and this name, indicated by such a number, is that of the Antichrist.

"Lucifer, the ancient serpent, the devil or Satan, the Red Dragon, becomes, in these last times, the Antichrist. The Apostle John already affirmed that whoever denies that Jesus Christ is God, that person is the Antichrist. The statue or idol, built in honor of the beast to be adored by all men, is the Antichrist.

"Calculate now its number, 666, to understand how it indicates the name of a man. The number, 333, indicates the divinity. Lucifer rebels against God through pride, because he wants to put himself above God. 333 is the number which indicates the mystery of God. He who wants to put himself above God bears the sign 666, and consequently this number indicates the name of Lucifer, Satan, that is to say, of him who sets himself against Christ, of the Antichrist.

"333 indicated once, that is to say, for the first time, expresses the mystery of the unity of God. 333 indicated twice, that is to say, for the second time, indicates the two natures, that of the divine and the human, united in the divine person of Jesus Christ. 333 indicated thrice, that is to say, for the third time, indicates the mystery of the Three Divine persons, it expresses the mystery of the Most Holy Trinity. Thus the number, 333, expressed one, two and three times, expresses the principal mysteries of the Catholic faith, which are: (1) the Unity and the Trinity of God, (2) the incarnation, the Passion and death, and the resurrection of our Lord Jesus Christ.

"If 333 is the number which indicates divinity, he who wants to put himself above God himself is referred to by the number 666.

"666 indicated once, that is to say, for the first time, expresses the year 666, six hundred and sixty-six. In this period of history, the Antichrist is manifested through the phenomenon of Islam, which directly denies the mystery of the divine Trinity and the divinity of Our Lord Jesus Christ. Islam, with its military force, breaks loose everywhere, destroying all the ancient Christian communities, and invades Europe and it is only through my extraordinary motherly intervention, begged for powerfully by the Holy Father, that it does not succeed in destroying Christianity completely.

"666 indicated twice, that is to say, for the second time, expresses the year 1332, thirteen hundred and thirty-two. In this period of history, the Antichrist is manifested through a radical attack on the faith in the word of God. Through the philosophers who begin to give exclusive value to science and then to reason, there is a gradual tendency to constitute human intelligence alone as the sole criterion of truth. There comes to birth the great philosophical errors which continue through the centuries down to your days. The exaggerated importance given to reason, as an exclusive criterion of truth, necessarily leads to the destruction of the faith in the word of God.

"Indeed, with the protestant Reformation, Tradition is rejected as a source of divine revelation, and only Sacred Scripture is accepted. But even this must be interpreted by means of the reason, and the authentic Magisterium of the hierarchical Church, to which Christ has entrusted the guardianship of the deposit of faith, is obstinately rejected. Each one is free to read and to understand Sacred Scripture according to one's personal interpretation. In this way, faith in the word of God is destroyed. The work of the Antichrist, in this period of history, is the division of the Church and the consequent formation of new and numerous Christian confessions which gradually become driven to a more and more extensive loss of the true faith in the word of God.

"666 indicated thrice, that is to say, for the third time, expresses the year 1998, nineteen hundred and ninety-eight. In this period of history, Freemasonry, assisted by its ecclesiastical form, will succeed in its great design: that of setting up an idol to put in the place of Christ and of his Church. A false christ and a false church. Consequently, the statue built in honor of the first beast, to be adored by all the inhabitants of the earth and which will seal with its mark all those who want to buy or sell, is that of the Antichrist.

"You have thus arrived at the peak of the purification, of the great tribulation and of the apostasy. The apostasy will be, as of then, generalized because almost all will follow the false christ and the false church. Then the door will be open for the appearance of the man or of the very person of the Antichrist!

"...Take courage! Be strong, my little children. To you befalls the duty, in these difficult years, of remaining faithful to Christ and to His Church, putting up with hostility, struggle and persecution. But you are a precious part of the little flock, which has the task of fighting against, and in the end of conquering, the powerful force of the Antichrist."

At LaSalette in 1846 Our Blessed Mother predicted, "Rome will lose the faith and become the seat of Antichrist, the Church will be in eclipse...."

A Crown Of Twelve Stars

A title is given to the Blessed Mother as Mother and Queen of all the Church. On December 8, 1989, the Feast of the Immaculate Conception, Our Blessed Mother gave Father Gobbi another message about her role as the Woman clothed with the sun and her role in waging the battle against the serpent.

"...At the end, I am seen as the Woman Clothed with the Sun, who has the task of fighting against the Red Dragon and his powerful army, to conquer him, to bind him and to drive him away into his kingdom of death, that Christ alone may reign over the world. Behold me, then, presented by Sacred Scripture in the splendor of my maternal royalty: 'And another sign appeared in the heavens: a Woman clothed with the sun, with the moon beneath her feet, and on her head a crown of twelve stars.'

"About my head there is therefore a crown of twelve stars. The crown is the sign of royalty. It is composed of twelve stars because it becomes the symbol of my maternal and royal presence in the very heart of the people of God.

"The twelve stars represent the twelve tribes of Israel, which compose the chosen people, selected and called by the Lord to prepare for the coming into the world of the Son of God, the Redeemer. Because I am called to become the Mother of the Messiah, my purpose is that of being the fulfillment of the promises, the virginal shoot, the honor and the glory of all the people of Israel....

"The twelve stars also signify the twelve apostles, who are the foundation upon which Christ has founded His Church. I was often with them, to encourage them to follow and to believe in Jesus, during the three years of His public mission. In their place, together with John, I stood beneath the Cross at the moment of the crucifixion, of the agony and of the death of my Son Jesus.

"I Am Mother And Queen Of All The Church.

"...The twelve stars also signify a new reality. Indeed the Apocalypse sees me as a great sign in Heaven: the Woman clothed with the sun who does battle with the dragon and his powerful army of evil. And so the stars about my head indicate those who consecrate themselves to my Immaculate Heart; who form part of my victorious army; and who allow themselves to be guided by me in order to fight this battle and to attain in the end our greatest victory....

"The twelve stars, which form the luminous crown of my maternal royalty, are made up of the tribes of Israel, of the apostles and of the apostles of these last times of yours."

The Mark On The Forehead And Hand

The Book of the Apocalypse describes a mark on the hand or forehead that will be imprinted on those that follow the beast:

"Then I saw another angel flying high overhead, with everlasting good news to announce to those who dwell on earth, to every nation, tribe, tongue, and people. He said in a loud voice, 'Fear God and give Him glory, for His time has come to sit in judgment. Worship Him who made Heaven and earth and sea and springs of water.' A second angel followed, saying: 'Fallen, fallen is Babylon the great, that made all the nations drink the wine of her licentious passion.'

"A third angel followed them and said in a loud voice, 'Anyone who worships the beast or its image, or accepts its mark on forehead or hand, you will also drink the wine of God's fury, poured full strength into the cup of His wrath, and will be tormented in burning sulfur before the holy angels and before the Lamb. The smoke of the fire that torments them will rise forever and ever, and there will be no relief day or night for those who worship the name'." (Revelation 14:6-11).

In a related message, Our Lady explained more about a sign on the foreheads of the faithful. In this apparition, Our Lady appeared to Matous Losuta, a forester in the village of Turzovka, Czechoslovakia, in 1958. For his faith, Matous was imprisoned for three years by the communist authorities. Mary has told Matous, **"All my children will receive and carry the sign of the cross on their foreheads. This sign only my chosen ones will see. These chosen ones will be instructed by my angels how to conduct themselves.** My faithful will be without any kind of fear during the most difficult hours. They will be protected by the good spirits and will be fed by Heaven from where they will receive further instructions. They will fall into a deathlike sleep, but they will be protected by angels. When they awake they will be like those newly born. Their bodies will be beautiful and their souls will be steeped in God. The earth will be beautiful and my chosen ones will see how God takes care of them."[3]

In a message dated September 8, 1989, to the Marian Movement of Priests, Mary further explained the Mark of the Beast: "Allow yourselves to be nourished and formed by me; allow yourselves to be led by me with docility; **allow yourselves to be signed by me with my motherly seal. These are the times when the followers of him who opposes himself to Christ are being signed with his mark on the forehead and on the hand.**

"The mark on the forehead and on the hand is an expression of a total dependency on the part of those who are designated by this sign. The sign indicates him who is an enemy of Christ, that is to say, the sign of the Antichrist. And his mark, which is stamped, signifies the complete belonging of the person thus marked to the army of him who is opposed to Christ and who fights against His divine and royal dominion.

"The mark is imprinted on the forehead and on the hand. The forehead indicates the intellect, because the mind is the seat of the human reason. The hand expresses human activity, because it is with his hands that man acts and works.

"Nevertheless it is the person who is marked with the mark of the Antichrist in his intellect and in his will. He who allows himself to be signed with the mark on his forehead is led to accept the doctrine of the denial of God, of the rejection of His law, and of atheism which, in these times, is more and more diffused and advertised. And thus he is driven to follow the ideologies in mode today and to make of himself a propagator of all the errors.

"He who allows himself to be signed with the mark on his hand is obliged to act in an autonomous manner and independently of God, ordering his own activities to the quest of a purely material and terrestrial good. Thus he withdraws his action from the design of the Father, who wants to illumine it and sustain it by His divine providence; from the love of the Son who makes human toil a precious means for one's own redemption and sanctification; from the power of the Spirit who acts everywhere to interiorly renew every creature.

"He who is signed with the mark on his hand works for himself alone, to accumulate material goods, to make money his god and he becomes a victim of materialism.

"He who is signed with the mark on his hand works solely for the gratification of his own senses, for the quest of well-being and pleasure, for the granting of full satisfaction to all his passions, especially that of impurity, and he becomes a victim of hedonism.

"He who is signed with the mark on his hand makes of his own self the center of all his actions, looks upon others as objects to be used and to be exploited for his own advantage and he becomes a victim of unbridled egoism and of lovelessness.

"If my Adversary is signing, with his mark, all his followers, the time has come when I also, your heavenly Leader, am signing, with my motherly seal, all those who have consecrated themselves to my Immaculate Heart and have formed part of my army."

And so a different perspective is seen which has not been understood previously. The devil and the Blessed Mother both sign all they call their own.

The people of God are being given adequate time to build an ark in preparation for the next "deluge" that will once again be sent to chastise the earth. This time the deluge will not be by a flood but by fire. Heaven's pattern is often to give information on a "need-to-know basis" and will usually give only little bits at a time. One source of information, Father Gobbi, has been speaking to us through the Marian Movement of Priests since 1973, offering guidance for our day.

We must listen to such visionaries if we expect to understand the times in which we are living.

7

"Why Am I Weeping?"

Mary went to Jesus, and as soon as she saw Him she threw herself at His feet, saying, "Lord, if you had been here, my brother would not have died." At the sight of her tears, and those of the Jews who followed her, Jesus said in great distress, with a sigh that came from the heart, "Where have you put him?" They said, "Lord, come and see." Jesus wept; and the Jews said, "See how much He loved him!"

John 11:32-36

The question must be asked, "Why are there tears?" Why does Mary weep? Throughout the world statues weep, icons emit a fragrance of perfume and roses, and the critical question continues to go unasked. Why is this phenomena taking place?

Besides the growing number of Marian apparitions, other miraculous phenomena are multiplying as well. From all across the world come reports of statues of Mary weeping, weeping for the sins of the world and for the disasters that appear to be ahead of us. Most recently, reports are that Mary has begun weeping tears of blood as a sign of the impending chastisement. As Jesus wept tears of blood in the Garden of Olives before His crucifixion, so too statues around the world are now turning from tears of water to tears of blood. A message is being sent.

Our Lady's message to Father Gobbi on July 13, 1973, "The Reason for My Tears," was her fourth message to him. The theme of tears has continued through the years, reaching a higher degree of urgency. Her tears are frequent, to help her children understand the days in which we are living.

Mary stated, "The reason for my tears, for a mother's tears, is my children who, in great numbers, live unmindful of God, immersed in the pleasures of the flesh, and are hastening irreparably to their perdition. For many of these my tears have fallen in the midst of indifference and have fallen in vain. Above all the cause of my weeping is the priests: those beloved sons, the apple of my eye, these consecrated sons of mine. Do you see how they no longer love me? How they no longer want me? Do you see how they no longer listen to the words of my Son?"

Mary further explained through Father Gobbi why her tears continue:

Why Am I Still Weeping?

"Why am I still weeping? I am weeping because humanity is not accepting my motherly invitation to conversion and to its return to the Lord. It is continuing to run with obstinacy along the road of rebellion against God and against His law of love. The Lord is openly denied, outraged and blasphemed. Your heavenly Mother is publicly despised and held up for ridicule. My extraordinary requests are not being accepted; the signs of my immense sorrow which I am giving are not believed in. Your neighbor is not loved; every day attacks are made upon his life and his goods...."

My Heart Is Bleeding

Mary spoke again through Father Gobbi on September 6, 1986, bringing the message to another level of urgency: "I am your most sorrowful mother. Again today, I am causing copious tears to fall from my merciful eyes. They want to make you understand how great the sorrow of the Immaculate Heart of your heavenly mother is. My heart is bleeding. My heart is transfixed with deep wounds. My heart is immersed in a sea of sorrow.

"You live unconscious of the fate which is awaiting you. You are spending your days in a state of unawareness, of indifference and of complete incredulity. How is this possible when I, in so many ways and with extraordinary signs, have warned you of the danger into which you are running and have foretold you of the bloody ordeal which is just about to take place? Because this humanity has not accepted my repeated call to conversion, to

repentance, and to a return to God, there is about to fall upon it the greatest chastisement which the history of mankind has ever known. It is a chastisement much greater than that of the flood. **Fire will fall from Heaven and a great part of humanity will be destroyed.** The Church of Jesus is wounded with the pernicious plague of infidelity and apostasy. In appearance, everything remains calm and it seems that all is going well. In reality, she is being pervaded with an ever widening lack of faith which is spreading the great apostasy everywhere. Many bishops, priests, religious and faithful no longer believe and have already lost the true faith in Jesus and in His Gospel. For this reason, the Church must be purified, with persecution and with blood....

"Sin is being committed more and more, it is no longer acknowledged as an evil, it is sought out, it is consciously willed and it is no longer confessed. Impurity and lewdness cover the homes built by your rebellion. This is the reason why my heart is bleeding: because of the obstinate disbelief and the hardness of your hearts."

Before 2000?

The words of Christina Gallagher echo those Our Lady spoke to other visionaries. "The chastisement has to come, to cleanse not only the world, but the Church, because the darkness is even in the Church," said Mrs. Gallagher. She believes that everything she has been shown or told about will be accomplished before the year 2000.

Our Blessed Mother has said: "My child, pray, pray, pray! You do not know the dreadful times which lie ahead for my children! Oh my little ones, there are dreadful times ahead of you, in battle! So many of my children will be destroyed and lost! The justice of God is unthinkable! **Oh, my heart weeps blood for my children, who do not listen, and continue in their sinful ways!** The angels and saints cry out to God to purify the world! My child, be not afraid, my peace be with you, Father, Son and Holy Spirit."[1]

The Plea From A Mother's Heart

The Blessed Mother told a young mother living in the midwestern United States the reasons for her tears. The woman receiving the locutions has sought anonymity to protect the privacy of family life. She uses the pseudonym "Mariamante."

The Blessed Mother told her: "I am speaking directly to your soul. This is by no ordinary means. Although God has given me this power, I have seldom used it in the past as it was not necessary in a more pious age when the Church was revered. Sadly, this is now not the case. This is why I must employ other means to speak to my children."

The Blessed Mother said to her on February 22, 1987: "God has given me the power to touch the hardest of hearts. Indeed, it has always been this way down through the ages. However, it is ever so urgent now that I must employ extraordinary means by which to reach my children so hardened by sin.... O, how I wish that I could persuade all my priest sons to return to their rosaries, but so many have become hardened in sin, it grieves me. They have forgotten how to pray. I plead with them from a mother's heart to return to prayer. This alone will save them. See my tears. I cry for their souls once so spotless and pure and now defiled by sin. Purity and humility, obedience and poverty, prayer and penance—this will lead them back to my Son Who also loves them so."

Rosa Mystica

Rosa Mystica (Mystical Rose) statues have been reported weeping tears as well as blood. Over eighty of these events have been witnessed and reported to the Vatican.

In 1947, the Blessed Virgin appeared to Pierina Gilli of Italy. Our Lady was sad, and her tears fell to the floor. Her breast was pierced by three swords. Our Lady said, *"Prayer, Penance, and Expiation"* and then was silent. On the second apparition, instead of swords piercing her breast, she had three roses: one white, one red, and one gold. Our Blessed Mother told Pierina that the first sword signified the loss of vocations. The second sword was for the priests, monks, and nuns who live in mortal sin. The third sword was for the priests and monks who commit the treason of Judas, meaning those who give up their vocation and often their faith and become enemies of the Church. The white rose is the spirit of prayer, the red rose is the spirit of expiation and sacrifice, and the gold or yellow rose is the spirit of penance. Additional apparitions displayed the displeasure of Heaven with those who sin against holy purity.[2]

The books and statues of the Rosa Mystica apparitions have been extremely popular with the laity and clergy. The messages to Pierina

Gilli from Our Lady about the priesthood seem quite prophetic in light of recent scandals with some clergy and the sexual molestation of children. Our Lady had emphasized the necessity for prayers and holy purity for religious.

Father James Bruse

Father James Bruse of Lake Ridge, Virginia, a suburb of Washington, D.C., is only the third priest in the history of the Roman Catholic Church to have the stigmata, the five wounds of Christ. (The other two priests were Padre Pio, who died in 1968 and Father Gino, who is currently living in Italy.) Legend has it that Saint Paul also had the stigmata. Father Bruse has received international media attention, including a *U.S. News and World Report* cover story on March 25, 1993, for the stigmata and various phenomena such as statues weeping, bleeding, and changing colors in his presence.

Since Christmas 1991, statues around Father Bruse have been weeping, bleeding, and changing colors. One of these statues at his rectory at Saint Elizabeth Ann Seton parish, wept blood; another statue of Our Lady of Fatima wept tears. The first statue that began weeping was Our Lady of Grace, a statue that belonged to Father Bruse's family. Two, thirty-six inch handcarved Medjugorje statues obtained by Signs of the Times, Sterling, Virginia, as Pilgrim statues were brought to Father Bruse to be blessed for their mission. One of these Medjugorje statues was blessed in April 1992 and wept for three hours in front of hundreds of people at Saint Elizabeth Anne Seton Church. This statue is now being sent over the east coast of the United States visiting various parishes. It has wept four times during the course of its journey. The second Medjugorje statue was blessed by Father Bruse in May 1992, and this too has wept. This pilgrim statue is also traveling on the west coast, and there have been stories of conversions and healings wherever the statue goes.

Father Bruse feels that these phenomena of the stigmata, conversions, healings, and the weeping statues are real but are pointing to Christ. He said: "Christ is the real power behind all these phenomena. Christ is preparing us for the Kingdom of God." Of course, this has always been the mission of His Church, "but perhaps Christ is preparing us more quickly; saying 'be prepared,' but shouting it out now. It's as if Christ is saying 'wake up! Let's get moving on our spirituality.' I believe it's building up to something big.... "

Father Bruse noted the extreme rapidity and depth of the conversions taking place: "Something that would normally have taken place over a lifetime is taking place, for many thousands of people, over a short period of time. Along with the conversions, many healings also have been taking place. There have been reports of healings of cancer and other diseases. The most important changes, however, have been the changed lives, the inner conversions."[3]

Father Bruse is presently under investigation by the Church authorities in his diocese.

8

LaSalette:
Satan in the World

Then the devil, taking Him up on a high mountain, showed Him all the kingdoms of the world in a moment of time. And the devil said to Him, "All this authority I will give You, and their glory; for this has been delivered to me, and I give it to whomever I wish. Therefore, if you will worship before me, all will be Yours." And Jesus answered and said to him, "Get behind me Satan! For it is written, 'You shall worship the Lord your God, and Him only shall you serve.'"

Luke 4:5-8

To Destroy The Work Of God

In trying to understand the role of Satan in the world today, we must ask ourselves that if the devil will tempt Jesus Christ Himself, and offer power, authority, and the wealth that accompany the worship of Satan, what is he capable of doing to us who are not as familiar with the strategies that have been used for thousands of years? We must humbly yet firmly rely on the wisdom of the ages and messages from Heaven that are applicable to the times in which we live if we expect to combat the evil in our midst.

One must remember at the very outset that the full attainment of the prize of eternal life is not achieved here on this earth. God's system of government is the Church, and man's system is power, Masonic lodges, wealth, avarice, and unjust governments. Who runs these places at the highest levels? Often times it is not the people of God. Ultimately the battle is of good versus evil, with the wars being waged for the hearts, minds, and souls of men.

The role of Satan in the world today is what it has always been. His sole mission is to destroy the work of God and that which is good. Prophets and apparitions warn us of his tactics. Words and phrases describing him include: seducer, evil one, snake, and an endless litany of foul things not of God. There is no good in him. However, the modern world has trivialized him as a harmless caricature with horns and a pitchfork rather than as the great destructive force he really is. His greatest source of power and comfort is that many believe that he does not exist.

Saint Paul speaks of arming ourselves for the spiritual world in which we live. "Put God's armor on so as to be able to resist the devil's tactics. For it is not against human enemies that we have to struggle, but against the sovereignties and the powers who originate the darkness in this world, the spiritual army of evil in the heavens" (Ephesians 6:10-11).

Warnings About The Evil One

Our Lady gave this message to Maria Pavlovic, a visionary in Medjugorje, on September 25, 1992: "Today I also wish to tell you: **I am with you also in these restless days in which Satan wishes to destroy everything which I and my son Jesus are building up. In a special way he wishes to destroy your souls. He wishes to guide you as far away as possible from Christian life as well as from the Commandments, to which the Church is calling you so you may live them. Satan wishes to destroy everything which is holy in you and around you. Therefore, little children, pray, pray, pray, in order to be able to comprehend all which God is giving you through my comings."**[1]

On January 25, 1991, the Blessed Mother spoke at Medjugorje of Satan's evil plan: "Satan is strong and wishes to destroy not only human life but also nature and the planet on which you live...."

On October 7, 1983, Mary said to Father Gobbi: "Today, Satan is successfully conquering everything with the spirit of pride and rebellion against God, and he is terrified by those who follow your heavenly mother along the road of littleness and humility."

On June 7, 1986 to Father Gobbi, Mary spoke of Satan's effective-ness: "There are evils of a social order, such as divisions and hatred, famine and poverty, exploitation and slavery, violence, terrorism and war. To be protected from all these evils, I invite you to place yourselves under shelter in the safe refuge of my Immaculate Heart. But, in these times, you have need above all of being defended from the terrible snares of my Adversary, who has succeeded in establish-ing his reign in the world. It is the reign which is opposed to Christ; it is the reign of the Antichrist. In this last part of your century, this reign of his will reach the peak of its strength, of its power, of its great seduction. **The hour is in preparation when the man of iniquity, who wants to put himself in the place of God to have himself adored as God, is about to manifest himself in all his power.**"

Saint Louis de Montfort addressed the conflicting roles of Heaven and hell: "What Lucifer has lost by pride, Mary has gained by humility. What Eve has damned and lost by disobedience, Mary has saved by obedience. Eve, in obeying the serpent, has destroyed all her children together with herself, and has delivered them to him [Satan]; Mary, in being perfectly faithful to God, has saved all her children and servants together with herself, and has consecrated them to His Majesty."[2]

The Warning Of LaSalette, France

Our Blessed Mother's message of September 19, 1846, given at LaSalette, France, is seldom mentioned. It was given to two children, Melanie Calvat and Maximin Giraud, during an apparition that was approved by the Church in 1851. Its message has been overlooked to the present day, partly because after the apparition several different versions of the secret were circulated and determining the authentic message was difficult. The version from which we quote here is generally believed to be the most authentic and is awe-inspiring in its prophetic and predictive power.[3]

The message was not only for France but for the Church and the whole world. The message tells of future world events in great detail; it has great relevance for our times. The message is stated in its entirety because of its importance in our day. The apostasy we are now living was all foretold at LaSalette. The message at LaSalette helps explain why the devil has so much dominion and power in our world today, although Mary says he is now losing power.

"Melanie, what I am about to tell you now will not always be a secret. You may make it public in 1858.

"The priests, ministers of my Son, the priests, by their wicked lives, by their irreverence and their impiety in the celebration of the holy mysteries, by their love of money, their love of honors and pleasures, the priests have become cesspools of impurity. Yes, the priests are asking for vengeance, and vengeance is hanging over their heads. Woe to the priests and to those dedicated to God who by their unfaithfulness and their wicked lives are crucifying my Son again! The sins of those dedicated to God cry out towards Heaven and call for vengeance, and now vengeance is at their door, for there is no one left to beg mercy and forgiveness for the people. There are no more generous souls, there is no one left worthy of offering a stainless sacrifice to the Eternal God for the sake of the world.

"God will strike in an unprecedented way. Woe to the inhabitants of the earth! God will exhaust His wrath upon them, and no one will be able to escape so many afflictions together. The chiefs, the leaders of the people of God have neglected prayer and penance, and the devil has bedimmed their intelligence. They have become wandering stars which the old devil will drag along with his tail to make them perish. God will allow the old serpent to cause divisions among those who reign in every society and in every family. Physical and moral agonies will be suffered. God will abandon mankind to itself and will send punishments which will follow one after the other for more than thirty-five years.

"The society of men is on the eve of the most terrible scourges and of gravest events. Mankind must expect to be ruled with an iron rod and to drink from the chalice of the wrath of God. May the curate of my Son, Pope Pius IX, never leave Rome again after 1859; may he, however, be steadfast and noble, may he fight with the weapons of faith and love. I will be at his side. May he be on his guard against Napoleon: he is two-faced, and when he wishes to make himself Pope as well as Emperor, God will soon draw back from him. He is the master-mind who, always wanting to ascend further, will fall on the sword he wished to use to force his people to be raised up.

"Italy will be punished for her ambition in wanting to shake off the yoke of the Lord of Lords. And so she will be left to fight a war; blood will flow on all sides. Churches will be locked up or desecrated. Priests and religious orders will be hunted down, and made to die a cruel death. Several will abandon the faith, and a great number of priests and members of religious orders will break away from the true religion; among these people there will even be bishops.

"May the Pope guard against the performers of miracles. For the time has come when the most astonishing wonders will take place on the earth and in the air.

"In the year 1864, Lucifer together with a large number of demons will be unloosed from hell; they will put an end to faith little by little, even in those dedicated to God. They will blind them in such a way, that, unless they are blessed with a special grace, these people will take on the spirit of these angels of hell; several religious institutions will lose all faith and will lose many souls.

"Evil books will be abundant on earth and the spirits of darkness will spread everywhere a universal slackening in all that concerns the service of God. They will have great power over nature: there will be churches built to serve these spirits. People will be transported from one place to another by these evil spirits, even priests, for they will not have been guided by the good spirit of the Gospel, which is a spirit of humility, charity and zeal for the glory of God. On occasions, the dead and the righteous will be brought back to life. (That is to say that these dead will take on the form of righteous souls which had lived on earth, in order to lead men further astray; these so-called resurrected dead, who will be nothing but the devil in this form, will preach another gospel contrary to that of the true Christ Jesus, denying the existence of Heaven; that is also to say, the souls of the damned. All these souls will appear as if fixed to their bodies).

"...The Vicar of my Son will suffer a great deal, because for a while the Church will yield to large persecution, a time of darkness, and the Church will witness a frightful crisis. The true faith of the Lord having been forgotten, each individual will want to be on his own and be superior to people of the same identity. They will abolish civil rights as well as ecclesiastical, all order and all justice would be trampled underfoot and only homicides, hate, jealousy, lies and dissension would be seen without love for country or family.

"The Holy Father will suffer a great deal. I will be with him until the end and receive his sacrifice. [Note: Father Gobbi uses this exact term to indicate the present Pope, John Paul II.] The mischievous would attempt his life several times to do harm and shorten his days but neither he nor his successor will see the triumph of the Church of God.

"All the civil governments will have one and the same plan, which will be to abolish and do away with every religious principle, to make way for materialism, atheism, spiritualism and vice of all kinds. In the year 1865, there will be desecration of holy places. In convents, the ...devil will make himself like the king of all hearts. May those in charge of religious communities be on their guard against the people they must receive, for the devil will resort to all his evil tricks to introduce sinners in to religious orders, for disorder and the love of carnal pleasures will be spread all over the earth.

"...France, Italy, Spain and England will be at war. Blood will flow in the streets. Frenchman will fight Frenchman, Italian will fight Italian. A general war will follow which will be appalling. For a time, God will cease to remember France and Italy because the Gospel of Jesus Christ has been forgotten. The wicked will make use of all their evil ways. Men will kill each other, massacre each other even in their homes. At the first blow of His thundering sword, the mountains and all nature will tremble in terror, for the disorders and crimes of men have pierced the vault of the heavens. Paris will burn and Marseille will be engulfed. Several cities will be shaken down and swallowed up by earthquakes. People will believe that all is lost. Nothing will be seen but murder, nothing will be heard but the clash of arms and blasphemy.

"The righteous will suffer greatly. Their prayers, their penances and their tears will rise up to Heaven and all of God's people will beg for forgiveness and mercy and will plead for my help and intercession. And then Jesus Christ, in an act of His justice and His great mercy will command His angels to have all His enemies put to death. Suddenly, the persecutors of the Church of Jesus Christ and all those given over to sin will perish and the earth will become desert-like. And then peace will be made, and man will be reconciled with God. Jesus Christ will be served, worshipped, and glorified. Charity will flourish everywhere. The new kings will be the right arm of the holy Church, which will be strong, humble, pious, poor but fervent in its imitation of the virtues of Jesus Christ. The Gospel will be preached everywhere and mankind will make great progress in its faith, for there will be unity among the workers of Jesus Christ and man will live in fear of God.

"This peace among men will be short-lived. Twenty-five years of plentiful harvests will make them forget that the sins of men are the cause of all the troubles on this earth. A forerunner of the Antichrist, with his troops gathered from several nations, will fight against the true Christ, the only Saviour of the world. He will shed much blood and will want to annihilate the worship of God to make himself be looked upon as a God.

"The earth will be struck by calamities of all kinds (in addition to plague and famine which will be widespread). There will be a series of wars until the last war, which will then be fought by the ten kings of the Antichrist, all of whom will have one and the same plan and will be the only rulers of the world. Before this comes to pass, there will be a kind of false peace in the world. People will think of nothing but amusement. The wicked will give themselves over to all kinds of sin. But the children of the holy Church, the children of my faith, my true followers, they will grow in their love for God and in all the virtues most precious to me. Blessed are the souls humbly guided by the Holy Spirit! I shall fight at their side until they reach a fullness of years.

"Nature is asking for vengeance because of man, and she trembles with dread at what must happen to the earth stained with crime. Tremble, earth, and you who proclaim yourselves as serving Jesus Christ and who, on the inside, only adore yourselves, tremble, for God will hand you over to His enemy because the holy places are in a state of corruption.... It will be during this time that the Antichrist will be born of a Hebrew nun, a false virgin who will communicate with the old serpent, the master of impurity, his father will be B. At birth, he will spew out blasphemy; he will have teeth, in a word, he will be the devil incarnate. He will scream horribly, he will perform wonders, he will feed on nothing but impurity. He will have brothers who, although not devils incarnate like him, will be children of evil. At the age of twelve, they will draw attention upon themselves by the gallant victories they will have won; soon they will each lead armies, aided by the legions of hell.

"**The seasons will be altered, the earth will produce nothing but bad fruit, the stars will lose their regular motion, the moon will only reflect a faint reddish glow. Water and fire will give the earth's globe convulsions and terrible earthquakes which will swallow up mountains, cities.... Rome will lose the faith and become the seat of the Antichrist.**

"The demons of the air together with the Antichrist will perform great wonders on earth and in the atmosphere, and men will become more and more perverted. God will take care of his faithful servants and men of good will. The Gospel will be preached everywhere, and all peoples of all nations will get to know the truth.

"I make an urgent appeal to the earth. I call on the true disciples of the living God who reigns in Heaven; I call on the true followers of Christ made man, the only true Savior of men; I call on my children, the true faithful, those who have given themselves to me so that I may lead them to my divine Son.... Finally, I call on the Apostles of the Last Days, the faithful disciples of Jesus Christ who have lived in scorn for the world and for themselves, in poverty and in humility, in scorn and in silence, in prayer and in mortification, in chastity and in union with God, in suffering and unknown to the world. It is time they came out and filled the world with light. Go and reveal yourselves to be my cherished children. I am at your side and within you, provided that your faith is the light which shines upon you in these unhappy days. May your zeal make you famished for the glory and the honor of Jesus Christ. Fight, children of light, you, the few who can see. For now is the time of all times, the end of all ends.

"**The Church will be in eclipse, the world will be in dismay. But now Enoch and Eli will come, filled with the Spirit of God. They will preach with the might of God, and men of good will believe in God, and many souls will be comforted.** They will make great steps forward through the virtue of the Holy Spirit and will condemn the devilish lapses of the Antichrist. Woe to the inhabitants of the earth! There will be bloody wars and famines, plagues and infectious diseases. It will rain with a fearful hail of animals. There will be thunderstorms which will shake cities, earthquakes which will swallow up countries. Voices will be heard in the air. Men will beat their heads against walls, call for their death, and on another side death will be their torment. Blood will flow on all sides. Who will be the victor if God does not shorten the length of the test? All the blood, the tears and the prayers of the righteous, God will relent. Enoch and Eli will be put to death. Pagan Rome will disappear. The fire of Heaven will fall and consume three cities. All the universe will be struck with terror and many will let themselves be led astray because they have not worshipped the true Christ who lives among them. It is time; the sun is darkening; only faith will survive.

"...Now is the time; the abyss is opening. Here is the king of kings of darkness, here is the Beast with his subjects, calling himself the Savior of the world. He will rise proudly into the air to go to Heaven. He will be smothered by the breath of the Archangel Saint Michael. He will fall, **and the earth, which will have been in a continuous series of evolutions for three days, will open up its fiery bowels; and he will have plunged for eternity with all his followers into the everlasting chasms of hell.** And then water and fire will purge the earth and consume all the works of men's pride and all will be renewed. God will be served and glorified."

Nearly all of the mystics and visionaries in our midst today speak about Satan in a very personal way. Never do they describe him as an ethereal, esoteric, impersonal, or imaginary being.

Satan Is Real

Patricia of Ecuador is aware of Satan's role in our world today. Our Lady told her: "...for there is a hell as there is a Heaven, but there is only one King, God the Father; for Satan exists who contains hatred, perversion and all that does not give peace to your hearts. My children, give your hearts over; do not allow Satan to penetrate your heart. Fight against evil and give your heart to the Sacred Heart of my Son and to my Immaculate Heart. And all that I tell you is in Sacred Scripture. Fulfill what I ask of you. Diabolic trends, and there are many in the world, try to affect and entangle my little souls. Satan will reach the summit, being adored by my children. His images will be idolized. A false prophet exists who will entangle them saying that he is God, but he is from the blood of the demon. He will betray the Father. And the one who has the heart and wisdom will realize that he [the false prophet] carries the number of the beast, "666" on his right hand. Satan is set loose to touch my little ones, but I am that Woman whom the Father announced, who will crush the head of the serpent that is Satan.

"...and so Satan has penetrated in the very depths of the Holy Church. But do not judge those who judge you.

"Another of Satan's victories is that young women, my little ones, give themselves to men before marriage. They have no right, for the body and the soul belong to God and they may do it only if He allows it through the blessed Sacrament [of Marriage], because what God unites man cannot separate.

"Another great victory of Satan is divorce. Those who fail in one of the greatest blessings, matrimony, having many lovers and try to separate and divide that which the Father has united. Another great victory is abortion, which is an attempt against the great blessing of the Father, life.

"Another great victory of Satan are fashions, styles, and the way young women dress for Mass, obscenely. They arouse temptation to sin. They should be respectful and dress in a way in which they will not be looked at sinfully, rather with honesty and respect. For you know that fashions and music are a great victory for Satan. For, with fashions he moves people to become slaves of money and of sin. For those who exhibit their body, and who do not repent, will be judged, because the Father did not give the body to be exhibited, but to take care of it as a temple of God.... Music [insulting God], in how many messages I have asked you to abandon it, for you know they are praises to Satan and they will remain engraved in your mind, for he infuses them and they will remain engraved in your life. He, through this music, makes mockery of the Father, of my beloved Son, and of the Spirit of God, and of me, His Mother. His great victory is to be idolized to the point of offering rituals with human blood and other human elements and [they] have even offered the sacrifice of their life in order to give their soul to Satan. He has managed that images be made to adore him, and they have their book which they say is sacred, for they have great temples for his adoration."[4]

Encounters With The Enemy

One feature common to most apparitions is that whenever Mary comes with a message of peace and conversion, a visit by Satan soon follows. There seems to be a sort of heavenly rule involved: **Those privileged to experience special graces must often suffer from diabolical attacks.**

One person to suffer from such an attack is Father Ken Roberts, the popular lecturer and evangelist. Father Roberts would often bring groups of teenagers over to Medjugorje for a pilgrimage. Being in Medjugorje often inspired most of the youths to commit themselves to living their faith. It was a place of great grace, and Father Roberts decided to capitalize on the opportunity for the conversion of rebellious teens. But a small number of the teens showed more interest in partying than praying.

One night one of these teens rushed into Father Robert's room and woke him with some startling news: Satan had come as a surprise guest to the nightly party and was now terrorizing the would-be revelers. Father at first thought this was another prank. But the fear in the boy's eyes made him think otherwise.

After entering the room, the priest noticed a severe drop in temperature. It had suddenly become bone-chillingly cold. Then he was overcome by the stench of sulphur. All doubt of a demonic presence left him when he heard an unearthly voice resound through the room: "Ha, ha, ha! I know who you are, priest of God!"

The voice was coming through the lungs and lips of a young seminarian. Father had brought him along to help oversee the teens on the trip. But this was not the seminarian Father Roberts knew. The man's face was contorted with rage with his eyes rolling wildly. His hand held a menacing switchblade. And his body—his skinny, unathletic body—was just barely restrained by the hold of four husky males.

Father had never been in such a situation before. As a post-Vatican II priest, he did not have much of an idea what to do. He tried laying hands on the seminarian and praying, but was assaulted with a string of curses and filth such as he had never heard before or since. He tried saying prayers in English, Latin, and French, only to hear the possessed seminarian mimic his every word—backwards. In desperation, the priest finally threw some holy water onto the young man. The seminarian returned to his senses. The smell of sulphur was cleansed from the air, and the coldness was gone. The demon had vanished.

The encounter did, however, have two long-lasting effects. The first was that the partying teens immediately became surprisingly sober. They exchanged their beer bottles and rock and roll music for Bibles and rosaries. The next day the teens sat through every Mass no matter the language! The second was that Father Ken Roberts realized it was time to brush up on some traditional exorcism prayers.

Christina Gallagher

Christina Gallagher, the Irish mystic, also speaks of Satan in a very personal way. Christina had an experience in which she saw Satan face to face. She was terrorized, and it took several days for her to recover from the experience.

The messages given since 1988 to Christina, and still continuing, have constantly referred to the vital importance of turning to God "while there is still time." They contain a note of great urgency.

Our Lady has indicated that the purification can be lessened if people change their ways and return to God. But she also has said that her pleas are being ignored. On May 30, 1989, Christina Gallagher received the following message. **"My children, so many of you cry out to me for help. I cannot help you unless you want help yourselves. You pray when in need. Sin in the world is causing so much destruction, disaster and illness of all sorts, but you remain blind. Satan is so strong now, he is destroying so many of my poor innocent children, because of the sinful ones. When are my children going to understand how much prayer, fasting, and sacrifice is needed to overcome all the darkness that overshadows the world? My children cry out to me only when everything else has failed. I want to help but you must decide. My children, the Purification is on the way. How my heart bleeds for my children who are blind and deaf....."[5]**

A Steady Decline

In the early part of the Eighteenth Century, French philosopher Alexis De Tocqueville was traveling throughout the United States. As a result of his travels, he wrote *Democracy in America*, a book filled with his insights and experiences. The book has become a classic on the early formative years of the Republic. He recognized that the United States was at that time already a great nation that would become a stronger presence throughout the world. He continued to ask himself, what was it about America that made it great? He said he looked for America's greatness in its cities and did not find it; he looked in the countryside and did not find it: he looked in its factories and did not find it, he looked everywhere and was not able to find it. Finally, as he went into its churches, he found what made America great. In a most prophetic way he stated in so many words America was great because America was good. In Medjugorje, Mary said that Satan is especially focused on destroying the United States because of the role God has given it in maintaining peace in the world.

As the post-communist world eases restrictions for religious worship, we in America and the West are heading in the opposite direction. In a public school, a teacher was forbidden to have a Bible on his desk. In Oregon, the Department of Education is endorsing a program to distribute an informational brochure to educate young school children on how to protect themselves for homosexual sex. The examples are numerous and become more perverse each passing year.

As we have stripped school prayer from our classrooms, silent or otherwise, we have seen a tremendous decline in our schools and in our society. All totalitarian regimes have known that if the symbols of a nation are taken away, it will lose its sense of identity. Inadequately prepared, the children of today are for the most part insensitive to spiritual truths.

Another area in which America has precipitously declined is popular culture. Nudity and themes of indecent behavior are the norm rather than the exception. What was considered unacceptable only a few years ago passes unchallenged today. Hollywood has replaced happy endings with themes of violence, sex, and four-letter words. When a movie delivers a "serious message," it is usually an attack on religion, patriotism, or the family. Hollywood has launched a wholesale assault on traditional values, and few seem to object. Those who do object are often ridiculed.

In a few short years we have drifted from goodness and truth. As we stray from the standards set by God, history has taught us through historians Arnold Toynbee, Will Durant, and others, that our high moral standards will only change through revolutions and turbulence. A likely outcome for the excesses in our culture is a totalitarian regime to control it. Anything in excess soon becomes its opposite.

Abortion—The Ultimate Child Abuse

The Lord said to Jeremiah, "Before I formed you in the womb I knew you; before you came to birth I consecrated you...." (Jeremiah 1:5). Abortion never could have happened in the world unless there was an apostasy of faith first. Much in the same way, apostasy could never have happened unless modernism and the various heresies preceded it. The erosion of faith is directly responsible for ushering in the abortion movement.

Nowhere do we see how we far we have drifted until we look at how we view abortion. In the United States today, there is an abortion every twenty seconds, over 4,300 per day, according to Human Life

International. That daily tally yields a ghastly annual total of an estimated 30 million abortions since *Roe v. Wade* in 1973.

The Freedom of Choice Act (FOCA), if passed by the U.S. Congress, will eliminate waiting periods, parental consent requirements, and "informed consent" for women. It will create a legislative structure that makes it legal to kill unborn children throughout the nine months of pregnancy. We are a nation that imposes a $5,000 fine on anyone who destroys an eagle's egg, yet we allow medical personnel to keep babies alive long enough to "harvest" their brains and other body parts for fetal tissue experimentation.[6]

Some studies show that the average number of abortions per woman in the former Soviet Union is seven per lifetime. Seventy out of every one hundred conceptions ends in abortion in the former Soviet Union. World-wide, the number of abortions is even more astounding. Communist China has approximately 1.4 billion citizens and imposes severe social and financial penalties for having more than one child; third trimester abortions are common. For the world, the number of abortions has reached into the hundreds of millions. **Here lies a major reason for the purification that lies ahead.**

Several years ago Mother Teresa said, "the fruit of abortion is nuclear war." She also said, "If we spent one hour before the Blessed Sacrament, abortion would stop."[7] Time will be our judge. Never could abortion have been so widely accepted if the churches in the world had taught the Gospel. The sin of abortion is one of the principal reasons for the threats of a chastisement upon the earth.

The Scriptures show us we may violate spiritual laws for a season, but at some point God the Father seems to say, "Enough is enough." Abortion is one of these instances.

Heaven's View Of Abortion

Following are excerpts from the messages from Jesus and Mary, as well as quotations from visionaries regarding the sin of abortion.[8]

The Blessed Virgin Mary to Bacco Umberto, Oliveto Citra, Italy August 6, 1986: "My children, I have come to earth for you, to open your hearts for God. My son, look around you: the world is full of sin, many of your brothers and sisters have been killed through abortion and God does not want this because they are His creatures. For these people He has reserved many punishments."

Visionary, on Our Lady's sorrow over abortion: Oliveto Citra, Italy, May 24, 1985: "*Like* Jesus, our heavenly mother defends the life and innocence of the children. When she asks for prayer and penance for the conversion of sinners who provoke the wrath of God, certainly she has in mind the provocation of God's justice by scandalizing the innocent. In one of the messages she spoke emphatically against the abominable crime of abortion, declaring...among those killed were priests and saints."

Visionary/locutionist Mike Slate, of Lubbock, Texas: "Once she came to us during the rosary all dressed in snow white. Then her beautiful white dress began turning blood red. As we knelt there amazed, she explained to us that her dress was turning red because of the blood being shed by aborted children.

The Blessed Virgin Mary to Steve Marino, Green Bay, Wisconsin, April 9, 1991: "...I ask you to keep on trusting me and believing. I want you to tell everyone just how much Jesus loves them. He loves everyone so much that he has withheld His hand of Justice to give me, your mother, time to bring more souls to my Son. The murdering of so many innocent and beautiful children in the wombs of their mothers, the great apostasy that is spreading through our Church, the sin of immorality—do you realize children that our bodies are the temple of the Holy Spirit? There is still time to convert, but you must not delay because the time is very short and everything will change. I, your mother, have come to show you the way. Prayer is the way, my children.... I pray before the cross of Jesus for your conversion."

The Blessed Virgin Mary to "Mariamante" March 7, 1987: "As you know, Satan has targeted the family and the priesthood because these are the holiest of vocations from which most of my children come to me in Heaven. Sadly, many children are not even born into families today, but are orphaned even before their birth by the choice of their parents who do not want them. This grieves my heart so. Cherish your children and give them the stable environment they deserve."

The Lord to Mariamante, March 8, 1987: "The Lord deals out vengeance with a two-edged sword and vengeance is Mine says the Lord. Those who have mutilated their bodies in the never ending attempt to prevent life are in need of repentance. They have sinned in a grievous manner and should remain chaste in atonement for their sin. Behold the sorrow which this aberration of today's society has caused, particularly to the children who are victims of it, victims in the sense of having all in the material realm but deficient in love due to having no brothers and sisters. The parents who have opted to destroy life even before it has begun have the modern world's thinking. They suffer from loneliness, lack of filial affection, and in all manner that is manifested directly from this aberration. To deny human life because of the whimsical and precarious excuses of today's person is an outrage against the divine order, and is directly responsible for much of the sin and tragedy that you witness today."

The Blessed Virgin Mary to J.D., District of Columbia, May 27, 1992: "My child, I have come to speak to the world. Multitudes know me under this image as Our Lady of Guadalupe, Our Lady of the Americas, and Patroness of the Unborn. I come here this evening as My Son requests that I be recognized in this image circulated around the world as a means of conversion and of bringing an end to the sins of abortion. Even as I speak, Satan mounts opposition to this plan. But the grace of my heart is greater than any power of darkness. Child, I give you this message through the grace of my heart. Now you must make it known."

Our Lord to Christina Gallagher, Melleray Grotto, County Waterford, Ireland, September 21, 1990: "The three sins which grieve my heart most deeply at this time are abortion, the killing of the innocents, the sacrificing of the innocents to Satan, and the abuse of the innocents."

The Blessed Virgin Mary to Father Don Stefano Gobbi, Italy, September 8, 1983: "To me, little ones are all those infants who, already conceived, are to be put to death purposely while still in the wombs of their mothers. The love and the anxiety of your heavenly mother, and of the Church, for their salvation, with the innocent blood being spilled by those who despise and disobey the Law of God, are a baptism of blood and desire saving all of them.

The Blessed Virgin Mary to Father Don Stefano Gobbi, Italy, November 15, 1990: "Abortions—these killings of innocent children, that cry for vengeance before the face of God—have spread and are performed in every part of your homeland. The moment of Divine Justice and of Great Mercy has now arrived. You will know the hour of weakness and of poverty; the hour of suffering and defeat; the purifying hour of the Great Chastisement."

Visionary Mirjana Dragicevic Soldo, Medjugorje, former Yugoslavia, June 1991, in answer to the question, "Did The Blessed Virgin Mary mention abortion in the United States?" — "Not only in the United States, but all over the world. In the second year of the apparitions, I asked the Blessed Mother about abortions, because I grew up in the city and in an environment where there are a lot of them. The Blessed Mother said that there is no sin for God which can't be forgiven. But for the abortion, you have to do penance all your life, not only the mother but both parents, mother and father. Mirjana asked the Blessed Mother what happened to the babies, and the Blessed Mother said that 'they are with me.'"

The Blessed Virgin Mary to an American man, August 4, 1990: "I want you to, immediately, place your entire pro-life force and efforts under my banner as your Lady of Guadalupe. I will give you my powerful protection and help. I will lead you to victory over the forces of death which are preying upon babies in the wombs of their mothers.... Together, my dear children, we will end the horrible evil of abortion. I will help you stop all abortions. There will be no exceptions. Together we will bring about a new era of protecting all human life, that is, each person, from conception to natural death.... I will put a stop to the present bloody human sacrifice like I did among the pagans after the miracle of my image began in 1531."

Our Lord to Zdenko "Jim" Singer, Canada, 1991: "Dear children, for your good I gave you the Law. Do not kill. Among these children [who are aborted] is a large number of them who were a gift to you for your own good. The Shining Darkness knows this and he still rules your hard hearts. These very ones, these innocent ones, were intended to deliver you from the despairs from which you now suffer. These innocent souls were intended to rule and advance this world which I gifted you, in the manner that I teach you, in My love."

Guadalupe, Mexico 1531

Nowhere has the role of the Blessed Mother been more magnificent than in what is now Mexico. In 1531, she introduced herself to the Americas in a little village in Guadalupe, Mexico. The story is so significant we have included details which should help you to understand her intervening role in history. It was the first apparition that had world-wide acclaim.

The armadas of Spain and Portugal primarily went to find new lands for the bounty of gold that would be brought back to their homeland. They pillaged, plundered, and ravaged the island nations in their relentless pursuit of wealth in what amounted to legalized genocide. Columbus had landed thirty-nine years earlier, and the clash of cultures began. In Mexican [Aztec] civilization, human sacrifice claimed tens of thousands of lives per year. This was the historical setting for the Blessed Virgin's intervention where she identified herself as the "Patroness of the Americas" although her banner title was, "The Mother of all My Children." She appeared on the highest point on the mountain (the Indians worshipped as high as possible to seek God) and the color of her tilma or cloak was the color of their own Aztec god signifying royalty.

In 1531, tensions were reaching the breaking point between the native Indians and the Spaniards in the New World. Cortez had conquered, but his forces were barbarously mistreating the Indians, who vastly outnumbered the Spaniards. Franciscan missionaries had recently come into what is now Mexico, to spread the Gospel. They were viewed with more trust than were the Spanish soldiers, but the territory was on the brink of a bloodbath. The Aztec religion required human sacrifice: an estimated 20,000 human beings were annually slaughtered and mutilated, their beating hearts cut out of their living breasts, as Aztec priests offered their sacrifices to appease the sun and serpent gods whom they worshipped.

Juan Diego Of Guadalupe

Early on the morning of December 9, 1531, a childless widower named Juan Diego, a fifty-seven-year-old Indian convert of five years, was walking to the Church of Saint James to attend Mass. He heard a heavenly choir, and then he heard a soft and gentle woman's voice calling him "Juan Diego! ...Juanito!" Juan climbed the hill, towards the sound. The sun had not yet risen, yet Juan gasped as he saw a young Indian girl, barely sixteen years of age, apparently pregnant, and incredibly beautiful. She was dressed in the aqua mantle reserved for royalty, with a black cross on the brooch at her neck and was bathed in golden beams of light. Rainbow colors of such intensity surrounded the apparition such that the very stones on the ground appeared like jewels. She spoke gently to Juan Diego, identifying herself as the Virgin Mary. She told him to convey to the bishop, Fray Juan de Zumarraga, that she desired a church to be built in this place, so that she might console and help all the people. The bishop suggested to Juan that the Lady provide a sign. Mary promised she would, if Juan would return at daybreak, on Monday, December 11. Mary instructed Juan Diego to climb to the top of Tepeyac Hill and pick the flowers he found there. Juan obediently made his way up the rocky and frost-covered hill where not much of anything could grow at any time, especially in December. There he found Castillian roses of all colors in full summer bloom, dripping with dew. He gathered them in his tilma and brought them back to the Lady. She rearranged them carefully on the tilma, tied them up tightly, and instructed Juan to present them to the bishop as his requested sign.

Juan Diego rushed to the bishop's residence. He told the bishop all the Lady had said. When he opened his tilma, the roses cascaded onto the floor. There was shock on the bishop's face. He fell to his knees before Juan Diego, yet he was not looking at the flowers, Juan saw, but at him—at his tilma. Juan looked down. The image of the beautiful Lady, as Juan had seen her, was taking form on the tilma, like a modern-day developing photograph. When the Bishop and the other Indians in the room saw the tilma, they all fell to their knees.

What did they each see? The bishop, of course, saw the Blessed Virgin Mary, as his faith had taught him she might appear. She was the "woman clothed with the sun and standing on the moon," the Mother of Jesus Christ. The Indians, not sharing a Christian heritage, saw something quite different. They saw someone from the heavens (with stars on her cape and standing on the moon), a queen dressed in the color aqua, reserved for royalty. She stood before the sun, indicating she was greater than the Aztec sun god, and atop the moon, symbolic of the serpent god, Quetzalcoatl. She wore the belt of her dress high, indicating she was pregnant. Her eyes were downcast, showing humility. Thus, although greater than the Aztec gods, she was not herself a goddess. Finally, she wore a black cross in her brooch. The Aztec princess had recently had a dream in which she had seen a black cross as the sign of the conqueror. Miracles of healing followed in the next few days. Mary's request for a church to honor her was granted. Over the next three years, a mass conversion never before or since seen within Catholicism occurred. The bloody pagan custom of Aztec human sacrifice ceased completely.[9]

The Sequel

Guadalupe is an Indian word which means "she who crushes the serpent." In 1990, Mary reportedly began appearing to a man in Seattle, Washington, as the "Virgin Of Guadalupe," asking that all the pro-life forces be assembled under her banner as "Protectress of the Unborn." Her purpose was to finally end abortion, just as she stopped the Aztec custom of bloody human sacrifice nearly 500 years ago. She told the Seattle visionary that she will end the Twentieth Century's bloody sacrifice of innocent human lives that we call abortion. Several replicas of her original image were commissioned by the Mexican bishops to travel throughout the Americas with this mission in mind. There have been many reported signs and wonders associated with the travels of these "Missionary Images" of Juan Diego's tilma, including healings, solar phenomena, and verified reports of rose petals materializing and cascading from the images. If Mary was a sign of hope in 1531, Our Blessed Mother is much more of a needed sign of hope in our day.

At this present moment, we can see no end to abortion. However, Our Blessed Mother is always several steps ahead of us, and with the symphony of prayers and the powerful intercession of Our Lady and Christ her Son, the scourge of abortion will be eliminated as was the Aztec horror of human sacrifice. We must, however, emphasize that Our Lady said, "together we will end abortion." She needs our prayers, sacrifices, and help.

Others Speak

Messages have come from Gladys of San Nicolas, Argentina, and stigmatist Julia Kim of Naju, Korea. They warn of Satan's activity in the world, particularly regarding abortion.

Gladys

"My children, in the large cities of the world, atheism and total indifference toward God are to be seen. The wicked one has risen like an effervescence, covering weak minds with his wickedness and dominating" (September 2, 1985).

"My daughter, the evil one is triumphant now, it is true, but it is a victory that will last briefly. The Lord is only giving him time, the same time that He gives man for him to return to God. That is why vices and worldly madness increase more every day. The weaknesses will have to become strengths, and in this I will be able to get rid of evil. As yet, man's heart is not totally invaded" (October 11, 1986).

"There are so many insane passions everywhere, my children, that blindness has taken hold of many people. Sin surpasses all measure. The devil wants to have full domination over the earth. He wants to destroy" (June 2, 1985).

"You know my daughter, a tempest has broken out, a terrible tempest, the work of the devil. It is that the Lord's Word is a stumbling stone for many sinners. But repeat what I so often said to you: the work of God is great, there is no evil able to stop it" (April 6, 1986).

"Daughter, the earth is inhabited, but it seems uninhabited, a very great darkness is over it. God's warning is over the world! Those who stay in the Lord have nothing to fear, but those who deny what comes from Him have" (October 14, 1986).

"Gladys, pray also for the children that are not born, that do not see the light of day. The abortions are so many, so many the attempts on lives that only belong to God!" (March 7, 1987).

Julia Kim: "I suffer most painfully when I behold children dying so soon after conception, put to death by the chemicals many women use to stifle life at its beginning. I plead with you to alleviate my anguish by your sacrifices and your prayer of reparation. I am pleading with priests everywhere: Please do not allow my tears to flow in vain. I desire that my dear priests would become victim souls for the conversion of sinners and for the salvation of mankind. Satan is disguising himself in various ways—outwardly good, charitable, intellectual and holy in appearance—but ultimately intending to create division, heresy and confusion. The best way to counteract these efforts of the evil one to weaken the church is to put my messages into practice" (June, 1989).

Satan's Final Hour

This message was received on October 13, 1987, at Fatima, Portugal, on the occasion of the seventieth anniversary of the Fatima apparitions. The message relayed information to the Marian Movement of Priests regarding Satan's final hour.

"These are seventy years during which I have descended from Heaven into your midst as the Woman Clothed with the Sun. These are seventy years during which my Adversary, Satan, has come up from the abyss into your midst, to manifest himself as the Red Dragon in all his terrible power. In fact, he has succeeded in extending his reign in many nations and in spreading his action of denial and of rebellion against God to every part of the earth.

"Thus, during the period of these seventy years, the Red Dragon has bound men with the chain of his slavery. He has made you slaves of pride and of haughtiness, with the deceptive illusion of bringing you to getting along without God, of putting your own selves in the place of God, so that in you he may be able to renew his act of rebellion and of defiance against the Lord. Thus he has spread everywhere the error of atheism and has driven humanity to build a new civilization without God."

Satan's authority and limited time is seen in Our Lady's message of January 1, 1992, to Father Gobbi: "Lift up your eyes from this dark epoch in which you are living and do not fear if, at present, Satan is the uncontested ruler of the world and the master of all humanity. Soon his reign will be reduced to a heap of ruins and his power will be destroyed, because I myself will bind him with a chain and will shut him up in his pool of eternal fire and death, from which he will be no longer able to get out. And it will be Jesus Christ, King of eternal glory, who will reign over the whole renewed world and thus bring about the beginning of the new times, which are on the point of arriving.... I announce to you that your liberation is near."

Mary's remedy for Satan's conquest was given to Father Gobbi on October 7, 1983: "Satan's pride will again be conquered by the humility of little ones, and the Red Dragon will find himself decisively humiliated and defeated when I bind him not by a great chain but by a very frail cord: the holy rosary."

We are now at the tail end of Satan's reign, near the time when the mystery of iniquity will surface and show his face for the world to see. The evils of abortion, homosexuality, and all impurities are today accepted as normal. Wrong has become right, and there are no objections from our clergy, elected leaders, or the majority of our citizens. Our cities are centers of violent crime, where it is unsafe even to walk in the evening. Drugs are pervasive and are destroying our youth on a world-wide scale. Many families are so ravaged by numerous ills that few are untouched in the immoral climate of our times.

Satan has had his reign, and the Woman clothed with the sun will soon crush the head of the serpent. The destruction has taken its toll to where there has nearly been a complete loss of faith. The predictions of LaSalette have all come true in "Satan's Century."

9

Fatima And The End Times

The edifice of modern civilization must be built upon spiritual principles which alone can support it, and even illuminate it and animate it. Such indispensable principles of superior wisdom can be found only...upon Faith in God.

Pope Paul VI, to the United Nations,
October 4, 1965

The Importance Of Fatima For This Century

After the failed assassination attempt on his life in 1981, and while he was recuperating from his wounds, Pope John Paul II reflected on Fatima. He told his friend Bishop Paul M. Hnilica, S.J.: "Paul, in these three months I have come to understand that the only solution to all the problems of the world, the deliverance from war, the deliverance from atheism, and from the defection from God is the conversion of Russia. The conversion of Russia is the content and meaning of the message of Fatima. Not until then will the triumph of Mary come."[1]

Fatima is the key Marian apparition of the Twentieth Century. Pope Pius XII noted that the message of Fatima is one of the greatest interventions of God through Mary in world history since the death of the Apostles. Only in the name of God does the Blessed Mother intervene. She does not say a word, does not take a step without the explicit will of God. The message of Fatima cannot be understood if you do not know atheistic communism, if you do not know what happened in Russia.[2]

Pope Pius XI said: "Today we see something that world history has never seen before: The waving of the flag of Satan in the battle against God and religion, against all peoples, and in all parts of the world; a phenomenon that outdoes all that happened before.[3]

In the history of all mankind nothing in our past rivals the brutality of man against man like communism. It passes in scope all former persecutions of the Church. Hitler is estimated to have been responsible for the deaths of approximately twelve million people, including Holocaust and war victims. Lenin, Mao, Stalin, and others after them collectively are thought to have been directly responsible for over 100 million deaths.

Nearly 300 million people in the Republics (former Soviet Union) and nearly 1.4 billion living in China have been subjected to this system of injustice. This does not include all of the other satellites that were in the grip of communist ideology. This is not the work of man; a higher and more cunning power is behind this.

Since the Revolution in 1917, Satan had been working tirelessly to control the heart and soul of Russia. Because the world did not heed the messages of Fatima, he succeeded to a significant degree. Not until the expanded role of the Blessed Mother in these times are we seeing change. She invites us to the highest calling possible: to become co-redeemers for our brothers in Christ. This is the message of Fatima, the message of peace.

The conversion of Russia is only a part of the overall message. It does not stand alone but is part of a larger message in the waning years of this century.

Prelude To Fatima

In Rue de Bac in Paris on November 27, 1830, Our Blessed Mother appeared to Catherine Laboure and gave her the "Miraculous Medal." Mary asked that the medal be struck showing two hearts: The Sacred Heart of Jesus and the Immaculate Heart of Mary, together on one side of the medal.

At LaSalette, France, in 1846, Our Lady told Maximin Giraud, "Afterwards, this peace shall be disturbed by the monster (communism). The monster shall arrive at the nineteenth, or at the latest, at the commencement of the Twentieth Century."⁴

In Hrushiv, Ukraine, in 1914, twenty-two peasants saw Our Lady. She predicted eighty or ninety years of hardship (remember, freedom of worship became possible only in the last several years). As at Fatima, she also warned that Russia would become godless and bring mankind precariously close to destruction. It was a significant link to what Sister Lucia of Fatima was told years later: if Russia did not return to Christianity, there might well be another world war, and whole nations would vanish.

The Fatima Apparitions

1916—The Angel of Peace Appears

In 1916, a time of persecution for the Church in Portugal, the Angel of Peace, the Guardian Angel of Portugal, appeared to three children: Lucia, Francesco, and Jacinta. He appeared on three separate occasions.

In the spring of 1916, the Angel of Peace asked the children to pray with him. He knelt down and bowed low and three times repeated the prayer, "O my God, I believe, I adore, I trust and love Thee. I beg pardon for those who do not believe, do not adore, do not trust, do not love Thee." He told them to pray this way.

In mid-summer of 1916, he appeared to the three children and said: "What are you doing? Pray! Pray a great deal! The Hearts of Jesus and Mary have designs of mercy for you! Offer unceasingly to the Most High prayers and sacrifices! Offer up everything within your power as a sacrifice to the Lord in an act of reparation for the sins by which He is offended; and of supplication for the conversion of sinners. Thus invoke peace upon your country. I am her Guardian Angel, the Angel of Portugal. Above all, accept and bear with submission the sufferings the Lord may send you."⁵

In the autumn of 1916, the Angel again appeared to the children holding a golden chalice in one hand; above it, in the other hand was a Host, which dripped blood into the chalice. The Angel left the chalice and Host suspended in the air and prostrated himself on the ground and three times repeated this prayer: "Most Holy Trinity, Father, Son and Holy Ghost, I adore Thee profoundly, and I offer Thee the Most Precious Body, Blood, Soul and Divinity of Jesus

Christ, present in all the tabernacles of the world in reparation for the outrages, sacrileges and indifferences by which He is offended. And through the infinite merits of His Most Sacred Heart and the Immaculate Heart of Mary, I beg the conversion of poor sinners." The Angel then gave Holy Communion to Lucia and to the other two children, as well as the chalice to drink from and said: "Take and drink the Body and Blood of Jesus Christ, horribly outraged by ungrateful men. Make reparation for their crimes and console your God."

Fatima In 1917—The Woman Clothed With The Sun

On May 13, 1917, at the Cova da Iria, just after noon, the three children had finished lunch and were going to play when they saw a flash of lightening, then another. A lovely Lady "more brilliant than the sun" appeared over a small holm oak tree. She said, "Do not be afraid. I will do you no harm. I am from Heaven." Lucia asked, "What do you want of us?" The Lady replied, "I want you to come here on the thirteenth day for six months at this same time, and then I will tell you who I am and what I want." The Lady asked them, "Would you like to offer yourselves to God, to accept all the sufferings which He may send you in reparation for the countless sins by which He is offended, and in supplication for the conversion of sinners?" Lucia, speaking for the three, said yes. The Lady replied, "Then you will have much to suffer, but the grace of God will be your comfort." She departed with the words, "Say the rosary every day to earn peace for the world and the end of the war."

On June 13, 1917, the Lady appeared a second time at the oak tree to the three children. Lucia asked the Lady what she wanted of her. The Lady replied, "I want you to come here on the thirteenth of the next month. Say the rosary, inserting between the mysteries the following ejaculation, 'O my Jesus, forgive us our sins. Save us from the fires of hell. Lead all souls to Heaven, especially those who have most need of Thy mercy.' I want you to learn to read and write and later I will tell you what else I want."

The Lady advised them that she would take Francesco and Jacinta to Heaven soon (An epidemic of flu claimed Francesco and Jacinta in 1919 and 1920, respectively). But the Lady said to Lucia, "You, however, are to stay here a longer time. Jesus wants to use you to make me known and loved. He wants to establish the devotion to my Immaculate Heart in the world. I promise salvation to those who embrace it and their soul will be loved by God as flowers placed by myself to adorn His throne." She promised Lucia she would never leave her. She said, "My Immaculate Heart will be your refuge and the way that will lead you to God."

On July 13, 1917, Our Lady again appeared over the oak tree. Lucia asked, "What do you want of me?" The Lady replied, "I want you to come here on the thirteenth of next month and to continue to pray the rosary every day in honor of Our Lady of the Rosary, in order to obtain peace for the world and the end of the war, for she alone can help. Continue to come here every month. In October, I will tell you who I am and what I want. And I will perform a miracle so that everyone may see and believe."

The Lady then told the children, "Sacrifice yourselves for sinners and say often, especially when you make some sacrifice, 'O my Jesus, it is for love of You, for the conversion of sinners and in reparation for the offenses committed against the Immaculate Heart of Mary." After saying this, she held out her hands from which light streamed, seeming to penetrate the earth, and the children were shown a vision of hell.

The Lady said to Lucia, "You have seen hell where the souls of poor sinners go. To save them God wants to establish throughout the world the devotion to my Immaculate Heart. If people will do what I tell you, many souls will be saved, and there will be peace. The war is going to end. But if they do not stop offending God, another and worse war will break out in the reign of Pius XI. **When you see a night illumined by an unknown light, know that is the great sign that God gives you, that He is going to punish the world for its crimes by means of war, hunger, persecution of the Church and of the Holy Father.** To forestall this, I shall come to ask the consecration of Russia to my Immaculate Heart and the communion of reparation on the First Saturdays. If they heed my request, Russia will be converted, and there will be peace. **If not, she shall spread her errors throughout the world, promoting wars and persecution of the Church; the good will be martyred, the Holy Father will have much to suffer, various nations will be annihilated; in the end, my Immaculate Heart shall triumph.** The Holy Father will consecrate Russia to me which will be converted, and some time of peace will be given to the world.... Do not tell this to anyone. To Francesco, yes, you may tell it."

On August 19, 1917, at Valinhos, near the Cova da Iria, the Lady appeared again to the children. The local officials had kidnapped the children and held them for several days to prevent them from going to the Cova da Iria on the thirteenth.

Lucia again asked "What do you want?" The Lady said, "I want you to continue to come to the Cova da Iria on the thirteenth and to continue to say the rosary every day." She promised Lucia that, "Yes, in the last month, in October, I shall perform a miracle so that all may believe in my apparitions. If they had not taken you to the village, the miracle would have been greater. Saint Joseph will come to bless the people. Besides, Our Lady of the Rosary and Our Lady of Sorrows will come." The Lady said "Pray! Pray a great deal and make sacrifices for sinners, for many souls go to hell from not having someone to pray and make sacrifices for them!"

On September 13, 1917, the Lady appeared. Lucia, as was her custom, asked, "What do you want of me?" The Lady replied, "Let the people continue to say the rosary every day to obtain the end of the war." Lucia begged her to perform a miracle. The Lady replied "Yes, in October, I will perform a miracle so that all may believe."

The Miracle Of The Sun

On October 13, 1917, a severe storm had raged through Europe. The ground was soaked and muddy. A crowd of people estimated between 50,000, and 70,000 made its way—drenched—to the apparition site.

The Lady appeared, and in reply to Lucia's usual question, "What do you want?" The reply was, "I want to tell you that they must build a chapel here in my honor, that I am the Lady of the Rosary; that they continue to say the rosary every day. The war will end and the soldiers will return to their homes soon."

As the Blessed Mother was leaving she opened her hands, and from them rays of light extended in the direction of the sun. Gradually the sun grew pale, appeared as a silver disk at which all could gaze directly, without shielding their eyes. Rays of multicolored light shot out from the sun in every direction; red, blue, yellow, green, and every color of the spectrum. Then the sun began to spin madly on its axis and appeared like a giant wheel of fire. The sun began to dance wildly. Suddenly the sun seemed to be torn loose from its orbit. It hurtled closer and closer to earth, and looked like it was going to plummet to the earth. The people were terrified and there arose cries of repentance and appeals for mercy. Many thought it was the end of the world. Then, just as suddenly, the sun stopped plummeting downwards, and in the same swirling motion it began to climb upward until it resumed its place in the sky. The rain-soaked clothes of the 50,000 to 70,000 people were immediately dry. This was an event reported by several newspapers of the day.

Sister Lucia, as of this writing, is still alive. She has continued to receive messages from Our Blessed Mother. Lucia has been told that she will see the fulfillment of all of the messages of Fatima. Lucy today is eighty-six years old.

Pope Paul VI, in his May 1967 encyclical entitled *Signum Magnum* identifies Our Blessed Mother at Fatima with "The Woman Clothed With the Sun," equating her directly with Revelation, Chapter 12.

Seventy-Five Years Of Events At Fatima

A series of important events associated with Fatima over the past seventy-five years are listed below.[6]

• December 10, 1925: The Blessed Virgin Mary, with the Child Jesus by her side, appeared to Lucia. Our Lady requested the five first Saturdays devotion in reparation to her Immaculate Heart.

• February 15, 1926: The Child Jesus appeared to Lucia and asked if she has spread this devotion (First Saturdays) of reparation to the Immaculate Heart of His Mother.

• June 13, 1929: In the convent at Tuy, Spain, Sister Lucia had a vision of the Blessed Trinity and Mary as the Virgin of Fatima. Mary was holding the Immaculate Heart in her hand and told Sister Lucia: "The moment has come in which God asks the Holy Father in union with all the bishops of the world to make the consecration of Russia to my Immaculate Heart, promising to save it by this means." Lucia conveyed this message to her spiritual director, Father Jose Bernardo Goncalves, and the priest turned it over to the bishop of Leira. There is no evidence that Pope Pius XI ever got the message. Eventually the message reached Rome, but in the meantime Russia was not consecrated and events continued on a disastrous course in the Soviet Union.[7]

- October 13, 1930: The bishop of Fatima declared the Fatima apparitions worthy of acceptance as of supernatural origin.

- September 12, 1935: The corpse of Jacinta was removed to Fatima. The casket was opened and the face of Jacinta appeared preserved. The bishop ordered Lucia to write everything she could remember about Jacinta's life. The First Memoir of Sister Lucia was written before December 25, 1935.

- November, 1937: The bishop of Leira, in whose diocese exists the parish of Fatima, ordered Sister Lucia to write the history of her life and the apparitions just as they happened. Her Second Memoir was written at that time.

- January 25-26, 1938: The lights predicted at Fatima on July 13, 1917, were seen in the United States and Europe. The people were startled by the display of lights which scientist termed an Aurora Borealis of "exceptional magnitude." Lucia, at the convent in Tuy, Spain, marveled at the spectacle. She sent a letter to the bishop, stating that "God made use of this to make me understand His justice was about to strike the guilty nations." Pope Pius XI had predicted that a great sign would be followed by horrible persecutions. Within several months Hitler had marched into Austria, annexing it to Germany. Hitler's aggression had commenced, and soon World War II began with the invasion of Poland on September 1, 1939.

- August 31, 1941, Sister Lucia wrote her Third Memoir, elucidating some details of Jacinta's life. In this Third Memoir Sister Lucia for the first time mentioned that the secret was in three distinct parts, and she revealed the first two. She stated that at that time she was not permitted to reveal the third part of the secret.

- December 8, 1941: Sister Lucia, in response to an order by her bishop on October 7, 1941, to write everything else she could remember about the events of Fatima, presented her Fourth Memoir.

- October 31, 1942: Pope Pius XII, in a Portuguese broadcast communication, consecrated the world to the Immaculate Heart of Mary.

- May 13, 1946: Pope Pius XII crowned the image of Our Lady of Fatima and proclaimed her "Queen of the World."

- June 13, 1946: Pope Pius XII in his encyclical *Deiparea Virginis Mariae* referred favorably to Our Lady's message at Fatima.

• July 7, 1952: Pope Pius XII consecrated the Russian people to the Immaculate Heart of Mary.

• November 12, 1954: Pope Pius XII raised the sanctuary shrine in Fatima to the rank of a basilica.

• December 13, 1962: Pope John XXIII instituted the feast of Our Lady of the Rosary in honor of Our Lady of Fatima.

• November 21, 1964: Pope Paul VI renewed Pope Pius XII's consecration of Russia to the Immaculate Heart, speaking to the Fathers of the Second Vatican Council. He did it alone, though in the presence of the Council Fathers.

• May 13, 1967: Pope Paul VI went to Fatima, where he called for renewed consecration to the Immaculate Heart.

• May 13, 1981: Pope John Paul II was seriously wounded by an assassin's bullets. The Pope was saved from death when he turned to look at a young girl in the crowd wearing a picture of the Virgin of Fatima. As the Pope turned, a shot aimed at his head missed. The assassin then shot twice more, striking the Pope in the abdomen. The Pope spoke with Lucia from his hospital room. While he was recuperating from his wounds he read everything he could about Fatima, corresponded with Lucia, and re-read the famous unreleased Third Secret.

• May 13, 1982: Pope John Paul II, in a visit to Fatima to thank Mary for saving his life, stated that the "message of Fatima is still more relevant than it was sixty-five years ago. It is still more urgent." Having sent letters to all the Catholic bishops of the world, the Pope attempted to "collegially" consecrate with them the world and therefore Russia to the Immaculate Heart. Many bishops did not respond, and Sister Lucia said afterwards the attempt did not fulfill all the conditions required by God.

• December 8, 1983, Pope John Paul II stated, **"Precisely at the end of the second millennium there accumulates on the horizon of all mankind enormously threatening clouds, and darkness falls upon human souls."**[8]

Controversy Number 1—The Third Secret of Fatima

On August 31, 1941, Sister Lucia wrote her third memoir elucidating some details of Jacinta's life. In this third memoir, Sister Lucia for the first time mentioned that the Secret was in three distinct parts. She wrote, "The Secret is composed of three distinct matters and I shall disclose two of them."

The first is the vision of hell and the designation of the Immaculate Heart of Mary as the supreme remedy offered by God to humanity, for the salvation of souls. Our Lady said, "In order to save them, God wishes to establish in the world devotion to My Immaculate Heart."

The second is the great prophecy concerning a miraculous peace which God wishes to grant to the world through the consecration of Russia to the Immaculate Heart of Mary, and the practice of communions of reparation on the first Saturdays of the month. "If people attend to my requests, Russia will be converted and the world will have peace." And there is also the announcement of terrible punishments if people persist in not obeying her requests. Sister Lucia stated that at that time she was not permitted to reveal the third part of the secret.

Bishop da Silva was given permission to read it, but he did not want the responsibility. He tried to get it to the Holy Office, but Rome refused to receive it. It was then agreed that if Bishop da Silva happened to die, the envelope would be entrusted to Cardinal Cerejeira, the Patriarch of Lisbon.[9]

In 1957, the Holy Office demanded the text of the third secret, which until then had been kept at the palace of the bishop of Leira. The auxiliary Bishop Venancio was entrusted with the delivery of the sealed document to Bishop Cento, then Apostolic Nuncio to Lisbon.

On April 16, 1957, the sealed envelope arrived in Rome. It was placed in the office of Pope Pius XII, in a little chest bearing the note, "Secret of the Holy Office."

It appears that Pope Pius XII did not read the secret. According to Cardinal Ottaviani and Monsignor Capovilla, secretary of Pope John XXIII, the envelope was still sealed when Pope John XXIII opened it in 1959, one year after the death of Pope Pius XII. Pope Pius XII had apparently decided to wait until 1960. He died on October 9, 1958, without having read the secret.[10]

In 1957, Sister Lucia confided to Father Fuentes: "The Most Holy Virgin has told me that the devil is about to engage in a decisive battle against the Virgin...and the devil knows what most offends God, and what will make him gain the most souls in the shortest possible time, he does everything to win consecrated

souls from God, for in this manner he will succeed in leaving the souls of the faithful defenseless, and so he will lay hold of them more easily."

On December 26, 1957, Sister Lucia told Father Fuentes, the Postulator of the beatification causes of Jacinta and Francisco: "The Blessed Virgin is very sad, for no one attaches any importance to her message. Neither the good nor the bad. The good continue on their way, but without paying attention to the message. I cannot give any other details, since it is still a secret. Only the Holy Father and His Excellency, the Bishop of Fatima would be able to know it in accordance with the will of the Blessed Virgin. But they haven't willed to know it as they did not want to be influenced."[11]

In 1959, there was a great wave of devotion in all Italy to the Immaculate Heart of Mary. On September 13, 1959, all the bishops of Italy solemnly consecrated Italy to the Immaculate Heart of Mary.[12]

On August 17, 1959, Pope John XXIII had the envelope brought to him at Castogandolfo, by Monsignor Philippe, then an official of the Holy Office. Pope John XXIII did not immediately open the envelope but stated, "I am waiting to read it with my confessor."[13]

Was The Secret To Be Revealed?

The secret was read a few days later, according to Monsignor Capovilla. Assistance in reading the Portuguese was given by Monsignor Paulo Jose Tavarez of the Secretariat of State. Later John XXIII had it read by Cardinal Ottaviani, Prefect of the Holy Office. On February 8, 1960, it was suddenly learned through a simple Portuguese press agency communique that the third secret of Fatima would not be published, and that it probably would never be disclosed. The Vatican communique ended: "Although the Church recognizes the Fatima apparitions, She does not desire to take the responsibility of guaranteeing the veracity of the words the three shepherd children said that the Virgin Mary had addressed to them."

Bishop Venancio, on his own initiative, decided to launch an appeal to all the bishops of the world and attempted to organize a world day of prayer and penance for the following October 13, but the Vatican turned a deaf ear to this proposal, and nothing was done. This did immense harm to the Fatima cause. It was from this date, after this public disregard for the "Secret of Mary," that devotion to the Most Blessed Virgin began to decrease in a perceptible and then alarming manner in the very bosom of the Church.[14]

This fault was to have incalculable consequences, according to Brother Michel, author of the four-volume set, *The Third Secret of Fatima*. He maintained that by disregarding the prophecies and requests of Fatima, it was the Virgin Mary—it was God Himself— who had been disregarded, who had been ridiculed in front of the world. The conditional punishment announced through the maternal warning of Our Lady was in consequence destined to be accomplished tragically, inevitably by disobeying the message of the Virgin.

Cardinal Ottaviani related that Pope John XXIII placed the Secret "in one of the those archives which are like a very deep, dark well, to the bottom of which papers fall and no one is able to see them anymore." Pope Paul VI straightway adopted the same attitude toward the third secret.

The Virgin had asked that the secret be made public in 1960 because, as Sister Lucia told Cardinal Ottaviani, "in 1960, the Message will appear more clear." Other statements from Sister Lucia have said that "the punishment predicted by Our Lady in the third secret has already begun."

We are now in the period of which the message speaks. We are now living through the third secret. We are witnessing the events that it announces.[15]

Catholics throughout the world by 1960 were waiting for the Pope to open the letter and reveal the third secret. But Pope John XXIII and the subsequent Popes have greatly disappointed the faithful by refusing to reveal its contents.[16]

Why this is so we are not sure. In Pope John XXIII's *Journal of a Soul*, the diary of his life, he says the Second Vatican Council was a success because of the Blessed Mother's intervention. **Pope John XXIII had read the secret of Fatima and said the secret did not pertain to the reign of his pontificate. Why several Popes did not reveal the secret is a mystery**.

There is continuing controversy concerning why Popes since Fatima have not revealed the Third Secret. Scholars disagree on whether or not the Third Secret was meant only for the eyes of the

Popes or if it was to be released to the general public. The comment by Pope John XXIII and others upon reading the secret—indicating that it did not pertain to their pontificates—lends credibility to this argument. Also, Pope John Paul II is under Mary's protective mantle, and he has not released the contents, either. It seems that the Third Secret was to be made available to the world from many sources.

On October 11, 1992, an interview took place between Sister Lucia and Anthony Cardinal Padiyara of India, Bishop Francis Michaelappa of India, and Father Francisco Pacheco of Fort Ceara, Brazil. Sister Lucia was asked by Cardinal Padiyara, **"Do God and Our Lady still want the Church to reveal the Third Secret?" Sister Lucia reportedly answered, "The Third Secret is not intended to be revealed. It was only intended for the Pope and immediate Church hierarchy. Our Lady never said that it was to be revealed to the public by 1960 at the latest. The Secret was for the Pope." Some respected priests doubt that this interview ever took place. The controversy continues.** [17]

The secrets of Fatima still have not been released by the Church, but through the intervention of the Blessed Mother at apparition sites we have a good idea of the contents.

We do know from the Akita message of October 13, 1973, and the May 13, 1990, message of Father Gobbi, that the secret seems to deal with the apostasy and chastisement.

"The Blessed Virgin has told us," confided Sister Lucia to Father Fuentes, that "many nations will disappear from the face of the earth, and Russia will be the instrument of heavenly punishment for the world, if we do not obtain beforehand the conversion of that poor nation."

Bishop Venancio named the late Father Alonso in 1966 as the official expert on Fatima. Father Alonso concluded that the Third Secret mainly refers to a spiritual chastisement which will be far worse, and even more fearsome, than famine, wars and persecutions, for it concerns souls and their salvation or their eternal perdition. His work consisted of fourteen volumes, which unfortunately he was forbidden to publish! However, before his death on December 12, 1981, he was able to make known his conclusions in various pamphlets and numerous articles in theological journals.

In a series of letters in 1969-1970, Sister Lucia reveals more: "It is indeed sad that so many people let themselves be dominated by the diabolical wave that is sweeping the world, and that they are blinded to the point of being incapable of seeing error! **Their principle fault is they have abandoned prayer;** in this way they have become estranged from God, and without God everything fails. The devil is very cunning and looks for our weak points in order to attack us. If we are not diligent and careful to obtain strength from God, we shall fall, for our age is very wicked and we are weak. Only the strength of God can keep us on our feet."[18]

Sister Lucia wrote: **"Let people say the rosary every day. Our Lady stated that repeatedly in all her apparitions, as if to fortify us against these times of diabolical disorientation, so that we would not allow ourselves to be deceived by false doctrines.... Unfortunately, the great majority of people are ignorant in religious matters and allow themselves to be led in any direction. Hence, the great responsibility of one who has the task of leading them.... A diabolical disorientation is invading the world, deceiving souls! It must be resisted."[19]**

On September 16, 1970, Sister Lucia wrote: "Our poor Lord, He has saved us with so much love and He is so little understood! So little loved! So badly served! It is painful to see such great confusion, and in so many persons who occupy positions of responsibility! The fact is the devil has succeeded in bringing in evil under the appearance of good; the blind are beginning to lead others, as the Lord tells us in His Gospel, and souls are allowing themselves to be deceived. Gladly I sacrifice myself and offer my life to God for peace in His Church, for priests and for all consecrated souls, especially for those who are so deceived and misguided!"[20]

Sister Lucia insists that, "the Virgin knew that these times of diabolical disorientation were to come."[21] To someone who was questioning her on the content of the Third Secret Sister Lucia one day replied: "It's in the Gospel and in the Apocalypse, read them." **She also confided to Father Fuentes that the Virgin Mary made her see clearly that "we are in the last times of the world."[22]**

The Greatest Danger To A Nation

Cardinal Ratzinger in August 1984 said that the Third Secret concerned "the dangers which threaten the faith and the life of

Christians." Responding to the question, "Why is the faith in crisis?" he stated, "The dangers threatening the faith, the importance of the last times and the fact that the prophecies contained in this Third Secret correspond to what Scripture announces."[23]

On September 10, 1984, Bishop Amaral of Leira, Portugal, declared in the great hall of the Technical University in Vienna, "The Secret of Fatima speaks neither of atomic bombs nor of nuclear warheads, nor of SS20 missiles. Its content concerns only our faith. To identify the secret with catastrophic announcements or a nuclear holocaust is to distort the meaning of the message. The loss of faith of a continent is worse than the annihilation of a nation; and it is true that the faith is continually diminishing in Europe." Father Alonso's thesis is now publicly confirmed by the bishop of Fatima. The message foretells a terrible crisis within the Church. **It is the loss of the faith, which the Immaculate Virgin predicted would occur in our era, if her requests were not sufficiently carried out. This loss of faith and all it entails is the drama that we have been witnessing since 1960.**[24]

Grave Circumstances

So we must ask why have such good and saintly men in the Chair of Peter such as John Paul II not disclosed the Third Secret of Fatima? In 1980, while speaking in Fulda, Germany, John Paul II stated in response to a question about the Third Secret that Lucia's text does speak of chastisements. In response to another question, he stated that, "the chastisements cannot be averted, it is too late." He stated that, "the die was cast. [The chastisements] can be mitigated by praying the rosary." He reiterated that he, as his predecessors in the Petrine Office, preferred to postpone publication so as not to encourage the world power of communism to make certain moves.

These questions also shed light on why he has not undertaken any papal-directed and comprehensive effort to reverse the continual and rapid deterioration of the Church. Pope John Paul II said at the Fulda meeting, **"No, the Church cannot be reformed at the present moment."**[25] He, too, chose not to disclose the Third Secret.

Understood in its depth and extent, John Paul's statement can be shocking: "so as not to encourage the world power of communism to make certain moves." For the Pope to come to such a conclusion illustrates how accurate the message of Lucia must be.

Father Malachi Martin in *The Keys of This Blood* writes about this issue: "In that 'Third Secret', Lucia's words are so explicit and so verifiable—and therefore so authentic—that, were the leaders of the Leninist Party-State to know those words, they would in all probability decide to undertake certain territorial and militaristic moves against which the West could have few if any means of resisting, and the Church would be plunged into further and deeper subjugation to the Party-State." This is the seriousness of Lucia's words. The capitalist West could be entrapped by the USSR. In Vatican parlance, Lucia's words have dire geopolitical meaning. They must not be treated as pious and devotional outpourings. Fatima relates to the fierce politics of nations. Ever since John XXIII opened and read those words, the Vatican has treated them gingerly. The "Secret" has to be buried, as Cardinal Ottaviani said in 1957, "in the most hidden, the deepest, the most obscure and inaccessible place on earth. If there was one dominant element to the 'Third Secret', it is Russia.[26]

"It must also be added, however, that the anti-Church partisans in the Vatican bureaucracy and throughout the Church abhor anything savoring devotion to Mary, to Fatima, and to divine revelation. They have forsaken the divine faith of Catholicism, of which Mary, the Mother of God, is an integral part. They also know the present Pope is under the special protection of Mary.[27] This Mary has said so many times to the visionaries of the world and most notably to Father Gobbi when she said, "he is the Pope of my secret." When Mary says, "and I will receive his sacrifice," she seems to point to a violent death of Pope John Paul II—soon.

"What is John Paul to do? He is precisely aware what the future holds with its chastisements, disasters, earthquakes, tidal waves, the betrayal of his churchmen, and the geopolitics of the world and its sensitive implications. While recuperating from his wounds inflicted by Mehmet Ali Agea, his attempted assassin, he came to realize the only hope for the world was the collegial consecration of Russia as requested at Fatima. Hoping for a mitigation of the coming tribulations—but only a mitigation—he attempted to consecrate the world to Mary, "with a special mention of Russia." John Paul's immediate step was to write all of his bishops, telling them he would do just that on May 13, 1982, in Fatima, and inviting them to join him —either by a physical presence or by parallel actions in their home dioceses.

The apostasy of the last fifty years produced an anemic response. Many of the bishops were no longer in union with Rome."[28]

Revealed In Other Apparitions?

Has the Blessed Mother revealed the Third Secret of Fatima in other messages? Many persons who have studied these messages clearly believe that Our Blessed Mother revealed it on October 13, 1973, to Sister Agnes Sasagawa at Akita, Japan. The apparitions at Akita have been approved by the local bishop.

The message was as follows: "As I told you, if men do not repent and better themselves, the Father will inflict a terrible punishment on all of humanity. It will be a punishment greater than the Deluge, such as one will never have seen before. Fire will fall from the sky and will wipe out a great part of humanity, the good as well as the bad, sparing neither priests nor faithful. The survivors will find themselves so desolate that they will envy the dead. The only weapons which will remain for you will be the rosary and the Sign left by my Son. Each day recite the prayers of the rosary. With the rosary, pray for the Pope, the bishops, and the priests."

"The work of the devil will infiltrate even into the Church in such a way that one will see cardinals opposing cardinals, bishops against other bishops. The priests who venerate me will be scorned and opposed by their confreres...churches and altars sacked; the Church will be full of those who accept compromises and the demon will press many priests and consecrated souls to leave the service of the Lord.

The demon will be especially implacable against souls consecrated to God. The thought of the loss of so many souls is the cause of my sadness. If sins increase in number and gravity, there will no longer be pardon for them.

"Pray very much the prayers of the rosary. I alone am able still to save you from calamities which approach. Those who place their confidence in me will be saved."[29]

Others point out that Our Lady seems to have revealed again the Third Secret in a locution to the Marian Movement of Priests on September 15, 1987, at Akita, Japan, the Feast of Our Lady of Sorrows: "A chastisement worse than the flood is about to come upon this poor and perverted humanity. Fire will descend from

Heaven and this will be the sign that the justice of God has as of now fixed the hour of His great manifestation. I am weeping because the Church is continuing along the road of division, of loss of the true faith, of apostasy and of errors which are being spread more and more without anyone offering opposition to them. Even now, that which I predicted at Fatima and that which I have revealed here in the third message confided to a little daughter of mine is in the process of being accomplished. And so, even for the Church the moment of its great trial has come, because the man of iniquity will establish himself within it and the abomination of desolation will enter into the holy temple of God."

Father Gobbi, in a locution on February 11, 1979, received this message (similar to the warnings of LaSalette): "This interior division sometimes even leads priests to set themselves against priests, bishops against bishops, and cardinals against cardinals, for never before as in these times has Satan so succeeded in finding his way into their midst, rending asunder the precious bond of their mutual love." On June 13, 1989, Father Gobbi received the following: "Thus errors are spread in every part of the Catholic Church itself. Because of the spread of these errors, many are moving away from the true faith, bringing to fulfillment the prophecy which was given to you by me at Fatima: The times will come when many will lose the true faith. **The loss of the faith is apostasy.**"

Cardinal Ratzinger

Cardinal Ratzinger has written in the *Ratzinger Report* that the Third Secret of Fatima has to do with what he called "de novissimis." The Cardinal had good reason to know, having previously read the still unrevealed "secret." The Latin expression "de novissimis" means "dealing with the end times," pertaining to the latter days or about the final events. These "end times" to which Cardinal Ratzinger and the Third Secret of Fatima refer, and about which Pope Paul VI and his predecessors spoke, are well known to Biblical scholars.[30]

Controversy Number 2: Was Russia Consecrated To The Immaculate Heart Of Mary?

Bishop Paul M. Hnilica, S.J., a personal friend of Pope John Paul II, who had been secretly ordained in a prison camp's hospital quarantine room and three months later ordained a bishop in a basement, built up the catacomb church in Czechoslovakia. His diocese titular is Moscow. He was a participant in 1963 in the Second Vatican Council. On March 25, 1984, while secretly in Russia, Bishop Hnilica made the Consecration of Russia to the Immaculate Heart of Mary at the altar at Saint Michael's Church in the Kremlin and then later the same day said a secret Mass at the altar of the Mother of God at the church called the "Assumption of Our Lady."He reported this to the Pope, who was convinced that this was a sign for him. He had great difficulty getting even some of the bishops and cardinals of Rome to perform that consecration in conjunction with him. Cardinal Ratzinger said it was not easy to accomplish this consecration. **Shortly after the 1984 act, Sister Lucia told the Papal Nuncio of Lisbon that the conditions God required for the collegial consecration of Russia were accomplished.**

On March 25, 1984, Pope John Paul II was joined by a moral totality of all Catholic bishops throughout the world in consecrating the world and therefore Russia to the Immaculate Heart of Mary. The consecration renewed the previous acts of consecration by Pius XII of the world in 1942 and Russia in 1952. For the 1984 Consecration, the Pope invited the Orthodox bishops of the world and some major Protestant leaders to join in the act. Many responded.

In July 1989, before the breakup of the communist empire, Lucia stated that the Collegial Consecration of Russia requested by Our Lady "has been accomplished" and "God will keep His word." A few months later the world began to witness the empire's collapse.

On May 13, 1990, at the Cova da Iria, Bishop Amaral of Leira, Portugal, announced that all indications are that the Collegial Consecration of Russia to the Immaculate Heart of Mary by the Pope, in union with the bishops of the world, had been accomplished as requested by Our Lady.

Bishop Hnilica stated that the message of Fatima signifies the activation of the powers of Heaven. All of Heaven takes part in achieving that victory; all saints, all angels, and the Blessed Mother.[31]

Results To Date Of The Reported Consecration
Of March 25, 1984

The Series of Events:
   • December 1, 1989: At the Vatican, Pope John Paul II met with

Soviet President Mikhail Gorbachev. The Pope said the meeting was prepared by Providence.

• December 1, 1990: Soviet President Mikhail Gorbachev met Pope John Paul II for the second time.

• May 1, 1991: Pope John Paul II in the encyclical *Centessimus Annus* (On the Hundredth Anniversary of *Rerum Novarum*) wrote of the peaceful fall of the Marxist empire.

• May 12-13, 1991: Pope John Paul II went to Fatima where he thanked Our Lady of Fatima for sparing his life in the 1981 assassination attempt. He thanked Our Lady of Fatima also for the fruits of the Collegial Consecration of "that memorable day, March 25, 1984."

• August 19, 1991: On the seventy-fourth anniversary of Our Lady's appearance at Fatima, the hardliners in Soviet Russia attempted a coup to return to the time before the liberation of peoples began in the Soviet republics.

• August 22, 1991: On the Feast of the Queenship of Mary, the coup attempt of the communist hardliners failed.

• September 12, 1991: Father Gobbi communicated the following message: "...In the Name of Mary, Marxist communism, which for decades had been exercising its rule and holding so many of my poor children in oppressive and bloody slavery, has been defeated in these countries. Not because of political movements or persons, **but through my personal intervention, has your liberation finally come about.** It will again be in the name of Mary that I will bring to completion my work with the defeat of Masonry...."

• December 8, 1991: The formation of the commonwealth of former Soviet republics began, each one to be independent, indicating the imminent collapse of the Soviet Union.

• December 25, 1991: The Soviet red flag with the hammer and sickle was lowered for the last time, and Soviet President Mikhail Gorbachev announced his resignation and the end of the Soviet Union. The former fifteen republics of the Union of Soviet Socialist Republics were free to become independent states or countries.

• March 3, 1992: Mikhail Gorbachev praised Pope John Paul II in an article published in numerous newspapers around the world. He said that Pope John Paul II played a major political role in the collapse of Communism in Eastern Europe. Pope John Paul II, conscious of the power of prayer and reparation of the universal Church, attributed the collapse not simply to his own actions but to those of the entire Church.

• March 14, 1992: *Pravda* (meaning "Truth" in Russian), the newspaper and propaganda organ founded by Lenin, was printed for the last time.[32]

Consecration Versus Conversion: The Key to World Peace

Has the Consecration of Russia been fulfilled? Many said yes as forms of freedom were obtained in the late 1980s with perestroika and glasnost. It was a beginning. Shortly after that, the larger institutional barriers came tumbling down. The proof is in the results of what was accomplished by Bishop Hnilica in 1984. The remaining issue is Russia's conversion, which has not been accomplished. These two issues of consecration and conversion seem to be creating confusion in the Catholic world. The Red Dragon of communism is still strong in China and North Korea and is weakening in Cuba and other satellite countries around the world. Many other countries in the world have leftist leanings. However, **the key to world peace is the conversion of Russia.**

Another View

The debate as to whether Russia has been consecrated according to Our Blessed Mother's request at Fatima continues. We will present some facts as we understand them. Father Gobbi to the Marian Movement of Priests stated the following on May 13, 1990, at an apparition in Fatima, Portugal: "Humanity has not accepted my motherly request to return to the Lord along the road of conversion of heart and of life, of prayer and of penance. Thus it has known the terrible years of the Second World War, which brought about tens of million of deaths and vast destructions of populaces and of nations.

"Russia has not been consecrated to me by the Pope together with all the bishops and thus she has not received the grace of conversion and has spread her errors throughout all parts of the world, provoking wars, violence, bloody revolutions and persecutions of the Church and of the Holy Father.

"**Satan has been the uncontested dominator of the events of this century of yours, bringing all humanity to the rejection of God and of His law of love, spreading far and wide division and** hatred, immorality and wickedness and legitimating everywhere divorce, abortion, obscenity, homosexuality and recourse to any and all means of obstructing life."

Several other messages from the Marian Movement of Priests provide insight into this controversy.

March 25, 1984

"Before I ask it of Pope John Paul II, the first of my beloved sons, who on the occasion of this feast, performed the consecration in a solemn manner, after writing to the bishops of the world and inviting them to do so in union with him. Unfortunately the invitation was not welcomed by all of the bishops; particular circumstances have not yet permitted the explicit consecration of Russia which I have requested many times. As I have already told you, this consecration will be made to me when the bloody events are well on the way to actuality."

May 13, 1987

"My request that Russia be consecrated to me, by the Pope together with all the bishops, has not been accepted and thus she has spread her errors in every part of the world."

Apostles Of The Last Era

On September 3, 1991, Our Blessed Mother said it was through her intervention that liberation came about: "In the name of Mary, Marxist communism, which for decades had been exercising its rule and holding so many of my poor children in oppressive and bloody slavery, has been defeated in these countries. Not because of political movements or persons, but through my personal intervention, has your liberation finally come about. **It will again be in the name of Mary that I will bring to completion my Work with the defeat of Masonry, of every diabolical force, of materialism, and of practical atheism**, so that all humanity will be able to attain its encounter with the Lord and be thus purified and completely renewed, with the triumph of my Immaculate Heart in the world."

"It will moreover be particularly important for the development of the great events which have been foretold to you by me if, during this year, there be at least carried out my request, made to my daughter, Sister Lucia of Fatima, that Russia be consecrated to me by the Pope together with all the bishops of the world."

Here are several other issues for consideration:

• The followers of Fatima contend that Sister Lucia has been told since 1917 that Russia would be the instrument of God's chastisement for the world. Are we presently in the midst of a false peace? Many say that there will be no lasting peace until Russia is consecrated to the Immaculate Heart in union with all the bishops in the world.

• In his book, *"New Lies For Old,"* Anatoliy Golitsyn, a former high ranking Russian KGB defector, stated that the Soviet Union has plotted a strategy for proposing change in its system since 1958. His book was published in the West in 1984. The Soviets realized they could no longer keep pace with the technological progress of the West. The thinking then was to lull the West to sleep by preaching peace and, using Western hard currency and technology, to continue to arm, that is, preach peace and arm for war. The name of the program was known as the "Shelepin Plan," and it was formally introduced in 1958.[33] The leaders of the USSR wanted to see how far they could go to allow apparent democracy in a nation and still fool the West. It was a long-term strategy that was to take them into the next century.

It was based upon two main principles: **Disinformation**—to eradicate truth and replace it with lies; and **Provocation**—to take steps against an enemy which will ultimately benefit the Soviet Union by making its enemy think the opposite. The first trial balloon for the Soviet Union was Czechoslovakia. The program ultimately failed, and the result was the Prague Spring in 1968 with the tanks rolling in to squash the uprising of Alexander Dubcek.

The Soviets learned a lot from this experiment and realized what went wrong. According to Golitsyn, the next step was to introduce perestroika and glasnost—modified versions of the Shelepin Plan based upon years of study and experimentation. Golitsyn also contended that all history of country occupation by the USSR was a prelude to glasnost. These experiments of occupying countries and the lessons learned were the testing grounds for the introduction of glasnost and other forms of social reform.

The former USSR today is in the last stages of the Shelepin Plan or the first stages of the restoration of Masonry. Due to the compartmentalization of Masonry operating on a need-to-know basis (as all intelligence agencies and secret sects), with each level not knowing the other's business, only time will tell. It is a fact that the old guard is still firmly entrenched in power in the former Soviet Union.

• Ezekiel Chapters 38 and 39 have been thought to refer to Russia invading Israel in the end times, according to Scripture scholars. If Russia is consecrated and converted, is this possible?

• Russia has not been converted and is an independent state. The Church today in Russia is weak to non-existent. The hunger for spirituality is clearly there, but the people have yet to be catechized into any faith. Moscow, a city of nearly ten million inhabitants, has about a dozen Catholic priests. Churches in Russia and other republics are attended principally by old women and small children. The total congregation numbers in the hundreds for cities with populations in excess of several million. Men still have a fear of worship because of the work camps of the very recent past. A good memory serves as a reminder of the cost of worship.

Russia will only be converted in the near future by direct intervention from Heaven. It will take a miracle along the lines of the warning and the miracle to turn the present situation around.

• At Fatima on July 13, 1917, Mary said to Lucia, "One day I will come to you and ask for the consecration of Russia to my Immaculate Heart." In Tuy, Spain, in 1929, Mary appeared to Lucia again and said, "what I told you in 1917 at Fatima, I am asking now." Lucia asked for the consecration of Russia under Pope Pius XI and nothing was done. In 1931, in Rianjo, Spain, Mary appeared to Lucia, and said, **"Make it known to my ministers: given that they follow the example of the King of France in delaying the execution of my command; like him, they will follow him into misfortune** [he was later killed]. **They will repent of it, and they will do it, but it will be late."**

Present Status

Noting all of the above, let us look at three issues. First, Mary said to Father Gobbi, "Russia has not been consecrated to me by the Pope with all the bishops..." Russia has not been consecrated by all the bishops as Our Blessed Mother had specifically asked in Fatima. Second, many of the bishops around the world were apostate, as was predicted at LaSalette; it would not make any difference to many clergy if a request came from Rome. Many were not in union with Rome by the mid-1980s. Also, the Curia often is not in union with the Pope's thinking. Third, through Sister Lucia, Mary said, "it would be done but late."

An Uncertain Future

Many people would argue that we have paid dearly because of the failure of some of our Church leaders, whatever the reason, to heed Our Blessed Mother's urgent messages from 1929 on. Error and confusion have spread throughout the Church, harming the faith of millions, with many souls being lost.

The message of LaSalette that Rome will lose the faith and become the seat of the Antichrist appears to be on the way to fulfillment. Our Blessed Mother also continued to give warnings in other apparitions throughout the world revealing her messages and plan. Again her warnings fell on deaf ears. The Soviet Union has collapsed into separate republics; Russia is a sovereign republic that has not been converted. Communism and the Red Dragon are still in control in many places in the world. However, Our Lady said at Fatima, "In the end, my Immaculate Heart will triumph." The final chapter on Fatima has not been written.

When the atomic bomb destroyed Hiroshima in 1945, eight men living near the blinding center of the nuclear flash miraculously survived the searing hurricane of blast and gamma rays, while everyone within a mile radius perished and others residing further afield continued to die from the lethal effects of radiation. For over thirty years, some two hundred scientists have examined these eight men, trying in vain to determine what could have preserved them from incineration. One of the survivors, Father H. Shiffner, S.J., gave the dramatic answer on television in America, "In that house, we were living the message of Fatima."[34]

10

Garabandal, Spain: Its Time Has Arrived

There are important links between LaSalette, France; Fatima, Portugal; Garabandal, Spain; Akita, Japan; and Medjugorje, Yugoslavia. They affirm and amplify one another, with similar themes: the importance and power of the rosary and of the priesthood; the emphasis on the Eucharist; the presence of angels (in several of the apparitions an angel precedes the appearance of Our Blessed Mother, and gives communion to the children); the emphasis placed on the sacraments; the secrets given which will be revealed at later dates; the urgent calls for prayer and penance; the emergence of a main visionary among the children; and visions of coming calamities.

At Garabandal and Medjugorje, Our Lady spoke about: 1) a Warning, a Miracle, and a Chastisement; 2) a visible sign to be left at the apparition site so that people would believe; and 3) instructions on fasting and the selection of a priest chosen to relay messages to the public.

According to the Medjugorje visionary Mirjana, the chastisement can be mitigated—but not eliminated—by prayer and penance. An evil which threatened the world already has been eliminated through prayer and fasting, Mirjana said. For that reason, the Blessed Virgin continues to ask for prayer and fasting. She reminds us, "You have forgotten that with prayer and fasting, you can ward off wars, and suspend natural laws."

The similarities among the apparitions of Fatima, Garabandal, and Medjugorje are striking. They build on one another. In fact, one might consider them as one extended apparition at different times, in different places, with slightly different messages that are relevant to the needs of the Church in the generation in which the vision occurs.

Events That Will Affect The Entire World

The apparitions at San Sebastian de Garabandal, Spain, took place from 1961 to 1965. Although there has been considerable confusion about these alleged apparitions, the Church has never condemned them. A new commission was formed by the bishop in 1986, and Garabandal currently is under ecclesiastical investigation by Vatican authorities.

The message of Garabandal contains prophecies of supernatural events that affect the entire world. Since we might be very near to these predicted events, it would be prudent for the faithful to be aware of Our Lady's messages, especially if the Church declares the apparitions "worthy of belief."

Things That Are To Come

The prophecies of Garabandal tell us that four of the greatest supernatural events in the history of mankind are about to take place:

1. **A world-wide warning:** It will come from God, and it will be experienced by everyone in the world.

2. **A great miracle**: God will perform the greatest miracle of all times.

3. **A permanent sign**: After the great miracle, a sign, something that has never been seen before upon the earth, will remain forever in "the pines" of Garabandal.

4. **The chastisement**: This is a punishment that is conditional upon the response of mankind to these messages.

When Will These Events Occur?

Mari-Loli, one of the visionaries of Garabandal, knows the year of the warning. She said that the warning will occur within one year before the miracle. Conchita, the oldest Garabandal visionary, knows when the miracle will occur.

The Village

The story of Garabandal began on the evening of June 18, 1961, when the Archangel Michael appeared to four young girls. He made eight silent appearances during the following twelve days. On July 1, the angel finally spoke to announce that on the following day the Blessed Virgin Mary would appear to them as Our Lady of Mount Carmel. San Sebastian de Garabandal is a tiny village of about 300 people located in the beautiful Cantabrian mountains of northwestern Spain, in the Diocese of Santander. About one-quarter mile to the north on a high ridge, nine pine trees tower over the village, marking the spot where Our Lady frequently appeared. Over the next four years, she appeared more than 2,000 times throughout the village.

The Visionaries

The visionaries were: Conchita Gonzalez (age twelve), Jacinta Gonzalez (age twelve), Mari Cruz Gonzalez (age eleven), none of whom are closely related, and Mari-Loli Mazon (age twelve). They described Our Lady as a beautiful young woman about eighteen years of age. She wore a white dress with a blue mantle and a brown scapular on her right arm. On her head she wore a crown of twelve stars. Her hair was deep brown and parted in the center. Her face was oval with a fine nose. The girls said, "No other woman looks like her or sounds like her."

The apparitions were preceded by three interior calls, which the girls described as joys, each one becoming stronger. After the third call, the girls would come running from different parts of the village and would arrive at the same time in the place designated by Our Lady, and they would fall to their knees in ecstasy.

During the apparition they were subjected by "investigators" to burns, spotlights in their eyes, and pinpricks without showing any physical response to pain. Reports indicate that four adult men had difficulty lifting one twelve-year-old girl, yet the girls could lift each other easily to kiss Our Lady goodbye. The apparitions were accompanied by other phenomena that seemed to defy natural law, such as ecstatic falls and running forward and backward over very rocky terrain. Many religious objects were kissed by Our Lady. The visionaries, while in ecstasy, would return the objects to their rightful owners even though their owners were unknown to them. The seers claimed that Our Lady guided them to the right person.

Our Lady promised: "Through the kiss I have bestowed on these objects, my Son will perform miracles, wonders, and prodigies before and after the Great Miracle." The fulfillment of this promise has been realized by the many conversions and cures of terminally ill and addicted persons around the world.

The Messages Of Garabandal

On July 4, 1961, Our Lady revealed her first message for the world. She told the girls to announce the message publicly on October 18, 1961. On this day, the children made known the message: "Many sacrifices must be made, much penance must be done. We must pay many visits to the Blessed Sacrament....but first of all we must be very good.... If we do not do this, punishment awaits us....already the cup is filling, and if we do not change we shall be punished."

On January 1, 1965, the Blessed Virgin told Conchita Gonzalez that the Archangel Michael would appear to her on the following June 18th to deliver a final message in Mary's name for the entire world, because her first message was not heeded. At the "Cuadro," Saint Michael appeared to Conchita while she was in ecstasy, which lasted approximately sixteen minutes. He delivered the following promised final message of Our Lady for the entire world: "Since my message of October 18 has not been complied with and has not been made known to the world, I will tell you that this is the last one. **Before, the chalice was filling, now it is overflowing. Many cardinals, many bishops and many priests are on the path of perdition and they take many souls with them. To the Eucharist, there is given less and less importance. We should avoid the wrath of God on us by our good efforts.**"

"If you ask pardon with your sincere soul, He will pardon you. It is I your Mother, who through the intercession of Saint Michael, wish to say that you amend, that you are already in the last warnings and that I love you much and do not want your condemnation. Ask us sincerely and we will give to you. You should sacrifice more. Think of the Passion of Jesus." Our Lady appeared wearing the brown scapular, an indication that we should also wear the brown scapular, and taught the children how to pray the rosary. Her greatest emphasis was placed on the Eucharist and prayers for priests. The last apparition for Conchita was on November 13, 1965, at "the pines."

Four Great Events Yet To Come

The visionaries tell us of four great and supernatural events that were prophesied at Garabandal. These predicted events, when they occur, will confirm the reality of Garabandal.

The Warning

The first event will be a world-wide warning from God. Conchita, wrote in a letter on January 1, 1965: "Our Lady said that a warning would be given to the entire world before the miracle in order that the world might amend itself. It will come directly from God and be visible throughout the entire world."

Conchita wrote on June 2, 1965: "The warning, like the chastisement, is a fearful thing for the good as well as the wicked. It will draw the good closer to God and warn the wicked that the end of times is coming. These are the last warnings." Conchita explained that the warning is a purification to prepare us for the miracle. She believes that after they occur, we will be near the end of times. Each person on earth will have an interior experience of how he or she stands in the light of God's Justice. Believers and non-believers alike will experience the warning. Mari-Loli, who knows the year of the warning, said, "We will see it and feel it within ourselves and it will be most clear that it comes from God."

Jacinta has said: "The warning is something that is first seen in the air, everywhere in the world and immediately is transmitted into the interior of our souls. It will last for a very little time, but it will seem a very long time because of its effect within us. It will be for the good of our souls, in order to see in ourselves our conscience...the good that we have failed to do, and the bad that we have done. Then we will feel a great love towards our heavenly Parents and ask forgiveness for all our offenses. The warning is for everybody because God wants our salvation. The warning is for us to draw closer to Him and to increase our faith. Therefore, one should prepare for that day, but not await it with fear. God does not send things for the sake of fear but rather with justice and love. He does it for the good of all His children so they might enjoy eternal happiness and not be lost."

The Great Miracle

Our Lady has promised that a great miracle will take place above the grove of the pine trees. It will occur on a Thursday evening, at 8:30

p.m., between the 8th and 16th of March, April, or May. The miracle will coincide with an important event in the Church and on the feast day of a young martyr of the Eucharist. Everyone in the village and on the surrounding mountains will see it. The sick who are present will be cured. Sinners and non-believers will be converted. It will be possible to photograph and televise this event. Russia will be converted after the miracle. Conchita, who knows the date of this miracle, must announce it eight days in advance. Conchita tells us in her diary that the reigning Pope will see the miracle from wherever he is.

According to Mari-Loli, the miracle will take place within one year after the warning. Mari-Loli does not know the date of the warning, only the year. She also said that the Blessed Mother told her: **"A time would come, when it would look like the Church was finished, when priests would have difficulty saying Mass and talking about holy things."** There would come a time when the Church would give the impression of being on the point of perishing. It would pass through a terrible test. When she asked Our Lady how this would happen, Our Lady called it "communism."

The Permanent Sign

A permanent sign will remain forever as a result of the great miracle. It will be of supernatural origin and something that has never been seen before on earth. Conchita has written: "A sign of the miracle, which will be possible to film or televise, will remain forever at the pines." No one, however, will be able to touch it.

The Chastisement

During July of 1962, Conchita, Mari-Loli, and Jacinta were shown a vision of the impending chastisement. Our Lady told the visionaries that, if we do not heed her warnings and mankind does not change after the warning and miracle, God will send the chastisement. In a note Conchita stated: "The punishment is conditioned upon whether or not mankind heeds the messages of the Blessed Virgin Mary." Conchita said in her diary: "If the world changes, the chastisement can be averted." In describing the vision of the chastisement, Mari-Loli said: "It would be worse than having fire on top of us—fire underneath us and fire all around us. She saw people throwing themselves into the sea, but instead of putting the fire out it seemed to make them burn more."

Padre Pio

Padre Pio was one of the only priests in the history of the Church to receive the stigmata from Our Lord. Blessed with many spiritual gifts from an early age, Padre Pio believed in the validity of Garabandal. An incident which confirms Padre Pio's belief in Garabandal occurred early in 1966. Conchita, who was only sixteen years old, was visiting Rome with her mother and Father Luna. She had been invited by Cardinal Ottaviani, Prefect of the Sacred Congregation for the Doctrine of Faith. During this visit, Conchita met privately with Padre Pio. On this occasion he took Conchita's hand and her crucifix that Our Lady had kissed in Garabandal and held them both in his own two hands. The crucifix had been passed through the hands of the child Jesus during the apparition of November 13, 1965.

It was also during this visit to Rome that Conchita had a private audience with Pope Paul VI. No report of this Papal audience has ever been made public, except that the Pope said, "Conchita, I bless you and with me the whole Church blesses you." On October 16, 1968, Conchita received a telegram requesting that she travel to Lourdes in order to accept a letter from Padre Pio. At Lourdes, she met Father Bernardino Cennamo, who informed her that he had been instructed by Padre Pio to give her a letter and the first veil that covered his face after death.

Conchita asked, "How is it that the Virgin told me Padre Pio would see the miracle before he died?" Father Cennamo answered, "He did see the miracle before he died. Pio told me so himself." The letter from Padre Pio was transcribed by Father Pelligrino, who attended Padre Pio in his final years. The letter reads as follows: "For Conchita, Padre Pio has said, 'I pray to the most Holy Virgin to comfort you and guide you always towards sanctity, and I bless you with all of my heart.'"

Jesuit Priest Sees The Great Miracle

Father Luis Marin Andreu, a thirty-eight-year-old Jesuit priest, was visiting Garabandal for the second time on August 8, 1961. Father Luis, while observing the visionaries during ecstasy, suddenly cried out, "Miracle!" four times. While driving home later that night with his friends, Father Luis said, "What a wonderful present the Virgin has given me! How lucky we are to have a mother like that in

Heaven! Today is the happiest day of my life!" Shortly thereafter, he lowered his head and died. In a later apparition, Our Lady told the visionaries that Father Luis had seen her and had also seen the great miracle. He died of joy. Our Lady also revealed to Conchita on September 14, 1965, that Father Luis Andreu's body someday will be exhumed and found to be incorrupt on the day after the great miracle.

Other Mysterious Phenomena

During the apparitions, the girls were able to detect and recognize priests who came to the village dressed in civilian clothes, trying to conceal their identities. Many times during the ecstatic walks, the visionaries would offer these priests their crucifix to be kissed. During one of Conchita's ecstasies in 1962, two priests were kneeling down in reverence. They were gently encouraged by Conchita to stand up, in order to emphasize the deep respect that Our Lady has for priests. She taught the children to greet the priest before greeting an angel, because a priest is more important, since only a priest can consecrate bread and wine into the Body and Blood of Christ during the Holy Sacrifice of the Mass.

Another remarkable event of Garabandal emphasized the importance of the Eucharist. An angel appeared bearing a golden chalice. The angel asked the children to think of the One whom they were going to receive. He taught them to recite the Confiteor, after which he gave them Holy Communion. He also taught them to say the Anima Christi in thanksgiving. These direct interventions occurred regularly whenever the priest from the neighboring village of Cosio was unable to come to Garabandal.

Many of these "Angelic Communions" were recorded on film, showing the movement of the girls' lips, tongue, and throat. However, since these hosts were only visible to the girls, many skeptics doubted that they were actually receiving Holy Communion.

When questioned about where the Hosts came from, since only a priest could consecrate, the angel told them that the Hosts were taken from the tabernacles of the church. Therefore, a priest and not an angel had consecrated the Hosts. On June 22, 1962, the angel told Conchita that God would perform a "special miracle." The people would be allowed to see the Sacred Host appear on Conchita's tongue at the moment she received Communion, in order that they might believe. Conchita's diary entry for June 30, 1962, stated: "While I was in the pines I heard a voice which said that the miracle would take place on the eighteenth of July." The angel later instructed her to reveal this message fifteen days in advance.

Visible Host

The miracle of the visible Host occurred at 1:40 a.m. on July 19, 1962. Hundreds of witnesses were present. The event was recorded on movie film by Don Alejandro, a businessman from Barcelona. This film was later submitted to the bishop of Santander. Witnesses said that Conchita knelt and put out her tongue to receive the Host. At first, nothing was visible. In a few moments, a white Host, thicker than usual, appeared on her tongue. It remained there for a few moments before being consumed. Conchita refers to this event as the "little miracle." It was chosen to call our attention to the reality of the Real Presence of Our Lord in the Holy Eucharist.

Significant Witnesses

Two significant witnesses who were present during some of the apparitions and whose lives were dramatically changed by the events of Garabandal are Joey Lomangino and Father Ramon Andreu, S.J.

Joey Lomangino

Joey Lomangino was born on October 5, 1930, in Brooklyn, New York. In June 1947, when Joey was sixteen years old, tragedy struck the Lomangino family. Joey was inflating a tire on one of his father's ice and coal trucks when suddenly the tire exploded in his face. The tire struck him between the eyes, severing his olfactory and optic nerves and causing the total loss of his sight and smell.

The following years were difficult. However, with much patience and perseverance, Joey completed his education and formed a sanitation business with his three brothers.

While on vacation in Italy in 1961, Joey met Padre Pio. This meeting changed his life dramatically. Joey recalls that he was not a very religious man at the time. However, this meeting began the process of conversion in his life.

Joey returned to Italy in 1963 to meet Padre Pio again. It was during this visit that Padre Pio encouraged him to go to confession. Joey states that as he blessed himself to begin his confession, Padre Pio interrupted him and began to list in perfect English all of the sins that

Joey had ever committed during his entire life! This overwhelming experience was just the beginning of what was yet to follow. A few days later, Joey was kneeling and waiting for Padre Pio to begin the Mass. As Padre Pio walked by, Joey experienced what he thought to be an explosion in his head. At that moment, Joey instantly regained his sense of smell. He was immediately aware of the scent of roses. Doctors described the miracle as, "a light bulb suspended in the center of the room, without wires attached, and was still capable of lighting." During this visit, Joey asked Padre Pio if Our Lady was appearing at Garabandal. His reply was "Yes." Joey also inquired if he should go there. The answer was "Yes, why not?" So began a series of events that would earn Joey the title of "Blind Apostle of Garabandal." He visited Garabandal many times and developed a close relationship with the visionaries.

On March 19, 1964, Conchita received an interior message from Our Lady at the pines. She was told that Joey Lomangino would see on the day of the great miracle. Conchita also was told that Joey would establish a "House of Charity" in New York that will bring great glory to God. Since 1963, Joey has traveled throughout the world giving his witness.

Father Ramon Andreu, S.J.

Father Ramon is the brother of the deceased Father Luis Andreu, the priest who saw the great miracle and later died of joy. Father Ramon received permission from his superiors to visit Garabandal. He also received authorization from the Apostolic Administrator of the diocese of Santander, Bishop Doroteo Fernandez. He was privileged to have witnessed more than 400 ecstasies. During his visits to the village, he kept a detailed record in his notebooks of everything he saw and heard. These notebooks represent some of the more valuable documentation, due to Father Ramon's keen analytical mind. The most startling event for Father Ramon was the revelation from the visionaries that they had conversed with his dead brother, Father Luis Andreu. Conchita's diary entries of August 15 and 16, stated the following:

"A few days after Father Luis' death, the Blessed Virgin told us that we were going to talk to him.... At eight or nine o'clock in the evening, the Blessed Virgin appeared to us smiling, very, very much, as usual. She said to the four of us: "Father Luis will come now and speak with you." A moment later, he came and called us one by one. We didn't see him at all but only heard his voice. It was exactly like the one he had on earth. When he had spoken for a while, giving us advice, he told us certain things for his brother, Father Ramon Maria Andreu. He taught us some words in French, German and in English and he also taught us to pray in Greek."

Father Ramon was told precise details of his brother's funeral and details of his personal life that were unknown to anyone but himself. On another occasion, Father Luis gave a message for his mother: "Be happy and content for I am in Heaven and I see you everyday." A message of great joy for his mother, who entered the convent, and a remarkable revelation about our loved ones who have gone to Heaven. Father Ramon is now living in California and is more than just an ordinary witness. He and his brother, Father Luis, were especially chosen by Our Lady to bear witness to the incredible events of Garabandal.

The Church's Position

Shortly after the apparitions began in 1961, Bishop Doroteo Fernandez, Apostolic Administrator of the diocese of Santander, set up a fact-finding board of inquiry consisting of three priests and two doctors to study the apparitions. Psychiatrist Luis Morales Noriega and Father Francisco Odriozola led the special study. This study was not considered a Canonical Commission. Included in the group was Father Juan del Val Gallo, who was later to become the present bishop of Santander. During the four years of apparitions, the members of this group went to the village only on three occasions. They never met as a body nor did they ever issue a common report. Dr. Morales, the leading expert on mental health in Santander, declared that the events had a natural explanation based on psychological theory.

He dismissed the whole affair as "child's play." In 1961, Our Lady told the visionaries: "A time will come when all four of you will contradict yourselves one with the other, when your families will also contradict themselves about the apparitions; you will even deny that you have seen me or Saint Michael." On this occasion witnesses heard the four visionaries while in ecstasy say: "How is it that one day we will say that we did not see you, since we are seeing you now?" Our Lady told them: "Because you are going to pass through the same confusion as the Church." These prophetic words did come to pass almost from the very beginning, and the children later denied receiving apparitions. Thus, the bishop and his successors had cause for serious reservations about the authenticity of the apparitions. Bishop Fernandez and his immediate successor Bishop Eugenio Beitia issued "Notas." These "Notas" advised caution and restricted priests from visiting the village without permission. They stated further that there was no evidence that any supernatural events had taken place.

However, it is significant to note that Bishop Beitia, in his "Notas" of July 8, 1965, stated: "...We would like to say, however, that we have found no grounds for an ecclesiastical condemnation either in the doctrine or in the spiritual recommendations that have been divulged in the events and addressed to the Christian faithful; furthermore, these recommendations contain exhortations to prayer, sacrifice, devotion to the Holy Eucharist and devotion to the Blessed Virgin under traditional, praiseworthy forms; there are also exhortations to a holy fear of the Lord, offended by our sins...." Bishop Puchol, who succeeded Bishop Beitia, was not as favorable. He denounced the events throughout the province with a media campaign. Due to Bishop Puchol's untimely death in an automobile accident on May 8, 1967, Enrique Cabo, the Vicar Capitular, headed the diocese until a new bishop could be appointed. The new successor, Bishop Cirarda, similarly discredited the apparitions by sending a letter to all the bishops, through the Church's Secretary of State.

From 1966 to 1983, the controversy over whether the events were supernatural continued. However, at no time were the apparitions officially condemned. In December 1971, Bishop del Val Gallo was appointed to head the diocese of Santander. He showed an openness towards the apparitions. While realizing the shortcomings of the original commission, he tried to establish a new one under the combined authority of Rome and Santander. These efforts were halted at the time, due to strong opposition.

A letter dated August 20, 1978, was hand-delivered to Bishop del Val Gallo. It was drafted by the priests who met at Lourdes to study all the events that occurred at Garabandal. The letter stated in part: "We want Your Excellency to know that some 200 Catholics, gathered from five continents, conducted a Marian Congress at Lourdes to enrich their love for Mary and her divine Son and to study in an atmosphere of serenity, under the guidance of the Holy Spirit, the events which took place at Garabandal. Among those present were some prominent theologians, two of them former consultants at Vatican Council II. There were also present some expert Mariologists, psychiatrists and other men of science. After fervent prayer, and encouraged by the presence of the 200 delegates from twenty-six countries, who reflected the sentiments of millions of Catholics, we feel confidently moved to convey to Your Excellency the following request:

"Many years have elapsed since the beginning of the events that occurred at San Sebastian and the Lord has already called home some of the leading witnesses of those happenings. Nevertheless, and thanks to Him, there are many such witnesses still alive. Consequently, and aware of the transcendental importance of the said events, we feel bound to ask Your Excellency, that without delay, you invite these same witnesses to submit their valuable testimonies for your archives. Although present circumstances may not advise the initiating of a new investigation at the official level, we feel that the disappearance of such precious testimonies, coming from serious and responsible witnesses, would constitute an irreparable loss. At the same time, we wish to assure Your Excellency that the request we are making does not imply in any way an anticipation of the final judgement by the Church in this matter."

Among the signatures in this letter was that of Father Joseph Pelletier, who has written extensively about Garabandal. Other signatures included Reverend A.J. Adikalam, Vicar General of Madras, India; Reverend Joseph Lee, S.D.B., Hong Kong; Father Francis Benac, S.J., India; and Father Francois Turner, O.P., France.

Dr. Luis Morales

A dramatic turning point in the events of Garabandal occurred on May 30, 1983, the eve of the Feast of the Visitation. Dr. Morales, the leading psychiatrist in Santander, delivered an historic address in which he retracted his original negative judgment and defended the reality of the apparitions. This startling reversal of judgment ended the twenty-two years of silence imposed by the Church authorities of Santander. In his opening remarks, Dr. Morales said: "I am here today to speak to you on the apparitions of Our Lady at Garabandal. It is because she herself has worked this change of attitude in me. Moreover, I am speaking with full permission of the ecclesiastical

hierarchy." He concluded by saying: "I will end my conference
pleading with the Virgin of Garabandal, that for the rest of my days,
she may keep me under her mantle and have mercy on me.

New Commission Appointed

In 1986, Bishop del Val Gallo appointed a new commission. He
announced to the Vatican during his visit to Rome that he was quietly
reopening the investigation on the events of Garabandal. One of the
prophecies of Garabandal stated that a future bishop of Santander
would at first not believe in the apparitions. However, after receiving
a sign, he would lift all restrictions that forbade priests to visit
Garabandal. In January of 1987, Father Gomez, the pastor of
Garabandal, was instructed by the bishop to allow visiting priests to
celebrate Mass in the village church. This change in policy lifted the
restrictions of 1962. The bishop in a statement carried by the Catholic
News Service explained that his decision had no connection with his
belief in the apparitions, but was merely out of respect for the priests
who arrive with pilgrims. Since this imposition has been lifted,
Conchita tells us that the time of the Miracle will be very close. "The
rest," she says "will not be long in coming." In 1991, all studies were
completed and submitted to Rome by the new bishop.

It should also be noted that all of the visionaries, except for Mari
Cruz Gonzalez, have formally retracted their denials in writing. As of
this writing, the Commission has completed the theological portion
of the investigation. The historical and sociological studies are in the
final stages of completion. When the studies are completed, the
bishop will submit all of the documentation to Rome for the Vatican
to make the ultimate decision, because the bishop retired on June 13,
1991, on the occasion of his seventy-fifth birthday. While we await
the decision of the Commission and the final judgement of the
Catholic Church, we should be guided by what Conchita wrote. On
September 14, 1965, she said, **"The Virgin Mary likes it very much
that we spread the message and she promised to reward everyone, but obedience to the Church must always come first because
this will give more honor and glory to God."**

Three More Popes

Conchita has said: " After Pope John XXIII died, Our Lady told
me, **'after Pope John, there will be three more Popes, one will**

reign only a short time, and then it will be the end of times.' When Pope Paul VI became Pope, Our Lady mentioned this to me again. She said, 'Now there will be two more Popes and then it will be the end of times, but not the end of the world.'" Because the meaning of these words is not yet understood, it would be well to point out that when the visionaries speak of the end of times they are not referring to the end of the world, but rather to the end of an era or space of time. The following references to "times" is not intended to interpret the meaning of this prophecy but rather to illustrate other meanings of the expression "times." For example, in the Old Testament, God the Father spoke to us through the Prophets (sometimes referred to as the era or times of the Jews). In the New Testament, God the Son spoke to us directly during His public life on earth (known as the time of the gentiles or the era of time that began with Saint Paul). Today, God appears to be speaking to us through Mary, the Mother of God. Pope John Paul II has called our century "Marian times."

Until the Magisterium of the Church renders a final judgment on Garabandal, which we the faithful will accept unconditionally, it would be prudent to ponder the following questions:

• Are we now living at the end of Marian times and at what has been sometimes called the time of God's Great Mercy?

• Will we enter into the time of God's Justice when the reign of Pope John Paul II ends?

The fourth and final prophecy of Garabandal tells us that the chastisement is conditioned on whether we heed the messages of the Blessed Virgin Mary.

What The Theologians Say

Father Michael O'Carroll of Dublin, Ireland, is a member of the Pontifical Marian Academy and of the French Society for Marian Studies. He has written a great deal on Marian theology and piety. He is probably best known for his work *Theotokos*, a theological encyclopedia of the Blessed Virgin Mary. When asked to comment about recent developments, Father O'Carroll said the following: **"Interest in Garabandal is very welcome at the present time for three reasons: first, the very many reported apparitions of Our Lady make it highly desirable that there be in each case an honest record available of what has happened, and of reactions from**

Church authority; secondly, there have been confusing and conflicting reports in circulation on the subject of Garabandal; and thirdly, the whole story has now one very distinctive feature; that it is the decision of the Bishop to reopen the investigation." This unusual decision means that attention will be focused anew on the phenomena . The inquiry and ultimate evaluation will consist of the sociological, theological, psychological, and spiritual aspects of the apparitions. The bishop is very considerate towards the seers, and he is in communication with Father Francois Turner, O.P., who has followed the story carefully and wisely for many years. The results should be valuable.

Father Edward O'Connor, author of many books and articles on Mary and a member of the Theology Department at the University of Notre Dame for fifty-one years, has written on the theology of Mary, and received the Dayton Library Award for his book, "The Dogma of the Immaculate Conception." Father O'Connor has followed closely all the modern day apparitions and shared the following thoughts on Garabandal. "I visited Garabandal in 1967, and met Jacinta and Mari-Loli, as well as the two parish priests who dealt with the visionaries. In going there, I did not know what to think of the apparitions, and tended to be skeptical. I came away convinced of their truth. Since then, I have studied the subject seriously, and all that I read confirms my conviction. There is no way four eleven- and twelve-year-old girls could fake the things they did."

Dr. Mark Miravalle, Director of the Marian Office of Contemporary Apparitions and Associate Professor of Theology at the Franciscan University of Steubenville, remarked: "The message of Garabandal fits well into the overall Marian messages to the modern world. Its emphasis on penance, Eucharistic adoration and devotion, as well as renewal of the priesthood, appears most timely for the contemporary Church and the world today. Garabandal manifests many signs of authenticity.[1]

The Warnings of Garabandal

Father Joseph Pelletier, the noted Marian scholar, asked Conchita several questions and offered further insight about the events of Garabandal. Conchita's answer on June 19, 1965, is as follows: "Here in writing is the warning that the Blessed Virgin gave me when I was alone at the pines on January 1st of this year, 1965. The warning that the Blessed Virgin will give us is like a chastisement. Its purpose is to draw the good nearer to God and to warn the others. I cannot reveal what the warning will consist of. The Blessed Virgin did not tell me to announce it. Nothing further. God would like that through this warning we amend our lives and that we commit less sins against Him." To the question posed by Marian and Garabandal scholar Father Laffineur whether the warning would cause death, she replied in writing: "If we die from it, it would not be from the warning itself, but from the emotional shock that we would experience in seeing and feeling the warning."[2]

September 13, 1965: Conchita's statement to some Americans follow. Two statements were made by Conchita in response to questions put to her:

Q. Will the warning be a visible thing or an interior thing or both?

A. The warning is a thing that comes directly from God. It will be visible all over the world, in whatever place anyone might be.

Q. Will the warning reveal his personal sins to every person in the world and to persons of all faiths, including atheists?

A. Yes, the warning will be like the revelation of our sins, and it will be seen and felt equally by believers and non-believers and people of any religion whatsoever.

October 22, 1965: Conchita's statement to a Spanish woman follows. In reply to a question whether the warning might be a comet that was approaching the earth, Conchita said: "I don't know what a comet is. If it is something that depends on man's will, I answer—no. If it is something that God will do, it is quite possible." When the woman expressed fear and asked Conchita to pray for her, the latter replied: "Oh, yes, the warning will be very fearful, a thousand times worse than earthquakes." To an enquiry concerning the nature of the warning, Conchita answered: "It will be like fire. It will not burn our flesh, but we will feel it bodily and interiorly." She added, "We shall comment on this later. All nations and all persons will experience it in the same way. No one will escape it. Even the non-believers themselves will experience the fear of God. Even if you hide in your room and close the blinds, you will not escape it. You will feel and see it just the same." And again, "Yes, it is true. The Blessed Virgin gave me the name of the phenomenon. It begins with an 'A.' But she did not tell me to reveal it to anyone."

As the lady again expressed her fear, Conchita added: "Oh, but after the warning, you will love the good Lord very much." To the question: "What about the miracle?" she said, "The miracle will not delay in coming." Conchita added an interesting observation: "Although it is taking time to come, it will not be late. God's time is always the appropriate time."

An important note should be added: when Conchita describes the warning as being "like fire," she means that in some way or ways it resembles fire but that it is not fire.

According to Conchita, the warning and fire have two things in common: they can be "seen" and "felt," and they are "very terrifying." The warning will be seen and felt by all men and will cause great fear in men's hearts, a fear so great that it could conceivably cause some to die. To want a precise and detailed description of the phenomenon in human terms is to seek the impossible. Also, it is not necessary. This should be enough to prompt us to take measures now so as to be ready for the warning when it comes.

The Warning In Perspective

Curiosity is a perfectly normal human trait. But it can easily become excessive. To be overly concerned about detailed descriptions of the warning could lead to a morbid curiosity that would be misleading and harmful. Because the warning is something supernatural, produced directly by God, human words will always be inadequate to describe it. The images and comparisons used can at best give but a partial picture of the reality. To take these images too literally will mislead us. There is also a very great probability that it will harm us by making us excessively fearful and fretful. This can cause us to lose the peace of mind and heart which are essential to good Christian living.

Fear of God is a good thing, as Holy Scripture tells us, but the fear of God that is good is not the kind of fear that obsesses us, causes us to worry constantly, and ultimately robs us of our peace of mind and heart and leads us away from God. The fear of God that is good is the fear that draws virtuous souls to God and prompts sinners to amend their lives. This is precisely the purpose that Conchita ascribed to the warning. It will cause a holy fear of God. Our concern at this moment should be to get closer to God, casting all sin from our lives and striving to love and serve Him better. If we do this, we will be ready for the warning when it comes. To be sure, it will strike fear in our hearts. However, this fear will not kill us. It will bring us closer to God because we fear offending Him as a son fears offending his father who is always good to him.

As predicted, there has been confusion and controversy in regard to the spread of the message of Garabandal. Jesus told Conchita on February 13, 1966: "Don't worry yourself with whether people believe or do not believe.... I shall do everything. But I will also give you suffering. I will be with whoever suffers for me.... You will have much to suffer for few people will believe you." Both the suffering of Conchita and the lack of belief in the apparitions were foretold by Our Lord. We are now in a period of waiting and expectancy in regard to Garabandal. During this time let us all, in faith, while living and spreading the message, pray and make sacrifices and place all in the hands of Our Lord. **Keep up your courage and remember there is nothing that so enlarges the capacity of the heart for God as does suffering. The suffering that you endure purifies your soul and is willed by God as gestures of His love for you. He is the King of Love and Peace. One who finds God, finds peace.**

Garabandal And The Synagogue

In August 1988, Father Francois Turner, the French Dominican, delivered a speech in a barn at the pines of Garabandal. For the last thirty years, Father Turner has been considered by almost everyone involved with the reported apparition to be one of Garabandal's leading authorities. For numerous reasons, Garabandal has not received the recognition that many of the other apparitions have in recent years. Shortly, it will receive world-wide focus. The following is a synopsis of a speech that Father Turner delivered.[3]

The Pillar Of Smoke At Garabandal

It is an established fact that Conchita was told by the Blessed Virgin that a sign would remain at the pines and it would remain there forever. It would be possible to photograph and televise it but not touch it, and it would appear as a thing not of this world, but it would originate from God. It would be miraculous, a permanent miracle. It is comparable to a pillar of smoke, but also to rays of sunlight, insofar as it can be seen but not touched. It will be made up of an unknown substance.

The Pillar Of Smoke In The Bible

All the Hebrews who followed Moses out of Egypt saw the "pillar of cloud by day and of fire by night" (Exodus 13:21), saving them from the Egyptians (Exodus 14:24), accompanying the Torah at Mount Sinai (Exodus 19:16-18,34:5), remaining present among His people, serving as their guide "wherever they halted on their journey," (Exodus 40:36), "marking out their encampments" (Deuteronomy1:33). It was the Lord who "appeared to them in this pillar of cloud that rose above them at the tabernacle door" (Deuteronomy 31:15).

The mysterious cloud invaded the Temple of Solomon (I Kings 8:10). Nehemiah celebrated the Lord "leading Thy people on their journey, hidden by day in a pillar of cloud, by night in a pillar of fire, to light the path they must tread" (Nehemiah 9:12,19). The Psalms mention it five times: as the guide of God's people (Psalms 77:17-21 and 78:14), overcoming the idolaters (Psalms 97:2-7), as protector (Psalms 105:39), as carrying His word: "His voice came to them from the pillar of cloud; so they heard the decrees, the law He gave them" (Psalm 9:7). The prophets announced it would come back, "a cloud and smoke by day, and the shining of a flaming fire by night" (Isaiah 4:5). "It shall come to pass that I will pour out my spirit upon everyone... and I will show wonders in the heavens and on earth, blood, fire, and pillars of smoke" (Joel 3:2, 3).

The luminous cloud has always been a choice subject of rabbinic thought and of Christian mystical theology. All Jews know what the pillar meant: a manifestation of God dwelling among His chosen people, tabernacling amidst them, guiding them, shedding light upon them, speaking to them. The other nations knew this (Numbers 14:14). It is the **Shekinah**, the most sacred and mysterious sign of the deity. The Shekinah Glory is Heaven itself. It is God's physical presence.

Conchita has said that it is like a pillar of smoke that will be the permanent sign above the pines. On November 18, 1961, a column of smoke by day and fire by night was seen by a number of people between the nine pines. Ramon Gonzalez, a shepherd about twenty years old, was tending his sheep and noticed a small fire about 50 centimeters in diameter. Again in Autumn 1962, this was seen by a number of people for a period of two or three months, all of whom provided written testimony. It was seen again on November 25, 1965, by four French witnesses. The column was seen at night, clear-cut and luminous.

The Likely Reaction From The Rabbis

For cultured Jews and Rabbis, a thorough knowledge of the Scriptures is a large measure of their religious life. In Israel, whatever their beliefs, all citizens have studied the Hebrew Bible as their only text of Hebrew classical literature. Whether or not they consider it as divinely inspired, they still know it. They know that it has been prophetically announced that, "your sons and your daughters will prophesy..." (see Song of Songs 3:6 and Acts 2:17-21). Thanks to the media that will cover the event, they will know at once that Catholic girls have announced that a pillar of smoke will appear in a Catholic village in Catholic Spain and remain there "para siempre." They will all be interested, especially the Sephardim, the Spanish Jews. Their interest will be extreme and lasting, because the miracle will inaugurate the permanent miraculous pillar.

Saint Bernard And Saint Thomas Aquinas

Historians consider that the first schism in the history of the people of God was between the Gentiles and the church of the Jews. This schism was caused by the refusal of the Synagogue to accept Jesus of Nazareth as the Messiah. For several centuries, this first schism was not fully effective. In the Roman Basilica of Santa Sabina (early Fifth Century), portentous figures of the Church from the Gentiles and of the Church from the Synagogue stand side by side as true believers. Saint Bernard (1090-1153) and Saint Thomas Aquinas (1226-1274) wrote that the Church would allow the Synagogue to enter into the fullness of her redemption. Saint Bernard wrote that the Synagogue has not in the eyes of God forsaken her birthright over her sister the Church. **Saint Thomas in his commentary on the Song of Songs taught the future reintegration of Israel would usher in the third era of the Church.** His authority is immense, and this view opens up great vistas.

Saints and popes alike, including John Paul II, have spoken about the mystery of the Church and the Synagogue. Paul wrote in Romans 11:15, "Since their [the Jews'] rejection meant the reconciliation of the world, do you know what their admission will mean? Nothing less than a resurrection from the dead." The Second Coming of the Lord and the prelude to it are expanded in 2 Thessalonians 2:7.

What we are trying to convey is not merely that there will be an "admission of" that part of Israel which hardened itself (Romans 11: 7-24), but it will come as a consequence of what will soon happen at Garabandal. It will happen soon because we know through Conchita the prophesied events are close at hand.

Saint Michael The Archangel

The first apparitions of Garabandal were of an angel, from June 18 to July 2, 1961. Michael was the forerunner of Mary and her messenger to Conchita alone on several occasions. A great deal has been written on Michael's role at Garabandal. Michael is named three times in the Hebrew Bible, each time as a guardian of Israel or as its Prince. Daniel 10:20 reads: "He said then, 'Do you know why I have come to you? It is to tell you what is written in the Book of Truth. I must go back to fight against the prince of Persia: when I have done with him, the prince of Javan will come next. In all this there is no one to lend me support except Michael your prince.'" Daniel 12:1-4 describes Michael again and his role in the latter times: "At that time Michael will stand up, the great prince who mounts guard over your people. There is going to be a time of great distress, unparalleled since nations first came into existence. When that time comes, your own people will be spared, all those whose names are found written in the Book. Of those who lie sleeping in the dust of the earth many will awake, some to everlasting life, some to shame and everlasting disgrace. The learned will shine as brightly as the vault of Heaven, and those who have instructed many in virtue, as bright as stars for all eternity. But you, Daniel, must keep your words secret and the book sealed until the time of the end. Many will wander this way and that, and wickedness will go on increasing."

Michael will "stand up in a time of great trouble," and thanks to him "thy people shall be delivered." His power is great as he is "one of the leading princes." Daniel 10:13 writes about the apparition of Michael, "The prince of the kingdom of Persia has been resisting me for twenty-one days, but Michael, one of the leading princes, came to my assistance." Although the Church applies this passage to itself, it is not possible to exclude "those who are Israelites," as they were the first to have Michael as their prince. Romans 9:4-5 speaks about the privileges of Israel. It reads: "They were adopted as sons, they were given the glory and the covenants; the Law and the ritual were drawn up for them, and the promises were made to them. They are descended from the patriarchs and from their flesh and blood came Christ who is above all, God forever blessed!"

Mary At Garabandal

For the first time in the history of Marian apparitions, as announced by Michael, the Blessed Mother appeared under a title which refers to a holy place—Mount Carmel. The three holy mountains of the ancient people of Israel were Mount Carmel, Mount Sinai or Horeb, and Mount Zion or Jerusalem. Mount Carmel is the mountain made holy by Elijah the prophet. It is the mountain which Mary had often seen from where she lived. Nazareth is the only holy village from which the mountain can be seen clearly. Moreover, of all religious orders, the Carmelites is by far the closest to Judaism. Elijah is considered by Carmelite friars and sisters as their founder and model. They celebrate his feast on July 20 of each year.

Conchita described Mary in her diary as a beautiful Jewish woman with dark and wavy hair, a perfect nose, full lips, and a rather dark complexion. In other apparitions Mary appears as a beautiful girl with the features of other beautiful girls of the country where she appears. Mari-Loli asked her one day if she was Jewish, and her answer was yes. It was the first time in the history of apparitions that the Blessed Virgin identified herself as such, saying that even in Heaven she belonged to the Jewish people. This was confirmed by the late Garabandal expert Father Laffineur. As was predicted, all of the visionaries would deny they had ever seen an apparition. The three eldest have since retracted their doubts and negations, and from January 1963, Mari Cruz continued to deny that she had ever seen the Blessed Virgin, even in front of the bishop of Santander who received her on June 24, 1965.

El Fin De Los Tiempos

Conchita announced prophetically that after John XXIII, there would only be three more popes before *el fin de los tiempos*, the end of our epoch. Let us remember that scriptural and God-inspired prophecies are not normally well understood before their accomplishments. A column of smoke by day and a fire by night without question will draw the attention of the Jews. As we compare the thoughts of Saint Thomas and Saint Bernard about the future reintegration of Israel ushering in the third era of the Church, the phrase *el fin de los tiempos* is of extreme importance.

Father Turner's documentation and sources are impeccable, and his history and scholarship are considerable. He has visited the village and has known the key people involved from the beginning. The world will soon focus on the tiny village in northern Spain. If the permanent sign is a pillar of smoke, this will have enormous repercussions for the Jewish world.

Few doubt that if the permanent sign that so many of the visionaries speak about were a pillar of smoke by day and a fire by night, how this would have enormous impact for the Jews. Many pilgrims who have visited Medjugorje and other shrines have seen a large white cross appear on the mountain. Often the vision of a staircase to Heaven is seen with an open door at many apparition sites as well. One or both of these phenomena may be factors in the miracle or permanent sign.

11

The Tears of Akita, Japan

Let the sea and all within it thunder;
the world, and all its peoples.
Let the rivers clap their hands
and the hills ring out their joy.
Rejoice at the presence of the Lord,
for He comes to rule the earth.
He will rule the world with justice
and the peoples with fairness.

Psalm 98

The Mother of God has entrusted a Japanese nun named Sister Agnes Sasagawa with important messages for the world. In 1973, the Blessed Virgin came to Japan, where approximately 0.3 percent of the population is Catholic. The religious order and convent visited by the Blessed Virgin is dedicated to adoration of the Holy Eucharist, so it is not surprising that the events preceding the messages started at the tabernacle. The first focus of the mystical events at Akita was to affirm the Real Presence of Our Lord in the Eucharist. Throughout the nine years of heavenly events, the existence and very active role guardian angels play in protecting their wards and the general function of all angels as adorers of God is shown repeatedly.[1]

Mary As Co-Redemptrix

The events that took place at Akita allude to the Blessed Virgin as Co-Redemptrix. The events at Akita focus on a weeping statue of Mary located in the convent. The message of Mary as Co-Redemptrix, Mediatrix, and Advocate comes through the image of the statue in several ways: (1) the statue is a reproduction of Our Lady of All Nations as she appeared in Amsterdam, when she announced a forthcoming dogmatic proclamation of Mary as Co-Redemptrix, Mediatrix, and Advocate; (2) the right hand of the statue bears a stigmata in the shape of a cross which bled, and (3) the statue sweat fluid and wept blood. The sweat and blood evoke images of Our Lord during His Passion. The Mother of Christ as Co-Redemptrix shares in Her Son's suffering. "If there is a particular conclusion to be drawn from the blood shed by Our Lady at Akita, it is that her mission as Co-Redemptrix has never ended, that it continues to this very day," said Father Jacques, the French missionary who worked in Japan for thirty years and was the superior to the Sisters

The role of co-redemption is shared by all who unite their sufferings with Christ and like Saint Paul "fill up these things that are wanting of the sufferings of Christ, in my flesh, for His body, which is the Church" (Colossians 1:24). This role for the laity was encouraged by the apparitions in Fatima when the Blessed Virgin said, "Pray a great deal and make sacrifices for sinners, for many souls go to hell for not having someone to pray and make sacrifices for them" (August 1917).

Feast Days

Another focus of the apparitions is the importance of liturgical feast days. The first time Sister Agnes heard her guardian angel speak to her was on the Feast of the Sacred Heart. Other messages from the guardian angel came on the Feasts of the Archangels (September 29), of the Guardian Angel (October 2), and of Saint Joseph the Worker (May 1). The statue of Our Lady stopped weeping on the Feast of Our Lady of Sorrows. The entire mystical events that took place in the convent ended on the Feast of the Visitation (May 31), which coincided that year with the Feast of Pentecost.

Devotional days were also emphasized in a dramatic way. The first two messages by the Blessed Virgin were given on First Fridays (significant in the devotion to the Sacred Heart) and the third on the anniversary of the miracle of the sun at Fatima (October 13). The right hand of the statue of Our Lady stopped bleeding on a First Friday; the statue started weeping on another First Friday.

Events Leading To The Messages

Our Lord in the Eucharist —1973

Sister Agnes went to the chapel alone and suddenly a brilliant light appeared to burst forth from the tabernacle. She prostrated herself immediately on the floor and remained there even after the light disappeared. Sister Agnes knew that Jesus in the Host had truly manifested His Real Presence.

June 14, 1973

Sister Agnes was praying with the community before the Blessed Sacrament when suddenly a light flashed from the tabernacle. Unlike the previous incident, the rays of the golden light were enveloped by a red flame. It seemed that the whole tabernacle was on fire.

June 28, 1973

While in the chapel praying, Sister Agnes felt as though something pierced the palm of her left hand. When she left the chapel she saw two red scratches forming a cross in the center of her hand. This little cross caused Sister Agnes intense pain. During Adoration of the Blessed Sacrament after Mass, Sister Agnes records the following in her personal diary: "Suddenly a blinding light shone from the Blessed Sacrament. As previously, something like fog or smoke began to gather around the altar and the rays of light. Then there appeared a multitude of beings similar to angels who surrounded the altar in adoration before the Host.... The brightness from the Host was so brilliant that I could not look at it directly. Closing my eyes, instinctively I prostrated myself."

June 29, 1973: Feast of the Sacred Heart

During adoration of the Blessed Sacrament, Sister Agnes began praying her rosary when a person appeared very close to her on her right side. This was the same person who had appeared to Sister Agnes four years before during one of her hospitalizations. The person taught her the following prayer to be said after each decade of the rosary: "Oh my Jesus, forgive us our sins, save us from the fires of hell, lead all souls to Heaven, especially those who are most in need of your mercy." It was the same prayer that Our Lady taught to the three children at Fatima.

Now the person was again standing next to Sister Agnes. This time this beautiful person prayed the rosary with Sister Agnes, but very slowly. Then the beautiful person prayed: "Most Sacred Heart of Jesus, TRULY present in the Holy Eucharist, I consecrate my body and soul to be entirely one with Your Heart, being sacrificed at every instant on all the altars of the world and giving praise to the Father, pleading for the coming of His Kingdom. Please receive this humble offering of myself. Use me as You will for the glory of the Father and the salvation of souls. Most Holy Mother of God, never let me be separated from your divine Son. Please defend and protect me as your special child. Amen."

(Note: This prayer was composed by Bishop Ito for the Institute of the Handmaids of the Eucharist. In the original, the first sentence did not contain the word "truly." At the request of the Blessed Virgin, the word "truly" was inserted.)

Sister Agnes realized this was an angel who was appearing in the form of a woman, and in due time she identified herself as Sister Agnes' guardian angel.

July 6, 1973: First Friday

During adoration, the angel again appeared and began to recite the rosary with Sister Agnes. Suddenly, a very sharp pain pierced her hand, but she continued to pray. Later, after examining the wound, Sister Agnes noticed that at the center of the two branches of the cross was now a hole from which blood flowed. The pain continued after the blood flow ceased. Sister Agnes spent that night tormented by pain.

Sister Agnes recorded in her diary that towards 3 a.m., "I had just changed the bandage again and was praying. Then I heard a voice which came from I know not where saying, "Do not fear. Pray with fervor not only because of your sins, but in reparation for those of all men. The world today wounds the Most Sacred Heart of Our Lord by its ingratitude and injuries. The wounds of Mary are much deeper and more sorrowful than yours. Let us go to pray together in the chapel." The voice was from her angel who later said, "I am the one who is with you and watches over you."

Sister Agnes hurried with the angel to the chapel. "At that time the statue was placed on the right side of the altar.... I suddenly felt that the wooden statue came to life and was about to speak to me. She was bathed in a brilliant light. Instinctively, Sister Agnes prostrated herself on the ground and heard the following message:

July 6, 1973: First Message of the Blessed Virgin

"My daughter, my novice, you have obeyed me well in abandoning all to follow me. Is the infirmity of your ears painful? Your deafness will be healed, be sure. Be patient. It is the last trial. Does the wound in your hand cause you to suffer? Pray in reparation for the sins of men. Each person in this community is my irreplaceable daughter. Since your Baptism you have always prayed faithfully for them. Continue to pray very much...very much. Tell your superior all that passed today and obey him in everything that he will tell you. He has asked that you pray with fervor." Sister Agnes understood, because of the pain in her left hand, that she was not to receive Communion in her hand. The pain was so intense she could not put her hand out to receive it.

July 7, 1973

Early in the morning, Sister Agnes was praying in the chapel and observed something unusual about the right hand of the statue of the Blessed Virgin. In the middle of the palm of the wooden hand was a wound in the shape of a cross. Where the two crossbeams intersected, blood flowed from a central hole, creating a most sorrowful sight. Overcome by a combination of fear and respect, Sister Agnes recalled the words spoken to her during the night: "Pray in reparation for the sins of men."

July 27, 1973

Sister Agnes had not been able to sleep for two days because of the painful wound in her hand. In the early afternoon of this First Friday, she was pierced with an excruciating pain. Sister Agnes fled to the chapel for refuge. Sister Agnes prostrated herself on the floor and immediately she heard her guardian angel say: "Your sufferings will end today. Carefully engrave in the depth of your heart the thought of the blood of Mary. The blood shed by Mary has a profound meaning. This precious blood was shed to ask your conversion, to ask for peace, in reparation for the ingratitude and the outrages towards the Lord. As with devotion to the Sacred Heart, apply yourself to devotion to the Most Precious Blood. Pray in reparation for all men."

To her surprise, Sister Agnes could not reply. Her angel continued: "Say to your superior that the blood is shed today for the last time. Your pain also ends today. Tell them what happened today. He will understand all immediately. And you, observe his directions." The angel ended with a smile and disappeared.

August 3, 1973

Sister Agnes went to the chapel in the early afternoon to meditate on the passion of Our Lord and later began to pray the rosary. Then she heard her guardian angel say: "You have something to ask. Go ahead, you have no need to be troubled." (The bishop had given Sister Agnes three questions to pose to the Blessed Virgin, and Sister Agnes was praying that the occasion might be given to accomplish the task given to her by the bishop). Then suddenly she heard a voice of indescribable beauty. Recognizing that it was the Blessed Virgin, Sister Agnes heard her second message:

August 3, 1973

"My daughter, my novice, do you love the Lord? If you love the Lord, listen to what I have to say to you. It is very important. You will convey it to your superior. Many men in this world afflict the Lord. I desire souls to console Him to soften the anger of the Heavenly Father. I wish, with my Son, for souls who will repair by their suffering and their poverty for the sinners and ingrates."

"In order that the world might know His anger, the Heavenly Father is preparing to inflict a great chastisement on all mankind. With my Son I have intervened so many times to appease the wrath of the Father. I have prevented the coming of calamities by offering Him the sufferings of the Son on the Cross, His Precious Blood, and beloved souls who console Him forming a legion of victim souls. Prayer, penance and courageous sacrifices can soften the Father's anger. I desire this also from your community. That it love poverty, that it sanctify itself and pray in reparation for the ingratitude and outrages of so many men. Recite the prayer of the Handmaids of the Eucharist with awareness of its meaning; put it into practice; offer in reparation [whatever God may send] for sins. Let each one endeavor, according to her capacity and position, to offer herself entirely to the Lord.

"Even in a secular institute prayer is necessary. Already souls who wish to pray are on the way to being gathered together. Without attaching too much attention to the form, be faithful and fervent in prayer to console the Master.

"Is what you think in your heart true? Are you truly decided to become the rejected stone? My novice, you who wish to belong without reserve to the Lord, to become the spouse worthy of the Spouse, make your vows knowing that you must be fastened to the Cross with three nails. These three nails are poverty, chastity, and obedience. Of the three, obedience is the foundation. In total abandon, let yourself be led by your superior. He will know how to understand you and to direct you."

September 29, 1973: Feast of the Archangels

As the community was finishing the office in the chapel, the statue became resplendent in light and began streaming as though with perspiration. Sister Agnes felt someone beside her. She lifted her eyes and saw the angel who said: "Mary is even sadder than when she sheds blood. Dry the perspiration." With great care and devotion, Sister Agnes and some of the other Sisters used cotton to soak up the perspiration. The entire statue was soaked. A liquid similar to heavy sweat oozed without stopping, especially on the forehead and the neck. Then suddenly, the Sisters noticed that the fragrance emitted from the cotton pads was of an unearthly delight. The fragrance lasted for quite a while in the chapel. Each time one entered, one had the impression of entering the realm of Heaven.

October 2, 1973: Feast of the Guardian Angels

At the moment of consecration at Mass a dazzling light burst from the tabernacle. "At the same moment there appeared the outline of angels in prayer before the shining Host. They were kneeling all around the altar in a semicircle, their backs toward us. There were eight of them...It was difficult precisely to describe their clothing. All that can be said is that they seemed to be enveloped in a sort of white light.... All eight were there to adore the Most Blessed Sacrament in an attitude of great devotion.

"At the moment of Communion, my guardian angel approached me to invite me to advance to the altar. At that moment I clearly distinguished the guardian angels of each member of the community close to their left shoulders, and the height a little smaller than each.

Like my guardian angel they gave truly the impression of guiding and watching over them with sweetness and affection."

October 13, 1973: Final Message of the Blessed Virgin Mary

Reciting the rosary during adoration of the Eucharist, Sister Agnes again saw the luminous splendor of the Blessed Sacrament. From the tabernacle the brilliant light seemed to spread into the whole chapel. At the same moment the statue of Mary gave off a celestial fragrance. She returned to her room after adoration, but soon returned to the chapel. Sister Agnes related that she entered the chapel and had barely finished making the sign of the cross with her rosary when she heard a voice of indescribable beauty come from the statue. From the first word, Sister Agnes prostrated herself on the ground and concentrated on the message being given to her, which was the final message. When the voice was quiet, Sister Agnes reflected on the message and later received the following message from the Blessed Virgin: "You have still something to ask? Today is the last time I will speak to you in a living voice. From now on you will obey the one sent to you [Father Yasuda] and your superior.

"Pray very much the prayers of the rosary. I alone am able to save you from the calamities that approach. Those who place their confidence in me will be saved.

"My dear daughter, listen well to what I have to say to you. You will inform your superior. **As I told you, if men do not repent and better themselves, the Father will inflict a terrible punishment on all humanity. It will be a punishment greater than the deluge, such as one will never have seen before. Fire will fall from the sky and will wipe out a great part of humanity, the good as well as the bad, sparing neither priests nor faithful. The survivors will find themselves so desolate that they will envy the dead. The only arms that will remain for you will be the rosary and Sign left by My Son. Each day recite the prayers of the rosary.** With the rosary, pray for the Pope, the bishops, and the priests.

The work of the devil will infiltrate even the Church in such a way that one will see cardinals opposing cardinals, bishops against other bishops. The priests who venerate Me will be scorned and opposed by their confreres ...churches and altars sacked, the Church will be full of those who accept compromises and the demon will press many priests and consecrated souls to

leave the service of the Lord. The demon will be especially implacable against souls consecrated to God. The thought of the loss of so many souls is the cause of my sadness. If sins increase in number and gravity, there will be no longer pardon for them.

"With courage, speak to your superior. He will know how to encourage each one of you to pray and to accomplish works of reparation."

January 4, 1975: Statue Weeps for the First Time

The angel told Sister Agnes: "Do not be so surprised to see the Blessed Virgin weeping. She weeps because she wishes the conversion of the greatest number. She desires that souls be consecrated to Jesus and to the Father by her intercession. He who directs you told you during the last sermon today; your faith diminishes when you do not see. It is because your faith is weak. The Blessed Virgin rejoices in the consecration of Japan to her Immaculate Heart because she loves Japan. But she is sad to see that this devotion is not taken seriously. Even though she has chosen this land of Akita to give her messages, the local pastor doesn't dare to come for fear of what one would say. Do not be afraid. The Blessed Virgin awaits you all, her hands extended to pour forth graces. Spread devotion to the Virgin. She rejoices in the profession of the lay members consecrated today by her intercession in conformity to the spirit of your Institute. You must not consider the lay members thus consecrated as of little importance. The prayer which you have the custom of saying, 'Grant to Japan the grace of conversion through the intercession of the Virgin Mary,' is pleasing to the Lord. You who have believed while seeing the tears of Mary, when you have permission of your superior, speak to the greatest number in order to console the Hearts of Jesus and Mary. Spread this devotion with courage for their greater glory. You will transmit my words to your superior and to him who directs you."

May 1, 1976: Feast of Saint Joseph the Worker

The angel told Sister Agnes after Communion: "Many men in this world afflict the Lord. Our Lady awaits souls to console Him. Remain in poverty. Sanctify yourself and pray in reparation for the ingratitude and the outrages of so many men. The rosary is your weapon. Say it with care, and more when for the intention of the Pope, of bishops and priests. You must not forget these words [of Mary]. The Blessed

Virgin prays continually for the conversion of the greatest possible number and weeps, hoping to lead to Jesus and to the Father souls offered to Them by her intercession. For this intention, and to overcome exterior obstacles, achieve interior unity, form a single heart. Let believers lead a life more worthy of believers! Pray with a new heart. Attach great importance to this day for the glory of God and of His Holy Mother."

September 29, 1981: Meaning of the Tears

During adoration of the Blessed Sacrament, Sister Agnes felt the presence of her angel at her side. She did not see the form of the angel, but instead an open Bible appeared before her eyes. When Sister Agnes recognized the passage, Genesis 3:15, the angel explained, "There is a meaning to the figure one hundred and one. It signifies that sin came into the world by a woman and it is also by a woman that salvation came to the world. The zero between the two signifies the Eternal God who is from all eternity until eternity. The first one represents Eve and the last, the Virgin Mary." Sister Agnes re-read the verse, then the angel and the vision of the Bible disappeared. (Father Yasuda comments that this passage of Genesis is called proto-evangelic and is considered the first promise of a Savior made by God to man. It is also the first verse of the Bible making allusion to the Immaculate Conception of Mary, and who was never under the domination of Satan.)

"The Message of Akita Is The Message Of Fatima...."

Bishop Ito, in whose diocese Akita is located, has noted the following similarities between Akita and Fatima:

Fatima: "Does this cause you to suffer a great deal? My Immaculate Heart will be your refuge and way...to God" (June 13, 1917).

Akita: "Does the wound in your hand cause you to suffer? Pray in reparation for the sins of men" (July 6, 1973).

Fatima: "The Holy Father will have much to suffer..." (July 13 1917).

Akita: "Pray very much for the Pope..." (July 6, 1973).

Fatima: "Say the rosary every day" (September 13, 1917).

Akita: "Each day recite the prayers of the rosary" (October 13, 1973).

Fatima: "...offer yourselves to God, to accept all the sufferings which He may send you..." (May 15, 1917).

Akita: "Offer in reparation [whatever God may send] for sins" (August 3, 1973).

Fatima: "He is going to punish the world for its crimes" (July 1917).

Akita: "The Father will inflict a terrible punishment on all humanity" (October 13, 1973).

Fatima: "Pray a great deal and make sacrifices for sinners..."(August 1917).

Akita: Pray in reparation for the sins of men" (July 6, 1973).

Fatima: "...persecution of the Church, the good will be martyred...various nations will be annihilated" (July 13, 1917).

Akita: "...will wipe out a great part of humanity, the good as well as the bad, sparing neither priests nor faithful..." (October 1973).

Bishop's Approval

Father Yasuda, Sister Agnes' spiritual director, witnessed the statue crying ninety-eight times of the total 101 times. Hundreds saw the statue weep. Faith was not required to see the miraculous events. In a recent television interview, Father Yasuda said that samples of the tears, blood, and sweat were sent to the laboratory of Akita University for analysis on January 29, 1979. According to signed testimony, the blood was type B and the body fluids were type AB. On November 30, 1981, the body fluids tested type 0. Father Yasuda suggests that creating three different types of blood is God's way of absolutely refuting the ectoplasm theory that critics advanced to discredit the bleeding and sweating statue. This theory says that Sister

Agnes transmitted her own blood "through the air" to the statue. The first commission investigating the Akita phenomena used this theory to discredit the events.

On Easter Sunday, April 22, 1984, the Most Reverend John Shojiro Ito, Bishop of Niigata, issued a pastoral letter declaring the events of Akita to be supernatural. In his pastoral letter, Bishop Ito cites the case of Teresa Chun, a Korean woman, who was reduced to a vegetative state because of a brain tumor. She was cured miraculously during an apparition of the Blessed Virgin of Akita. Another miraculous cure was that of Sister Agnes, who was cured of her deafness. The Blessed Virgin Mary announced the nun's cure during the Benediction of the Blessed Sacrament.

12

Medjugorje: Its Messages, Secrets, And Warnings

I will give you messages like never before in all of history, and I come to tell you God exists.

Our Lady to the Visionaries of Medjugorje

On June 24, 1981, in a little village in Yugoslavia, the Blessed Mother appeared to two children on the feast of John the Baptist. The two youths, sixteen-year-old Mirjana Dragicevic and fifteen-year-old Ivanka Ivankovic, were walking along a road at the foot of Mount Podbrdo and saw a beautiful luminous figure of a young woman radiating tremendous light. Ivanka pointed to the Lady and exclaimed, "Look, Mirjana, it's the Gospa [Our Lady]!" Mirjana, without looking, said, "Come on! Would Our Lady appear to us?" They continued on their way. When they returned from the village of Bijakovici, they encountered the same Lady again when leaving the village with Milka Pavlovic, who was then rounding up sheep. This time seventeen-year-old Vicka Ivankovic and sixteen-year-old Ivan Dragicevic joined them and also saw the Lady. As the five young people saw the distant vision, Our Lady beckoned them to come closer. They were fearful at first and then experienced a deeper peace and joy. The vision lasted for about forty-five minutes.

On the second day, June 25, 1981, four of the youths, Ivanka, Mirjana, Vicka and Ivan, felt attracted to Mount Podbrdo. This time they decided if they saw the vision again, they would get their two friends, Maria Pavlovic and ten-year-old Jacov Colo. They approached Mount Podbrdo around six p.m., and again Ivanka was the first to see the vision. Vicka also could see the vision and, remembering her promise to Maria and Jacov, ran to get them. They came immediately. Now all six children saw the Blessed Mother. She was very beautiful and spent about fifteen minutes with them. Our Lady bade the young people goodbye as she was leaving with the words, "Go in the peace of God."

She has continued to appear to these young people up to the present day. Our Lady is often preceded by a bright light resembling lightning. Each of the young people was told by Our Lady that he or she would receive ten secrets. Mirjana and Ivanka have now received all ten secrets and only see Our Lady infrequently. Ivan, Jacov, Vicka, and Maria each have nine secrets and still see Our Lady daily. Our Lady's main messages are prayer, fasting, faith, conversion, and peace. She stressed that peace can only come from conversion or reconciliation with God and with one's neighbor.

Our Lady's apparitions at Medjugorje are very important, for they appear to be a central focal point for messages for the world. In the United States alone, one can see the tremendous influence that Medjugorje has had on the spiritual life of the visionaries in such places as Scottsdale and Phoenix, Arizona; Denver, Colorado; Marlboro, New Jersey; Conyers, Georgia, and many others. Many of the visionaries in the world have been to Medjugorje, and for them, this was the genesis of the acute awareness of the reality of Jesus in their lives. In many respects, other apparition sites are satellites of Medjugorje.

The Hub Of The Wheel For Apparitions

Medjugorje has been a beacon of light to the world. It has been a special place of pilgrimage calling the world back to God. The messages of Fatima and Garabandal were not heeded. In Medjugorje, the Blessed Mother is blowing the trumpet for all to take notice as she gives messages like never before in all history. It seems to be a final attempt by Heaven to be heard in a world that is too busy to listen. At first, some of the messages about peace seemed repetitive, but now we see how prophetic these messages are regarding the current destructive political situation. Who would have believed that a diabolical ethnic cleansing would have begun, which continues to shock the entire world. The war in Bosnia-Herzegovina is televised almost every night; Our Lady's messages become clear. We now see why she chose this area of the world to appear and give messages.

Just as Mary appeared in Fatima to warn the world of atheistic communism and other evils, she is appearing in Medjugorje to sound the alarm. As the ethnic conflict intensified, so did Mary's pleadings for prayer and penance. In the messages of September 25, 1992, Mary explained to us how Satan is trying to destroy the plans of Heaven: "Dear children! Today also I wish to tell you: I am with you in these restless days in which Satan wishes to destroy everything which I and my Son Jesus are building up. In a special way he wishes to destroy your souls. He wishes to guide you as far away as possible from Christian life as well as from the commandments, to which the Church is calling you so you may live them. Satan wishes to destroy everything which is holy in you and around you. Therefore, little children pray, pray, pray, in order to be able to comprehend all which God is giving you through my coming!"

In the October 25, 1992, message, she warned us that Satan is strong and wishes to make as many souls as possible his own. She pleaded for us to trust in her and she said that she is here to help and guide us. Mary also hinted that these apparitions will soon be ending. When this happens, events foretold will unfold rapidly. We are told at Medjugorje that these are the last apparitions on earth and that when they cease in Medjugorje they will cease everywhere:

"Dear children, I invite you to prayer now when Satan is strong and wishes to make as many souls as possible his own. Pray, dear children, and have more trust in me, because I am here in order to help you, and to guide you on a new path towards a new life. Therefore, dear little children, listen and live what I tell you, **because it is important for you, when I shall not be with you any longer, that you remember my words and all which I told you.** I call you to begin to change your life from the beginning and that you decide for conversion not with words but with your life."

We are told, through the visionaries, that when these apparitions cease, three warnings will come to the world and then the visible sign will be given. After the visible sign appears, "those who are still alive will have little time for conversion." Our Lady said that her appearances at Medjugorje are a great grace from God. She reiterated this in words she gave on July 25, 1992: "... thank God for the gift of my being with you, because I am telling you: this is a great grace...."

It appears that soon this great grace of these heavenly visitations will cease and that our world will be colliding with God's Justice. We will then need to live all that has been said in Scripture and over the last twelve years in Medjugorje.

Medjugorje Pilgrims Experience A Warning, 1992

Very recent reports from pilgrims in Medjugorje describe how they experienced an illumination of conscience, seeing their entire life pass before their eyes as in a film. They reported that they were able to see precisely and clearly each event of their life when they had said "Yes" to God, and each time when they said "No." Their consciences were flooded with such light that they saw themselves as in an X-ray from the Holy Spirit, "with the shadows of sin and the light of love which they had given." They felt a profound repentance. They all received at the same moment a great healing, physical and spiritual. One, a drug addict, was completely freed from drug addiction. These pilgrims now have only one desire: to put God and His love above everything else in their lives.[1] Could this be a foreshadowing of the world-wide warning that visionaries at Garabandal and other apparition sites have proclaimed?

The Messages

The messages remain the central focus at apparition sites. Therefore, we have focused our attention on these central themes rather than on the personalities receiving them. The next several pages concerning these messages are from the book by Mary Joan Wallace, *Medjugorje: Its Background And Messages.*[2]

The critical messages involve seeking a right relationship to God through conversion and reconciliation, a process which goes on throughout one's entire life. "Peace is necessary for the world to be saved," emphasizes our Blessed Mother. She invites us to the peace that the world cannot give but only God can give—interior peace and serenity of heart that come from prayer, fasting, penance, conversion, reconciliation, and faith.

As Queen of Peace, Our Lady has referred to peace over and over; she usually has exhorted at the close of each apparition, "Go in God's peace!" On the third day when Maria was descending from Mount Podbrdo, Mary appeared to her with an empty cross, from which were shining many colors of the rainbow. "Peace, peace, peace!" she tearfully cried. "Only peace! Do not be afraid of injustice," she advised on the next day. "It always has existed." When sufferings come," she later recommended," offer them up as a sacrifice to God." She said on July 25, 1990, "You should do everything out of love! Accept all annoyances, all difficulties, everything with love! Forgive! Reconcile! I desire to bring all of you to the peace which only God gives, and which enriches every heart. I invite you to become carriers and witnesses of my peace to this unpeaceful world. Let peace rule in the whole world, which is without peace and longs for peace!"

Urgently Needed Conversion And Reconciliation

Another message involves surrendering to God—reaching out to Him in prayer and saying "Yes" to His will. "I want to be with you to convert and to reconcile the whole world," Mary explained on the third day. "Give up everything that goes against conversion!"

Reconciliation with God and with one another are necessary for interior peace and for world peace, Our Lady has explained. "Dear children, today I am calling you to a life of love towards God and your neighbor! Without love, dear children, you cannot do anything!" In other messages she implored, "Open your hearts to Jesus! I am calling you to prayer and to complete surrender to God! Today I beg you to start loving with the burning love with which I love you!" These messages remind us of Jesus' teaching (in Mark 12:28-33) about our being called to love God with all our hearts, souls, minds, and strength, and our neighbors as ourselves.

"I beg you to help me present you to God... to lead you on the way to salvation!" Mary has pleaded. "They, too [those separated from God], are my children. I grieve for them, because they do not know what awaits them if they do not turn back to God. Pray for them!" Mary has said that she usually prays daily before the Mt. Krizevac cross for God's forgiveness for mankind and for conversions.

"If you pray with all the heart, dear children, the ice-cold hearts of your brothers will melt, and every barrier will disap-

pear. Conversion will be easy for all those who want it. This is a favor which you must beg for your neighbor," she instructed on January 23, 1986. "Especially I call you to pray—so that all those who are far away from God may be converted!"

She emphasized in August 1982 that the Sacrament of Reconciliation is important in the process of ongoing conversion. Mary pointed out: "One must invite people to go to Confession each month, especially the first Saturday.... Monthly Confession will be a remedy for the Church in the West. One must convey this message to the West!" Mary's requests for monthly Confession immediately were implemented by the priests of Saint James and followed by parishioners and pilgrims. The visionaries and other Medjugorje parishioners, including some youth prayer group members, have attended Confession not only monthly but weekly. Of the pilgrims coming to Medjugorje, more come for conversion than for healing.

Mary said that the great sin of the world consists in the fact that so many people are not interested in God, even when they have the capacity to know that He exists. In self-centeredness and pride, people do not reach out for God.

Expressing concern for the people of the West in October of 1981, Mary explained: "The West has made civilization progress, but without God, as if they [its people] were their own creators. Whole regions of the Church would be healed if believers would go to Confession once a month!" She later exclaimed, "You who believe, be converted! Hasten your conversion!"

Because the world is in great sin, Mary asks that family members pray together in particular for conversions each evening. In 1917, at the Fatima apparitions, Mary requested prayer for the conversion of Russia. Now Mary also is asking for prayer for the West.

Faith

Mary frequently has encouraged faith, and she did so often in the first year of apparitions. Faith comes with trust, she emphasizes; and without prayer, faith and trust cannot be kept alive. "Many believers do not pray," she has stated sadly. Mary smiles when hearing the Apostles' Creed, one of her favorite prayers. This and the traditional praying of the Our Father, Hail Mary, and Glory Be seven times (the

Medjugorje Prayer) are to help us review and develop faith in basic Christian beliefs.

Through Jelena, a young woman who receives interior locutions supplementing the visionaries' messages, Mary asked for Thursday evening readings of the Gospel of Matthew 6:24-34, with its emphasis on trusting God and seeking first His Kingdom. She has encouraged us to do Bible reading either before the Blessed Sacrament or at home with the family.

Every fear and every conflict in our families and in the Church are an indication of the lack of faith, says Mary. "Reject fear!" Jelena has reported that she received this message from Mary in an inner locution: "If you want to be very happy, lead a simple, humble life; pray a great deal; and do not sink into your problems—but leave it to God to resolve them."

Through the visionaries, Mary asks priests to believe and to develop firm faith. Many priests have been accompanying those on pilgrimages to Medjugorje and studying the messages. In *The Medjugorje Messenger*, a quarterly magazine of the Medjugorje Center in England, Father Richard Foley, S.J., D.D., editor, wrote in early 1989 that some 14,000 priests had been to Medjugorje since the start of the apparitions. The estimated number today is 15,000.

Fasting And Penance

"Through fasting and prayer one can stop wars; one can suspend the laws of nature," emphasized Mary on July 21, 1982. "Everyone except the sick has to fast." She has recommended that we fast for the sick and for those in difficulty. She usually links the word fast with the word pray. "Fast and pray with your hearts. Fast and pray out of gratitude to God for allowing me to remain this long in this parish." When asked the best fast she replied, "bread and water."

In an unexpected apparition to Ivan at his home on August 14, 1984, the day before the Feast of the Assumption, Our Lady made this important request: "I ask the people to pray with me these days as much as they can. Fast strictly on Wednesdays and Fridays. Every day pray at least one rosary—joyful, sorrowful and glorious mysteries." In Medjugorje those fasting do so often in remembrance, preparation, and thanksgiving for the Sacrament of the Eucharist, instituted by Jesus on the first Holy Thursday. The early Christians also fasted on Wednesdays and Fridays, recalling on Wednesdays Judas' betrayal of Jesus and on Fridays Jesus' sacrificial death for the sins of mankind.

In explaining reasons for fasting, Father Slavko Barbaric, a spiritual adviser to the visionaries, has said that fasting should not be done to make one suffer. We should look at fasting in a positive way. Fasting was recommended and done by Jesus. Throughout Scripture, fasting has been recommended and followed for overcoming Satan and the power of his darkness. It is to help us become more open before our Eternal Father and more sensitive to the hungers and needs of others. In putting material things aside, we become more open to the spiritual. Fasting helps us, too, in better recognizing the heavenly bread of the Eucharist. Pray for the gifts of fasting, prayer, and love, he has encouraged.

In Medjugorje the people eat very wholesome, home-baked bread, sometimes fortified with potatoes. The water they drink during fasting is often mineral water. The visionaries and members of three youth prayer groups sometimes have fasted several days a week, especially when Mary has requested additional prayer for specific needs. They have fasted, too, for three to nine days before major feast days.

If not able to follow "the best fast" of bread and water, don't give up fasting altogether, say spiritual advisers. To keep going, some people have a little soup, fruit, yogurt, and/or vegetables. If not physically able to fast from food, follow some other form of fasting or penance, suggests Mary. Practice self-denial for the sake of Jesus Christ and for the Father's intentions for conversions and the spreading of His peace. You can fast from alcohol, smoking, or television, she suggests. She has pointed out that TV often can be a great source of sin, because after watching so many programs people feel incapable of praying. Mary has suggested fasting other than from food on Thursdays, perhaps giving up some leisure-time activity.

Many expressions of such penance can be witnessed at Medjugorje, as when some visionaries, youth prayer group members, and others climb the steep and rocky path of Mt. Krizevac at night—all the way up to the large cross at the top. En route they pray at each station of the cross for Mary's intentions, while offering up their own sacrifices as penance. A special call for prayer has been issued for priests and bishops.

Prayer

Mary's most frequent messages have concerned prayer with the heart—spending time in loving concentration on God's presence and on the words being exchanged in prayer. "The most important thing in life is to pray," she said in December of 1983. "Prayer is a conversation with God. To pray means to listen to God," she explained on October 20, 1984. "Prayer is useful for you, because after prayer everything is clear. Prayer makes one know happiness," she continued.

Mary has said that every kind of prayer is pleasing to God— conversational prayer, formal prayer, prayer with use of the Bible, and simply being quiet in God's presence. One only learns to pray through doing it, she taught. "You wish to live all that I tell you, but you are not successful in it because you do not pray enough." "Therefore, from today decide seriously to dedicate time to God!" she repeated on October 25, 1989. "Pray, pray, pray."

Frequently Mary has encouraged seeking help from the Holy Spirit in prayer, as before and during Mass. **"The important thing is to pray to the Holy Spirit so that He may descend on you. When one has Him, one has everything,"** she emphasized on October 21, 1983. Continuing on that day she commented, "People make a mistake when they turn only to the saints to request something."

Consecrate each day to the Holy Spirit, and ask for His help when starting prayer, Mary has requested. Ask Him for understanding and for assistance in following God. Pray for His blessings on Church authorities and the whole world. Request His help for being open to God and surrendering to His will.

In a message on April 17, 1986, Mary said, **"Dear children, you are preoccupied with material things, and thus you lose everything that God wants to give you. Pray then, dear children, for the gifts of the Holy Spirit. They are necessary for you, in order that you may give witness to my presence here and to everything that I give you."**

Some particularly relevant messages are the following.

Weekly and monthly messages in "the school of prayer"

From March 1984 until January 1987, Mary provided weekly messages for parishioners and for those throughout the world wishing to live these messages. In what some call "the school of prayer" and "the school of holiness," messages were given about prayer and love. Messages given since then on the twenty-fifth of each month provide spiritual instruction to the faithful all over the world.

"Pray to Jesus. I am His mother, and I will intercede with Him. I will help. I will pray with you... We always are close when called upon. I always want you to be closer to your Father. Open your hearts to God like flowers in spring, yearning for the sun. Let prayer be LIFE for you!" Mary has described prayer as a sign of our surrender to God—a surrender which she is requesting more and more, "A COMPLETE SURRENDER."

On May 25, 1987, Our Lady explained, "I am your mother, and I desire to lead all of you to complete holiness. I wish for each of you to be happy on earth and then to be with me in Heaven. This, dear children, is my purpose in coming here, and my desire."

Prayer at Mass and Eucharistic Adoration

"I am calling you to more attentive prayer, and to greater participation in the Mass! I want you to experience God within yourselves at Mass!" In a series of different messages about the Mass, Mary emphasized the following: **"Come in love and accept the Holy Mass! Let everyone coming to Mass be joyful! The Mass is the greatest prayer from God, and you will never understand the greatness of it. Let Holy Mass be your life!"**

"Be humble at Mass. Prepare for it. I want Holy Mass to be the gift of the day for you! Before Mass it is necessary to pray to the Holy Spirit! Prayers to the Holy Spirit always should accompany the Mass. Jesus Christ gives Himself to you during Mass. Give thanks! Adore continually the Most Holy Sacrament of the Altar... I always am present when the faithful are in adoration. Then special graces are being received."

Prayer with Scripture

Frequently Mary encourages parishioners and others to practice family prayer and Bible reading. "Read what has been written about Jesus!" Mary recommended on June 2, 1983. "Meditate on it and convey it to others! Today I ask you to read your Bible in your home every day," she urged on October 18, 1984. "Place it in a visible place there, where it will remind you to read it and to pray."

Through Jelena, Mary said: "If you want to be stronger than evil, make an active conscience for yourself. Pray a reasonable amount in the morning. Read a text of Holy Scripture. Plant the divine Word in your heart, and try to live it during the day—especially in moments of trial. So you will be stronger than evil." In March 1984, through Jelena, Mary asked for the reading of Matthew 6:24-34 by parishioners when coming together for the weekly Thursday messages.

Prayer with the rosary

"I beg the families of the parish to pray the family rosary," requested Mary on September 27, 1984. Through Jakov on October 8, 1984, Mary had this to say about the rosary: "All the prayers which you recite in the evening in your homes, dedicate them for the conversion of sinners, because the world is immersed in a great moral decay. Recite the rosary each evening. Pray and let the rosary always be in your hands as a sign to Satan that you belong to me." On a visit to California in December of 1989, Ivan recommended taking time for quality prayers. He suggested that those praying the rosary sometimes read small portions of the Bible before or after each decade, meditate on how the passages apply to one's own life, talk to God in one's own words, and then thank Him.

Through Jelena, members of the youth prayer groups in Medjugorje were encouraged to pray the Jesus Rosary. It contains thirty-three Our Fathers and reflections about Jesus, such as His trust and sacrificial love.

On June 25, 1985, when Mary was asked what was desired for priests, she responded: "I urge you to ask everyone to pray the rosary. With the rosary you will overcome all the troubles which Satan is trying to inflict on the Catholic Church. Let all priests pray the rosary. Give time to the rosary."

Prayer for the souls in purgatory

All six of the visionaries have seen Heaven and purgatory, and four have seen hell. They say that more souls go to purgatory than to Heaven or hell. In purgatory there are many different levels, some close to Heaven and some close to hell. Mary has recommended praying at least seven each of the Our Father, Hail Mary, and Glory Be, plus the Apostles' Creed, for the souls in purgatory and for their

204 THE THUNDER OF JUSTICE

intentions. Souls there are waiting for your prayers and sacrifices, Mary has emphasized.

Vicka and Jakov have said they actually were taken to Heaven, hell, and purgatory. Vicka has described seeing a vast area of grayness in purgatory but tremendous joy in Heaven on the faces of those she viewed there. She reported that on Christmas Day more souls enter Heaven from purgatory than on any other day in the year.

"Today I invite you to pray every day for the souls in purgatory," Mary has told us through the visionaries. "Every soul needs prayer and grace in order to reach God and His love. By this way, dear children, you will gain new intercessors, who will help you during your life to discern that nothing on earth is more important for you than striving for Heaven. For that, dear children, pray without respite, so that you may be able to help yourselves and others to whom your prayers will bring joy." Mary gave this message on November 6, 1986.

Prayer of protection

Satan temporarily has been allowed power in this Twentieth Century, reports Mary. However, through prayer and fasting we can disarm him totally and ensure our happiness. Even now he has begun to lose his power and has become aggressive. He is destroying marriages and creating divisions among priests. He is responsible for obsessions and murders, Mary explained.

"Protect yourselves through prayer and fasting, and especially community prayer. Restore the use of holy water." On July 18, 1985 Mary said, "Today I invite you to put more blessed objects in your homes, and may every person carry blessed objects... because you are armored against Satan, he will tempt you less."

"You know that I promised you an oasis of peace; but you do not know that around this oasis is a desert, where Satan watches and tries to tempt each one of you. Dear children, it is only through prayer that you will be able to overcome every influence of Satan, wherever you may be. I am with you, but I cannot deprive you of your free will," she declared on August 7, 1986.

Prayer for healings

On July 25, 1982, the feast of the parish patron, Saint James, Our Lady recommended the following as being important: praying the

Apostles Creed; praying the Our Father, Hail Mary, and Glory Be seven times; and fasting on bread and water.

"It is good to impose one's hands on the sick and to pray. It is good to anoint the sick with holy oil. All priests do not have the gift of healing. In order to receive this gift, the priest must pray with perseverance and believe firmly."

Those participating in services at Medjugorje have taken very seriously their responsibilities to unite in fervent and loving prayers for the needs of those present and those for whom prayers are offered. Healing prayers and occasional anointings with oil by priests have followed evening Masses.

It is believed that such caring and concerned prayer in this atmosphere of reconciliation, love, and unity—united with Our Lady's intercession—has helped produce a large number of remarkable healings. The people at Medjugorje have been setting a beautiful example of what can be done to help bring about healing throughout the world.

Prayer before the cross

"**Dear children, I wish to tell you these days to put the cross at the center of your life. Pray especially before the cross, which is the origin of great graces. In your homes make a special consecration to the cross of the Lord. Promise that you will not offend Jesus and that you will not insult Him or the cross.**" This was a message of September 12, 1985.

On February 20, 1986, Our Lady urged: "Renew your prayer before the cross. Dear children, I am giving you special graces; and Jesus is giving you special gifts from the cross. Take them and live! Meditate on the passion of Jesus. Unite your life to Jesus!"

Prayer of total surrender

"I want to call you to prayer and to a total surrender to God. I come here in order to show you the way of peace and that of the salvation of your soul. I beg you, dear children, to give yourselves totally; and you will be able to live all I tell you." On January 25, 1990, Mary exclaimed: "...choose Him before everything and above everything, so that He may work miracles in your life and that, day by day, your life may become a joy with Him.

"Little children, do not forget that your life is fleeting like a spring flower—so beautiful today and totally disappeared tomorrow. Therefore, pray, so that your prayer and your surrender to God may become a sign. Thus your testimony will be of value not only to yourselves, but to everyone throughout eternity."

Prayer within families and with the community

Our Blessed Lady has encouraged community prayer and family prayer most of all. "May prayer hold the first place in your families," she begged as our mother. "Each family **must** pray and read the Bible," she emphasized on February 14, 1985, one of only a few occasions when she used a Croatian word meaning **must**. Mary has asked that family members pray together regularly for unbelievers, for those sinning, and for the living of the messages. "Encourage the very young to pray and go to Holy Mass. You are all important, especially the elderly within families. Invite them to pray. Let all the young people by their lives be an example for others. Let them be witnesses for Jesus.

"Love your neighbors, especially those who hurt you. Begin by loving your own families and everyone in the parish, and then you will be able to accept and love all those coming. Spiritual renewal is needed for the entire Church. Pray for the outpouring of the Holy Spirit to renew your families and your parish." When asked on April 11, 1982, whether it was necessary to establish prayer groups in the parish, Mary responded by saying, "Communities of prayer are necessary in all parishes."

Father Tomislav Vlasic's Letter To The Pope

The following is a letter sent to the Pope by Father Tomislav Vlasic of Medjugorje on December 2, 1983, providing information to the Vatican on the apparitions and their messages. Father Tom is from Yugoslavia; he has followed the apparitions of Medjugorje from the very beginning and is considered one of the principal sources of valid information. In the letter he addressed the issues of peace, the visible sign, and the ten secrets. Father Vlasic eventually became the pastor of Saint James parish. The letter reads as follows:

"After the apparition of the Blessed Virgin on November 30, 1983, Maria Pavlovic came to see me and said, "The Madonna says that the Supreme Pontiff and the Bishop must be advised immediately of the urgency and great importance of the message of Medjugorje."

"This letter seeks to fulfill that duty.

"1. Five young people (Vicka Ivankovic, Maria Pavlovic, Ivanka Ivankovic, Ivan Dragicevic, and Jakov Colo) see an apparition of the Blessed Virgin every day. The experience in which they see her is a fact that can be checked by direct observation. It has been filmed. During the apparitions, the youngsters do not react to light, they do not hear sounds, they do not react if someone touches them, they feel that they are beyond time and space.

"All of the youngsters basically agree that:

- "We see the Blessed Virgin just as we see anyone else. We pray with her, we speak to her, and we can touch her."

- "The Blessed Virgin says that world peace is at a critical stage. She repeatedly calls for reconciliation and conversion."

- "She has promised to leave a visible sign for all humanity at the site of the apparitions of Medjugorje."

- "The period preceding this visible sign is a time of grace for conversion and deepening the faith."

- "The Blessed Virgin has promised to disclose ten secrets to us. So far, Vicka Ivankovic has received eight. Marija Pavlovic received the ninth one on December 8, 1983. Jakov Colo, Ivan Dragicevic and Ivanka Ivankovic have each received nine. Only Mirjana Dragicevic has received all ten."

- "These apparitions are the last apparitions of the Blessed Virgin on earth. That is why they are lasting so long and occurring so frequently."

"2. The Blessed Virgin no longer appears to Mirjana Dragicevic. The last time she saw one of the daily apparitions was Christmas 1982. Since then the apparitions have ceased for her, except on her birthday (March 18, 1983). Mirjana knew that this would occur.

"According to Mirjana, the Madonna confided the tenth and last secret to her during the apparition on December 25, 1982. She also disclosed the dates on which the different secrets will come to pass. The Blessed Virgin has revealed to Mirjana many things about the future, more than to any of the other youngsters so far. For that reason I am reporting below what Mirjana told me during our conversation on November 5, 1983. I am summarizing the substance of her account, without word-for-word quotations.

"Mirjana said that before the visible sign is given to humanity, there will be three warnings to the world. The warnings will be in the form of events on earth. Mirjana will be a witness to them. Three days before one of the admonitions, Mirjana will notify a priest of her choice. The witness of Mirjana will be a confirmation of the apparitions and a stimulus for the conversion of the world.

"After the admonitions, the visible sign will appear on the site of the apparitions in Medjugorje for all the world to see. The sign will be given as a testimony to the apparitions and in order to call the people back to the faith.

"The ninth and tenth secrets are serious. They concern chastisement for the sins of the world. Punishment is inevitable, for we cannot expect the whole world to be converted. The punishment can be diminished by prayer and penance, but it cannot be eliminated. Mirjana says that one of the evils that threatened the world, the one contained in the seventh secret, has been averted, thanks to prayer and fasting. That is why the Blessed Virgin continues to encourage prayer and fasting: 'You have forgotten that through prayer and fasting you can avert war and suspend the laws of nature.'

"After the first admonition, the others will follow in a rather short time. Thus, people will have some time for conversion.

"That interval will be a period of grace and conversion. After the visible sign appears, those who are still alive will have little time for conversion. For that reason, the Blessed Virgin invites us to urgent conversion and reconciliation. The invitation to prayer and penance is meant to avert evil and war, but most of all to save souls.

"According to Mirjana, the events predicted by the Blessed Virgin are near. By virtue of this experience, Mirjana proclaims to the world: 'Hurry, be converted; open your hearts to God.'

"In addition to this basic message, Mirjana related an apparition she had in 1982, which we believe sheds some light on some aspects of Church history. She spoke of an apparition in which Satan appeared to her disguised as the Blessed Virgin. Satan asked Mirjana to renounce the Madonna and follow him. That way she could be happy in love and in life. He said that following the Virgin, on the contrary, would only lead to suffering. Mirjana rejected him, and immediately the Virgin arrived and Satan disappeared. Then the Blessed Virgin gave her the following message in substance:

"Excuse me for this, but you must realize that Satan exists. One day he appeared before the throne of God and asked permission to submit the Church to a period of trial. God gave him permission to try the Church for one century. This century is under the power of the devil; but when the secrets confided to you come to pass, his power will be destroyed. Even now he is beginning to lose his power and has become aggressive. He is destroying marriages, creating divisions among priests and is responsible for obsessions and murder. You must protect yourselves against these things through fasting and prayer, especially community prayer. Carry blessed objects with you. Put them in your house, and restore the use of holy water.

"According to certain Catholic experts who have studied these apparitions, this message of Mirjana may shed light on the vision Pope Leo XIII had. According to them, it was after having had an apocalyptic vision of the future of the Church that Leo XIII introduced the prayer to Saint Michael which priests used to recite after Mass up to the time of the Second Vatican Council. These experts say that the century of trials foreseen by Leo XIII is about to end.

"Holy Father, I do not want to be responsible for the ruin of anyone. I am doing my best. The world is being called to conversion and reconciliation. In writing to you, Holy Father, I am only doing my duty. After drafting this letter, I gave it to the youngsters so that they might ask the Blessed Virgin whether its contents are accurate. Ivan Dragicevic relayed the following answer: 'Yes, the contents of the letter are the truth. You must notify first the Supreme Pontiff and then the Bishop.'

"This letter is accompanied by fasting and prayers that the Holy Spirit will guide your mind and your heart during this important moment in history."

Yours, in the Sacred Hearts of Jesus and Mary,
Father Tomislav Vlasic
Medjugorje, December 2, 1983

Life Like The Ancients

After a taped interview, Father Tomislav gave a little information about the secrets on August 15, 1983. They (the seers) say that with the realization of the secrets entrusted to them by Our Lady, life in the world will change! What will change and how it will change, we don't know, given that the seers don't want to say anything about the secrets."[3]

Father Tomislav continued, **"Life in the world will change. Afterwards men will believe like in ancient times.** These few words imply a lot about extraordinary events, that lie ahead and for which Our Lady came to prepare the world at Medjugorje." This theme is consistent with the severity and urgency of other apparitions that are mentioned in this book. It must be remembered that Quito, Ecuador, Fatima, Akita, and many of those we mention have either a stigmatist in their midst, full approval by Rome, or approval by the local bishop. To date, Medjugorje has not been approved by Roman Catholic authorities nor has it been condemned but is presently being investigated. Pope John Paul II does not discourage anyone regarding Medjugorje. On April 21, 1989, Bishop Paul Hnilica, SJ, Auxiliary Bishop of Rome, reported that he had been admonished by the Holy Father for not stopping in Medjugorje on his return trip to Rome after a meeting in Moscow on behalf of the Pope. The Pope said to Bishop Hnilica, "If I wasn't the Pope, I'd be in Medjugorje already."[4] Those who know this Pope are aware of his long-standing devotion to Our Blessed Mother.

The messages of Medjugorje have simultaneously been a source of warning and inspiration for untold millions. It has been a beacon of light as its messages lift our spirits as the Blessed Mother places the world under her protective mantle. Medjugorje's impact throughout the world is unprecedented in Church history with its fruits reaching peoples of all nations. It has been a great gift from Heaven.

Book III
Signs And
Tribulations

The Twin Pillars of Don Bosco. "The vision he had of the Church in the end days with the Eucharist on the larger pillar and the Blessed Mother on the lesser pillar. Don Bosco said, "There will be chaos in the Church. Tranquillity will not return until the Pope succeeds in anchoring the boat of Peter between the Twin Pillars of Eucharistic Devotion and devotion to Our Lady. This will come about one year before the end of the century." (Prediction made in 1862 for the end of the 20th Century).

In addition to his prophetic dreams, so many miraculous occurrences happened to and around Don Bosco that Pope Pius XI said of his life, "The supernatural almost became natural, and the extraordinary ordinary."

The Virgin of Revelation as she appeared to Bruno Cornacchiola at Tre Fontane, Italy, in 1947. The Blessed Mother said, "I am the Daughter of the Father, the Mother of the Son, the Spouse of the Holy Spirit." When the Blessed Mother appeared to Bruno he was on his way to assassinate the Pope.

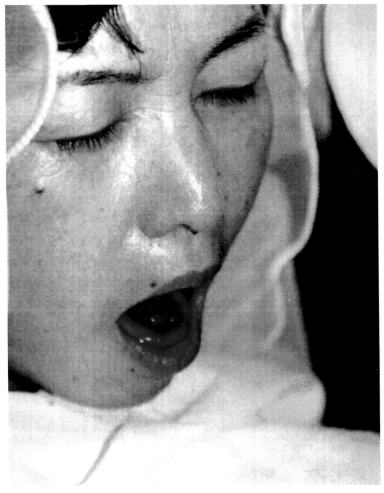

Eucharistic Miracle of Julia Kim, stigmatist, on Sept. 22, 1995 at a Mass concelebrated by Bishop Roman Danylak of Toronto in Naju, Korea.

Julia Kim with the Papal Nuncio. The Papal Nuncio (right) was sent by the Vatican to investigate Julia's Eucharistic phenomena and while receiving communion, she experienced another Eucharistic Miracle.

Julia Kim, stigmatist, of Naju, Korea with Cardinal Sin of the Philippines, 1992.

Statue in the home of Julia Kim.

The statue weeping tears of blood in the home of Julia Kim. The reason for the tears of blood as told to us by Our Lady: ABORTION. Julia is a victim soul for the world because of the sin of abortion.

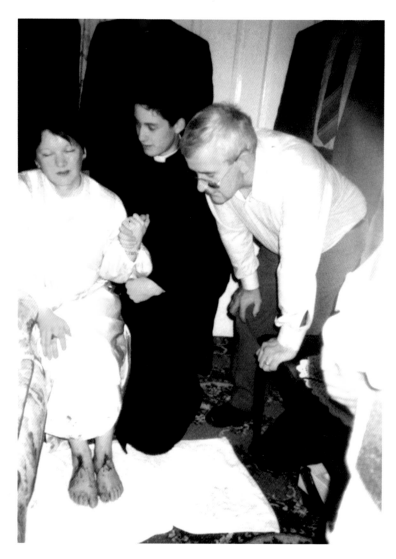

Christina Gallagher, stigmatist and visionary, of County Mayo in Ireland, experiencing bleeding like the wounds of Jesus. Christina's messages speak heavily about the loss of faith in the world.

Padre Pio under obedience shows his stigmata in 1919.

Padre Pio of Italy (1887-1968) as an older man saying Mass with the visible stigmata. Padre Pio once said, "It would be easier for the world to exist without the sun than the Holy Sacrifice of the Mass."

Eucharistic Miracle at Saint Vincent de Paul parish of Yardsville, New Jersey, in 1994 on the Feast of Divine Mercy. This miracle was prophesied in advance by Our Lady as a sign to show the authenticity of the apparitions of Joe Januszkiewicz of Marlboro, New Jersey. The Eucharist has bled several times since the first occurrence.

The statue of "Our Lady of Lourdes Yellow Rose of Peace" at the home of Joe Januskiewicz, visionary of Marlboro, New Jersey.

Dr. Francis Hennessey, Peg Hennessey, Colleen Flynn, Joe and his wife, Ronnie Januszkiewicz at his home in Marlboro, New Jersey in 1995. (Left to Right).

Eucharistic Miracle of Father Sweeney of Ogden, Utah in 1995. The cloth on the altar has blood stains. This occured on the Feast of Corpus Christi.

Eucharistic Miracle of Santarem, Portugal in 1247 being held in a monstrance, 1994.

Pope John Paul II and Father Stefano Gobbi of Milan, Italy. Father Gobbi is the founder and leader of the worldwide movement, the Marian Movement of Priests (MMP).

Pope John Paul II with the Bulgarian assassin Ali Agea in his prison cell. On May 13, 1981, Pope John Paul II was seriously wounded as the Communist backed plot to kill the Pope failed.

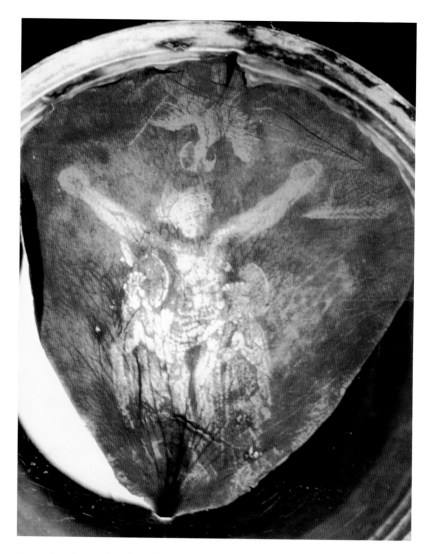

Miraculous image found on the rose petal in Quezon City, Philippines that fell from the sky during Our Lady's apparitions. The image is of Jesus on the Cross with a dove over His head and the image of two women at the foot of the cross. On enlarged photographs of the rose petal, the images are crystal clear. Hundreds of rose petals have different images of the life of Jesus and the Holy Family. At the apparition site where she appears, she came under the title of, "Mother of the Eucharist and Grace."

Another miraculous rose petal of the Blessed Mother in the image of the Miraculous Medal. By her right hand are the easily detectable words, 'O Mary conceived without sin, pray for us who have recourse to thee.' This inscription encircles the image as it does on the Miraculous Medal of St. Catherine Laboure.

"Our Lady of the Eucharist" painting as seen by visionary Luz Amparo Cuevas of Escorial, Spain.

Picture taken of the "Sun Dancing" where a Eucharist appeared in the center of a chalice in Escorial, Spain, 1984.

Picture taken at Garabandal, Spain in 1984 where an image of a chalice appeared. Messages on the Eucharist were of significant emphasis at Garabandal during the apparitions from 1961 – 1965 where the Blessed Mother appeared over 2,000 times. The Blessed Mother foretold of attacks on the EUCHARIST and the priesthood.

The children of Garabandal, Spain, in ecstasy. Mari Loli and Jacinta fall inside the village church in Garabandal, Spain.

Left to right: the children of Garabandal, Spain: Mari Loli, Conchita, Mari Cruz and Jacinta.

Conchita as an adult now living in New York City.

The "Miracle of the Eucharist" — December 8th, 1991, Betania, Venezula — A very rare phenomenon — a modern day miracle.

The grotto in Betania, Venezula, where hundreds of thousands visit.

Maria Esperanza of Betania, Venezula. The miraculous as ordinary for a good part of her life. Healer, mystic, and visionary. Many occurrences of the supernatural grace her.

Maria outside the church in Betania with a group of pilgrims.

The picture of St. Joesph with the child Jesus. St. Joseph is Patron and Guardian of the Universal Church. At many apparitions throughout the world, St. Joseph is present as he was at Fatima, Portugal in 1917.

Danny Flynn at Garabandal, Spain in the chapel in front of a statue of St. Michael the Archangel.

The church today in the mountains of La Salette, France. A glorious and magnificent setting.

The visionaries of La Salette, France: Melanie Calvat and Maximin Giraud at the time of the visions of the Blessed Mother in 1846. The messages are relevant today.

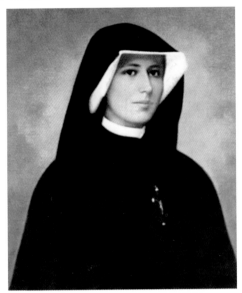

Blessed Sister Faustina Kowalska of the Most Blessed Sacrament. "My mission will not come to an end upon my death . . . I will draw aside for you the veils of heaven to convince you of God's goodness" (Diary, 281). Sister Faustina was beatified in April, 1993.

The "Divine Mercy" vision of Jesus given to Sister Faustina of Poland with the rays of love flowing forth from His heart to the world.

A statue of "Our Lady of Lourdes" located at Signs of the Times Catholic Resource Center in Sterling, Virginia. The statue teared for over six weeks beginning March 21, 1991. Our Lady has told Father Gobbi, "I am weeping because, in great numbers, the souls of my children, are being lost and going to hell."

Reyes and Estela Ruiz near the cross which is prominent in their yard in Phoenix, Arizonia. Estela has been receiving apparitions and messages from Our Lady since December 1990 with many messages for the United States.

Bernardita, Patricia Talbot, and Patricia's mother at a Papal Audience in April 1990. Patricia is presenting the Holy Father with a special message from Our Lady.

Patricia Talbot in ecstasy in the garden sanctuary in February, 1990. It was raining at the time. "Pachi" started receiving messages and apparitions in the late 1980's.

Our Lady of Fatima, 1917. Our Blessed Mother said, "If men do not repent, then Russia will spread her errors throughout the world." This was said by Our Lady before the Communist revolution. In this century we have seen how truly prophetic were her words.

This is a marble replica of the angel at Fatima, Portugal holding the Eucharist and appearing to the three young children Jacinta, Francisco, Lucia in 1917. At Fatima, the Blessed Mother predicted World War II and the role of Russia for this century.

This picture was taken in March 1972 on the eve of Roe vs. Wade (legalizing abortion in the U.S. in 1973) as a part of a French nuclear test explosion. Note Jesus on the cross in the middle and Our Lady on the top left.

Left to right: Nicolas Kripakov of Denver, Colorado; Father Slavomir of Lublin, Poland; Ted Flynn and Father Tadduez of Poland at a church reconstruction site in Gomel, Belarus. Rebuilding the churches where the Communists made church destruction into an art form. Under Stalin, if you were active in the church you would be taken away in the middle of the night and never heard from again.

The "dead zone" above Chernobyl where the food chain is contaminated for thousands of years. Thousands of houses were evacuated overnight and permanantly abandoned. The winds brought fallout as far north as Finland in less than two days and contaminated soil for thousands of miles in many directions. Mary appeared at Hrushiv, Ukraine on the first anniversary of Chernobyl to the minute. The fruit of Communism was CHERNOBYL. Mary has said, "Chernobyl is a sign for the world."

The church in Hrushiv, western Ukraine, where hundreds of thousands saw the Blessed Mother appear above the church — a suffering church granted the grace of seeing.

Josyp Terelya formerly of the Ukraine and religious prisoner with Ted Flynn and a peasant, in front of the miraculous well in the tiny church at Hrushiv.

Portrait of Josyp Terelya. Josyp Terelya spent over twenty years in the Soviet gulag system as a prisoner because of his unbending faith and his unwillingness to submit to the atheistic Soviet totalitarian system. He has had many visions of future world events.

St. Maximilian Maria Kolbe founded the Knights of the Immaculata. Their purpose was simple: to conquer all souls for Christ through Mary Immaculate. Father Kolbe wrote, "Modern times are dominated by Satan and will be more so in the future. The conflict with Hell cannot be engaged by men, even the most clever. The Immaculata alone has from God the promise of victory over Satan." (Picture courtesy of Ave Maria Institute, from I Knew Blessed Maximilian Kolbe, by J. Mlodozeniec).

"Our Lady of All Nations", as seen by Ida in Amsterdam. Note the similarity to the statue of "Our Lady of Akita".

"Our Lady of Soufanieh", Damascus, Syria. Mirna, the visionary has had this icon where oil has come from it for many years.

The statue of "Our Lady of Akita", in Akita, Japan. The statue wept 101 times in 1973. The statue is very similar to the picture of "Our Lady of All Nations" in Amsterdam.

The international "Pilgrim Virgin" (Our Lady of Fatima) and the miraculous statue of Our Lady of Akita. Bishop Ito said: "The message of Akita is the same as that of Fatima."

Sister Anna Ali of Nigeria, stigmatist with strong messages for the world about the days in which we live. Her messages have Archbishop approval. Sister Anna says this about Our Lord, "He was in great pain because of the way those to whom He entrusted souls are treating Him. Some of them abuse Him in the Holy Eucharist and want to destroy Him there. They want to abolish the sacrifice of the Holy Mass. He is also unhappy about the spiritual life of souls consecrated to Him and those whose salvation is in danger, and also for many souls for whom His blood is in vain."

Mother Teresa of Calcutta: Model of love, work, and humility; a sign of contradiction in the world today.

Mark Treanor and Christina Gallagher of Ireland. Both have received apparitions and messages from Our Lady. Christina has the stigmata.

On March 25, 1858, on the Feast of the Annunciation, Our Lady proclaimed to young Bernadette, "I am the Immaculate Conception."

"Our Lady's Tears." The Missionary Image of Our Lady of Guadalupe appears in this photograph weeping tears of oil in front of a Christian Congregation in 1994. The angel told Sister Agnes of Akita, Japan, that Our Lady's statue wept tears "because she wishes the conversion of the greatest number. She desires that souls be consecrated to Jesus and to the Father by her intercession." Our Lady's tears belong to the order of signs: they testify to the presence of the Mother in the Church and in the world. A mother weeps when she sees her children threatened by evil, be it spiritual or physical. In the picture below is the same Missionary Image where the Shekinah Cloud of Fire appears above Our Lady of Guadalupe. For many years pilgrims visiting apparition sites around the world thought film was overexposed upon developing. It has been revealed that the light surrounding these holy objects is the Shekinah Glory. See Numbers 9:15-16.

Vicka Ivankovic, visionary of Medjugorje with pilgrims, 1990.

The Pilgrim Statue of Medjugorje weeps tears. Over many years, this statue has wept dozens of times in front of thousands of people as it has visited hundreds of homes and churches in the U.S.

The famous statue of "Our Lady of Grace", that once was in the church of Father Jozo from Medjugorje.

Danny and Colleen Flynn with Ivan Dragicevic of Medjugorje in the Flynn home, 1992.

St. James Church, Medjugorje. An estimated 20 million pilgrims have visited this site since 1981, where the Blessed Mother has said, "I will give you messages like never before in all of history, and I come to tell you God exists." The apparitions at Medjugorje will be the last of the Blessed Mother on earth.

The cross at Mount Krizevac, overlooks the village of Medjugorje. It was built in 1933.

A miraculous photograph of a picture taken at Medjugorje and when developed, the Blessed Mother was holding all fifteen decades of the Rosary.

A statue seen weeping blood in Agoo, Philippines in February 1993.

The Blessed Mother above the Coptic Church in Zeitoun, Egypt, where millions of people witnessed her image in 1968.

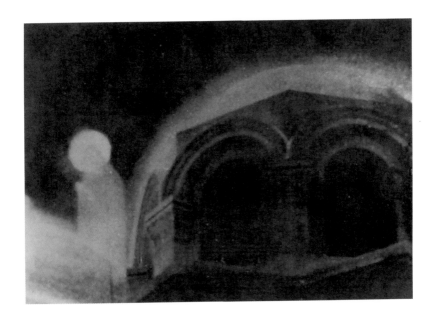

Painting of "Our Lady of the Most Blessed Sacrament".

"Mary: The Mystical Rose" The color of the white rose means the spirit of prayer. Red-expiation. Yellow or golden means the spirit of penitence. Over 70 Rosa Mystica statues have wept around the world.

Jim Singer, visionary of Toronto, Canada, with wife Natalie, daughters Ingrid (left) and Alpina. The Lord prophesied about the war in Bosnia before it occured. The Lord said to Jim, "Satan is the 'shining darkness.'"

Josefina-Maria, (white shirt) visionary of Melbourne, Australia, greeting the Pope. Her messages speak of the necessity of devotion to the Twin Hearts. The Blessed Mother said to Josefina, "In this century, many of you will see the Triumph of My Miraculous Heart."

Los Angeles Earthquake, January 1994. A world not connected to the things of Heaven. Messages foretell earthquakes and natural disasters of unprecedented proportions in the years ahead.

A truly remarkable photo of the icon of Jesus King of All Nations being carried through the square at Fatima in 1992. During the procession, a white dove landed on the painting as if to say, "I saw the Spirit descend like a dove from the sky, and it came to rest on Him." (John 1: 32) This was also the 75th Anniversary of Fatima.

Emmanuel Segatashya, one of the seven visionaries of Kibeho, Rwanda, Africa. Jesus told Emmanuel, "I am coming to prepare you for my second coming." Emmanuel was martyred during the war. The Blessed Mother said in Rwanda: "It will become a river of blood unless there are conversions." Over one million are dead since the beginning of the war.

The Holy Face, The Shroud of Turin is thought by a team of scientists to be the tablecloth of the Last Supper and the burial garment of Jesus.

The Blessed Mother appearing to Saint Catherine Laboure at Rue de Bac, Paris, France in 1830. The Blessed Mother held a golden globe up to God, with her eyes raised heavenward; her lips praying for the whole world in its great need—for every person in particular. Rays (graces) streaming from her hands, fell upon the large globe on which she stood. The Blessed Mother ushered in the Marian Age at this site.

The statue of the Blessed Mother in the church at Rue de Bac, Paris, coming under the title as the Virgin of the Globe. Directly under the statue is the incorrupt body of Saint Catherine Laboure.

Father James Bruse of Kilmarnock, Virginia. Father Bruse has had the stigmata since December 1991. Many conversions and healings have occurred through the prayers of this priest. He is only the third priest in the history of the church (known) with the stigmata. He is one of the spiritual directors for the Jesus King of All Nations Devotion.

This photo was taken of the Pope's plane SHEPHERD I, (in the U.S., TWA) by an employee of TWA upon arriving in Baltimore, Md. in October, 1995. As in many photo's the Shekinah Glory appears. For many years this was thought to be a problem in developing the film. See Numbers 9:15-16.

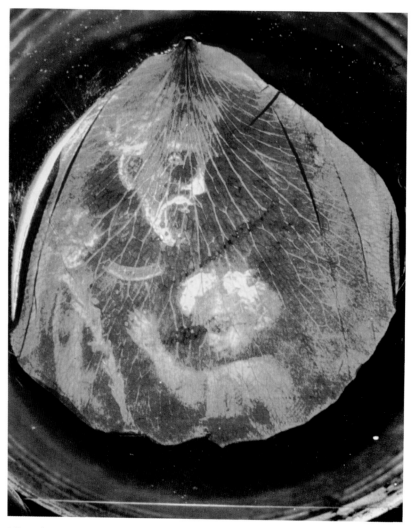

Miraculous rose petal in Quezon City, Philippines of St. Joseph and the child Jesus.

Therese Neumann (1898-1962) mystic and stigmatist of Germany. She did not eat, drink, sleep, or have body functions for 40 years—a well documented fact in light of being so contemporary. She lived solely on the Eucharist. When asked in 1945 after World War II if America would ever be destroyed or invaded by war, she responded, "No, at the end of this century America will be destroyed economically by natural disasters." This corresponds with the message of Father Gobbi on November 15, 1990 about America, "The moment of divine justice and of great mercy has now arrived. You will know the hour of weakness and of poverty; the hour of suffering and defeat; the purifying hour of the great chastisement....it is the hour of the great trial."

"Our Lady of the Second Coming" as found in a remote city in Belarus, formerly Byelorussia of the Former Soviet Union. The discovery of the icon was prophesied by a visionary in 1993.

13

Smoke Enters
The Church

But when the Son of Man comes, will he find faith on earth?

Luke 18:8

After the Second Vatican Council, Pope Paul VI remarked that the smoke of Satan was seeping into the Church of God through cracks in the wall. On October 13, 1977, Pope Paul VI told the world: "The tail of the devil is functioning in the disintegration of the Catholic world. The darkness of Satan has entered and spread throughout the Catholic Church even to its summit. Apostasy, the loss of the faith, is spreading throughout the world and into the highest levels within the Church." The tactic of Satan has been to gain control by destroying the Roman Catholic Church. As Mary has so frequently stated, he has been very effective.

Our Blessed Mother revealed the coming of this darkness and apostasy at the apparitions of LaSalette, France, in 1846, and Akita, Japan, in 1973. Our Blessed Mother also revealed this to Father Don Stefano Gobbi of the Marian Movement of Priests in interior locutions. As we have seen, it appears that information about this apostasy was contained in the unrevealed third secret of Fatima.

At LaSalette, France, the Blessed Mother on September 19, 1846, appeared to Melanie Calvat and Maximin Giraud. Mary told Melanie, **"In the year 1864, Lucifer together with a large number of** demons will be unloosed from hell; they will put an end to faith little by little, even in those dedicated to God. Woe to the Princes of the Church who think only of piling riches upon riches to protect their authority and dominate with pride. The Vicar of my Son will suffer a great deal, because for a while the Church will yield to large persecution, a time of darkness, and the Church will witness a frightful crisis.... Rome will lose the faith and become the seat of the Antichrist. **For now is the time of all times, the end of all ends. The Church will be in eclipse, the world will be in dismay....** Now is the time; the abyss is opening. Here is the king of kings of darkness, here is the Beast with his subjects, calling himself the savior of the world."

Maximin Giraud spoke of a monster—most likely communism—which was about to come into the world. "The monster shall arrive at the end of this Nineteenth Century, or at latest, at the commencement of the Twentieth." Our Blessed Mother told Maximin, **"For behold, the age of ages, the end, the extremity is at hand! The Church passes into darkness. The world will be in a state of consternation, perplexity and confusion."**[1]

At the time of and after these apparitions, the Church was under siege from the adherents of false philosophical systems, the Freemasons, associated secret societies, and the state. The Illuminated Freemasons in 1829 met in New York and formed a committee which later financed Karl Marx, the chief architect of atheistic communism. Communism under Lenin and Trotsky replaced the ruling monarchy in Russia by murder and revolution. In 1917, the Russian veterans of World War I overthrew the czar. A short-lived revolutionary government was formed by Alexander Kerensky and in several months was overthrown by Lenin and Trotsky. Thus Soviet Russia, the first large country operating under the tenets of atheistic communism, the Red Dragon, was formed—*at the beginning of the Twentieth Century!*

Pope Pius IX in 1846 in his *Syllabus of Errors* pronounced a solemn condemnation of the erroneous propositions of the modern philosophies, secret societies, and communism. *The Communist Manifesto* was published two years later in 1848. The Church was aware of the seductive power of communism and published other encyclicals condemning it. Pope Leo XIII in 1884 in his encyclical *Humanum Genus* exposed and condemned the propositions of the Freemasons, the affiliated secret societies, and the philosophy of the

Masons which he identified as naturalism. He noted that communism was the sequel to naturalism.

Pope Leo XIII in his encyclical *Quod Apostolici Muneris* defined communism as "the fatal plague which insinuates itself into the very marrow of human society only to bring about its ruin."[2]

In an apparition at Akita on October 13, 1973—an apparition approved by the local bishop—Our Blessed Mother said to Sister Agnes Sasagawa, "As I told you...the work of the devil will infiltrate even into the Church in such a way that one will see cardinals opposing cardinals, bishops against other bishops. The priests who venerate me will be scorned and opposed by their own confreres...the Church will be full of those who accept compromises and the demon will press many priests and consecrated souls to leave the service of the Lord. The demon will be especially implacable against souls consecrated to God."

Our Blessed Mother through Father Gobbi of the Marian Movement of Priests revealed on November 20, 1976: "Satan has now pitched his tents even among the ministers of the sanctuary and has brought the abomination of desolation into the holy temple of God...."

On August 26, 1983, Mary told Father Gobbi: **"Error is being taught and propagated beneath the ambiguous formulas of a new cultural interpretation of the truth; the spirit of the world finds welcome; it spreads its malignant influence and leads so many souls to accept sin, to justify it and to live in it; loss of faith is becoming a deluge, and in many places of worship the images of the saints have been removed, even those of your heavenly mother. The apostasy has now been spread into every part of a Church betrayed even by some of its bishops, abandoned by many of its priests, deserted by so many of its children, and violated by my Adversary."**

On September 15, 1983, she stated to Father Gobbi: "I am beneath the cross being carried today by the bishops who remain faithful, while the number of those who prefer to go their own way grows ever greater, heedless of and refusing to follow the Holy Father, whom Jesus has placed at the very foundation of His Church. They are preparing another Church, one separated from the Pope, and this will cause a further scandal, that of a sorrowful division."

On September 6, 1985, she told Father Gobbi: "There has also entered into the Church disunity, division, strife and antagonism.... These are the times foretold by me, when cardinals will be set against cardinals, bishops against bishops and priests against priests, and the flock of Christ will be torn to pieces by rapacious wolves, who have found their way in under the clothing of defenseless and meek lambs. Among them there are even some who occupy posts of great responsibility and, by means of them, Satan has succeeded in entering and in operating at the very summit of the Church."

Ecclesiastical Masonry

In the message of June 13, 1989, the Blessed Mother warned Father Gobbi of the danger of Ecclesiastical Masonry. Mary said that this form of Masonry:

"1) Works to obscure God's Divine Word, by means of natural and rational interpretations and, in the attempt to make it more understandable and acceptable, empties it of all its supernatural content. Thus errors are spread in every part of the Catholic Church itself. Because of the spread of these errors, many are moving away today from the true faith, bringing to fulfillment the prophecy which was given to you by me at Fatima: The times will come when many will lose the true faith. The loss of the faith is apostasy;

"2) Works, in a subtle and diabolical way, to lead all into apostasy;

"3) Has the aim of justifying sin, of presenting it no longer as an evil but as something good and of value.... The pernicious fruit of this accursed cancer, which has spread throughout the whole Church, is the disappearance everywhere of individual confession;

"4) Favors those forms of exegesis which give the Gospel a rationalistic and natural interpretation, by means of the application of the various literary genres, in such a way that it becomes torn to pieces in all its parts. In the end, one arrives at denying the historical reality of miracles and of the resurrection and places in doubt the very divinity of Jesus and His salvific mission;

"5) Seeks to destroy the Mystical Body of Christ which is the Church;

"6) Seeks to destroy the reality of the hierarchical Church, that is to say, the Pope and the bishops united with him by false ecumenism, which leads to the acceptance of all Christian churches, asserting that each one of them has some part of the truth. It develops the plan of founding a universal ecumenical Church, formed by the fusion of all the Christian confessions, among which is the Catholic Church;

"7) In many subtle ways, seeks to attack the ecclesial devotion towards the sacrament of the Eucharist. It gives value to the meal aspect, tends to minimize its sacrificial value, seeks to deny the real and personal presence of Jesus in the consecrated Host. In this way there are gradually suppressed all the external signs which are indicative of faith in the real presence of Jesus in the Eucharist, such as genuflection, hours of public adoration and the holy custom of surrounding the tabernacle with lights and flowers; and

"8) Seeks to destroy the foundation of unity of the Church, through a subtle and insidious attack on the Pope."

On May 13, 1990, Mary said: "The Church will know the hour of its greatest apostasy. The man of iniquity will penetrate into its interior and will sit in the very Temple of God, while the little remnant which will remain faithful will be subjected to the greatest trials and persecutions."

The Blessed Mother warned Father Gobbi on November 15, 1990: "How great is your responsibility, O Pastors of the holy Church of God! You continue along the path of division from the Pope and the rejection of his Magisterium; indeed, in a hidden way, **there is in preparation a true schism which could soon become open and proclaimed.** And then, there will remain only a small faithful remnant, over which I will keep watch in the garden of my Immaculate Heart. The great trial has arrived for all humanity. The chastisement, predicted by me at Fatima and contained in that part of the secret which has not yet been revealed, is about to take place. **The great moment of divine justice and mercy has come upon the world."**

The Origin Of The Problem

Reasonable persons who are emotionally and intellectually honest with themselves will ask how we have drifted so far from God in so short a time. To understand fully where we are today, we must trace our current confusion to its roots. In the Garden of Eden, Yahweh warned Eve not to eat of the forbidden fruit: "The serpent was the

most subtle of all the wild beasts that Yahweh God had made. It asked
the woman, 'Did God really say you were not to eat from any of the
trees in the garden?' The woman answered the serpent, 'We may eat
the fruit of the trees in the garden. But of the fruit of the tree in the
middle of the garden God said, 'You must not eat it, nor touch it, under
pain of death.' Then the serpent said to the woman, 'No! You will not
die! God knows in fact that on the day you eat it your eyes will be
opened and you will be like gods, knowing good and evil.' The
woman saw that the tree was good to eat and pleasing to the eye, and
that it was desirable for the knowledge that it could give. So she took
some of its fruit and ate it. She gave some also to her husband who was
with her, and he ate it. Then the eyes of both of them were opened and
they realized that they were naked. So they sewed fig leaves together
to make themselves loin-cloths" (Genesis 3:1-7).

There are three players in this exchange: God, the subtle serpent or
the devil, and man. From the beginning, the devil tempted man to be
like God. The serpent offered man intellectual knowledge to become
like God. Man did not heed the warning of God; he ate the forbidden
fruit and suffered the consequences. The participants in the human
drama are the same today as they were then, and the battle for the soul
of man in a never-changing war continues in the heavens. Satan
initially trapped Adam and Eve through appealing to their minds so
he could ensnare their souls. **The battle for our souls usually starts
in the mind with the pride of intellect.**

The attack is aimed at separating man from union with God by
encouraging him to think he can replace or equal God. The devil
encourages us to let reason dominate faith. The early Church Fathers,
on the other hand, combined faith with reason to understand the
world. The early saints and Doctors of the Church developed a
method to comprehend our universe, **inclusive** of God, called Scholasticism.

Early Thinking

Scholasticism is a method of theological and philosophical speculation which aims at a better understanding and deeper penetration of
revealed truths and Christian doctrine through the intellectual pro-
cesses of analogy, definition, speculation, coordination, and system-
atization of these materials.[3] The foundations of Scholasticism were
laid by Saint Augustine. In his *De Doctrina Christiana*, he urged the

use of dialectics to study Christian doctrine, and in his *De Praedestinatione Sanctorum* he claimed that belief was to ponder with assent. Saint Anselm, another foundation-layer of Scholasticism, asserted the duty of reason is to gain fuller understanding of what was given in faith.

When Scholastic philosophers and theologians obtained translations from the Greek of Aristotle, the period of high Scholasticism began. Saint Albert the Great (Albertus Magnus, the teacher of Aquinas) and Saint Thomas Aquinas tried to harmonize Augustine and Aristotle. Lines were drawn between the declarations of faith and reason by the use of argument, counterargument, and resolution of the dispute.[4]

The pervasive and continuing conflict between religion, science, and philosophy has helped produce the secularism of our times. How did it come about that a major part of the educated classes in Europe and America has lost faith in the theology that for nearly sixteen centuries gave supernatural sanctions and supports to the precarious and uncongenial moral code upon which Western civilization has been based? What are the effects—in morals, literature, and politics—of this silent but fundamental transformation?

The living drama began in the Eighteenth Century with the Age of the Enlightenment. The wandering and agitated life of the French thinker Voltaire merely represented the times of this turbulent era as the seeds of dissent were sown. Because of this dissension, what had once been sacred became profane. The thinking of Voltaire, Rousseau, Diderot, and others ignited a world-wide revolution. Man succumbed again to the enticement of the subtle serpent, tempting the pride of the intellect in the absence of faith with old lies for the new epoch.

Saint Thomas Aquinas gave rise through his writings to the contemporary philosophy of Thomism. His *Summa Theologica* is the summit of Catholic thought, synthesizing previous truths and wisdom. Scholasticism and Thomism had stood the test of time for centuries. Yet in the space of a few years, modernism had declared these philosophies unacceptable for higher education.

The Subversion Of The Mind

The principal desire of Satan is to take us away from God. Initially, he works to entice man through subtly distracting his mind, leading him to seek answers within himself. If men think solutions are within themselves, they have no reason to commune with God. Self-reliance through strength of will becomes their focus, rather than dependence on God. Prayer, Church, Scripture, and the sacraments become disposable. This is a direct contradiction of the words of the Blessed Mother at the apparition sites, who continually stresses the importance of these things. Mary's way is prayer from the heart.

Satan's ultimate target is the destruction of the papacy and the Holy Roman Catholic Church. The primary assault is aimed at banishing religion from the realm of the state, causing factions and divisions and bringing about ungodly laws. Once this is accomplished, the secondary assault weakens the Church from within. Satan's strategy is a powerful one: divide and conquer. Silence the generals, and the soldiers become confused and scatter.

There is widespread confusion and dissent in the Church over even the most basic doctrines. A deadly disease has spread so far, so quickly we do not realize how we evolved to our present state. It may be helpful to give a short synopsis of some of the leading philosophical thought which has poisoned our thinking and led to this state of confusion and division. This division has led to apostasy, the loss of faith, principally over the last 100 years, as the views of the Enlightenment found their way into European and North American classrooms.

In the Eighteenth and Nineteenth Centuries, the **Enlightenment** and the **Age of Reason** produced thinkers such as **Rousseau, Voltaire, and Diderot,** who were rationalists; that is, they placed reason over faith. This **philosophic rationalism** derived its methods from science and natural philosophy, which was to replace religion as the means of knowing nature and the destiny of humanity. The Enlightenment's understanding of human nature was one that emphasized the right to self-expression and human fulfillment, the right to think freely, and express one's views publicly without censorship or fear of oppression. **Rousseau** sought human nature in the wholly private realm of intuition and conscience. He looked inward for the fundamental source of moral obligation. **Voltaire,** the most influential figure of the Enlightenment, was a self-styled reformer who raised the slogan "Crush the Infamous" against the Church and Christianity. He was a Deist—one who believes God has no dealings with His creation after it was created. Numerous philosophies evolved from these movements such as liberalism, religious rationalism, positivism, secularism, naturalism, secular humanism, indifferentism, individualism, socialism, Communism, Marxism, theological liberalism, radical feminism, deism, agnosticism, atheism, and pantheism. The New Age movement is another tactic of Satan to replace faith with reason. It simply lacks an "ism" at the end of the name.

It was this mixture of modern philosophical systems which forsook Scholasticism and produced a large number of errors concerning God, Jesus Christ, the Church, the papacy, Church dogma, and the sacraments. These errors were condemned by Pope Pius IX, Vatican Council I, Pope Leo XIII, Pope Saint Pius X, Pope Pius XI, and Popes to the present day. These false modern philosophies were all strongly condemned by Pope Pius IX, who in *The Syllabus of Errors* listed eighty principal errors of his time under ten headings. The Syllabus was published on December 8, 1864.[5] Many Catholics today are unaware that previous Popes have condemned these errors. In fact, most do not understand how these subtle and deceptive philosophies have deeply penetrated our churches and culture.

In 1907, Pope Saint Pius X issued his encyclical *Pascendi Dominici Gregis* on modernism, a synthesis of all heresies founded upon the false modern philosophical systems which attack the Church, the divinity of Christ, Church dogmas, discipline, authority, and the papacy. He stated that modernism leads to pantheism and atheism. He then suppressed modernism in the Church.[6]

By this time, modernism was no longer an intellectual idea but a formidable force wreaking large-scale moral destruction. Pope Pius XI wrote *Divini Redemptoris* as the major encyclical against socialism and communism in 1937. In his most ominous warnings against the dangers of communism, he wrote to his bishops to "See to it, venerable brothers, that the faithful do not allow themselves to be deceived. Communism is intrinsically wrong, and no one who would save Christian civilization may collaborate with it in any undertaking whatsoever."[7]

Pope Pius XI gave three basic reasons for the rapid spread of communism: 1) Too few people had been able to grasp the nature of communism; 2) A propaganda campaign for communism so diabolical that the world has perhaps never witnessed its like before, and 3) The conspiracy of silence on the part of a large section of the non-Catholic press of the world.

Modernism: The Synthesis Of All Heresies

We could never have reached this state of apostasy in our Church unless philosophical errors had reached into the depths of Catholic thought. Pope Pius X issued an encyclical in 1907 on modernism. He knew that modernism would be perhaps the ultimate attack on the Church in our time. He stated, "We must now break silence, in order to expose before the whole Church, in their true colors, those men who have assumed this bad disguise." As the Vicar of Christ on earth, Pope Saint Pius X was warning us that modernism is the sum of all the errors of these modern philosophical systems as they relate to God, Jesus Christ, Sacred Scripture, Tradition, the Holy Fathers, the Church, sacraments, dogma, the papacy, ecclesiastical authority, hierarchy, state, and man.

Pope Pius X stated that he had exposed the doctrines of the modernists at some length, "to refute their charge that we do not understand their ideas. We desired to show their system does not consist in scattered and unconnected theories, but is a perfectly organized body, all parts which are solidly joined so that it is not possible to admit one without admitting all. **We define modernism as the synthesis of all heresies,** attempting the task of collecting together all the errors that have been broached against the faith and to concentrate the sap and substance of them all into one. It means the destruction not of the Catholic religion alone, but of all religion."[8]

Furthermore, modernism changes with the age to conform to the age. Pope Paul VI said: "It is the most dangerous revolution the Church has ever had to face and it is still scourging her severely. This revolution is a process of self-demolition and it aims at driving the Church to the end of the road to perdition. The trinity of parents responsible for the perversion known as modernism are: 1) Its religious ancestor is the Protestant Reformation; 2) Its philosophical parent is the Enlightenment; 3) Its political pedigree comes from the French Revolution."

Pope Pius X pointed out that "the whole system, with all its errors, had been born of the alliance between faith and false philosophy. Modernists place the foundation of religious philosophy in that doctrine which is usually called agnosticism."

As one of their principal points, modernists discuss dogma (religious formulas), which they hold arise as secondary propositions based on primitive and simple formulas. They consider them to be symbols and instruments; that is, images and vehicles of truth which are subject to change and ought to evolve and be changed. Pope Pius X stated: "They audaciously charge the Church both with taking the wrong road from inability to distinguish the religious and moral sense of formulas from their surface meaning, and with clinging tenaciously and vainly to meaningless formulas whilst religion is allowed to go to ruin." He further says, "modernists do not deny, but actually admit, some confusedly, others in the most open manner, that all religions are true."[9]

In addition, he stated: "The modernists recognize that the three chief difficulties for them are scholastic philosophy, the authority of the Fathers and Tradition, and the Magisterium of the Church. On these they wage unrelenting war. For scholastic philosophy and theology they have only ridicule and contempt. Whether it is ignorance or fear, or both, that inspires this conduct in them, it is certain that the passion for novelty is always united in them with a hatred of Scholasticism, and there is no surer sign that a man is on the way to modernism than when he begins to show his dislike for the system."[10]

Methods Of Destruction

Pope Pius X then pointed out that, "Modernists seize upon chairs in the seminaries and universities, and gradually make of them chairs of pestilence. From these sacred chairs they scatter, though not always openly, the seeds of their doctrines; they proclaim their teachings without disguise in congresses; they introduce them and make them the vogue in social institutions. Under their own names and under pseudonyms they publish numbers of books, newspapers, reviews.... If they write history, it is to search out with curiosity and to publish openly, on the pretext of telling the whole truth and with a species of ill-conceived satisfaction, everything that looks to them like a stain in the history of the Church." Pope Pius X finally stated: "Modernists try in every way to diminish and weaken authority. They propose to remove the ecclesiastical Magisterium itself by sacrilegiously falsifying its origin, character, rights, and by freely repeating the calumnies of its adversaries."[11]

Some modernist tenets condemned by the Popes are as follows:

• Faith is subject to science;

- The Church and State must be separate, but the Church is subject to the State;
- The Catholic must be separate from the citizen;
- The Church and the Sacraments were founded mediately but not directly by Christ;
- The Sacraments are mere symbols or signs;
- The Bible is inspired by God, but not in the Catholic manner of belief. Modernists' belief allows them to state that there are many errors in the Bible referring to science or history;
- Christ Himself manifestly erred in determining the time when the coming of the kingdom of God was to take place;
- The dogmas of the Church brim over with flagrant contradictions;
- There are two Christs, the real Christ and the Christ of faith. Christ, according to what modernists call real history, was not God and never did anything divine;
- It is permissible to grant that the Christ of history is far inferior to the Christ who is the object of faith;
- The Resurrection of Christ was not a fact of the historical order;
- The divinity of Christ is not proved from the Gospels. It is a dogma which the Christian conscience derived from the notion of the Messiah;
- Christ did not always possess the consciousness of His Messianic dignity;
- It is impossible to reconcile the natural sense of the Gospel texts with the sense taught by our theologians concerning the conscience and the infallible knowledge of Jesus Christ;
- Not everything Saint Paul says about the institution of the Eucharist is to be taken historically.[12]

Post Vatican II—Neo-Modernism

Today we are witnessing the final fruits of that pernicious doctrine and the complete attempt to liberate man from God. These godless philosophies are now commingling into a system of thought, manipulating and governing the masses who remain unaware of its intellectual underpinnings. Neo-modernism is unified in its basic inspiration—hatred of God and religion. There is such an apostasy of faith in many of our Catholic schools that the Antichrist would find himself right at home in the atmosphere that pervades campuses and classrooms.

When the Blessed Mother speaks of the institutional abandonment of the faith by the leaders in the Church, she is referring to those who have turned their back on faith in favor of the fashionable liberalism of the day. One example would be the wholesale retreat of the educators. Father Miceli, S.J., in his book *Antichrist*, writes: "In 1967-1972 the leaders of the Catholic institutions and the Vatican held meetings in which the leaders rejected any institutional, statutory, academic allegiance to the teachings of Jesus Christ as transmitted to His Church through the Magisterium. This is institutional apostasy from Christ and His Church."[13]

"The leaders, lusting after secular academic excellence, huge student bodies, expensive scientific complexes, publicity, political clout, and financial power somehow lost sight of the purpose and spirit of the Catholic university. In today's Catholic university, intellectualism is preferred to Catholicism, scientism to faith, and relativism to truth.[14]

"In the name of total liberation, the public demands widespread use of contraception, the right to free and state-financed abortion, the right to trial marriages, the right to choose homosexuality, and the right to enter lesbian and homosexual marriages. These are not marginal demands but are essentially linked to the movement of the total liberation of man from God, from morality, from restrictive positive laws, and from the canons of reason. Progressively these demands deny the very nature of man; they are now moving to the denial or the cancellation of the marriage institution as such.[15] These apostates have legislated these movements into existence and thus the law is now on their side. The Christian view is now outside the law.

"The first aim of Catholic modernists is to convert the Church of Rome to modernism and then to convert the Universal Church. They seek to create a Church in their own image and likeness—a small, Gnostic, elite Church of worldly-wise intellectuals who will dominate the religious thinking and practice of the whole human race.

"Today, in the post-Christian era, neo-modernism has regrouped its forces under such titles as 'Catholic Opposition' or 'Catholic

Dissent' or 'Christian Critics.' This dissent and criticism is leveled against 'the institutional Church,' not against the enemies of the Church."[16]

This century has seen the errors—which arose from rationalism, naturalism, secularism, humanism—that lead to modernism, the synthesis of all heresies. Condemned by Saint Pope Pius X, modernism went underground in the seminaries and universities, only to rise again after the Second Vatican Council as neo-modernism. Neo-modernism masquerades under various names and guises: the spirit of Vatican II, feminism in the Church, liberation theology, and the conciliar Church, among others. This misinterpretation and the incorrect implementation of Vatican II led numerous cardinals, priests, nuns, and laity to lose the faith, following instead what many call the "New Christianity."

The five main characteristics of this "New Christianity" are:

1) **Anthropocentrism**: Man, not God is the center of religion. God is found solely in the face, functions, fortunes, and future of man. The primacy of man is identified with the primacy of God.

2) **Immanence in the world**: The kingdom of God is not hereafter. Salvation means liberation from social sin, i.e., from ignorance, hunger, underdevelopment, political oppression, economic exploitation. Personal sin is no longer relevant in today's historical context. The new Catholics, enlisting under socialism's banner, must achieve the kingdom of God by destroying capitalism.

3) **The New Evangelism**: The true meaning of the Gospel is economic rather than spiritual, arising from service to the poor; only the poor and their socialistic champions can understand the Gospels. The Magisterium has misinterpreted the meaning of the Gospel these past two thousand years, using it to exploit the poor and remain in power with the mighty of this world.

4) **The New Ecclesiology**: The Church is part of the world; she does not exist for herself, but to serve the world. Hence, she must dissolve all her own institutions. In her liturgical life, any members may function as priests. In her jurisdictional life, local churches must be autonomous, for all authority comes from the faithful who share co-responsibility.

5) **The New Passion for Christ**: This love is not for Christ the God-Man. Rather it is for Christ who is only a great man—the Man-

for-others, the friend, the defender, the liberator of the poor, indeed, the revolutionary and grand subverter, aiding the poor to overthrow all corrupt institutions, the institutional Church included.

Weakness was found in the Church leaders and especially among its prestigious intellectuals. It took the Second Vatican Council to reveal that too many of its own members had been nurturing for a long time a secret desire to join the world; now, abusing the Council itself as an authoritative pretext, such lovers of this world are opening the gates of the Church so as to bring the faithful into contact with the stultifying and deadly energies of neo-modernism. These New Church Catholics have become scandalized over the Catholic Church's allegedly intransigent and dogmatic policies.

Serious divisions exist among Catholics on essential matters of faith and morals: errors concerning God, the historicity of the Gospels, the Real Presence, the divinity of Christ, the infallibility of the Pope, the Resurrection, the nature of the Church and its salvation ministry, and many, many other points too numerous to mention. All have divided and mutilated the flock of Christ.

It is hardly surprising that Satan, in his attack on the Catholic Church, concentrates his big guns on two major doctrines that constitute the heart of the Catholic faith: **1) the Eucharist as the Real Presence of Jesus Christ; and 2) the Virgin Mary as the Mother of God. Both of these mysteries are reduced to being Christian development of old pagan myths, fables that attempt to explain the origin of the universe through monistic and cosmological forces.**[17]

The New Order of the Mass as it was presented by those who drew it up for Pope Paul VI stressed the communal meal aspect of the liturgy and forgot the Sacrifice. Cardinal Ottaviani of the Holy Office intervened with the Pope, who had the sacrificial aspect reinserted. Liturgical change in the Mass has led to the majority of Catholics today—as shown by a recent poll—holding that the Kiss of Peace is the main part of the Mass. A large number of Catholic laity, priests and nuns, appear not to believe in the Real Presence of Christ in the Eucharist as taught by the Catholic Church. In some churches the kneelers have been removed. The altar rails in the churches in the United States have been removed so that the faithful may not kneel out of reverence and respect for the Lord to receive communion. The tabernacle has been moved to the side of the church and in some churches it has been removed from the church into a chapel, away from the main altar.

In one private revelation a visionary likens this to a guest of honor at a banquet being asked to go off and sit to the side. The Lord has allegedly said to a visionary, "Put me back in the center." Our Lady has echoed the theme: "Let the Holy Mass be the center of your life."

Ecclesiastical Masonry: The Enemy In The Camp

Nowhere is an enemy more destructive than when he is in your own camp. Satan's primary ploys were to divide Church from state and the Church from within itself. To date, Satan's plan has been successful. This leads us to the topic of Freemasonry. It is a complex subject with its leaders having access and control in most economic, political, judicial, and social spheres. It is a huge world-wide network that the Blessed Mother calls the "secret sect," which has common goals and an agenda all its own. Briefly, there is a vast network in place which is more for earthly goals of wealth and creature comforts than heavenly ones. Sadly, this network extends into the very Church itself. What could be worse than people in high places within your camp working against you? This strategy of deceit in the Church is called Ecclesiastical Masonry.

The reasons for corruption in the Church are numerous. However, one area of widespread destruction has been what Pope Paul VI called the "auto-demolition" of the Church; that is, destruction "from within." He was directly pointing to subversive movements in the Church looking to do harm from within.

One such effective movement is revealed in the book *AA-1025— The Memoirs of an Anti-Apostle*. It is the book of a French Catholic nurse in the 1960s attending to an auto crash victim who died within hours of being brought into her hospital. The man had no identification on him, but he had a briefcase of biographical notes which contained information about how the Communist Party commissioned him to enter the priesthood to subvert and destroy the Church from within.

Seeing the value in these papers she published them. It is an account of this man's time in the seminary in the early 1940s and his deceptive plots year after year to destroy all that was Roman Catholic. Using all of the intelligence methods of the KGB, the notes provide information on the systematic plan to break down the Church from within. For this 'anti-apostle' it all began with an uncle in the Communist Party saying, "I am now going to send you to practice a militant and international atheism. You will have to fight all religions, but principally the Catholic, which is better organized. To do so, you will enter a seminary and become a Roman Catholic priest." The notes then told of the murder of a Polish bishop who spotted his role, a hierarchy of authority and command established for him, thousands of churches closed in Russia, infiltration and placement of priests into high positions, the attempts to abolish Catholic traditions, the ultimate goal of establishing all religions into a universal religion, the gathering of writers to promote these views, the supply of rubles from Russia to support his programs, and a complete agenda of diabolical extremes. When the man was recruited, he was the 1,025-man in a program that was sending "seminarians" all over the world.[18]

Our Lady has spoken to Patricia Talbot (known as "Pachi") of Cuenca, Ecuador, about the destruction in the Church. **"Pray much for [priests] because Satan is penetrating into the depths of the Holy Church. Do not let Satan penetrate you. I am the Guardian of the Faith.** My children, Satan wants to destroy the missions which Heaven has granted you, children of the light. In the same way he will try to destroy the Church, but his attempts will be in vain if you convert. Pray the rosary, which is a shield against evil. Use the scapular which will protect you. Place the Heart of Jesus in your homes for it will keep you united and in peace. Do penance and fast, and with prayer you will reach the heart of my Son. Go to Mass and visit the Blessed Sacrament. Pray to me and I will keep you under my mantle and in the Heart of my Son."

New Wine In Old Skins

From the state of the world today, it looks as if the "subtle serpent" has won. The divisions have been most intense in the last thirty years over the Real Presence in the Eucharist, the Divinity of Christ, papal infallibility, the Resurrection, the nature of the Church, and numerous other issues which have divided the Body on a scale which has not been seen since the Reformation. The Blessed Mother's messages deal specifically with this crisis. The voice of Mary and Scripture speak of these difficult days. The corruption around us has been predicted by many. And so the slide continues. The program of the enemy has been effective and he has proven himself a formidable adversary. It is the extremely rare Christian university that teaches faith and morals in truth. Liberation theologians and dissident academics have had a significant impact on students over many years. The feminization or neutrality of language has gained a foothold and each year firmly plants itself and gains acceptance. New Age creeps in with large numbers of disciples and is merely an old heresy by another name. It is a recycled lie enticing the mind once again: "Ye shall be like gods."

In his book *Trojan Horse in the City of God*, scholar Dietrich Von Hildebrand summed up the problem. He wrote: "Like a beseiged city, the Church is surrounded by the errors and dangers of our time. Unfortunately, some Catholics are not only not aware of these dangers, but are in varying degrees infected by them."

The Climax Of The Battle

All that is happening today has been predicted at sites of many of the Marian apparitions. All events are positioned for the Woman clothed with the sun to crush the head of the serpent. There will be many more events as a prelude to this, but there will be three of great significance.

The first major falling away from the faith will be occasioned by the new catechism that was signed and approved by Pope John Paul II on December 8, 1992. It is an orthodox version of the faith that some of the Catholic hierarchy will find themselves unable to accept. It will further divide the opposing camps and provide a prelude to the messages of LaSalette: "cardinal against cardinal, bishop against bishop." The split in the Church is a *de facto* schism that to date has been for the most part hidden and contained. Soon it will be open.

A document related to the new catechism is John Paul's new encyclical on morality, scheduled to be released in the late fall of 1993. It is an encyclical promoting views on morality as taught by the Magisterium of the Church—not liberal theologians. Liberal Catholic Americans will be troubled by Rome's views. This will pose a stumbling block for those who call themselves "progressive thinkers." The "American Catholic Church" and the Roman Catholic Church gather distance between them with each passing year.

The battle lines are drawn. The Pope and those bishops in union with him, in an attempt to correct modernist errors of interpretation of the Catholic faith after Vatican II, have given us an authoritative, in–depth presentation of the true Catholic faith. Modernist cardinals, bishops, priests, nuns, and laity will become more firmly entrenched in their own views as they read the new documents. We are on the way to a new schism of huge proportions. It will be so large it will drive underground the Church that is in union with the Pope and Rome. Shortly, to the undiscerning eye, it will be difficult to tell the true Church from the apostate church. The message of Our Lady on June 17, 1989, stated through the Marian Movement of Priests: **"The Apostasy will be as of then generalized, because almost all will follow the false christ and the false church."**

The last major event will be the proclamation of the Blessed Mother as Co-Redemptrix, Mediatrix, and Advocate—the last and final Marian dogma of the Catholic Church. To many it will seem to be a doctrine of demons, and for those who adhere to such a doctrine, it will actually bring on persecution. These events will pave the way for the movement of the anti-church and the anti-pope.

Today, many Catholics are lukewarm and indifferent. With the proclamation of the above encyclical, they will openly oppose the Pope. Most will fall away from the practice of the one true Faith because of the great apostasy.

A Schism Already

The break from Rome each year in faith and doctrine is gradual. Many bishops are not obedient to the instructions of the Pope. The Pope as of this writing has not given permission for the inclusive language of the American lectionary. Yet it appears one U.S. bishop has ordered its use in his diocese on the basis that it will be approved soon even though there are grave misgivings concerning mistranslations of the Latin text into English. This has been done to placate radical feminists as the politically correct thing to do in the Church, without the consultation of other members of the Church. Many radical feminist nuns support abortion, contraception, lesbian-ism, and other doctrines contrary to Catholic moral teaching. Many Catholic priests do not believe in the Real Presence of the Eucharist. Also, many Catholics do not believe in the Real Presence; personal mortal sin; the need for sacramental reconciliation; the evils of abortion, homosexuality, divorce, drug abuse, and pre-marital sex;

and the authority of the Magisterium of the Holy Roman Catholic Church.

When Mary is proclaimed Co-Redemptrix, as she herself has stated, conditions will further deteriorate inside the Church. It will be a combination of events such as an economic and social collapse which will lead mankind to the acceptance of the Antichrist and his ecclesiastical puppet—the antichurch. As Mary predicted at LaSalette, "Rome will loose the faith and become the seat of Antichrist."

The elements of the apostasy have been given to us in great detail: Freemasonry, ecclesiastical apostasy, the worship of man over God, and extreme division on earth, the setting up of an idol to put in the place of Christ and the Church, and a false christ and a false church. All that has been predicted is being fulfilled. The messages of those warning the world have been more specific with each passing year. Satan is firmly planted in the corridors of ecclesiastical power, and the prophecy of LaSalette, France, is coming to fruition.

Our Lady, in her apparitions, speaks of this widespread and nearly total loss of faith before the return of Jesus Christ. The passion of the Mystical Body is being played out as the Passion of Jesus. As Good Friday comes before Easter Sunday, we will see the death of the Catholic Church before its resurrection in a new form in the glorious era of peace.

14

The Great Apostasy: The Loss Of Faith

Let no one deceive you in any way. For unless the apostasy comes first and the lawless one is revealed, the one doomed to perdition, who opposes and exalts himself above every so-called god and object of worship, so as to seat himself in the temple of God, claiming that he is a god, do you not recall that while I was still with you I told you these things? And now you know what is restraining, that he may be revealed in his time. For the mystery of lawlessness is already at work. But the one who restrains is to do so only for the present, until he is removed from the scene. And then the lawless one will be revealed, whom the Lord Jesus will kill with the breath of His mouth and render powerless by the manifestation of His coming, the one whose coming springs from the power of Satan in every mighty deed and in signs and wonders that lie, and in every wicked deceit for those who are perishing because they have not accepted the love of truth so that they may be saved. Therefore, God is sending them a deceiving power so they may believe the lie, that all who have not believed the truth but have approved wrongdoing may be condemned.
2 Thessalonians 2: 3-12

The Apostasy Was Predicted

We are at the state of such a loss of faith that Paul's letter to the Thessalonians is in the final stages of being fulfilled. The great apostasy must come before the lawless one, the Antichrist, is revealed. The Second Letter of Paul to the Thessalonians is clear, as are the words of Mary: there will be a loss of faith. The century of Satan is in its final act, and the reign of Mary has begun. She soon will crush the head of the serpent.

The Marian Era has begun. With the great battle of the angelic powers, the Archangels (Gabriel, Michael, and Raphael) and the angels of Heaven are fighting under the mantle of the Woman clothed with the sun against Satan and his wicked spirits. To Father Gobbi, on November 15, 1990, Our Blessed Mother told of the war being waged with her adversary. She stated: "Satan is battling against the apostles of these last times, who have been chosen to combat courageously against the power of him who places himself in opposition to Christ, in order to obtain, in the end, my greatest victory."

Akita

In the apparition of Akita, Japan, October, 13, 1973, Our Blessed Mother told Sister Agnes Sasagawa: "As I told you...The work of the devil will infiltrate even into the Church in such a way that one will see cardinals opposing cardinals, bishops against other bishops. The priests who venerate me will be scorned and opposed by their own confreres....the Church will be full of those who accept compromises and the demon will press many priests and consecrated souls to leave the service of the Lord."

From November 25-27, 1992, the Episcopal Conference of Japan called a meeting which was attended by many Bishops and Marian leaders to discuss the significance of the Akita apparitions. During one of the conferences, a question was asked of Father Michael O'Carroll (a leading Marian scholar and one of the attendees) how the third secret of Fatima related to Akita. He responded: "If you are interested in the third secret of Fatima, read the messages of Akita." Although we know the third secret is the Apostasy of the faith, there is more to the message of Fatima. The Fatima expert for Pope John Paul II was a priest named Father Joseph de St. Marie, now deceased. He drafted the speech for the Pope's address given at Fatima during his visit in 1982. There, Pope John Paul II publicly thanked Our Lady of Fatima for saving his life during the assassination attempt. Father St. Marie knew of the contents of the Fatima secret. When asked of the secret several years later, he responded, "Do you know what the people did during the miracle of the sun?" The reply was, "they fell to their knees and repented." Father Saint Marie answered, "It will be the same, however many will not repent even though the events will be catastrophic; the miracle of the sun will be a prefigurement or foreshadowing of what will happen in the future." The messages of Fatima were completed with those of Akita, Japan. The messages from both apparitions give us a more complete view of the chastisement and the apostasy.[1]

Father Gobbi

The Blessed Mother told Father Gobbi on a number of occasions about the coming difficulties.

On September 6, 1986 Mary stated: "There has also entered into the Church disunity, division, strife and antagonism. The forces of atheism and Masonry, having infiltrated within it, are on the point of breaking up its interior unity and of darkening the splendor of its sanctity. These are the times, foretold by me, when cardinals will be set against cardinals, bishops against bishops, and priests against priests, and the flock of Christ will be torn to pieces by rapacious wolves, who have found their way in under the clothing of defenseless and meek lambs. Among them there are even some who occupy posts of great responsibility and, by means of them, Satan has succeeded in entering and in operating at the very summit of the Church. Bishops and priests of the holy Church of God, how great today is your responsibility! The Lord is about to demand of you an account of how you have administered His vineyard. Repent, seek pardon, make amends and, above all, be once again faithful to the task which has been entrusted to you."

On May 13, 1990, she stated: "Now you are beginning the last decade of this century of yours.... I am coming down from Heaven, so that the final secrets may be revealed to you and that I may be able thus to prepare you for what, as of now, you must live through, for the purification of the earth.... My third secret, which I revealed here to three little children to whom I appeared and which up to the present has not yet been revealed to you, will be made manifest to all by the very occurrence of events.... The Church will know the hour of its greatest apostasy.... **The man of iniquity will penetrate into its interior and will sit in the very temple of God, while the little remnant which will remain faithful will be subjected to the greatest trials and persecutions."**

On November 15, 1990, Mary said: "The great trial has arrived for your Church. Those errors which have brought people to the loss of the true faith have continued to spread.... There is in preparation a true schism which could soon become open and proclaimed.... The great trial has arrived for all humanity. **The chastisement, predicted by me at Fatima and contained in that part of the secret which has not yet been revealed, is about to take place. The great moment of divine justice and mercy has come upon the world.**"

On May 13, 1991, she revealed to Father Gobbi: **"My Pope, John Paul II.... I confirm for you is the Pope of my secret; the Pope about whom I spoke to the children during the apparitions; the Pope of my love and my sorrow.... When this Pope will have completed the task which Jesus has entrusted to him and I will come down from Heaven and receive his sacrifice, all of you will be cloaked in dense darkness of apostasy, which will then become general."**

On May 13, 1992, Mary said, "Beloved children, today you are observing the seventy-fifth anniversary of my first apparition, which took place at Fatima, in the Cova da Iria, on the 13th of May, 1917.... At the time, I predicted the times of the loss of the true faith and of the apostasy, which would be spread throughout every part of the Church. You are living the times of which I foretold you.... At that time, I predicted the times of the war, and of the persecution of the Church and the Holy Father, because of the spread of theoretical and practical atheism, and of the rebellion of humanity against God and His law.... At that time, I predicted the chastisement and that, in the end, my Immaculate Heart would have its triumph."

The Mystery Of Being Tested

The apostasy is the loss of faith in the Church. It appears that the testing of the faithful is near its completion. In Chapter 12 on Medjugorje, in the letter that Father Tomislav Vlasic wrote to Pope John Paul II on December 2, 1983, this testing time is mentioned. Father Vlasic, quoting what Mary said to one of the seers, wrote: "...you must realize that Satan exists. **One day he appeared before the throne of God and asked permission to submit the Church to a period of trial. God gave him permission to try the Church for one century.** This century is under the power of the devil; but when the secrets confided to you come to pass, his power will be destroyed.

Even now he is beginning to lose his power and has become aggressive. He is destroying marriages...."

Another person who believed this century was under the power of the devil was Pope Leo XIII. *Soul Magazine* provides this anecdote in its May/June 1984 issue: "On October 13, 1884, Pope Leo XIII had just finished Holy Mass when he heard a deep and guttural voice say: 'I can destroy your Church...to do so I need more time and more power.' Then the Pope heard a gentle voice asking: 'How much time? How much power?'.... The guttural voice responded: 'Seventy-five to one hundred years and a greater power over those who will give themselves to my service.' The gentle voice replied: 'You have the time...'. Deeply troubled, Pope Leo XIII commanded a special prayer to be said to Saint Michael the Archangel at the end of every Mass:

"Saint Michael the Archangel, defend us in battle, be our safeguard against the wickedness and snares of the devil. May God rebuke him, we humbly pray, and do thou, O Prince of the Heavenly Host, by the power of God, cast into Hell Satan and the other evil spirits who prowl about the world for the ruin of souls, Amen."

This prayer continued to be recited after Mass through the remainder of the Nineteenth Century and until September 26, 1964, when the Constitution of the Sacred Liturgy decreed: "Leonine prayers after Mass are no longer to be said."

Confirming the validity of the dialogue that Pope Leo XIII heard, in the November 9, 1984, message of the Marian Movement of Priests, Mary stated: **"The apostasy arising from Satan's trial of the Church is now in its final stages. The Lord has granted him this space of time, because the end of the pride of the Red Dragon will be broken and conquered by the humility, the littleness, and the power of your heavenly Mother, the Woman clothed with the sun, who is now gathering all her little children into her army, drawn up for battle."** At the turn of the Twentieth Century, Pope Saint Pius X stated in his encyclical that modernism in the Church is the genesis of heresy. He predicted—prophetically—that the modernist and secular heresy would bring about the apostasy.

Those in Leadership Are Held Responsible

Throughout Scripture and the messages of Mary, considerable blame is directly tied to priests and those in leadership positions in the Church. Accusing words were often spoken by Jesus to the Pharisees and Sadducees. Calling the lawgivers and those in spiritual control a "brood of vipers and whitened sepulchers" did not make Jesus popular with those in authority. They subsequently plotted to kill Him because His mission was not in line with their own. The following Scriptural text taken from Hosea is clear regarding the holding of worldly position and authority, and the responsibility of those who hold ecclesial positions of leadership:

Priests, nobles and kings are the ruin of the nation
Listen to this, priests,
attend, House of Israel,
listen, royal household,
you who are responsible for justice,
for you have been a snare at Mizpah,
and a net outspread on Tabor.
They are entrenched in their deceitfulness
and so I am going to punish them all.
I know all about Ephraim,
Israel has no secrets for me;
yes Ephraim, you'd have played the whore,
Israel has defiled himself.
Their deeds do not allow them to return to their God;
since a prostituting spirit possesses them;
they do not know Yahweh.
The arrogance of Israel is his own accuser,
the iniquity of Ephraim knocks him down
and down comes Judah with him.
Though they go in search of Yahweh with their sheep and oxen,
they do not find him;
for he has withdrawn from them.
They have proved unfaithful to Yahweh.

Hosea 5:1-7

Our Lady has been firm in her messages about faith and obedience. Following is the message of March 13, 1990, to Father Gobbi and Our Lady's reference to the Second Letter to the Thessalonians. Those who advocate rebellion to the Magisterium, pastors absorbed with liberal theology, and those who neglect ordained priestly duties are reprimanded. Our Lady also says her activities will be more "vigorous" as the day of the Second Coming approaches. The Blessed

Mother stated: "You read in the Gospel: 'When the Son of Man returns, will He still find faith on earth?' Today I want to invite you to meditate on these words, uttered by my Son Jesus. They are grave words which cause one to reflect and which succeed in making you understand the times through which you are living. First of all, you can ask why Jesus has uttered them: to prepare you for His Second Coming and to describe for you a circumstance which will be indicative of the proximity of His glorious return. This circumstance is the loss of faith. Also, in another part of Holy Scripture, in the letter of Saint Paul to the Thessalonians, it is clearly announced that, before the glorious return of Christ, a great apostasy must take place. The loss of the faith is a true apostasy. The spread of the apostasy is therefore the sign which indicates that the Second Coming of Christ is, as of now, close at hand...."

Christina Gallagher Of Ireland

Revelations of the apostasy were given to Christina Gallagher of Ireland.

"My child, there are many of my children, sons and daughters in religious life, who serve in the name of God. But the true Spirit of God is not in them. They only serve God in mockery. It wounds my heart to see this. The power of darkness overshadows my Church and the world" (July 23, 1988).

"Catherine of Siena came in remarkable beauty. She said, 'Pray for the Pope every day, for priests and cardinals, and for my sisters, the nuns.' Then her eyes filled with tears. When I asked her why she was unhappy she did not reply but went on: we are in the time of battle but only at the beginning stage..." (September 19, 1990).

Gladys of San Nicolas, Argentina

Gladys, a visionary from Argentina, has been given similar messages: "My daughter, how much hatred there is enclosed in men, how much mistrust and despair! They feel this for lack of faith and love, because God is absent in their hearts. Those children will perish if they continue in ignorance. It would be enough only to ask for love of the Lord; it would be enough to ask the Lord for help and He would transform them, remember that God protects. Glory be to the Everlasting Father" (January 28, 1985).

Understanding the apostasy and the messages of LaSalette and Akita sheds enormous light on how we have arrived at our present state of depravity throughout the world. Scripture is clear: in 2 Thessalonians, Paul says the apostasy precedes the lawless one—the Antichrist who then seats himself in the very temple of God.

The New Age Movement

Adolph Hitler said, "tell a lie, tell it often enough, and people will believe it." Perhaps no religious threat to Catholicism today is as seductive as the New Age movement. Its greatest deception lies in the fact that it is so close to the truth, thus many are ensnared. Randall Baer, a former leader in the New Age movement, has written a book called *Inside the New Age Nightmare* that exposes the inner workings and intent of the Movement.[2] New Age is the religion of the New World Order because of its inclusiveness. Its hallmark is man at the center of the universe—man as deity, the same old lie. Mr. Baer's unique insights offer a deep understanding of New Age. Therefore, we quote directly from him:

"What exactly is New Age? Essentially, it is a Satan-controlled, modern-day mass revival of occult-based philosophies and practices in both obvious and cleverly disguised forms. In effect, it is an end-times 'plague of the spirit' propagating the 'powerful delusion that they should believe the lie.' It is nothing more than a glitteringly seductive, broad road leading only to eventual destruction. Over the last three decades, however, an enormous and unprecedented massive revival of occult-based practices has been taking place, some of it disguised as being non-occult in nature. The magnitude and momentum of this movement is to such an extent that is poses one of the nastiest-growing threats to Christianity today, especially in the years ahead as the end times unfold.

"What do most people think of when they hear the term New Age? Shirley MacLaine? Harmonic convergence? Reincarnation? Crystal power? Channeling? Psychic readers? In fact these are only a part of a very broad spectrum of different New Age forms, strategies, and practices. To make matters all the more difficult, the term New Age is sometimes not even used when something is actually New Age at the core.[3]

"This movement can actually best be understood as a broad spectrum of non-Christian philosophies and practices that can be categorized as New Age Spiritual Humanism. The cornerstone of this humanism is the belief that man is divine in nature, and therefore essentially 'God' or an enlightened 'God-man'. New-age man, believing himself to be divinely perfect and ultimately all-powerful, sets himself up on a cosmic throne. Man becomes his own deity.

"Just as secular humanism offers its own type of anti-religious deceits to certain types of people, so does spiritual humanism offer spiritually based counterfeits to an entirely different strata of people in our society, people who hunger for and search for spiritual meaning, truth and fulfillment in their lives.[4]

"The New Age is an extremely difficult movement to define with anything other than generalized statements. There are no centralized organizations controlling all doctrines, activities, or agendas. No single committee, council or organization dictates the doctrines or agenda, or controls all activities. The landmark manifesto, *The Aquarian Conspiracy*, terms it 'a leaderless but powerful network.' This characteristic has allowed room for an immense variety of philosophies and phenomena to flourish via all manner of diverse individuals and organizations.

"Furthermore the New Age has so many faces and directions to its overall agenda that it has infiltrated into every facet of American society in both obvious and very subtle, deeply underlying ways. From religion, business, and politics to music, education, and science the New Age has wormed its way in the very cornerstones of Western civilization—more so than many people realize. New Age thought encompasses all aspects of human experience. It is an attempt to revolutionize every aspect of life on the personal, interpersonal, societal, and global scale.[5]

"There's a basic credo that says 'create you own reality according to what feels right for you.' For example, whether a person chooses to be homosexual, bisexual, monogamous, polygamous or whatever is OK as long as 'It's right for me' or 'It's done with love and no one's hurt.' It is all relativistic.[6]

"There are two overlapping but different major schools of New Age thought: the first viewpoint of New Age thought as 'Consciousness Renaissance.'

"Consciousness Renaissance sees humankind currently experiencing the beginning of a new spiritual and socio-political awakening, a modern-day super-Renaissance destined to lead man into a new era of enlightened spiritual humanism. Spurning the thought of man needing divine intervention to assist in the creation of a global utopia, this perspective sees the awakening of 'unlimited human god-potential' as the means by which 'Heaven on earth' will become manifest. In essence, as man achieves higher states of 'god-consciousness' through New Age practices, Heaven will dawn on Earth only through the dawning of man's enlightened 'higher consciousness.'[7]

"The second major branch of New Age thought can be termed 'Quantum Leap of Consciousness.' This says we are on the brink of a new age, a whole new world. In the twinkling of an eye, mankind's awareness, our collective consciousness, is going to make an instantaneous quantum leap into the heavens. Everything will change in a flash of divine Light. Get ready. Your heavenly heritage awaits. Come on in; the water's fine. He who hesitates is lost. He who chooses life is found.

"When sufficient momentum is generated by enough people having developed 'higher consciousness,' then the entire world will be ready to make a collective quantum leap into a higher dimension of the heavenly realm. Earth and humanity will literally leap in a flash of light into the heavens above. This Quantum Leap of Consciousness model is directly tied to some form of divine intervention. Furthermore, this school of thought maintains that some other 'World Teacher' or 'Council of Ascended Masters' will have divine authority in the New Age, not Christ.

"Another variation of this skewed theme is that it is not the personal and visible Jesus who returns, but rather 'Christ consciousness' that descends into the minds of all earthly inhabitants. Some new age fundamentalists do predict that a literal apocalypse is imminent and that it will be brought about by mystical, extraterrestrial, or cosmic forces.

"Many of the Consciousness Renaissance camp tend to focus on integrating increasingly socially acceptable New Age values into personal and societal life. This is the side of the New Age that has made especially strong inroads into areas such as the corporate business world, psychology, entertainment media, education, health care, and science. In terms of value-system and practical-level infiltration into mainstream American culture, this aspect of the New

Age has proven the more successful of the two schools of thought due to its subtler humanistic approach.

"The Quantum Leap of Consciousness viewpoint is much more predisposed to the metaphysical-occult end of the spectrum. In particular, the predominant themes lie much towards mediumship, spiritism, witchcraft, psychic powers, and sorceries in myriad shapes and forms. One of the primary dangers from this branch of the New Age is its major contribution to the historically unprecedented unleashing of demonic forces into the world today...." [8]

"Channeling, crystal power, contacting your 'Higher Self,' going to geographical 'vortexes' (occult 'power spots'), goddess worship, world peace meditations, psychic readings, self-empowerment seminars, occult-based success and prosperity seminars, interpersonal development and sex workshops, and telepathically contacting UFOs...." [9]

"Most New Age prophecy foresees a millennial transition time during which those who accept the message and mark of the 'New World Order' become a part of the greatly proclaimed New Age. In effect, as the Antichrist forces come to greater world power, a revamped and upgraded New Age-based philosophy is to be applied toward 'purifying' the planetary populace of those who are not 'ready' to make the next step into becoming a superior race of godmen. This should ignite memories of Hitler's blood 'sacrifice' of the Jewish people....

"A thorough reading of New Age literature will show that some New Agers sanction the persecution of Christians. They do so on the basis of the need to remove those who may refuse to accept or attempt to 'prevent' a spiritual uniting of humanity. If true globalism—or world unity—is eventually to be a reality, then by definition all dissenting voices must either be converted, silenced, or removed. That, of course, is the 'rub'—the New Age of love and harmony may have to be repressive for a time to usher in their version of peace on Earth...." [10]

15

Satan's 100 Years: Antichurch, Antipope, Antichrist

In these days there was no king in Israel, every man did that which was right in his own eyes.

Judges 21:25

The Twentieth Century has been ruled by Satan, the Lord of the earth, the Prince of Darkness. It is the century granted by God to Satan, who requested this time to test the Church.

On October 13, 1884, Pope Leo XIII experienced a vision in which he heard Satan ask God for 100 years. Satan boasted that, if he were given sufficient time and power, he could destroy the Church and drag the world to hell.

In 1982, Our Blessed Mother told Mirjana, one of the visionaries at Medjugorje: "Excuse me for this, but you must realize that Satan exists. One day he appeared before the throne of God and asked permission to submit the Church to a period of trial. God gave him permission to try the Church for one century. This century is under the power of the devil, but when the secrets confided to you come to pass, his power will be destroyed. Even now he is beginning to lose his power and become aggressive. He is destroying marriages, creating division among priests, and is responsible for obsessions and murder. You must protect yourselves against these things through fasting and prayer, especially community prayer. Carry blessed objects with you. Put them in your house, and restore the use of holy water."

In 1634 in Quito, Ecuador, Our Blessed Mother warned about our present times. In an apparition approved by the Church, Mary appeared as Our Lady of Good Fortune to Mother Anne of Jesus Torres, while she was praying in front of the Blessed Sacrament. The sanctuary light went out. While she was trying to relight it, a supernatural light filled the church; in this light, the Mother of God appeared. She told Mother Anne, "The sanctuary lamp burning in front of the Prisoner of Love, which you saw go out, has many meanings."

"First meaning: At the end of the Nineteenth Century and for a large part of the Twentieth Century, various heresies will flourish on this earth, which will have become a free republic. The precious light of the faith will go out in souls because of the almost total moral corruption. In those times there will be great physical and moral calamities, in private and in public. The little number of souls keeping the faith and practicing the virtues will undergo cruel and unspeakable sufferings....

"Second Meaning: My communities will be abandoned; they will be swamped in a fathomless sea of bitterness, and will seemed drowned in tribulations. How many true vocations will be lost for lack of skillful and prudent direction to form them! Each mistress of novices will need to be a soul of prayer, knowing how to discern spirits.

"Third Meaning: In those times, the air will be filled with the spirit of impurity which like a deluge of filth will flood the streets, squares and public places. The licentiousness will be such that there will be no more virgin souls in the world.

"Fourth Meaning: **By gaining control of all the social classes, the sects will tend to penetrate with great skill into the hearts of families and destroy even the children. The devil will take glory in feeding perfidiously on the hearts of children. The innocence of childhood will almost disappear. Thus priestly vocations will be lost. It will be a real disaster. Priests will abandon their sacred duties and will depart from the path marked for them by God.**

"Then the Church will go through a dark night for lack of a Prelate and Father to watch over it with love, gentleness, strength and prudence, and numbers of priests will lose the spirit of God, thus placing their souls in great danger.... Satan will take control of this earth through the fault of faithless men who, like a black cloud, will darken the clear sky of the republic consecrated to the Most Sacred Heart of my divine Son. This republic, having allowed entry to all the vices, will have to undergo all sorts of chastisements: plagues, famine, war, apostasy, and the loss of souls without number. And to scatter these black clouds blocking the brilliant dawning of the freedom of the Church, there will be a terrible war in which the blood of priests and of religious will flow.... That night will be so horrible that wickedness will seem triumphant. Then will come my time: in astounding fashion I shall destroy Satan's pride, casting him beneath my feet, chaining him up in the depths of hell, leaving Church and country freed at last from his cruel tyranny.

"Fifth Meaning: Men possessing great wealth will look on with indifference while the Church is oppressed, virtue is persecuted, and evil triumphs. They will not use their wealth to fight evil and to reconstruct the faith. The people will come to care nothing for the things of God, will absorb the spirit of evil and will let themselves be swept away by all vices and passions."[1]

Remember that in 1846 Our Lady of LaSalette told the visionary Melanie that Lucifer together with a large number of demons would be released from hell in 1864. She said they will put an end to faith little by little, even in those dedicated to God. Evil books will be abundant on earth. The spirit of darkness will spread everywhere. For a while the Church will yield to a large persecution, a time of darkness and a frightful crisis.

Antichurch

Father Malachi Martin, in his book *The Keys of This Blood*, wrote that throughout the Church, at the level of parish and diocese, among laypersons, nuns, priests, and bishops, is the belief that the One, Holy, Apostolic Roman Catholic Church ceased to exist after the Second Vatican Council. Its place was taken by the "Conciliar Church," animated by the "spirit of Vatican II." It was no longer called the "Roman Catholic Church" but instead the "people of God" or the "Church."

Father Martin pointed out that the Church that now exists differs radically from the pre-Conciliar Church on four major points:

1. The Conciliar Church lays no claim to exclusive possession of the means of eternal salvation. All of us—Catholics, non-Catholics, and non-Christians—are pilgrims approaching the same goal by different roads.

2. In the Conciliar Church, the local "community of faith" is the source of religious enlightenment, guidance, and authority. Correct beliefs and correct moral practice no longer come from a hierarchy of bishops submissive to the central teaching authority of the Bishop of Rome.

3. The world-wide clusters of "communities of faith" have as their prime function cooperating with "mankind in building and assuring the success of world peace and world reform in the use of the earth's resources so as to eliminate economic oppression and political imperialism."

4. The rules of the "former" Roman Catholic Church on issues such as contraception, marriage, death, and sexuality must be brought into fraternal alignment with the outlook, desires, and practices of the world at large.[2]

The Conciliar Church And The Mass

In 1963, Pope Paul VI established the Concilium, which consisted of some 200 individuals, many of whom had functioned as Conciliar *periti* ("experts") during Vatican Council II. It was to this committee that Pope Paul VI entrusted the duty of carrying out the liturgical reform mandated by Vatican II. At its head was Archbishop Annibale Bugnini, who allegedly enjoyed well-established connections with Freemasonry. The Concilium was helped by six Protestant "observers," whom Paul VI publicly thanked for their assistance in re-editing new liturgical texts.[3]

According to the statements of Paul VI, the changes were made: 1) to bring the Church's liturgy into line with modern mentality; 2) in obedience to the mandate of Vatican II; 3) to take cognizance of progress in liturgical studies; 4) to return to primitive practice; and 5) for "pastoral" reasons.[4]

Archbishop Bugnini, the Secretary of Consilium, and the Reverend Peter Coughlan stated that the Instruction would treat of theological principles, constitute a full theological exposition of the new rite, describe the New Mass from a doctrinal point of view, and serve as an "introduction of a doctrinal character."[5]

Archbishop Bugnini, Pope Paul VI's executive officer in the creation of the Novus Ordo Missae (New Order of the Mass), described the result as "a new song" and as "the conquest of the Church." Cardinal Benelli, one of the principal architects of the new liturgy, stated that it reflects a "new ecclesiology."[6]

The "New Mass," or the Novus Ordo Missae, was first offered publicly in the Sistine Chapel before a Synod of Bishops in October 1967. At that time it was called the Missa Normativa, or Normative Mass. The bishops present were polled as to whether it should be implemented: seventy-one voted yes, sixty-two voted yes with reservations, and forty-three rejected it outright. To accommodate the wishes of this last group, a number of minor changes were made, including restoration of two of the traditional Offertory prayers.[7]

Some worried bishops intervened in what is now called the Ottaviani Intervention. The central contention of the Ottaviani Intervention is that the New Order of Mass teems with dangerous errors in doctrine and represents an attack against the Catholic teaching on the Mass. The authors of the Intervention stated that their intention was not to present an exhaustive treatment of all the problems the New Mass poses, but rather to point out those deviations from Catholic doctrine and practice which are most typical of the New Mass. Among these the Intervention lists are the following:

• A new definition of the Mass, as an "assembly," rather than a sacrifice offered to God;

• Omissions of elements emphasizing the Catholic teaching (utterly repudiated by Protestants) that the Mass makes satisfaction for sins;

• The reduction of the priest's role to a position approximating that of a Protestant minister;

• Implicit denials of Christ's Real Presence and the doctrine of Transubstantiation;

• The change of the Consecration from a sacramental action into a mere narrative retelling of the story of the Last Supper;

• The fragmenting of the Church's unity of belief through the introduction of countless options; and

- Ambiguous language and equivocation throughout the rite which compromise the Church's doctrines.[8]

Pope Paul VI promulgated the New Order of the Mass after responding to the Ottaviani intervention. The use of the Roman Missal of 1962 was authorized by Pope John Paul II in October 1984, only as long as those using it agreed that the New Order of the Mass is valid. The Holy Spirit continues to guide the Church and vouchsafe its authority under the guidance of the Magisterium, Scripture, and Tradition.

Divine Appeal Revelations

Sister Anna Ali, born December 29, 1966, in Kenya, and baptized in April 1979, was brought up in the Moslem faith. Her father was a devout Moslem but her parents split over the issue of the Catholic faith of the mother. Sister Anna has apparitions of Jesus, and writes down His words. Her revelations focus on Eucharistic devotion. Sister Anna's messages have been approved by her bishop.[9]

The Holy Sacrifice Abolished?

Our Lord has told Sister Anna that the devil is making every effort to abolish His Presence and the Holy Sacrifice of the Mass. The devil is using many lost souls and even many consecrated ones, who are working hard in this endeavor. More than ever before, says the Lord, the Freemasons attack His Divine Sacrament of Love in the tabernacle. They have all agreed to abolish the Mass.

In the Divine Appeal Number 4: Our Lord said: "Pray a great deal for humanity; the world is growing from bad to worse. **The devil is making every effort to abolish the Holy Sacrifice of the Mass. Divine Justice is prepared to act with My eyes fixed on Heaven.** It will be terribly frightful as if it were the end of the world. But the end has not arrived" (September 23, 1987).

In Divine Appeal Number 35, Our Lord said, "Pray for the many lost souls and many of My Own consecrated ones. The devil is using them in order to abolish the Sacrifice of the Holy Mass" (November 1, 1987).

In Divine Appeal Number 46, He said, "These times are My difficult hours when the devil is making every effort to abolish the Holy Sacrifice of the Mass.... Pray, pray for those who ridicule, abuse, condemn and more than in the past, step on Me in order to abolish My Presence in the Sacrament of Love" (December 5, 1987).

In Divine Appeal Number 47, He said, "My own...are labouring hard to abolish My Presence and the Holy Sacrifice of the Mass" (December 6, 1987).

In Divine Appeal Number 53, He said, "The devil is giving battle against My Divine Sacrament of Love. I am so abused and blasphemed. My own...are labouring hard to abolish My Presence in the Holy Sacrifice of the Mass" December 14, 1987).

In Divine Appeal Number 54, Our Lord said, "These are the dark hours when the devil is using My Own...who are labouring hard to destroy the Holy Sacrifice of the Mass and to destroy souls in order to lead them to perdition. My sacraments are abandoned and despised; My mysteries are blasphemed. Continuously, and more than ever before, the Freemasons attack My Divine Sacrament of Love in the tabernacle" (December 15, 1987).

In Divine Appeal 70, He said, "Time is approaching when My church will be devastated and sacked. My Own...have become like enraged lions. There are many sacrileges committed against My Presence in the tabernacles. Many have lost their dignity and light of reason. The devil has chained their hearts. Led by him they labour hard to abolish the Holy Sacrifice of the Mass. The chalice is filled" (January 18, 1988).

In Divine Appeal 71, Jesus said, "The Freemasons are abusing Me in the tabernacles and in My very Gospel. The iniquity is repugnant. Unite your heart to My tears of blood. These are the moments they are laboring hard to abolish My Holy Sacrifice of the Mass.... Evil concerns are in the hands of the Freemasons. They have all agreed to abolish the Mass.... Satan is in the midst of their ranks. I assure you that souls are allied with Satan. My great love for mankind keeps me day and night in the Blessed Sacrament. How much pain do I receive from their treason and indignity! With many sins, revenge cries out on My Eternal Father's behalf. I desire mankind to be saved. No one goes to hell without his consent. I am calling all back to My sheepfold. The world has lost its senses" (January 19, 1988).

Scripture also speaks of the abolition of the daily sacrifice. Daniel 12: 4-13 speaks of the daily sacrifice actually being abolished for a period of 1, 290 days: "As for you, Daniel, keep secret the message and seal the book until the end time; many shall fall away and evil shall increase."

"I, Daniel, looked and saw two others, one standing on either bank of the river. One of them said to the man clothed in linen, who was upstream, 'How long shall it be to the end of these appalling things?' The man clothed in linen, who was upstream, lifted his right and left hands to Heaven; and I heard him swear by Him Who lives forever that it should be a year, two years, a half-year; and that, when the power of the destroyer of the holy people was brought to an end, all these things should end. I heard, but I did not understand; so I asked, 'My lord, what follows this?' 'Go, Daniel,' he said, 'because the words are to be kept secret and sealed until the end time. Many shall be refined, purified, and tested, but the wicked shall prove wicked; none of them shall have understanding, but the wise shall have it. **From the time that the daily sacrifice is abolished and the horrible abomination is set up, there shall be one thousand two hundred and ninety days. Blessed is the man who has patience and perseveres until the one thousand three hundred and thirty-five days. Go, take your rest, you shall rise for your reward at the end of days.'"**

The December 31, 1992, message of Our Lady to Father Gobbi stated: **"The Holy Mass is the daily sacrifice, the pure oblation which is offered to the Lord everywhere, from the rising of the sun to its going down. The sacrifice of the Mass renews that which was accomplished by Jesus on Calvary. By accepting the protestant doctrine, people will hold that the Mass is not a sacrifice but only a sacred meal, that is to say, a remembrance of that which Jesus did at His Last Supper. And thus, the celebration of Holy Mass will be suppressed. In this abolition of the daily sacrifice consists *the horrible sacrilege* accomplished by the Antichrist, which will last about three-and-a-half years, namely, 1, 290 days."**

Further Schisms Prophesied

Several people recognized by the Church have spoken about the predicted schism and events related to it:

Blessed Anna-Katarina Emmerick

In the 1820s, Blessed Anna-Katarina Emmerick, an Augustinian nun and stigmatist, had visions of the Church in the future. On May

13, 1820, she stated, "I saw also the relationship between the two popes....I saw how baleful would be the consequences of this false church. I saw it increase in size; heretics of every kind came into the city [of Rome]. The local clergy grew lukewarm, and I saw a great darkness.... Once more I saw that the Church of Peter was undermined by a plan evolved by the secret sect, while storms were damaging it.

"But I saw also that help was coming when distress had reached its peak. I saw again the Blessed Virgin ascend on the Church and spread her mantle [over it]. I saw a Pope who was at once gentle, and very firm.... I saw a great renewal, and the Church rode high in the sky."

On September 12, 1820, she said: "I saw a strange church being built against every rule.... No angels were supervising the building operations. In that church nothing came from high above.... There was only division and chaos. It's probably a church of human creation, following the latest fashion, as well as the new heterodox church of Rome, which seems of the same kind.... I saw again the strange big church that was being built there [in Rome]. There was nothing holy in it.... Everything was being done according to human reason. I saw all sorts of people, things, doctrines, and opinions. There was something proud, presumptuous, and violent about it, and they seemed to be very successful. I did not see a single angel nor a single saint helping in the work. But far away in the background, I saw the seat of a cruel people armed with spears, and I saw a laughing figure which said: 'Do build it as solid as you can; we will pull it to the ground.'"

From August to October 1820: "I see more martyrs, not now but in the future.... I saw the secret sect relentlessly undermining the great Church. Near them I saw a horrible beast coming up from the sea.... When the Church had been for the most part destroyed [by the secret sect], and when only the sanctuary and altar were still standing, I saw the wreckers enter the Church with the Beast. There they met a Woman of noble carriage who seemed to be with child because she walked slowly. At this sight, the enemies were terrorized, and the Beast could not take but another step forward. It projected its neck towards the Woman as if to devour her, but the Woman turned about and bowed down [towards the altar], her head touching the ground. Thereupon, I saw the Beast taking to flight towards the sea again, and the enemies were fleeing in the greatest confusion.... Then, I saw that the Church was being promptly rebuilt, and she was more magnificent than ever before."

On October 1, 1820: "The Church is in great danger. We must pray so that the Pope may not leave Rome; countless evils would result if he did. They are now demanding something from him. The Protestant doctrine and that of the schismatic Greeks are to spread everywhere. I now see that in this place [Rome] the [Catholic] Church is being so cleverly undermined, that there hardly remain a hundred or so priests who have not been deceived. They all work for destruction, even the clergy. A great devastation is now near at hand."

On April 20, 1820: "I had another vision of the great tribulation. It seems to me that a concession was demanded from the clergy which could not be granted. I saw many older priests, especially one, who wept bitterly. A few younger ones were also weeping. But others, and the lukewarm among them, readily did what was demanded. It was as if people were splitting into two camps."

On April 22, 1823: "I saw that many pastors allowed themselves to be taken up with ideas that were dangerous to the Church. They were building a great, strange, and extravagant Church. Everyone was to be admitted in it in order to be united and have equal rights: Evangelicals, Catholics, sects of every description. Such was to be the new Church.... But God had other designs."

"I see that when the Second Coming of Christ approaches, a bad priest will do much harm to the Church. When the time of the reign of Antichrist is near, a false religion will appear which will be opposed to the unity of God and His Church. This will cause the greatest schism the world has ever known. The nearer the time of the end, the more the darkness of Satan will spread on earth, the greater will be the number of the children of corruption, and the number of the just will correspondingly diminish."[10]

Antipope, No Pope

Nothing is new under the sun. The Church in her history has often been plagued by schism, apostasy, and two popes simultaneously claiming the same throne. Prophecies as well as some recent events seem to indicate we may be headed in the same direction: The Petrine Keys of John Paul II may soon be sought by another, as dissenters and false teachers in the Vatican become more open and rebellious.

Richard Langley in *Signs of the Times* has illustrated the historical precedent for the Antipope. "There have been at least thirty-seven Antipopes in history. The Great Western Schism came about after the election of Pope Urban VI, April 8, 1378. On August 2, 1378 the Cardinals issued a statement that the election was invalid, claiming they were pressured into electing him out of fear. They demanded that Urban VI resign his office. He refused so they elected another pope, who called himself Clement VII, who went to Avignon. Each pope excommunicated the other and claimed him to be schismatic and deposed. Both appeared to be validly elected. Countries, saints of the Church, and religious orders were split by this. The Franciscans elected two Master generals of their order, one supported one pope, the other the other pope. Confusion reigned. Who to follow? A Council was called in Constance in 1414 to resolve this.

"The Council of Constance declared that general councils were superior to the pope, and had set up, in the resolution of the Western Schism, the mandate that the Church be ruled by general councils. After the Council of Constance, this idea originally subscribed to by the opposing sides was subsequently ignored and refuted by Martin V and his successors, who did however call some general councils. The canons of the council mandating this were declared invalid, but the remaining ones for the most part were accepted as valid and the Council of Constance was listed as a valid ecumenical council.

"Although the principle had been that only a pope could call a general council, the idea grew that the real authority was vested in the episcopate as a whole and that general councils were superior to the authority of the pope at any time and not in emergencies, a view known as conciliarism. The pope was considered a figurehead. Subsequent popes had to fight to restore their supremacy over councils and bishops.

"This problem plagued the Church until the declaration of the Infallibility of the Pope by Vatican I, July 18, 1870. This Council was permanently suspended during the Italian Revolution, due to the entrance of Garibaldi's troops into Rome in July of 1870, leaving incomplete the Church's position on the collegial relationship between all the bishops of the world as a body and the pope. This was partly resolved in Vatican II, at which time, out of three competing interpretations, Pope Paul VI's position, after his intervention with a

Preliminary Explanatory Note, was accepted by the Council. His position was that the pope personally was the subject of supreme power in the Church, and also the college of bishops when united to its head, the pope. **This meant that the episcopal college could not exercise its supreme power independently of the pope.**"

Mr. Langley further stated: "There is a direct connection between the national episcopal conference's rise to power and the notion of collegiality. The national episcopal conferences, councils of bishops...are purely human institutions, since as Cardinal Ratzinger has publicly stated they are not hierarchically instituted. They have however begun to act at times independently of Rome. This tends to foster the idea of a "national church" which could lead to schism."[11]

Catholic prophecy warns us of severe problems threatening the papacy in these end times. One realistic scenario for our time centers on the persecution of Catholics who follow the teachings of the true Church. When Pope John Paul II is among us no longer, the general indication from today's seers—as well as from thoughtful observers of the Church—is that chaos will be in our midst. An Antipope will seize papal authority, and the faithful element in the Church will be subjected to intense persecutions. Prophecy tells us of persecution like never before in history for those who follow the teachings of the Church. It will be those who hold fast to the truths of the faith who will be labelled as the perpetrators of this horrible schism, according to some visionaries.

The Pope Overthrown

Blessed Joachim (d. 1202): "Toward the end of the world, Antichrist will overthrow the pope and usurp his See."[12]

Pope Flees Rome

John of Vitiguerro (Thirteenth Century): "The pope will change his residence and the Church will not be defended for twenty-five months or more because, during all that time there will be no Pope in Rome.... After many tribulations, a Pope shall be elected out of those who survived the persecutions."[13]

Blessed Anna-Maria Taigi (Nineteenth Century): "Religion shall be persecuted, and priests massacred. Churches shall be closed, but only for a short time. The Holy Father shall be obliged to leave Rome."[14]

No Pope

Maria Steiner (Nineteenth Century): "I see the Lord as He will be scourging the world and chastising it in a fearful manner so that few men and women will remain....The Holy Church will be persecuted, and Rome will be without a shepherd. But the Lord showed me how beautiful the world will be after this awful punishment."[15]

The Pope is Killed

Saint Hildegard (d. 1179): "One of the remaining Mohammedans will be converted, become a priest, bishop and cardinal, and when the new Pope is elected (immediately before Antichrist) this cardinal will kill the pope before he is crowned, through jealousy, he wishing to be pope himself; then when the other cardinals elect the next pope this cardinal will proclaim himself Anti-Pope, and two thirds of the Christians will go with him."[16]

Venerable Bartholomew Holzhauser (d. 1658), "Antichrist and his army will conquer Rome, kill the Pope and take the throne."[17]

Two More Popes

At Garabandal, Spain, Our Blessed Mother in 1962 told Conchita, one of the visionaries that, "there would be only two more popes after Pope Paul VI and that one of the popes would have a very short reign. But this does not mean that the world will come to an end."[18]

Antichrist

Antichrist in the broad sense of the word is anyone who denies that Jesus is the Christ (1 John 2:18-22). Throughout history the spirit of antichrist is spoken of with a small "a." The Scriptures speak of the **Antichrist** as a person, an individual. It is the physical manifestation of a man. At LaSalette Mary warned, "Rome will loose the faith and become the seat of Antichrist." In the Marian Movement of Priests on June 17, 1989, Our Lady spoke at length about the Antichrist. She said that at the peak of the apostasy and tribulation the door would be open for the appearance of the Antichrist. Echoing Scripture, she said that people would not be able to buy or sell without the mark of the Beast.

"Before the coming of our Divine Savior there were many prophecies and figures given of Him. It shall be the same for Antichrist. The prophet Daniel speaks of him in a literal and mystical sense in four different chapters (namely, 7, 9, 11, and 12), while Saint Matthew (24), Saint Mark (13), Saint John (5), Saint Paul's Second Epistle to the Thessalonians, Saint John in his first and second Epistles, and especially the Apocalypse (13), etc., tell us of his future or coming event. A few decades ago it was quite a difficult problem for theologians to explain how Antichrist would bring the whole world under his political and religious dominion."[19]

Antichrist is a person who rules for a period of time according to the end day prediction in the book of Daniel. In the book of Daniel, the Archangel Michael is spoken about as the great prince who protects the people in the end days. Daniel writes, **"There will be a time of distress such as has not happened from the beginning of nations..." (Daniel 12:1).** The passages speak of great distress and the perpetual sacrifice of the Mass being abolished for three-and-a-half years. The abomination being erected could be the Antichrist sitting in Rome during his reign causing distress and nearly unbelievable pain on the earth, "such has not happened from the beginning of the nations."

The religious and secular stages have been set for his imminent appearance. Our Blessed Mother in her locutions to Father Gobbi, on September 18, 1988, hinted at the ominous events awaiting us in the next few years: **"In this period of ten years there will come to completion that fullness of time which was a pointed out to you by me, beginning with LaSalette all the way to my most recent and present apparitions.... In the period of ten years the mystery of iniquity, prepared for by the ever increasing spread of apostasy, will become manifest."**

Our Blessed Mother at LaSalette spoke about the Antichrist: "It will be during that time that the Antichrist will be born of a Hebrew nun, a false virgin who will communicate with the old serpent, the master of impurity, his father will be B. At birth, he will spew out blasphemy; he will have teeth, in a word, he will be the devil incarnate. He will scream horribly, he will perform wonders, he will feed on nothing but impurity. He will have brothers who, although not devils incarnate like him, will be children of evil. At the age of twelve, they will draw attention upon themselves by the gallant victories they will have won; soon they will lead armies, aided by the legions of hell....

"Rome will lose the faith and become the seat of the Antichrist. The Church will be in eclipse, the world will be in dismay. But now Enoch and Eli will come, filled with the spirit of God. They will preach the might of God, and men of good will believe in God, and many souls will be comforted. They will make great steps forward through the virtue of the Holy Spirit and will condemn the devilish lapses of the Antichrist. There will be bloody wars and famines, plagues and infectious diseases. It will rain a fearful hail of animals. There will be thunderstorms which will shake cities, earthquakes which will swallow up countries. Voices will be heard in the air. Men will beat their heads against walls, call for their death, and on another side death will be their torment. Blood will flow on all sides. Who will be the victor if God does not shorten the length of the test?

"All the blood, the tears, and the prayers of the righteous, God will relent. Enoch and Eli will be put to death. Pagan Rome will disappear. It is time; the sun is darkening; only faith will survive. Now is the time; the abyss is opening. Here is the king of kings of darkness, here is the Beast with his subjects, calling himself the Savior of the world. He will rise proudly into the air to go to Heaven. He will fall, and the earth, which will have been in a continuous series of evolutions for three days, will open its fiery bowels; and he will have plunged for eternity with all his followers into the everlasting chasms of hell. And then water and fire will purge the earth and consume all the works of men's pride and all will be renewed. God will be served and glorified."

Several past prophets in Church history have written about the physical manifestation of the mystery of iniquity becoming a man who rules. The Fathers and Saints of the Church have pondered deeply over what Scripture tells us about the Antichrist and his reign:

Saint **Hippolytus** (d. 235): "John says, 'I will give power unto my two witnesses, and they shall prophecy a thousand and two hundred and threescore days, clothed in sackcloth. That is the half of the week whereof Daniel spake. These are the two olive trees and the two candlesticks standing before the Lord of the earth...For this is what the prophets Enoch and Elias will preach.

"Let us observe somewhat in detail what Daniel says in his visions. For in distinguishing the kingdoms that are to rise after these things, he showed also the coming of Antichrist in the last times, and the consummation of the whole world. Daniel says: 'And one week will make a covenant with many, and it shall be that in the midst (half) of the week my sacrifice and oblation shall cease.' By one week, therefore, he meant the last week which is to be at the end of the whole world....

"In every respect that deceiver seeks to make himself appear like the Son of God. Christ is a lion, and the Antichrist is a lion. Christ is King of things celestial and things terrestrial, and Antichrist will be king upon earth. The Savior was manifested as a lamb; and he, too, will appear as a lamb, while he is a wolf within.

"When Daniel says, 'I shall make a covenant for one week,' he indicated even years; and the one half of the week is for preaching of the prophets, and for the other half of the week—that is to say, for three years and a half—Antichrist will reign upon the earth. And after this his kingdom and his glory will be taken away. And by reason of the scarcity of food, all will go to him and worship him; and he will put his mark on their right hand and on their forehead, that no one may put the sign of the honorable cross upon his forehead with his right hand; but his hand is bound.... And his seal upon the forehead and upon the right hand is the number, six hundred threescore and six."[20]

Origen (d. 254): "When the close of the times draws nigh, a great prophet [Elias] shall be sent from God to turn men to the knowledge of God, and he shall receive the power of doing wonderful things. Wherever men shall not hear him, he will shut up the heavens, and cause it to withhold its rains; he will turn their water into blood; and torment them with thirst and hunger; and if any one shall endeavor to injure him fire shall come forth out of his mouth, and shall burn that man.

"By these prodigies and powers he shall turn many to the worship of God; and when his works shall be accomplished, another king shall arise out of Syria, born from an evil spirit, the overthrower and destroyer of the human race [Antichrist], who shall destroy that which is left by the former evil, together with himself....

"But that king will not only disgrace himself, but will also be a prophet of lies; and he will constitute and call himself God; and power will be given him to do signs and wonders, by the sight of which he may entice men to adore him. He will command fire to come down from Heaven, and the sun to stand and leave its course, and an image to speak, and these things shall be done at his words—by which miracles many even of the wise shall be enticed by him.

"Then he will attempt to destroy the temple of God, and persecute the righteous people; and there will be distress and tribulation, such as there never has been from the beginning of the world. Power will be given him to desolate the whole earth for forty-two months. That will be the time in which righteousness will be cast out, and innocence be hated; in which the wicked shall prey upon the good as enemies; neither law, nor order, nor military discipline be preserved."[21]

Saint John Chrysostom (d. 407): "The world will be faithless and degenerate after the birth of Antichrist. Antichrist will be possessed by Satan and be the illegitimate son of a Jewish woman from the East."[23]

Saint Augustine (d. 430): "Daniel prophesies of the Last Judgment in such a way as to indicate that Antichrist shall first come, and to carry on his description to the eternal reign of the saints.... But he who reads this passage, even half asleep, cannot fail to see that the kingdom of Antichrist shall fiercely, though for a short time, assail the Church before the last judgment of God shall introduce the eternal reign of saints. For it is patent from the context that the time, times, and half a time, means a year, and two years, and a half a year, that is to say, three years and a half."[24]

Saint John Damascene (d. 770): "He will be known as Antichrist who shall come about the end of the world. His mother will proclaim she gave birth to him while remaining a virgin. He will reign from ocean to ocean. Antichrist shall be an illegitimate child, under the complete power of Satan, and God, knowing his incredible future perversity, will allow the devil to take a full and perpetual possession of him from his very sinful conception."[25]

Saint Hildegard (d. 1179): "The Son of Corruption and Ruin will appear and reign only for a short time, towards the end of the days of the world's duration.... He shall come in the last days of the world. He shall not be Satan himself, but a human being equaling and resembling him in atrocious hideousness. His mother, a depraved woman, possessed by the devil, will live as a prostitute in the desert.... She will maintain that her son was presented to her by God in a supernatural manner, as was the Child of the Blessed Virgin. She will then be venerated as a saint by deceived people.

"Antichrist will come from a land that lies between two seas, and will practice tyranny in the East. After his birth false teachers and doctrines will appear, followed by wars, famines, and pestilence.... He will be raised at different secret places and will be kept in seclusion until full grown. He will lure the people to him by giving them complete exemption from the observance of all divine and ecclesiastical commandments, by forgiving them their sins and requiring of them only their belief in his divinity. He will spurn and reject Baptism and the Gospel. He will say Jesus of Nazareth is not the son of God, only a deceiver....

" He will say I am the Savior of the world...especially will he try to convince the Jews that he is the Messiah sent by God, and the Jews will accept him as such...yet by his moral laws he will try to reverse all order on earth. Therefore he is called in Holy Writ the 'Lawless One'.... He will discard all laws, morals, and religious principles, to draw the world to himself. He will grant entire freedom from the commandments of God and the Church and permit everyone to live as his passion dictates.... Religion he will endeavor to make convenient. He will say that you need not fast and embitter your life by renunciation.... It will suffice to love God.... He will preach free love and tear asunder family ties...maintain sin and vice are not sin and vice.... **Immediately preceding Antichrist there will be starvation and earthquakes.**"[26]

Saint Bridget of Sweden (d. 1373): "The time of Antichrist will be near when the measure of injustice will overflow and when wickedness has grown to immense proportions, when the Christians love heresies and the unjust trample underfoot the servants of God.

"At the end of this age, the Antichrist will be born. As Christ was born from the highest type of womanhood [Virgin] so Antichrist will be born from the lowest [prostitute]. He will be a child-wonder at birth. His mother will be an accursed woman, who will pretend to be well-informed in spiritual things, and his father will be an accursed man, from the seed of whom the devil shall form his work. The time of this Antichrist, well-known to me, will come when iniquity and impiety shall above measure abound, when injustice shall have filled the measure to overflowing, and wickedness shall have grown to immeasurable proportions.... He will reign during three years, and shall have dominion over the whole earth.... **In the year 1980 the wicked shall prevail**."[27]

Jeanne Le Royer (d. 1798), also known as Sister Mary of the Nativity: "Many precursors, false prophets, and members of infernal secret societies, worshippers of Satan, shall impugn the most sacred dogmas and doctrines of our holy religion, shall persecute the faithful, shall commit abominable actions; but the real and extreme abomination and desolation shall more fully be accomplished during the reign of Antichrist, which shall last about three years and a half. Woe, woe, woe to the last century which is descending! What tribulations precede its commencements. Out of this mighty voice I recognized that these woeful tribulations will make their appearance in the age before the judgment. And as I pondered over and weighed, in God, the century, I saw, that which begins with 1800 will not yet be the last. I see that when the Second Coming of Christ approaches, a bad priest will do much harm to the Church.

"When the time of the reign of Antichrist is near, a false religion will appear which will be opposed to the unity of God and His Church. This will cause the greatest schism the world has ever known. The nearer the time of the end, the more the darkness of Satan will spread on earth, the greater will be the number of the children of corruption, and the number of the just will correspondingly diminish.

"Antichrist will kill the Pope, probably by crucifixion. As a child of ten he will know more than anyone else in the world and when he is thirty he will begin his real work. Fifteen days after the ascension of Enoch and Elias into Heaven, terrible catastrophes will come upon the earth: most severe earthquakes, tidal waves inundating much of the earth's surface, culminating in a thick darkness over the entire earth."[28]

The Stage is Set

Events in the world are happening at such an accelerated pace that we can barely comprehend them. Our human faculties have difficulty understanding and following the strategic movements of Heaven and hell as they battle for control of the world and its people. The mystery of iniquity is in our midst. Major precursors of the Antichrist such as Hitler, Lenin, Stalin, and Mao have all come and gone in this century.

According to the 1982 revelations to Eileen George of Massachusetts from God the Father, another precursor is due to arrive in the Middle East between 1990 and 1999, followed by the Antichrist who is already alive and who supposedly comes from Syria. The identity of these two, the precursor antichrist and the Antichrist, is at the present time masked under a cloak of secrecy.[29]

The battle is being waged in the areas of finance, politics, society, family, and religion. As Scripture tells us, Satan is the Prince of this world. In contrast, Jesus specifically said His kingdom is not of this world. All that is of God, Satan hates and seeks to destroy.

The one-world government introduced by many of the antichrists has been planned over many generations. As Franklin Delano Roosevelt said, "In politics, nothing happens by accident. If it happens, you can bet it was planned that way." The structure has been developed gradually through the years by the secret societies of the Beast. The hidden agenda, known only to the privileged few, is nothing short of one-world government, under one ruler. It is to be in place between 1995 and 1998 and will replace all sovereign nations.

The United Nations is the enforcement body of the structure in its present evolutionary form. President Bush during the Persian Gulf War spoke about the New World Order, a term which surprised almost everyone by its frequent use—all but those few powerful persons in the know. Soviet Prime Minister Edward Shevardnadze told the United Nations in reference to Iraq's assault on Kuwait, "An act of terrorism has been perpetrated against the emerging New World Order."[30]

Annoying disruptions in the New World Order, if they are not in the plans of those in control, are promptly crushed. Economic control is one tentacle of this octopus-like movement. The control will always be in the hands of the large multinational banks. They will admit only those nations who will play by the rules they set. Because the need for capital is so great, no nation can survive without the help of large lending institutions. The lending agencies have enjoyed controlling the destinies of nations for a very long time. This control will increase. Conformity to the world lending rules is a must for the survival of a nation. A nation must conform or perish.

Technological advances will also help to allow a world-wide government to rule. With transactions of all sorts speeding around the globe through fiber optics, satellites, very small aperture terminals, compatible computers, centralized data bases, mobile telephones, and other methods of communicating via wireless means, new vistas have opened up for the world. The credit card with a microprocessor chip will allow debit and credit from anywhere at anytime. All transactions will feed into a few main databases—under the control ultimately of Big Brother. The chip will store massive amounts of information and will become each person's identity on plastic. An identity like a social security number will be issued to eliminate credit card abuse. The bar code or universal product code will be a very effective tracking method for all purchases. All transactions will be scanned, and the use of the physical property of money will gradually decrease. The personal computer that began in a very primitive form in a California garage in 1979 now has powerful workstations and distributed architecture.

With geometric growth in technology each year, the speed of change will go beyond our grasp to understand. Tom Peters, the author of *In Search of Excellence* and *Liberation Management* recently said, "technology will cause us to go bonkers this year, bonkers squared next year, and bonkers cubed the year after."[31] The free flow of information along data highways being piped into our homes and offices will permit unimaginable control by a small elite.

Ecclesiastical control has been accomplished through the secret societies, modernism, and the World Council of Churches, with the goal of one New Age or watered-down ecumenical church. The breakdown of Catholicism needed to happen first before this could take place. In the past, the Roman Catholic Church was too well-organized and too strong. It had to be dismantled, and it had to happen first from within. Recall earlier where the book *AA 1025* was discussed; the book detailed how a communist secret agent infiltrated the Church. One thousand and twenty-four men are said to have preceded the anti-apostle AA 1025 into Catholic seminaries—and hundreds more followed him into the Church as priests.

Our Blessed Mother, through Father Gobbi, has told us a great deal about Ecclesiastical Masonry and the damage it is doing. At LaSalette, Our Blessed Mother told us about this destruction in great detail. Today we are in the final act as the Church fights for its survival. The one hundred-year reign of Satan has taken its toll.

One-World Government

The armies are poised for battle. Satan has his cohort; Mary has hers. The tactics could not be more dissimilar. Mary's plan, which is God's plan, is prayer, fasting, penance, reconciliation. We are to love one another, be humble, little, docile. We are to become as little children, to be guided by Mary our mother and by Our Lord. Satan's plan uses the false idols of money, power, lust, greed, clothed in pride.

The political, financial, and ecclesiastical clout of the people working behind the scenes for the development of a one-world government is overwhelming. Were it not for the apparitions of Mary, the Mother of God, the Prophetess of Our Times, and her detailed messages to Father Gobbi and others, we would know little about the evolving Satanic plan which has nearly come to fruition.

For an in-depth account of how masterfully this Satanic plan is being executed on all powerful secular and ecclesiastical fronts read the account by Gary Kah in his book, *En Route to Global Occupation.* It outlines in detail the structure of secular control through reputable organizations which are household names. He warns that national sovereignty will soon be a thing of the past. Political forces around the world are now cooperating in an unprecedented fashion to achieve their goal of uniting the people of this planet under a New World Order.

The umbrella organization actually charged with the task of bringing us into the New World Order is called *The World Constitution and Parliament Association* (WCPA). It has many financial supports. The agenda of the New World Order is being funded by literally hundreds of organizations. One is the Lucis Trust—called at first the *Lucifer Trust.* To name a secular organization the Lucifer Trust shows the boldness and confidence of the men behind this movement. But the use of such a name is really not surprising; the philosophy driving the creation of the New World Order is heavily indebted to the New Age, old pagan practices, Masonry, and the occult.

The members proposing a New World Order are a Who's Who of the world establishment, secular and ecclesiastic. Their agenda is control; their tactics, deceit. Most of the key players sit on the boards or committees of a few powerful organizations: the Council of Foreign Relations (CFR), the Trilateral Commission, the Bilderbergers, and the Club of Rome. Often members of one organization will be involved with several of the others as well.

On September 17, 1973, the Club of Rome published a special, highly confidential report called the "Regionalized and Adaptive

Model of the Global World System," which was sent to the power elite to be implemented. **This document reveals that the Club has divided the world into ten political/economic regions, which it refers to as "kingdoms"**—a designation that tracks eerily with the terminology used in the Book of Revelation, Chapter 13:1-2. In 1974 the authors of the report, Mihaljo Mesarovic and Edward Pestel published their findings in a book *Mankind at the Turning Point.* However, in this book, which is intended for public consumption, they have dropped the word "kingdom."[32]

The people belonging to these powerful organizations are high-ranking United Nations officials, noted world leaders, noted politicians, bankers, World Bank and International Monetary Fund officials, clergy, members of the World Future Society, top-level Masons, and people either inadvertently or purposely promoting a one-world government. The systems which they have developed are now in place to allow such a government with a leader to surface and rule between 1995 and 1998.

The foundation for this one world government was planned consciously by a political and financial elite. Much of the groundwork was laid 16 years ago, when the Constitution for the Federation Earth was adopted in June 1977.

This Constitution was first adopted at Innsbruck, Austria, at a meeting of the World Constituent Assembly—an event sponsored by the WCPA. The WCPA does not consider the United Nations part of its planned New World Order, but more than 20 percent of WCPA members belong to the United Nations. The WCPA plans to replace the UN—much like the UN replaced the League of Nations.

The Constitution for the Federation Earth was signed by 135 participants from twenty-five countries, and is intended to replace the UN Charter to become the centerpiece of the New World Order.

Gary Kah has a detailed "Diagram Of World Government under the Constitution For The Federation of Earth." The WCPA cites forty-nine problems of international concern, which it says point to the need for a one-world government. Fifteen deal with the environment, seven with military concerns (disarmament, prevention of war and terrorism), six with world hunger and poverty, four with international monetary matters. The WCPA bases its main argument for a New World Order on the threat of an impending climactic crisis.[33]

The environmental movement is probably the most powerful lobby today for a one world government—it is the trigger to send the bullet for conformity. Indeed, no one can deny the need to clean up the planet. Chernobyl is a prime example. Chernobyl fallout traveled over thousands of miles and as far north as Sweden and Lapland in a matter of days. Chernobyl showed that the whole Soviet system was in a meltdown—and in a few seconds it blasted into oblivion the claim that communism had shaped a society technologically superior, more caring, more efficient, and more honest than that of the corrupt West—and was more caring of its people, more efficient, and more honest. Chernobyl had become a symbol of the whole rotting communist system, with its callous, self-seeking bureaucrats, its barbarous robot-like enforcers, and its deceitful ideologists, whose lies were designed to tranquilize the Russian people into mindless docility. In the view of the other nations, what went on inside the country was permissible, but exporting lethal fallout to the West was an entirely different matter.

Here was a huge opening for the globalists. The money masters of the world could now anoint Mother Earth as the official queen before whom all must kneel. How could one logically disagree in light of Chernobyl? Chernobyl would be the vehicle to drag the world body of nations into its orbit. It is an ingenius strategy because no one can object to protecting the planet from the rot and stench of pollution.

The Rio, or Earth, Summit in Brazil in June 1992 provided an opportunity for the nations of the world to conform on much more than an environmental level; its connections to the New Age movement and Masonry are well-established. Rio was not solely about clean air, clean water, and containment of acid rain. It was about the massive redistribution of wealth from the industrial countries to the poor countries, global socialism, people control, and world government. Lester Brown, president of Worldwatch Institute, said, "I think when we look back, we will see the Rio conference as the event that marked the end of an era and the start of a new one."

The operative word again is "conformity"—if a nation stays within the rules set by the governing bodies, loan applications will be approved. Environmental compliance is only the first kind of conformity that can be forced on cash-starved nations needing access to world capital markets.

The environmental movement has clout that transcends all party affiliations. Vice President Albert Gore is a chief proponent of the movement and has in fact written a best-selling book on environmentalism. He is the "man of destiny" in the Clinton administration. Support for his policies exists across the political spectrum. Data from the Federal Election Commission reveal that Republican organizations took in contributions of $71.1 million in calendar year 1988, while Democratic institutions took in $18.6 million the same year. The Environmental Party had an operating budget of $336 million in 1988 with a donor base of 10 million persons more than both political parties. The Environmental Party has nearly four times the funding of the Democrats and the Republicans combined. Twelve organizations constitute the base support of the Environmental Party: Center for Marine Conservation, Clean Water Action Project, Environmental Defense Fund, Greenpeace USA, National Audubon Society, National Wildlife Federation, Natural Resources Defense Council, Nature Conservancy, Public Interest Research Group, Sierra Club, Wilderness Society, and World Wildlife Fund. It is only the people on the top who are aware of the true intent of its members' movements.[34]

The WCPA projects that the formation of the world government will occur sometime between 1995 and 1998. When will the Antichrist arrive on the world scene? All indications are that the stage is set on the secular and religious levels. **Once this world government is in place, the structure for the reign of Antichrist will be ready.** Gary Kah states, "The WCPA effort to form a New World Order is not based on need but on the hidden agenda of the occult secret societies to bring the world under their control in order to usher in the reign of their "World Teacher": the Antichrist."[35]

The World Powers

In history, seldom do events happen by chance. Jim Singer, of Ontario, Canada, has been receiving messages from Our Lord from May 1989 to September 1989 on a very consistent basis. Since then, the messages have been infrequent. On May 27, 1993, the Lord spoke to Jim Singer about the role of preplanned events and the earthly bodies which carry out these plans.

Jesus' first message to Jim was as follows: **"Dear children, the time has come that you can no longer survive without my direct** intervention. **The one you call Satan is the Shining Darkness who has poisoned all of your souls and has deprived you of the dignity with which I gifted each one of My children.** I created each one of you good. To each of you I gifted a whole and pure soul. Among you, children, there are no more souls which are whole. I am the truth and there is only one truth." Jesus is telling Jim Singer that He must intervene or we no longer can survive the onslaught of the devil.

For years, the United Nations has become the enforcement body of the world rulers. Premiers and presidents of nations will not go against the rulers of this institution. Who are these men? Most notably, the clout inside the United Nations is from the Group of Seven (G-7 nations)—the single most powerful body in the world controlling finance. These nations are the United States, Canada, Great Britain, France, Italy, Germany, and Japan—the world's major industrialized economies. Prime Minister John Major was the chairman in 1991, coordinating the West's policies toward the economic plight of the Soviet Union. The former Soviet Union is being given billions of dollars with the West knowing it can never be repaid. It is now under the world's financial mantle and in its controlling orbit. No nation today can go against the strength of this body. Saddam Hussein recently tried. Action was swift and effective.

"Revelation 13:1-7 states: "Then I saw a beast come out of the sea with ten horns and seven heads; on its horns were ten diadems, and on its heads blasphemous names. To it the dragon gave its own power and throne, along with great authority. I saw that one of its heads seemed to be mortally wounded, but this wound was healed. Fascinated, the whole world followed after the beast. They worshipped the dragon because it gave its authority to the beast; they also worshipped the beast and said, 'Who can compare with the beast or fight against it?' The beast was given a mouth uttering proud boasts and blasphemies, and it was given authority to act for forty-two months.... It was also allowed to wage war against the holy ones and conquer them, and it was granted authority over every tribe, people, tongue, and nation. All the inhabitants of the earth will worship it, all whose names were not written from the foundation of the world in the book of life, which belongs to the Lamb who was slain."

In concert with Daniel 12, the beast rules for forty-two months. The Black Beast, Masonry, the one-world government, Antichrist is given dominion over the earth for this period of time. The one-world government is allowed to wage war against the holy ones of God and conquer them, even to the point of abolishing the Holy Mass ("abolishing the perpetual sacrifice," as Daniel states it). The one-world ruler is given authority over every tribe, people, tongue, and nation. All inhabitants will worship it. Antichrist will appear to have the answers for our troubled world.

The role of Russia is unclear in many respects. In the September 18, 1992, message of Josyp Terelya from Marmora, Ontario, Our Lady said that Russia is preparing for world-wide revolution. Mr. Terelya had seen the face of Satan in Boris Yeltsin in his 1987 vision—before the coup. Mikhail Gorbachev has risen to head of the International Green Cross, taking over the environmental movement with governmental blessing. Isn't this odd? A former premier ousted in a coup by hardliners now is in the present government. Is Russia a mainstream player with the world body of the United Nations or an independent international villain?

On May 27, 1993, the Lord showed Jim Singer that the United Nations is the vehicle of planned events. Our Lord said: "...Look at what Satan is inflicting upon you; 326,000 of My children and all the agony which you are seeing today in your ancestral homeland [Jim originally is from Croatia] alone is just a prelude of sadistic fury and hate that Satan wants to pour out upon you. Out of His mercy and grace, the Father has gifted you the Queen of Peace, yet nations prostitute themselves in the United Nations and My children continue to pay deep homage to the *dead head which now lives again* in that city by the ocean. Know that it is...Satan's own servants who toil tirelessly to deliver My children into his clutches. Just as they contaminate and poison so much in your lives, they are the ones also who are overseeing the aims of that organization—the UN. Know that all their aims, each one of their moves and actions, are always preplanned. In their labors of deceit, even truth has become a sweet bait to be exploited by Satan and his earthly stewards. They lure away even your shepherds, My apostles, along with the entire flocks of My children.

"Today, as you stand at the threshold, you are the only ones who choose how much more suffering you must bear. I call My children to hear My mother's calls, to focus on her. Listen and respond to all that she asks of you. Be sure that the triumph of her heart is near. It is My mother, your Queen of Peace, who ardently wishes to show you the way and bring you all back to Me."

(Authors' note: Josyp Terelya, in his Marmora, Ontario, vision, uses this term "dead head" in reference to the United Nations. Jim's footnote is as follows: "Our Lord's reference to the United Nations as 'this dead head which now lives again' is peculiar and puzzling. A number of possible explanations for this term have been offered, both biblical and non-biblical. Although this term is not used anywhere in the Bible, there are a number of similar terms which do appear throughout the Scriptures. Chapter 13, verse 3 of Revelation makes reference to one of the beast's mortally wounded heads, but the mortal wound was healed. Even more interestingly, in Chapter 17, verse 8 of Revelation, the beast is said to 'have existed once and now exists no longer, and yet it will exist again.'")

On January 12, 1991, Our Lord appeared to Jim Singer and gave a message in which He stated: **"The Shining Darkness, that malefactor, is drawing your attention to the great evil which he threatens you with—the sort of catastrophe that your minds cannot begin to imagine, while he, in the meantime, is multiplying his evils in other parts of the world.** From the beginning you have been warned through this, My child, that these two years are the decisive years for all My children. Through your conversion all of you have been called into My secure embrace of love. More than half of that time has passed, but your hearts remain enslaved in thorns of evil. Today you have the choice of what kind of world you will have after these three days. **The evils to which you will soon be witnesses because of your disobedience and hard hearts towards Me will multiply among you. You have already been warned about them. In your apprehension of evil you have taken all the steps to protect yourselves from the horrors. But few are My children among you who have recognized the malefactor's hand among you.** Three days remain for you, by your free will, to consecrate your hearts to Me, to enjoy My rewards and victory over the malefactor. Three days remain for you to allow the malefactor seven years of his particular aggression and oppression among you. Through the ages you have been warned what the malefactor is preparing for you during these final times. Only by your conversion and sincere love will you be protected...."

During the April 22, 1991, apparition of Our Lord to Jim, He told him that, "Without My intervention you can no longer completely triumph over the evil one, for My earthly children are surrounded with traitors. Even among those who enjoy the confidence of My earthly children, there are those who are in the service of Satan. They consciously victimize My flock—their own brothers and sisters."

Our Lord's message of September 23, 1991, to Jim contained no secrets but stated in part, "Tell My children of the world to look at the satanic oppression in your ancestral homeland, for I have already warned you many times about the evils that this malefactor is preparing for you all. [Concerning the war in Bosnia]: tell My children to recognize that Satan is attacking My children of Croatia precisely because I have chosen them to be the model of My love to all My children of the world. **Do you not remember that I have warned you about the particular aggression that the Shining Darkness desires to unleash among My children of the Soviet Union?** I invite you all—evict the malefactor from your midst. Fill your hearts with My love. I call you again, return to My embrace, use My gifts. I will protect you. Satan aggressively wants to bring his hell into the Soviet Union. Not only will his fury be unleashed upon My children of that land, but the malefactor will utilize all his powers from hell to spill his rage from that land, through his earthly servants, to other lands as well. Son, only because of their firm and complete faith in Me will My children of Croatia be able to enjoy the victory over the Shining Darkness. **But, precisely because of their faith in Me, these children will also not be spared from the renewed vicious satanic attempt with which the malefactor will endeavor to flood, from the USSR, all the countries of the east. While they are convinced that they are enjoying liberty and freedom, Satan's rage will not spare My children of the Western world, either. Never have My children delighted in sin as now. In Noah's age, I cleansed the world of sins much lesser than these in which my children now take delight. Today many of My children's enjoyment is murderous sin. Many of My children are fully conscious of this. The faith of many who remain in My flock is lukewarm.**"

Jim stated: "In one of my conversations with the Lord, I asked the Lord to explain Revelation. The Lord's answer to this question was that the dragon with seven heads and ten horns now dwells in our world. The Lord said, "Look to the West.""

On May 28, 1992, Our Lord told Jim: "Babylon, too, has been rebuilt. It stands again. Soon in your midst and in full view will also stand a grand image (statue) of a false god. **The symbol of this image** will be worshipped by many, in almost every language....The beast has laid his vicious seven heads in the lands that you know as the G-7, while its body continues to crush My children in Russia."

On January 13, 1991, Jim also was shown that Satan, the malefactor, is allowed seven years of aggression and opposition. This brings us to the year 1998. This corresponds with the decisive period of ten years separating us from the end of this century, revealed in Our Blessed Mother's message to Father Gobbi on September 18, 1988, in which she said: "**there will come to completion that fullness of time beginning with LaSalette all the way to my most recent and present apparitions; the purification will come to its culmination; there will come to completion the time of the great tribulation, foretold in Holy Scripture, before the Second Coming of Christ; the mystery of iniquity, prepared for by the ever-increasing spread of apostasy, will become manifest; all the secrets which I have revealed to some of my children will come to pass and all the events which have been foretold will take place.**"

This also corresponds with the period of time for the onset of the events (revealed by God the Father to Eileen George) beginning between 1990 and 1999. Then there would be a long era of peace.

Our Blessed Mother told the Marian Movement of Priests on June 17, 1989, that, "Lucifer, the ancient serpent, the devil or Satan, the Red Dragon, becomes, in these last times, the Antichrist. The Apostle John already affirmed that whoever denies that Jesus Christ is God, that person is the Antichrist. The statue or idol, built in honor of the beast to be adored by all men, is the Antichrist...666 indicated thrice, that is to say, for the third time, expresses the year 1998, nineteen hundred and ninety-eight. In this period of history, Freemasonry, assisted by its Ecclesiastical form, will succeed in its great design: that of setting up an idol to be put in the place of Christ and his Church, a false christ and a false church. Consequently, the statue built in honor of the first beast, to be adored by all the inhabitants of the earth and which will seal with its mark all those who want to buy or sell, is that of the Antichrist. You will have thus arrived at the peak of the purification, of the great tribulation and of apostasy....almost all will follow the false christ and the false church. Then the door will be open for the appearance of...the very person of the Antichrist."

16

Wars, Disasters, And Tribulations

Certain events are willed by the Lord of History, and they shall take place.

Stefan Cardinal Wyszynski

On December 31, 1984, Our Blessed Mother told Father Gobbi how she will send signs so we may understand the times in which we live. She states: "Then, with the same familiarity that a mother has for her children, I will reveal to you the cares, the anxieties and the deep wounds of my Immaculate Heart and, at the same time, I will help you to understand and to interpret the signs of your times. Thus you can cooperate in the plan of salvation, which the Lord has for you and which He wishes to carry out in the course of the new days which await you.

"You are living under an urgent request made by your heavenly mother, who is inviting you to walk along the road of conversion and of return to God. Beloved children, share in my anxious motherly concern as I see that this call of mine is neither welcomed nor followed. And yet I see that the only possibility of your salvation is bound up uniquely with the return of humanity to the Lord, with a strong commitment to follow His law. Be converted and walk along the road of the grace of God and of love. Be converted and build up days of serenity and peace. Be converted and take part in the plan of divine mercy."

The Consequences Of Sin

For years, the world has been undergoing a great apostasy, with people and governments making decisions unmindful of God or His precepts. From January to March 1979, the Blessed Mother, through Father Gobbi, gave us four major signs which would indicate that the purification is near:

The First Sign: Confusion

"Beloved children, take refuge in my Immaculate Heart. The glorious reign of Christ will be preceded by a great suffering which will serve to purify the Church and the world and to lead them to their complete renewal. Jesus has already begun His merciful work of renewal with the Church, His spouse. Various signs indicate to you that the time of purification has come for the Church: the first of these is the confusion which reigns there. This in fact is the time of the greatest confusion. Confusion is spreading within the Church, where everything in the field of dogma, liturgy, and discipline is being subverted. These include truths revealed by my Son and which the Church has defined once and for all, through her divine and infallible authority. These truths are unchangeable, as the very truth of God is unchangeable. Many of these form part of real mysteries in the strict sense of the word, because they are not and never can be understood by human intelligence...."

The Second Sign: Lack of Discipline

"Thus, lack of discipline is spreading in the Church and reaping victims, even from among her very pastors. This is the second sign which indicates to you that, for the Church, the final time of purification has come: a lack of discipline which has spread throughout all levels, especially among the clergy. How many there are among the priests, who allow themselves to become absorbed in excessive activity and who no longer pray!"

The Third Sign: Division

"Today, my Immaculate Heart trembles and is anguished to see the division within the Church. This division...is the third sign which indicates to you with certainty that the final moment of her painful purification has come. If...the Church has many times been torn by division..., I nevertheless obtained from Jesus the singular privilege of her interior unity...."

The Fourth Sign: Persecution

"The fourth sign, which indicates to you that the culminating period of the Church's painful purification has come, is persecution.... She is persecuted in a subtle and painless manner, by being deprived bit by bit of the oxygen she needs to live."

One does not need great spiritual discernment to notice the significant increase in natural and man-made disasters in our midst. Wars and disasters often are sent for the punishment of sins. Tony Fernwalt, the stigmatist from Akron, Ohio, received a message from Our Lady on January 22, 1993, about the United States of America. This was the day President Clinton signed the bill allowing the testing of fetal tissue, and revoked the "gag rule," for federally-funded family planning clinics to counsel women to get abortions. January 22, 1993, was the twentieth anniversary of the landmark Supreme Court decision *Roe v. Wade*, legalizing abortion in the United States. With a defiant ceremony at the White House, President Clinton signed into existence federally-funded genocide of the unborn. By the summer of 1993, when President Clinton's fetal tissue research measure was enacted, he hailed it as the most significant piece of legislation thus far in his presidency.

Jesus said through Tony Fernwalt: "As of today you will find all that I have told you will soon start. Your country has truly become immoral and a godless nation. As your President has signed the papers to legalize the killing of the innocent, there is no one to blame for what will come from this signing.... Even my Pope, John Paul II, will speak out....the turmoil will soon begin.... It will be hard for the faithful....the storms will be of nature and man....as you have been told, these things will begin.... Do not fear criticism from any man. **Your country has fallen from grace,** and the world has fallen from grace also.... Fear no man; only fear God!"[1] We have brought these problems upon ourselves, and have only ourselves to blame.

The United States And Rome

The actions of the President of the United States on abortion and homosexuality are leading to an open confrontation with the Catholic Church united with Rome. If the Pope speaks out against the official U.S. administration position, retaliatory means might be taken—ever so subtly. Speaking in Denver on August 15, 1993, Pope John Paul II described American culture as a "culture of death" and encouraged the youth to be vocal against abortion and to shout it from the housetops.

The Catholic Church will be driven further away from the United States government, specifically if the Pope speaks out against government's increasing promotion of abortion. The Roman Catholic Church and the liberal agenda of President Clinton are incompatible. We should not be surprised if, under the guise of needing revenue, President Clinton attempts to tax churches in America.

The Signs Of Decline

Many signposts indicate our decline. The demise of our financial structures is one sign of our interior decay. Yesterday the Savings and Loan, today the commercial banks, and tomorrow the insurance companies and pension funds will all rapidly evaporate. Over two-thirds of the world goes to bed hungry or dying from starvation. AIDS is another crisis, clearly pointing to the dangers of unbridled lust—and also to the hard hearts of men, who refuse to change destructive habits, even in the face of God's merciful chastising. Incurable diseases will multiply as homosexuality in the world's major cities will continue to grow.

In the United States violence is exploding. Syndicated columnist George Will recently pointed out that here in the U.S. "firearms cause more deaths among those fifteen to twenty-four than all natural causes combined. In the span of just one generation, deviant behavior has soared to levels Americans flinch from recognizing."[2]

William Bennett, the former Secretary of Education and drug czar under the Reagan and Bush Administrations, and now at the Hudson Institute, has studied leading cultural indicators. He recently noted that "over the last three decades we have experienced substantial social regression," particularly in matters relating to families and children. Since 1960, he reported, "there has been a 560 percent increase in violent crime; more than a 400 percent increase in illegitimate births; a tripling of the percentage of children living in single-parent homes; a quadrupling of divorce rates; more than a 200 percent increase in the teenage suicide rate; and a drop of almost 80 points in the SAT (pre-college scholastic aptitude test) scores."[3]

In 1990, a special commission issued a report on the health of today's adolescents entitled "Code Blue." This team of prominent

experts wrote, "Never before has one generation of American teenagers been less healthy, less cared for, or less prepared for life." The
1981 McCready opinion poll surveyed 4,000 U.S. and Canadian
Catholics from fourteen to thirty years old and found 75 percent do
not believe in papal infallibility, 90 percent reject the Church's stand
on birth control, 80 percent believe premarital sex is not wrong, and
only 11 percent agree that divorced people should not remarry
without the Church's sanction.[4] The difference in moral values
between 1981 and now is substantial.

Hurricane Andrew recently ravaged Florida and the Gulf Coast,
becoming the costliest natural disaster in United States history—until
the Midwest floods. Newscasts mentioned that 1992 was the costliest
year ever on record for disasters in the United States—until 1993.
Each year the damage increases by the billions. There were floods in
France and Italy, and Mount Pinatubo erupted in the Philippines. The
list goes on and on and on. Storms will continue to hit our coastal
areas. These are the signs of our time. There will be a price for man
to pay after 1 billion abortions. This we will not escape.

Financial Collapse And Other Signs

There are signs all around us that beg us to take notice. The stakes
continue to get higher as the world falls more rapidly into economic
and moral decline. Wars and disasters threaten to add to the economic
downturn, and could easily turn what is now a lingering, world-wide
recession into a full-blown depression and economic chaos. World-
wide famine will soon engulf us.

The world financial system is poised for collapse. Bank failures
have cost taxpayers hundreds of billions according to banking experts
Edward W. Hill and Roger J. Vaughn, authors of *Banking on the
Brink*. They say another 1,000 U.S. banks are in the process of "dying
and on the lip of insolvency." The losses caused by bank failures
could run as high as $95 billion—on top of the billions lost through
present bank failures.[5]

As a nation we are bankrupt. Although this book is not about
banking or finance, it is not hard to see that if the world economy
collapses, then society will deteriorate quickly. Natural disasters will
quicken our decline as we will no longer be able to pay for nature's
destructive deeds. If the bankrupt Weimar Republic looked to the
rising star of a madman paper hanger from Linz—Adolph Hitler—

during the depression of the 1920s and 1930s, what can we expect today, when people have much less patience, perseverance, and moral fortitude?

The Antichrist who will take control to manage the crisis will bring a false peace and a false economic stability. Predictions have indicated that he will arrive shortly. Mary stated to the Marian Movement of Priests on September 18, 1988: "In this period of ten years there will come to completion that fullness of time, which was pointed out to you by me, beginning with LaSalette all the way to my most recent and present apparitions...sufferings will become greater for all.... In this period of ten years there will come to completion the time of the Great Tribulation which has been foretold to you in the Scripture.... The mystery of iniquity, prepared by the ever increasing spread of apostasy, will become manifest.... All secrets will come to pass."

The economy, natural disasters, AIDS, apparitions throughout the world, the formation of a one-world currency, weeping statues, the stigmata upon the laity, abortion, distribution of pornographic material on television and in print, are all signs of where we are and indicators of where we soon will be.

Sister Anna Ali of the *Divine Appeal Revelations* has received messages from Jesus about illness, disasters of all kinds, and incurable diseases. Three of these Divine Appeal messages from Jesus follow:

Divine Appeal 29: "My daughter, pray and atone. I am pierced by many swords, but I forgive all those who will come to repent.... I warn this world, full of horrors, for which a tremendous punishment is prepared. The thin line that separates it from the precipice will break; there will be no other way to salvation because there are many who do not want to hear My Call.... If they continue to live in corruption, there will be no mercy, but rather tears, mourning, earthquakes, **floods** and sickness of all kinds. These poor people are blind and deaf to My Call of Love. The air is contaminated and everywhere is full of sin. Men's hands are armed, and a great punishment will befall them. I love them; this is why I warn them before it is too late for them to repent. They should pray more" (October 24, 1987).

Divine Appeal 40: "The world advances towards the precipice from one day to the next. Reflect upon what is happening...in all humanity. There is too much hatred, there are too many enemies of

My Eternal Father. The Freemasons and all other devil worshippers want to obliterate fraternal love in the world, substituting it with division and blood wounds.... I am calling everyone to penance and pray. Do not be afraid.... On the contrary, flames will be cast down from Heaven which will destroy all sinners and the work of the Evil one: abysses, mountains and flaming lava will swallow up entire villages. Earthquakes, floods, electrocutions, tempestuous seas, suicides, drugs, and illnesses of all kinds. What a great desolation— children who rebel against their parents, innocent souls who are killed, divorce, communists, and all sinners. A just rigor weighs down on them" (November 22, 1987).

Divine Appeal 184: "In the world and My Church there are distractions of all kinds. This is a grave moment. Time is short for saving souls. There are many diseases, as an admonishment. Pray a great deal to atone and appease the wrath of My Eternal Father. I beg you not to allow My Word to die. If you do not do what I tell you, then you will be captured by Satan, the Red Lucifer, who is very conscious of this serious moment. These are times of overwhelming violence. **Time is approaching and there will be many diseases which will be allowed by My Eternal Father.** There will be no physician or medicine to cure them. If souls listen to Me and respond to My Call of Mercy, then it will be their salvation and peace. Make people pray more and love one another. My heart is filled with pain. I ask many souls to return to Me. Lucifer has taken possession of many souls and he tells them that My Eternal Father does not exist. What more could I have suffered for mankind?" (July 21, 1988).

AIDS And Cancer

In the United States, the AIDS virus is primarily the result of drug abuse and homosexuality. Through sexual promiscuity and adultery, it is now spreading to the heterosexual population.

Major parts of Africa will be nearly wiped out from AIDS. In Uganda, AIDS is known by the name SLIM—as it makes those with the disease slim and emaciated. The World Health Organization estimates millions of people in Africa alone will die of AIDS by the year 2000. The effects of its devastation are just beginning.

Many cities in Asia will also suffer greatly. Gene Antonio, author of the book *AIDS: Rage & Reality*, writes: "AIDS is the most significant threat to the human race in the modern era. AIDS has the potential for killing more people world-wide than those who died in both World Wars. The potential for an infectious disease to cause the devastation of human life on a mass scale is not without precedent. The bubonic plague wiped out one-third of the population of Europe before it was finally brought under control."[6] He continues: "It has become evident that AIDS has become a politically protected disease. The basic priority of protecting the well-being of society as a whole has been completely subverted. Simply put, the sexual comfort and privacy of those infected with AIDS have been given total supremacy over the rights of the uninfected members of society.[7]

Dr. Arthur Mann, Director of the International AIDS Center at Harvard University, has written: "The world's vulnerability to the spread of AIDS is increasing, not decreasing. The pandemic is spreading to new areas and communities. The disease has not peaked and will reach every country by the end of the decade. An estimated 110 million people will have contracted HIV disease by the year 2,000.[8] The estimated federal spending to treat an AIDS patient is $50,000. Counting private spending on top of federal funds, estimates are nearly $75,000 per person. In contrast, cancer is $3,500 per person. Per capita federal spending for AIDS far outweighs that of any other life-threatening illness in history. **In the mid 1990s, the cost of treating all people with HIV diseases in the United States alone is estimated to exceed ten billion dollars annually.**"[9]

When Gene Antonio wrote an article several years ago for *Barrons,* the financial newspaper, the estimate of one billion dollars sounded extreme. He now estimates that this number of ten billion dollars may be low. It is not very difficult to see the devastation this will wreak on our economy. Many health carriers will be wiped out; and for those with insurance, premiums will escalate sharply.

It should not come as a surprise to see AIDS as an epidemic. The responsible use of freedom is a forgotten principle. The loss of faith has meant that few restrictions or controls remain on personal freedoms. Promiscuity has led to a world-wide epidemic of sexual maladies. There are 685,000 new cases of sexually transmitted diseases per day—in other words, more than 28,000 new cases per hour, or 250 million such cases per year, according to the World Health Organization. WHO officials state that sexually transmitted diseases represent "a grave menace for reproductive health" and that the current high incidence of such maladies is "unacceptable."

In the publication *Progress in Human Reproduction Research,* which discusses among other things sexually transmitted diseases, the WHO estimated that, at a minimum each year, there are world-wide 25 million cases of gonorrhea, 50 million cases of genital chlamydial infections, 3.5 million cases of infectious syphilis, and 2 million cases of chancroid. Moreover, 20 million persons each year contract genital herpes and 30 million others suffer genital human papillomavirus infection.

Dr. John Platt, Ph.D., biophysicist, wrote in *Futurist Magazine*: "Aids is likely to cause the U.S. economy—built on consumer growth—to stagnate. Hospitals will be desperately overcrowded, and many AIDS patients will die at home or be abandoned.... Fear of AIDS will affect a broad range of activities—even those non-intimate activities where contracting AIDS would seem unlikely. The disease will ultimately shift the world's balance of power. Some countries will be destroyed by it, some badly hurt, and some almost unharmed. Those that suffer least will tend to dominate afterwards, as in previous epidemics. AIDS could make overpopulation, famine, environmental destruction, or the extinction of species seem like minor complaints."[10]

The Angel Of The First Plague—AIDS

The Book of Revelation depicts the angels pouring out God's wrath: "Then I saw in Heaven another sign, great and awe-inspiring: seven angels with the seven last plagues, for through them God's fury is accomplished" (Revelation 15:1).

"I heard a loud voice speaking from the temple to the seven angels, 'Go and pour out the seven bowls of God's fury upon the earth.' **The first angel went and poured out his bowl on the earth. Festering and ugly sores broke out on those who had the mark of the beast or worshipped its image**" (Revelation16:1-2).

The angel of the first plague is AIDS. Our Lady has spoken of the first plague as having arrived. It is one we know well. It is cancer and AIDS. We have seen the lives lost from cancer over the last several decades. The malignant tumors Mary has spoken about are cancer. Since the 1930s we have seen a steady rise in cancer rates among the population of the world. Many people attribute this to the environmental hazards and widespread pollution in our midst.

Our Blessed Mother gave Father Gobbi the following message on October 13, 1989: "**It has begun to corrupt the consciences of little children and of youth, bringing them to the conviction that impure acts committed by oneself are no longer sins; that relations before marriage between those engaged is licit and good; that families may behave as they please and may also make use of the various means of birth control.** And they have come to the justification and the exaltation of impure acts against nature and even to the proposing of laws which put homosexual cohabitation on a par with marriage.

"**Never as today have immorality, impurity and obscenity been so continually propagandized, through the press and all the means of social communication. Above all, television has become the perverse instrument of a daily bombardment with obscene images, directed to corrupt the purity of the mind and the heart of all. The places of entertainment—in particular the cinema and the discotheques—have become places of public profanation of one's human and Christian dignity.**

"The Angel of the first plague cuts—into the flesh of those who have allowed themselves to be signed with the mark of the monster on the forehead and on the hand and have adored his image—with a painful and malignant wound, which causes those who have been stricken by it to cry out in desperation. This wound represents the physical pain which strikes the body by means of grave and incurable maladies. The painful and malignant wound is a plague for all humanity, today so perverted, which has built up an atheistic and materialistic civilization and has made the quest for pleasure the supreme aim of human life.

"Some of my poor children have been stricken by it because of their sins of impurity and their disordered morals and they carry within their own selves the weight of the evil they have done. Others, on the other hand, have been stricken, even though they are good and innocent; and so their suffering serves for the salvation of many of the wicked, in virtue of the solidarity which unites you all.

"The first plague is that of malignant tumors and every kind of cancer, against which science can do nothing notwithstanding its progress in every field, maladies which spread more and more and strike the human body, devastating it with most painful and malignant wounds. Beloved children, think of the spread of these incurable maladies, throughout every part of the world, and of the millions of deaths which they are bringing about.

"The first plague is the new malady of AIDS, which strikes, above all, my poor children who are victims of drugs, of vices and of impure sins against nature."

The Lord has also told Canadian visionary Jim Singer that some diseases in the future will have no earthly cure: "Dear children, convert back to me, hear my admonishments, for you do not have much time left. The Shining Darkness has sown among you various vicious diseases. AIDS mows down your lives. **By your conversion back to Me, you shall prevent two more vicious sexually transmitted diseases which the malefactor is preparing as his future 'gift' to you.** Despite all of the earthly technologies and sciences you shall not eradicate these diseases. Because of your conversion to Me, out of My Love for you, I shall protect you."

The Pace Quickens

What may be Satan's chief weapon in causing widespread destruction is the onslaught of sex education in our schools. First, prayer was banned in our public school system; now, educators are allowing youth to be morally corrupted through school-based sex education, which is really nothing more than Planned Parenthood propaganda modified. Surely the words of Jesus in Luke 17:2 apply in this case: "To those who harm these little ones it would be better for them to tie a millstone around their neck and be cast into the sea."

Never do we hear the media discuss the causes of AIDS. The Magic Johnsons of the world suddenly become heroes and overnight experts on national policies. Each year, as we give our approval by our silence, the moral standards of Scripture drift further from the nation's conscience. Abstinence is mentioned with embarrassment, if not completely scorned.

As abortion has been accepted into mainstream thinking, so too has homosexuality. The edifice of our faith is slowly chipped away piece by piece. A Cabinet official in the Clinton Administration was heard to say she wanted sex education to begin in kindergarten. The sexually conservative, she stated, are not in the mainstream. The moral corruption reaches each year into the younger grades.

Let us not be lulled into thinking that things are really not that bad. In a message dated December 31, 1987, to the Marian Movement of Priests called "The Great Tribulation," the Blessed Mother states the signs of the tribulation: "First of all, a great apostasy is spreading in every part of the Church, through the lack of faith which is flooding even among its very pastors. Satan has succeeded in spreading everywhere the great apostasy, by means of his subtle work of seduction, which has brought many to be alienated from the truth of the Gospel to follow the fables of the new theological theories and to take delight in evil and in sin, sought after as an actual good.

"Then, in your time, overturning of the order of nature are multiplying, such as earthquakes, droughts, floods, and disasters which cause the unforeseen death of thousands of persons, followed by epidemics and incurable diseases which are spreading everywhere.

"Moreover, your days are marked by continual rumors of wars which are multiplying and are reaping, each day, innumerable victims. Conflicts and dissensions within countries are increasing; revolts and struggles between various peoples are propagating; bloody wars are continuing to extend themselves, notwithstanding all the efforts which are being made to attain peace.

"Finally, in your time, there are occurring great signs in the sun, on the moon, and in the stars. The miracle of the sun which took place at Fatima was a sign which I gave you to warn you that the times of these extraordinary phenomena which are taking place in the heavens have now arrived. And how many times during my present apparitions have you yourselves been able to contemplate the great prodigies that are taking place in the sun.

"Just as the buds which sprout forth on the trees tell you that Spring has now arrived, so also these great signs which are taking place in your time are telling you that even now there has come to you the Great Tribulation, which is preparing you for the new era which I have promised you with the Triumph of my Immaculate Heart in the world."

On December 31, 1983, through Father Gobbi, the Blessed Mother gave several reasons for the destruction that is upon us. She stated: "The signs the Lord sends are neither understood nor accepted; **the dangers pointed out by 'my Pope' who courageously and anxiously is predicting the storm awaiting you, are not believed. The** messages which I give, through simple and little souls chosen by me in every part of the world, are not taken into consideration. The appearances which I am still making, often in faraway and dangerous places, are ignored. And yet you are only inches from your ruin. When all will be shouting for peace, a new World War could suddenly fall upon you, spreading death and destruction everywhere."

Chernobyl: A Disaster Few Really Know About

"...and a great star fell from Heaven, blazing like a torch, and it fell on a third of the rivers and on the springs of water. The name of the star is Wormwood, and many died from the water, because it was made bitter."

Revelation 8:10

In the Ukrainian language the word Chernobyl means "wormwood" (bitter), which is another name for Satan in the Book of Revelation.

The Chernobyl nuclear power plant is on the northeastern Ukrainian border only miles from the Republic of Belarus. The plant contaminated parts of Sweden, Poland, Finland (as far as Lapland where tens of thousands of reindeer were slaughtered due to contamination), significant parts of Russia, Ukraine, Hungary, and Czechoslovakia. The world is unaware of the destruction that is levied for a thousand years and thousands of miles due to a problem at one plant. There are twenty-six such plants in the former Soviet Union of the same 2,000 megawatt design. Nine should have been shut down years ago. However, there is no money to retrofit the plants to make them safe, for the republics are not able to pay the Western companies for their work. According to Asea, Brown, Boveri (ABB), the largest electrical contractor in the world, these plants are another disaster waiting to happen.

The Soviet government tried to keep the Chernobyl disaster quiet until an American satellite photographed a brown forest two days after the accident. The word was out in the West, but the Soviet government hid the facts from its own citizens for as long as possible. Approximately 40,000 people have died, and another several hundred thousand are in and out of the oncology wards. Official estimates are that over 250,000 people have relocated away from areas with contaminated soils.

A clock tower in Gomel (a town of approximately 700,000 residents just north of Chernobyl) posts the time, date, and radiation level. The people have something called a nuclear smile: a scar from the thyroid gland being cut out, since this is where the radiation collects and stores in the body. Scientists, psychologists, and others have been using Gomel as a test case for what happens when trauma strikes a community. Over seventy percent of the people suffer from depression and hope has largely vanished from their eyes.

Although several years have passed since that fateful day of April 26, 1986, the scope of the disaster and its long-term effects are only now coming to light. Now the contamination is in the soil and experts estimate the repercussions of active plutonium in the soil will affect agriculture for thousands of years. As we read in the verse of Revelation quoted above—"and it fell on a third of the rivers"— could more nuclear accidents pollute rivers and waters world-wide? To the pilgrims at the Hrushiv, Ukraine, apparition site, Our Blessed Mother said, **"Chernobyl is a sign for the world."**[11]

Events That Will Shake The World

Josyp Terelya, a visionary from the Ukraine, recently experienced some apparitions and messages from the Mother of God in Marmora, Ontario, Canada. We give considerable weight to his messages. A full account of Mr. Terelya's life is contained in his book *Witness,* written with Michael Brown. It is a fascinating account of his twenty years as a prisoner of conscience in the former Soviet Union.[12]

Sunday, September 13, 1992: Our Lady said: "Pray constantly for Russia, for these people will suffer again exceedingly and will perish in their sins without grace and repentance. Pray in this chapel for peace and for love in this country of Canada. **People are not aware that the prophesied times are upon them.** My heart grieves; I weep with maternal tears for all sinners, but what of this.... People have torn themselves loose of all restraints. There is no authority; there is no peace; there is no truth nor justice. There is no true piety.

"My child, I tell you that the final times are near. My children, **you are on the threshold of the day of judgment.** God is now calling all to Himself as never before, to mutual understanding, to brotherly love among all. Respect your parents.... And again I ask devout Christians to pray; to pray constantly for the Pope that God might give him the wisdom and strength to lead the Church to its triumph and to the glory that He has predestined for her. The destruction in the Church began during the pontificate of Pope Paul VI. They began destroying the Church from within.

"...His authority as Pope is being eroded in disastrous fashion. But God has given the Church strength even here, notwithstanding the internal shortcomings brought about by apostates. The faith of Christians throughout the entire world is being renewed and strengthened through the pilgrimages of the Pope."

Friday, September 18, 1992: The Mother of God said: "I have come because there are terrible events that will befall a godless humanity that does not want to receive my Son. Josyp, my son, the time is at hand. So many events of greater or lesser magnitude have already affected many nations. But there is an event coming that will shake the entire world. A great war, the greatest that has ever been until now is imminent. So many will not survive it; only those who accept Christ the King and obey God's Commandments. I am telling you this so that devout Christians might be able to obtain the knowledge that will enable them to defend themselves. All this has been written in the Holy Book in the Gospel of Christ. Everywhere the servants of the Antichrist, the sons of Satan, will come proclaiming peace and quiet, but Satan is preparing a great war, such as has never been seen until now. His power is invisible, and this power will drive people to arm themselves.

"...It is Satan himself who speaks through the false prophet of the Organization of the United Nations using the corpse of the Organization of United Nations to deceive mankind...

"From antiquity, when God changed the name of Lucifer and gave him the name the Dragon, the Serpent and Satan, because of his rebellion against the Lord, he always opposes God's plans. We are in those times, when the end is near and remember what the Lord said about Satan and his visible and invisible forces on earth. In the end times Satan will be punished and all his forces destroyed. The devil knows well that his time is short, the time to prepare for the great battle and his purpose is to destroy all mankind rather than seeing all men serve God. This is the age-old despair of the devil, for he knows that he can never win against God. Satan knows that he cannot win his duel with God, the Almighty and All-Merciful One. This is why for some time I have been speaking across the globe about the imminent coming of God's kingdom under Christ, that this kingdom is the hope of the world. This is why the devil is in such a frenzy to drag all the nations of the world into a great war, in order that he might destroy God's creation. This is why the Organization of the United Nations was established through the agency of the devil, that through this diabolic exchange he might change God's kingdom into a kingdom of darkness. The devil is now using the Organization of the United Nations to deceive and to blind the nations before God's truth, to keep people from placing their trust in the kingdom of God, which alone is the hope of the world.

"...Today as never before we see the servants of Satan, all the evil spirits and antichrists, openly proclaiming their hatred of God, saying, We are rejecting God and His kingdom, because we shall govern the earth ourselves as we ourselves want.

"How many priests and bishops there are today who give glory to God with their lips but not with their hearts. How many are the priests that deny the Bible today, especially those sections which proclaim Jesus as the Savior and King of the world.

"...Some governments will begin to protect homosexuality and all sorts of abominations of the devil. Congresses and parliaments will make laws against truth, and some have already done so. Those who speak the truth will be considered criminals. It is then that the general persecution of Christians will begin. The law will prohibit the truth and the law of God.

"In Russia preparations are under way for a world-wide revolution; the forces of hell that control the world will continue to say that everything they are doing is for the sake of peace and the welfare of the people, but at the same time they will continue to take away the freedom and free will from the people. They will continue to persecute the Church, but in another way. The overseer leaders of the Red Dragon are so sure that they have defeated the nations. And as their dictatorial power throttles the throats of the people it says 'Now you have peace and security,' but there will be no security."

The Signs Of Our Times

On December 31, 1992, the Blessed Mother, through Father Gobbi, pointed out to us the signs of the last times. She said, "I have announced to you many times that *the end of the times* and the coming of Jesus in glory is very near. Now, I want to help you understand the signs described in Holy Scriptures, which indicate that His glorious return is now close.

"These signs are clearly indicated in the Gospels, in the letters of Saint Peter and Saint Paul, and they are becoming a reality during these years.

"*The first sign* is the spread of errors, which lead to the loss of faith and to the apostasy.

"*The second sign* is the outbreak of wars and fratricidal struggles, which lead to the prevalence of violence and hatred and a general slackening off of charity, while natural catastrophes, **such as epidemics, famines, floods, and earthquakes, become more and more frequent. When you hear of reports of wars, close at hand or far away, see that you are not alarmed; for these things must happen.**

"*The third sign* is the bloody persecution of those who remain faithful to Jesus and to His Gospel and who stand fast in the true faith.

"*The fourth sign* is the horrible sacrilege, perpetrated by him who sets himself against Christ, that is, the Antichrist. He will enter into the holy temple of God and will sit on his throne, and have himself adored as God. One day, you will see in the holy place he who commits the horrible sacrilege. The prophet Daniel spoke of this. Let the reader seek to understand (Matthew 24:15).

"...In order to understand in what this horrible sacrilege consists, read what has been predicted by the prophet Daniel: 'Go, Daniel; these words are to remain secret and sealed until the end of time. Many will be cleansed, made white and upright, but the wicked will persist in doing wrong. Not one of the wicked will understand these things, but the wise will comprehend.

"'**Now, from the moment that the daily sacrifice is abolished and the horrible abomination is set up, there shall be one thousand two hundred and ninety days.** Blessed is he who waits with patience and attains one thousand three hundred and thirty-five days.'

"*The fifth sign* consists in extraordinary phenomena, which occur in the skies. 'The sun will be darkened and the moon will not give its light; and the stars will fall from the sky; and the powers in the heavens will be shaken' (Matthew 24:29).

"I am always with you, to tell you that the coming about of these signs indicates to you with certainty that the end of the times, with the return of Jesus in glory, is close at hand."

Patricia ("Pachi") Talbott, of Cuenca, Ecuador, has received similar messages. On January 1, 1989, the Blessed Mother told Pachi: "The third World War threatens the world...earthquakes will come, hurricanes, the sky will shower fire, all this will come from the Father, the Son, and the Spirit of God."[13]

Many national security experts feel that the incubator for the next World War is in Bosnia. The killings and brutality have been on a scale that this generation has not seen. Ten years ago the scenario that is taking shape there was not even imaginable. Former Yugoslavian dictator Marshall Tito had kept a firm grip on the region for nearly forty years and had prevented it from being under the total domination of the Soviet Union. The beautiful Adriatic was a mecca for European vacationers. In the space of a few short years, this region has become a scourge of Western civilization.

The Balkan region is potentially the breeding ground for the next World War. The Russians are siding with the Serbs, and Muslims as well as Christians continue to be massacred. Russian mercenary troops in Serbia further complicate the scenario. Europe sits back and watches anemically while the ethnic tensions continue to escalate to the point where the United Nations Security Council goes through the motions of problem-solving but continues to do nothing. The Balkans have always been a hotbed of ethnic tension. Today's fighting could easily evolve into a Christian versus Muslim conflict, with world powers taking sides. Is this the war so many of the mystics and visionaries have alluded to? Or is it North Korea with its nuclear capability? "There will be wars and rumors of wars...."

Jim Singer Of Canada

Jim Singer, a native of Zagreb, Croatia, now living in Canada, in 1989 started receiving apparitions of the Father, Jesus, and the Blessed Virgin Mary.

On December 14, 1989, Our Lord gave the message that we shall soon witness tragic events in the countries of the Eastern world because of the vicious aggression by the Shining Darkness and the weak faith of God's children. "Our Lord warned us that difficult and tragic times threaten our ancestral homeland. [Authors' note: This message predates the war.] Out of the vicious aggression of the Shining Darkness our ancestral homeland shall be on the front news of the media. Our Lord's message is that He will destroy the malefactor's intentions and to His children in our ancestral homeland He will give peace and love, if children in sufficient numbers sincerely surrender their hearts to Him."

"On January 1, 1990, Our Lord's message is that we are to follow His teachings, to use His gifts, and we will be shielded from the Shining Darkness.... the decisions which the leaders of the world's countries will make over the next several weeks will be lasting and of enormous consequence....even the individuals who will make these decisions have no concept of the significance of their decisions. Our Blessed Mother encouraged the Lord's children to conversion, sacrifices, and many contrite prayers. She promised that by... prayers we can prevent the evils...which the hellish enemy is preparing...."

"The future two years (1990 and 1991) are decisive for all My children.... This malefactor shall multiply his evil powers.... By the power of My presence you will soon be rewarded with the first victory in this final battle. Communism shall crumble before your eyes, but many of My children will not recognize My hand among you. Many of My children among you will again be deceived and seduced. Remember, wherever I am with you, the evil one has already sown his seed of poison to hinder your return to My embrace...."

"Dear children, be alert, for you are now entering into the age of great viciousness by the Shining Darkness. Constantly keep in mind that he uses all possible deceptions and evil powers.... These next two years (1990 and 1991), are of particular significance to you. The consequences of your earthly decisions shall be permanent. Do not rejoice in the disintegration of the evil powers too soon. Your rejoicing will become deservedly glistening only when you completely eradicate every drop of the malefactor's poison which he has sown deeply among you children. The power of faith in Me, by each one of My children, is the only way to the total triumph over the evil enemy of My children's bodies and souls.

"My dear son, out of my love for My earthly children I shall devastate the evil communist empire of the Shining Darkness. My

son, even your ancestral homeland shall not be left short of My power. Remember My teachings. You have been warned that anyone who cleans and tidies his/her home of the evil spirit, must urgently receive Me under his/her roof. Any home into which I am not called shall be filled with seven new evil spirits, much more vicious than the first one.

"To My Church I send the message to awaken the love for Me in My every child more potently, thoroughly, and courageously. I warn you to beware of the delights of the malefactor's poison and his particular attention to My children of the Western world. These children are in need of My love equally as urgently. Under the Shining Darkness they are becoming the ever more powerful instrument of evil, but in My Love they are called to be the guardians of Truth, Justice and Peace."

Our Lord told Jim: "For your conversion I give you the gift of Medjugorje. **In the gift of Medjugorje you possess all the messages which the Immaculate Mother brings you.** They are the only method for you to eliminate the Shining Darkness from your lives. His poisoned gifts lead you to eternal damnation."

"In China the Shining Darkness will appear as the victor, since far too few of you have enough faith in divine intervention. **I tell you that the time when you will be witnesses of My Intervention into your earthly lives is soon coming.** But, I admonish you to examine your love and faithfulness to me. The Shining Darkness will multiply his powers.

"The Shining Darkness is preparing for you great bloodshed in the Eastern world, especially the USSR. In the Western world my children shall meet with great injustices, violence, oppression, and an ever deeper and greater loss of dignity with which I gifted you.

"Because of your conversion the Shining Darkness shall lose this battle. But, the victims among you shall be many. In these special times you will soon be witnesses of My graces. Many among you who were tortured, disgraced, banished, exiled and persecuted will soon take their place among those that are first. Convert and through My love you shall be the victors. The tragedies which the Shining Darkness is preparing as his 'gift' to you My children, will be thwarted by your faith."

Julia Kim Of Naju, Korea

Julia Kim of Naju, a stigmatic, is only one of the mystics through-out the world saying the world is in serious trouble. Like other visionaries around the world—most of whom have had no contact with each other—Julia has been warned by Our Lady of dire future events: "To prevent fire from falling on the earth, I am constantly praying for my children who are victims of sin and corruption and I am suffering in their place offering up the sacrifices they should be making to the Almighty. However, if people still continue to compromise with the world, without paying attention to the will of God and without trying to live the spiritual life, it will be too late to avert disaster. You know what was the sad state of the world at the time the Tower of Babel was built and the years before the deluge. Well, what happened then will occur again unless there is a reformation in morality and a change for the better in the lives of men" (January 8, 1989).

"Feet that should be turned in the direction that leads to the worship and service of God are now running in the opposite way. That is, on the broad road to evil and destruction. Lips that should be used to praise and bless the Lord are blaspheming and insulting Him. That is the reason why the world is slowly being surrounded with darkness and obscurity—a condition that will not fail to provoke the displeasure of the Almighty. If my children do not live evangelical lives, heed my messages and do all they can to alleviate my tears and anguish, they will...have no way of escaping the sufferings caused by all kinds of evil disasters" (October 14, 1990).

"Before long the world will come face to face with extraordinary disaster. My children must forsake the way of evil and put into practice the messages I am giving you. Recall how the people of Israel obeyed Moses and left Egypt to go in the direction of the promised land. I am pleading with you now and with tears in my eyes in the same way that God, through Moses, appealed to the Jewish people to follow Him on the way to freedom and away from paganism and bondage. What would have been the lot of mankind if Noah, who had been instructed by God to build the ark for his own salvation, had neglected to obey the Divine command? Take my urgent appeals to heart and inscribe them on your hearts because I am making them with blood and tears in my eyes—why are so many so bland and so drab? My heart is aflame with sad concern for families, for the Church and for society, because all these have been touched and weakened by evil and corruption" (October 14, 1989).

Oliveto Citra, Italy

The messages of Oliveto Citra, Italy, given to twelve boys, warn that the world is on the edge of the abyss—and say that time before the catastrophe is very short. Oliveto Citra, south of Naples, Italy, is a small town of 3,500 people. Apparitions have been occurring since 1985 in a church by the name of "Our Lady of Mercy."[14]

December 15, 1985: Tarcisio, one of the visionaries, said: "Our Lady appeared to me...and she said to me, 'Tell the pilgrims that I do not need flowers and candles, that I need prayers because the time left before the catastrophe is very short.'"

December 20, 1985: "Our Lady told me [Tarcisio] that the arm of her Son is held back, but we should remember that what the Lord has put in the world he can remove."

January 10, 1986: Our Lady to Mafalda: "My dear children, God sends me on earth to come to save all because the whole world is in danger. I come among you to bring peace to your hearts. God wants that peace to reign in the hearts of all mankind, and He wants the conversion of all peoples.

"Therefore, my dear children, pray, pray, pray; if you do not pray, you will receive nothing. **The time that you have left is short; there will be earthquakes, disasters, and famines for the inhabitants of the earth.... I will pray that God will not punish you. God says, Save yourselves, pray much, and do penance, and be converted, with prayer you can obtain everything.** People should not bow only before God, but also toward their own brothers and sisters who suffer fighting hunger in the world. Mankind is full of serious sins that offend the love of God. Peace on earth is about to end, the world cannot be saved without peace, but the world will find peace only if mankind returns to God. My children, I beg you to pray for the conversion of all peoples; do penance and save yourselves from hell. I will engage in the final struggle against Satan which will conclude with the triumph of my Immaculate Heart and with the coming of the kingdom of God in the world.

"Those who refuse God today will go far from Him tomorrow into hell. I have presented myself to you as the Immaculate Virgin Mother of Jesus, and I come to bring to you, dear children, mercy, forgiveness, and peace in the name of God the Father.

"**Have this message read to priests, and I want it to be communicated to everyone as soon as possible. Do not be ashamed of my message, but say it to everyone you meet. For the spreading of my message is a great apostolic work, because with information about the apparitions and with knowledge of the messages, many people will pray more.**"

February 11, 1986: Mafalda's message for the people of Oliveto Citra from Our Lady: "My dear children, I invite you to pray much in these days because Satan has made himself evident in a particular way in this town. So pray, pray, pray so that all I have planned may come about. That way, Satan can't do anything."

April 1986: Mafalda wrote: "I asked Our Lady if there is danger of a third World War. Our Lady answered me with this message: "Dear children, do not ask, but be converted, and pray much. I, Mary, will not leave you, but I want you to understand once and for all that the world is at the edge of the abyss. Mankind is sliding toward a frightening precipice; therefore, my children, pray, pray, pray; be converted and do penance. The three-fold way to save yourselves from sin and punishment is: prayer, conversion, and penance."

Dozens of visitors have seen Our Blessed Mother at Oliveto Citra, where she first appeared to twelve young boys. Since then, others have also witnessed her appearances.

Book IV
The Purification
Of
The World

17

Where Mercy And Justice Meet

You are priests; you are not social or political leaders or officials of a temporal power...

Pope John Paul II to the Mexican Bishops

The cries of the prophets are unanimous in conveying the gravity of Our Lady's messages: convert your heart now before the time of grace and mercy becomes the moment of Justice. We are told that at some point during the chastisement it will be too late for conversion. Mary has counseled us for the last twenty years not to fear but rather to come under her mantle, persevere in faith, and stay under the guidance of the Pope and the Magisterium of the Church. For the future, there is only spiritual refuge.

The recent messages coming to us from all over the world say that the time of Justice is at hand. The Blessed Mother is warning her children—as any mother would—that there is danger in the near future. She has been preparing us and providing us with the information necessary to endure the chastisement ahead. Since 1973, when the Marian Movement of Priests began, the level of intensity has increased each year.

The messages of the early years were never casual; however, the degree of detail and urgency we now see was missing. When the storm is very close, you race to the harbor for safety. Years ago, images and statues of Our Lady wept human tears. Today, we are told by Julia Kim and others that she sheds tears of blood because the chastisement is near.

Purification, Justice And Love

All indications are that we are approaching the end of God's era of mercy. Here lies a very delicate and confusing matter. Does God's mercy ever end? If God is a God of love, how could He do these terrible things to us? How can He allow these chastisements to strike us?

In the Old Testament the Jews were brought into the land of Israel on a promise by Yahweh. While on the journey they traveled under the Shekinah Glory, which was God's physical presence among His people: a cloud by day and a fire by night. What should have been a very short journey took forty years because of sinfulness. From the beginning, man has been given a free will to do as he chooses. God has never forced His will upon us, as He did not force His will upon His chosen people in the desert. This is a great act of love in itself. As the Israelites chose not to obey, God withdrew His protective graces, and they were left to their own devices. The result was chaos. "It has been your sins which have separated you from God" (Isaiah 59:2). The mantle of His covering was absent. Calamity often struck in the desert as a result of disobedience to God. They thought they had a better way and ignored every opportunity to repent.

The Purging Of Sin

In Ezekiel, the people of Jerusalem were given over to depravity and fell into a deep state of sin. Yahweh speaks about how the country was "filled with bloody murders and violent crime. I am going to summon the cruelest of the nations to seize their houses. I will break the pride of their grandees; their sanctuaries will be profaned. Anguish is on its way: they will look for peace and there will be none. Disaster will follow on disaster, rumor on rumor, they will pester the prophet for a vision; the priest will be at a loss over the law and the elders on how to advise. The King will go into mourning, the prince plunged in grief, the hands of the country people tremble. I mean to treat them as their conduct deserves, and judge them as their own verdict merits; and so they will learn that I am Yahweh" (Ezekiel 7:23-27). Yahweh takes Ezekiel on a tour of the city in the next chapter and shows him abominations in every corner of Jerusalem. Each one is more depraved than the one before it. Yahweh says to Ezekiel: "Have you seen what the elders of the House of Israel do in the dark, each in his painted room? They say Yahweh cannot see us; Yahweh has abandoned the country...you will see them at filthier practices still" (Ezekiel 8:12). Again, each abomination is worse than the one before, and at this point Ezekiel has no argument before God. He too, has seen enough.

The remainder of the story is how God ordered the slaughter of the city sparing only **those who remained pure to Him by placing a seal on their forehead.** Only these people were to be spared death. "Show neither pity nor mercy; old men, young men, virgins, children, women, kill and exterminate them all. But **do not touch anyone with a cross on their forehead.** Begin at my sanctuary...." (Ezekiel 9:5-6). The blessing is now gone from the people of Israel. Two things remain to be done. First, the glory of Yahweh is taken from the temple. In an elaborate ceremony, the physical presence of God is taken from the temple. God has abandoned his people. "The glory of Yahweh came out from the Temple threshold and paused over the cherubs. The cherubs spread their wings and rose from the ground to leave, as I watched the wheels rose with them" (Ezekiel 10:18). At the second and final blow Yahweh says, "I shall drive you from the city and hand you over to foreigners, and I shall carry out my sentence on you; you will fall by the sword on the soil of Israel; I shall execute justice on you; and so you will learn that I am Yahweh.... I am going to execute justice on you on the soil of Israel; and so you will learn that I am Yahweh, whose laws you have not obeyed and whose observances you have not kept; instead you have adopted the manners of the nations around you" (Ezekiel 11:11-13).

In the New Testament Paul writes: **"Therefore, God handed them over to impurity through the lusts of their hearts for the mutual degradation of their bodies. They exchanged the truth for a lie and revered and worshipped the creature rather than the Creator—Therefore, God handed them over to degrading passions...."** (Romans 1:24). Again, God does not force His people to obey Him. After a time of mercy, He hands the unrepentant over to the consequences of sin.

The messages today from all over the world speak about our sinful world. Mary has stated that impurities today are worse than at the time of Noah and the flood. She has stated many times, **"the world will be purged by the fire of His justice." God does not inflict the pain on us; our sin allows it to happen. Sin has its consequences.** At some point, it seems, God says, "Enough is enough. I have loved you, cared for you, provided for you, and you continue to disobey." To create something new, He will "purify with the strong action of justice and of love" (Marian Movement of Priests—July 3, 1987). The purification is an act of mercy, not vengeance.

Hell

If there is a doctrine in the world today that is not understood by the majority of people, it is most probably hell. Visionaries throughout history, including some in our present day, have been shown Heaven, hell, and purgatory. Jesus tells us in Mark 9:41-47 to avoid hell at all cost.

The three little children of Fatima were shown hell in a vision. After seeing hell they all responded by doing severe penances. In doing so, they were responding to Mary's request to "pray and offer sacrifices for poor sinners, for many go there [to hell] because they have no one to pray for them." Little Jacinta, one of the three children said, "if only men knew what awaits them in eternity, they would do everything to change their lives." Some of the children of Medjugorje have reportedly been shown hell along with Heaven and purgatory.

Pope Paul VI reiterated Church teaching in his Credo of the People of God: "those who refuse God's love and mercy to the end, will go to the fire that will never be extinguished." Francis Johnston in his book, *Fatima, the Great Sign*, comments on how many "liberal theologians inside the Church regard the doctrine of hell as being unsuitable for the mentality of modern man and are infecting others with their view." He states that, "such liberal theologians are quick to admit God's love and mercy but not His justice. They maintain this stance despite Jesus stressing the existence of hell some fifteen times in Holy Scripture." It is significant that as hell is never mentioned from the pulpit, confessionals are emptying and sin is abounding as never before.[1]

Cardinal Hoeffner of Cologne stated at Fatima on October 13, 1977: " Today, we are witnessing a great rebellion against the holy will of God. Moral behavior has deteriorated to such a degree that it couldn't be imagined twenty years ago...."

The bishop of Fatima in a similar address on December 10, 1975, said: "In light of the Fatima message, sin is not a phenomena of the sociological order but is, in the true theological concept, an offense against God with necessary social consequences. Perhaps no other century has had a life so sinful. But there is something new added in the sins of this century. **The man of today, more sinful than those who came before him, has lost the sense of sin.** He sins, but laughs and even boasts of his sin....man of today has arrived at this stage because he has placed a division between himself and God....believing that when God is ignored, everything is possible."[2]

Regarding purgatory, Our Blessed Mother on November 2, 1992, said to Father Gobbi: "Those souls in purgatory who, while on earth, had formed part of my cohort, now enjoy a special union with me, feel in a special way my presence which sweetens the bitterness of their suffering, and shortens the time of their purification. And it is I myself who go to receive these souls into my arms, that I may lead them into the incomparable light of paradise. "

The Greatest Sign

As Abraham negotiated with God and asked for His mercy for the few righteous men before God destroyed the city of Sodom, Mary has approached the throne of Heaven asking grace for her children. This is the role of an intercessor—to pray for another. Christina Gallagher of Ireland was recently in California, praying on a balcony overlooking a city. She had been told by the Blessed Mother this city was going to be destroyed. She begged God that this would not happen. At this point she was shown the "Book of Life" with all of the sins that city contained in it. Like Ezekiel before her, Christina had no argument. The sins were too great.

The greatest sign in our midst today is the Blessed Mother. Only in the name of God does the Blessed Mother intervene. She does not say a word or take a step without the explicit will of God. All she does is appointed by God. She is **the** messenger for our time. In the message of December 8, 1990, Mary specifically stated to Father

Gobbi how she was "chosen by the Holy Trinity to become the Mother of the Second Advent, and thus my motherly task is that of preparing the Church and all humanity to receive Jesus, who is returning to you in glory." She has been sent to warn and remains our greatest gift. It is the will of the Father.

No apparition in history has been on the scale of Medjugorje. Messages at Fatima were few, as were those of Lourdes, Rue de Bac, and Garabandal, compared to the frequency of those today. Mary has given several hints that her time may be coming to a close—very shortly. On October 25, 1992, she stated at Medjugorje, "at a time when I am no longer with you...." Messages have been received from the Philippines and other places that public apparitions may be coming to a close.

The visionaries of Medjugorje have informed us of several relevant points. First: The apparitions of Medjugorje are the last of the Blessed Mother on earth, and for this reason they are lasting so long and occurring so frequently. Second: A visible sign will be left there. Before this visible sign will be a time of grace for conversion and the deepening of faith. Third: Before the visible sign is given to humanity, there will be three warnings given to the world. The warnings will be events on earth. Mirjana will witness to them three days beforehand and will notify a priest. This will serve as confirmation of the apparitions and a stimulus for the conversion of the world. Fourth: After the admonitions, the visible sign will appear on the site of the apparitions in Medjugorje for all the world to see. Fifth: After the first admonition, the others will follow in a rather short time. Thus, people will have some time for conversion. Sixth: That interval will be a period of grace and conversion. After the visible sign appears, those who are still alive will have little time left for conversion.

Christina Gallagher, Josyp Terelya, and others are saying that God's hand can no longer be held back. We will soon live the Thunder of His Justice. When this will be precisely we do not know for sure. But as we see destructive natural forces increase around us, it appears that the day may well be upon us and will grow in intensity. Our hearts and ears have been deaf to the Gospel (see Appendix on Selected Scriptures).

Mary told the Marian Movement of Priests at the beginning of the Marian Year in 1987 that the great chastisement and the great mercy coincide. What appears to be contradictory in our eyes is not so in the eyes of Heaven. The days of the warning, the miracle, and the chastisement are God's acts of mercy. He is giving us a chance to repent and amend our lives before time runs out.

The message of the Blessed Mother to Father Gobbi of July 3, 1987, spoke of the chastisement. Mary stated: "These are the times of the great chastisement. The cup of divine justice is full, is more than full, is flowing over. Iniquity covers the whole earth; the Church is darkened by the spread of apostasy and of sin. **The Lord, for the triumph of His mercy, must as of now purify with His strong action of justice and of love. The most painful, most bloody hours are in preparation for you.** These times are closer than you think. Already during this Marian Year, certain great events will take place, concerning what I predicted at Fatima and have told, under secrecy, to the children to whom I am appearing at Medjugorje.... These are the times of the great return. Yes, after the time of the great suffering there will be the time of the great rebirth and all will blossom again. Humanity will again be a new garden of life and of beauty and the Church a family enlightened by truth, nourished by grace, consoled by the presence of the Holy Spirit. Jesus will restore His glorious reign. He will dwell with you and you will know the new times, the new era. You will at last see a new earth and new heavens."

Blessed Sister Faustina

In the Divine Mercy writings of Sister Faustina we see the merciful and loving God. Sister Faustina was beatified in Rome, on April 18, 1993. Beatification is a step along the way to canonization in the Roman Catholic Church. Though she died more than fifty years ago in 1938, Sister Faustina kept a diary of her experiences—which included apparitions by Jesus—that have relevance for today. The following material is from her numbered entries into that diary.

Jesus speaks: 50. **"I desire that priests proclaim this great Mercy of Mine towards souls of sinners. Let the sinner not be afraid to approach Me. The flames of Mercy are burning Me— clamoring to be spent; I want to pour them out upon these souls, distrust on the part of souls is tearing at My insides. The distrust of a chosen soul causes Me even greater pain; despite My inexhaustible love for them they do not trust Me. Even My death is not enough for them. Woe to the soul that abuses these gifts."**

177. "After the renewal of vows and Holy Communion, I suddenly saw the Lord Jesus, who said to me with great kindness, **My daughter, look at My merciful Heart.** As I fixed my gaze on the Most Sacred Heart, the same rays of light, as are represented in the image as blood and water, came forth from it, and I understood how great is the Lord's mercy. And again Jesus said to me with kindness, **My daughter, speak to priests about this inconceivable mercy of Mine. The flames of mercy are burning Me—clamoring to be spent; I want to keep pouring them out upon souls; souls just don't want to believe in My goodness.**"

186. "Today Jesus said to me, **I desire that you know more profoundly the love that burns in My Heart for souls, and you will understand this when you meditate upon My Passion. Call upon My mercy on behalf of sinners; I desire their salvation. When you say this prayer, with a contrite heart and with faith on behalf of some sinner, I will give him the grace of conversion.**"

474. "The Origin of the Chaplet of Divine Mercy: In the evening, when I was in my cell, I saw an angel, the executor of divine wrath. He was clothed in a dazzling robe, his face gloriously bright, a cloud beneath his feet. From the cloud, bolts of thunder and flashes of lightning were springing into his hands; and from his hand they were going forth, and only then were striking the earth. When I saw this sign of divine wrath which was about to strike the earth, and in particular a certain place, which for good reasons I cannot name[3,] I began to implore the angel to hold off for a few moments, and the world would do penance. But my plea was a mere nothing in the face of divine Anger. Just then I saw the most Holy Trinity. The greatness of Its majesty pierced me deeply, and I did not dare to repeat my entreaties. At that very moment, I felt in my soul the power of Jesus' grace, which dwells in my soul. When I became conscious of this grace, I was instantly snatched up before the Throne of God. O, how great is Our Lord and God and how incomprehensible His holiness! I will make no attempt to describe this greatness, because before long we shall all see Him as He is.... Never before had I prayed with such inner power as I did then. The words which I entreated God are these: 'Eternal Father, I offer You the Body and Blood, Soul and Divinity, of your dearly beloved Son, Our Lord Jesus Christ, in atonement for our sins and those of the whole world.'" The next day, Our Lord dictated the Chaplet of Divine Mercy to Sister Faustina.[4]

According to Irish visionary Christina Gallagher, "the alarm has been set." Exactly what this means we are not sure, but we do know it foretells something awful and frightening about the just anger of God. "'My people, my people! Why do you not respond to the cries of My Most Sacred Heart? Where are My shepherds to lead my flock? My flock is crying out for shepherds!' He was silent for a moment and then He said: 'I am the One True Shepherd. I will lead My flock who have strayed. I gather My little ones of the world, to be My army of love and truth. You, My people who serve the flesh and its desires before My Mercy, I will cut you down in the light of My Justice. Oh, you say to yourselves. This will not be. I tell you, it is close! The clock, its alarm is set. It cannot be turned back. Your cries will be heard now, if you throw yourselves under My mercy and turn away from sin and your evil ways.'"

Recently, Our Lady's warning that her Son, Jesus, would soon release His hand in justice and the world would be "plunged into the depth of its sin" was followed by advice to Christina's spiritual director to read the Apocalypse and "the Seven Seals of God, especially the seventh Seal...."[5]

Fire And Blood

On May 30, 1982, the message to the Marian Movement of Priests spoke of the "Hour of the Holy Spirit" as a gift of His merciful love. However, the same message reiterates how fire and blood will renew the whole world: "In the cenacle of my Immaculate Heart, prepare yourselves to receive the fire of the love of the Holy Spirit, which will lead my Church to live the joyous moment of its Pentecost and which will renew the whole face of the earth. This is its hour. It is the hour of the Holy Spirit who, from the Father and by means of the Son, is given to you ever more and more as a gift, as a sign of the merciful love of God who wants to save mankind. By the fire of the Spirit of Love, the work of the great purification will be quickly accomplished. The Church groans as it awaits His merciful work of purification. Through interior sufferings and by means of trials which will bring it to relive the bloody hours of the Passion through which my Son Jesus lived, the Church will be led to its divine splendor. It will be healed of the wounds of error, which have spread like a hidden cancer and which threaten the deposit of faith. It will be cured of the leprosy of sin, which obscures its sanctity. It will be deprived of its earthly goods and purified of many of its means of power, that once again it may become poor, humble, simple and chaste. In its pastors and its flock, it will again be crucified, that it may give perfect witness to the Gospel of Jesus. Through the power of fire and of blood, the whole world will also be renewed. Humanity will return once again to the glorification of the Father, through Jesus, who will at last have established His reign in your midst."

18

The World-Wide Warning: God's Ultimate Act Of Mercy

The Warning

The Lord in His infinite love and mercy for humanity continues to provide every opportunity for His people to make amends. Much evidence, from many sources in the Church today, indicates that the day of reckoning is soon to come upon us. As prophets like Amos, Jeremiah, and Isaiah warned their people of impending judgments, we too are being warned by the prophets in our midst that earth-shaking events are soon to happen. The warning will be an event on a scale unprecedented in Church history.

The warning is an event that will allow every man, woman, and child to see the state of their own souls through the illumination of conscience. The fire of divine truth will enable all of God's people to "see" their lives in the form of a miniature judgment. This will be one of several final acts of mercy coming from Heaven to allow us to change the direction and focus of our lives.

On the Feast of Pentecost, May 22, 1988, the message from Our Lady to the Marian Movement of Priests was clear: "...The Holy Spirit will come, as a heavenly dew of grace and of fire, which will renew all the world. Under His irresistible action of love, the Church will open itself to live the new era of its great holiness and will shine resplendently with so strong a light that it will attract to itself all the nations of the earth. The Holy Spirit will come, that the will of the Heavenly Father be accomplished and the created universe once again reflect His great glory.

"The Holy Spirit will come, to establish the glorious reign of Christ and it will be a reign of grace, of holiness, of love, of justice and peace. With His divine love, he will open the doors of hearts and illuminate all consciences. Every person will see himself in the burning fire of divine truth. It will be like a judgment in miniature. And then Jesus Christ will bring His glorious reign in the world.

"The Holy Spirit will come, by means of the triumph of my Immaculate Heart."

On October 2, 1992, the Blessed Mother again told Father Gobbi how miraculous the warning actually will be. The Blessed Mother said: "What will come to pass is something so very great that it will exceed anything that has taken place since the beginning of the world. It will be like a judgment in miniature, and each one will see his own life and all he has done, in the very light of God."

If one is not moved by these passages, there is either an insensitivity of spirit or a general unawareness of the profound meaning of this event and its potential impact on world thinking. Although we have gone to great extremes to stay away from specifying dates and believe it is wrong to be a part of a guessing game, this date may be approaching. Mary stated through Father Gobbi that "there will come to completion the time of the great tribulation" during the period from 1988 to 1998.

A Period Of Ten Years

In the message of September 18, 1988, Mary said to Father Gobbi: "In this period of ten years there will come to completion that fullness of time which was pointed out to you by me, beginning with LaSalette all the way to my most recent and present apparitions.

"In this period of ten years there will come to its culmination that purification which, for a number of years now, you have been living through and therefore the sufferings will become greater for all. In this period of ten years there will come to completion the time of the great tribulation, which has been foretold to you in Holy Scripture, before the Second Coming of Jesus.... In this period of ten years the mystery of iniquity, prepared for by the ever increasing spread of apostasy, will become manifest.... In this period of ten years all the secrets which I have revealed to some of my children will come to pass and all the events which have been foretold to you by me will take place."

Past Prophets

Jesus used the example of birthpangs to illustrate the events preceding the Second Pentecost. The birthpangs He was referring to are wars and rumors of wars, famines, earthquakes, violence, and natural disasters—all signs that are increasing at an alarming rate. The Blessed Mother is clarifying exactly what these signs are. For example, Mary indicated to Father Gobbi on October 13, 1989, that the angel of the First Plague spoken of in Revelation 16:2 is AIDS. Revelation 16: 2 reads, "The first angel went and emptied his bowl over the earth; at once, on all the people who had been branded with the mark of the beast and had worshipped its statue, there came disgusting and virulent sores."

The way of Heaven is to enlighten when there is a need. The demons of hell are loosed and waging a full-scale war on the faithful. For this reason, the Trinity and Mary are forewarning us in very certain terms.

Blessed Anna Maria Taigi

These messages are in concert with those of Blessed Anna Maria Taigi and others who spoke of a great chastisement which would come to the world, preceded by an illumination of conscience in which everyone would see themselves as God sees him or her. She indicated that this illumination of conscience would result in the saving of many souls because many would repent as a result of this "warning," this miracle of "self illumination."

Beatified in 1920, and a model for women and mothers, Anna Maria Taigi was not only a prophetess of our time, but one of the most extraordinary mystics in the history of the Church. From the time she was twenty years old until she died at the age of sixty-three, she was accompanied by a mysterious light in which she saw past, present, and future events, some relating to struggles among nations, some relating to individual souls.

Blessed Anna Maria gazed into that light only when she felt an interior impulse, a sort of direction from Our Lord and the Holy Spirit. When she looked into the light she was asked to offer some special suffering for a special need of the Church or an individual.

In that light, Anna Maria saw a great chastisement coming upon the world in the future, but at the same time a great blessing. She spoke about the illumination of the consciences of men, just as though suddenly every man was given the same kind of light that accompanied her, in which they would see themselves as God sees them.[1]

Blessed Sister Faustina Kowalska

Sister Faustina Kowalska (1905-1938), of Cracow, Poland, experienced on a personal basis a "judgment" where she was allowed to see her sins as God sees them. She wrote about this spiritual experience: "Once I was summoned to the judgment [seat] of God. I stood alone before the Lord. Jesus appeared such as we know Him during His Passion. After a moment, His wounds disappeared except for five, those in His hands, His feet and His side. Suddenly I saw the complete condition of my soul as God sees it. I could clearly see all that is displeasing to God. I did not know that even the smallest transgressions will have to be accounted for.

"What a moment! Who can describe it? To stand before the Thrice-Holy God! Jesus asked me, **'Who are you?'** I answered, 'I am Your servant, Lord.' **"You are guilty of one day of fire in purgatory.'** I wanted to throw myself immediately into the flames of purgatory, but Jesus stopped me and said, **'Which do you prefer, suffer now for one day in purgatory or for a short while on earth?'** I replied, 'Jesus, I want to suffer in purgatory, and I want to suffer also the greatest pains on earth, even if it were until the end of the world.'

Jesus said: **'One [of the two] is enough; you will go back to earth, and there you will suffer much, but not for long; you will accomplish My will and My desires, and a faithful servant of Mine will help you to do this. Now, rest your head on My bosom, on My heart, and draw from it strength and power for these sufferings, because you will find neither relief nor help nor comfort anywhere else. Know that you will have much, much to suffer, but don't let this frighten you; I am with you.'"[2]**

Her life and writings were silenced by the Church for over twenty years. The diary of Sister Faustina, called *Divine Mercy in My Soul,* is considered a spiritual classic today. Pope John Paul II initiated the reinvestigation of her life and writings while he was Archbishop of Cracow. She was declared Blessed in April 1993, the first step toward canonization.

The Signs Of All Time

Over thirty years ago, the warning was predicted by the Mother of God, who communicated her message through four young girls from the mountain village of Garabandal, Spain. The message was plain and not really new in content, for she had been repeating it generation upon generation as she visited one place after another for several hundred years. Yet at this moment she had spoken of it with special urgency. Time was running out. People would have to change their lives and stop offending God, or else they would suffer the most terrible consequences.

The four children who saw her were informed of great events that would overwhelm the world. These occurrences were to happen, by God's great mercy, so that the whole world would be converted. They would bring about the conversion of humanity. But unless men heard the message and changed soon, conversion would happen only after great suffering.

She told them of the warning, a **"correction of the conscience of the world," which all would experience as a kind of disaster in their lives, but none would die of if, except perhaps from the shock of it.** She also spoke to them of a great miracle to be worked by the Lord at Garabandal so that all might come to believe, but she would not permit the disclosure of the exact time this would happen. Conchita, one of the four children to receive the apparition, knows the date of the miracle and must announce it eight days before it happens. Lastly, Mary revealed to them the punishment that would descend upon us "directly from God" if people did not repent in time to avert it.

God gives us the warning and the miracle as His ultimate acts of mercy. **These will be the signs of all time** meant to warn the world. We must understand what to do to be saved, and then we must do it. Our fate hangs in the balance. In the end, there will be peace. The messages of Garabandal and Medjugorje appear to be identical in this prophecy.

What is the warning? Will the whole world be involved in such a powerful, direct way? Is it the end of the world? No, it is the prelude to the end of an age or an epoch as Our Lady has stated to the Marian Movement of Priests and others. The material presented from Garabandal has been available for thirty years, but only now is it receiving world-wide attention. Only now has there been a piercing of the darkness and a lifting of the veil.

The Prediction Of The Warning

The warning was predicted by Our Lady of Mount Carmel at Garabandal, where she prophesied three great events to come: the warning, the
miracle, and the punishment. Mari-Loli knows the date of the warning,
and Conchita knows the date of the miracle. **The miracle will come
within a year of the warning.**

The warning will be like the conversion of Saint Paul the Apostle, who
was penetrated by the same light we will soon endure. He was on the
Damascus road, journeying to persecute the newly-converted Christians.
In a glorious vision it was revealed to him that he was assailing not only
the members of the Church, but Jesus Himself. The blinding light of the
Risen Christ convicted him of sin. Paul heeded the warning Jesus had
given him; he repented and became the Lord's faithful follower. Saul, one
day a killer stoning the first Christian martyr, became the great Paul, a
saint, after the "illumination of soul." The same grace granted to Saul will
penetrate every human heart in a single, sudden burst of divine light. Each
of us must embrace our own road to Damascus.

The warning will make us aware of God. Everyone, unbelievers as well
as believers, will declare that God has touched us with His immeasurable
power. He will intervene in an unprecedented manner to make all people
aware of His existence, His mercy, His sovereign rulership, His love for
us and His concern for our salvation. There is a God, and He is good. The
warning will make God evident beyond all speculation and doubt.

Our Sins Revealed

The warning will show us our sins much in the same way Dorian Gray
saw the state of his life, except it will not be on a canvas but in our souls.
It will be a "correction of the conscience of the world." The Scriptures
foretold long ago that Jesus would send the Holy Spirit to "convict the
world of sin." If we did not fully understand before what that meant, we
will by the power of the warning.

Sin—our resistance to becoming the loving kind of person God is—
results in many unloving deeds, decisions, and attitudes. These will all be
vividly clear in the brilliant light which God shines in our souls. Our
consciences will be thoroughly illuminated at that moment, exposing all
the self-deception we indulge in so often, pulling out the dead memories
that have never been leavened with love, uncovering the lies we told
ourselves and the compromises we made.

We will see so blatantly the many harsh, stubborn, and unkind decisions we have made, the times we cruelly trod on the feelings of other people, coveted their possessions, envied their good fortune and rejoiced at their failures. Then we will groan with anguish when God reveals to us the neglect, the refusal to help, the undone deeds and the unfulfilled plans. We will hear Him say to us, "Why have you persecuted Me?"

It will no longer be possible, because of the warning, to hide from ourselves. All we ever did will be before our eyes, seen all at once, in a single glance. We will know then how God's gaze crosses all barriers and grasps the uttermost secrets. We will see the true internationalism of Heaven with no barriers of color, race, or creed. He will share with us, for our conversion, how He sees us, and in a mercifully brief instant, whatever in us was displeasing to Him. We will understand our eternal state and the lightness or blackness of our soul. We will suffer for a moment the pain of our sin, the pain of separation from God, the pain of purgatory or hell. We will see it all whether we wish to or not.

The warning is mercy from God. By the warning, we will become aware that we are not yet what He wants us to be. His will is for us to become like Himself and to become close to Him. Sin is the only impediment to that. It prevents us from achieving perfect, eternal happiness. Our sinfulness will be unveiled in the warning, not out of revenge, for vengefulness is foreign to His heart, but rather out of love and mercy.

Garabandal Is Key

The warning is a sign for the future, the major turning-point in world history, and probably the greatest sign of all time. The parting of the Red Sea and manna from Heaven were powerful divine interventions for small numbers of people. **The world-wide warning and the miracle will be much greater interventions, for they will affect every man, woman, and child on earth.**

The warning will prepare all the world's people for the message of the Gospel, prepare them all for Jesus and His life. By the warning we will all know our sinfulness. We will know we need a Savior. Without knowing our own sins, we would never understand how much we need Jesus and His forgiveness.

The warning is a direct intervention from God. This "sign" shows again the depth of His love for us. **Never before has God acted directly and universally to make every person in the world completely aware of his** or her sinfulness before His holiness. Never before in history has He acted with such power, such precision, such immediacy.

But time is running out. This current epoch is about to end, and a new age of peace is promised. The warning will be the first dramatic sign to all that the old age is ending. It is not God's wish that we be among those who refuse to repent in time. Not in all the ages is it ever His wish that even a single one of His little ones be lost.

We have made the choices, and in the past we have not chosen the way of the Cross. For this reason He has intervened, so that the danger would be manifest, the evil of the present age unmasked, and the darkness of false "enlightenment" exposed. If the world has not wanted to listen to the truth, and the Father's little ones are being misled, He, in His sovereign majesty and power, will compel us to listen. With the Warning, He will sweep away all the sophistry and deception with which Satan has obscured the light of the Gospel.

The Warning As Preparation

The warning calls us to prepare for the miracle. A great miracle has been foretold by Our Lady of Mount Carmel, which will take place in the little village of Garabandal. The wisdom of Heaven is perfect: we are unable to grasp its complexities with our finite minds. We must rely on a wisdom greater than our own. The warning is a preparation for the future: less than a year will pass until the greatest miracle the Lord has ever worked for the world will take place at Garabandal.

Another sign for all time is the miracle, another act of mercy. A similar miracle, also predicted in advance, was granted at Fatima in 1917, in what has come to be known as "The Miracle of the Sun." The sun spun in the sky and hurtled toward earth. Some 70,000 spectators witnessed it. Marvelous as that may sound, it is even more amazing that the miracle will be experienced by so many people! What an event indeed is the great miracle going to be at Garabandal! Millions will undoubtedly journey there to behold its glory, to be healed, converted, and comforted.

They will travel there because they have been prepared to accept the miracle with faith. The warning will send multitudes to that remote Spanish mountain village. It will alert the entire populace of the earth to the impending event of the miracle and open hearts to the message and the action of God that will be revealed there.

The news about Fatima took many decades to spread throughout the world. When the great miracle bursts forth at Garabandal, television, radio, newspapers and the countless witnesses viewing the miracle will spread the story speedily to the farthest corners of the planet in a matter of hours. The warning will prepare us to hear God together at Garabandal, where His people will be gathered once again, just as they were on Sinai, under the protective covering of the Shekinah Glory: the cloud or pillar of smoke by day and a fire by night, offering a protective shield and guidance for the people of God. The place of the miracle will become a destination place.

The warning and the miracle are inseparable. They are two aspects of the same intervention of the Lord. Neither can be understood properly without knowing the other. The warning prepares us for the miracle, and it will offer further proof of the truth of all that was spoken by the visionaries throughout the world.

Sign Coming

Christina Gallagher has been told that all the people of the world will be given a warning, through a sign; if the sign is not accepted, chastisement will follow. **"There will come a sign, when everyone in the world will experience an inner awareness, and will know that this is of God, and see themselves as they really are. It is up to those who believe to pray, so that our prayers will be used, to allow everyone to respond to that Sign, and be saved for God. Our Lady is relying on those of us who do believe to pray that others who are in darkness will receive the grace to come back."**

"We must think not only of praying for our own souls and for our relatives and friends, **we must pray and make reparation for everyone, because that is what is expected of all believers, as God's children and members of Christ's Mystical Body.** When we respond to God's grace, we can help others who cannot help themselves at that time to be saved.

Christina Gallagher believes that the supernatural sign is not very far away. "I can feel it within myself. I can feel it coming at a great speed," she explained.

She believes that everything she has been shown will happen before the end of the century.

Other visionaries have similar things to say:

Theresa Lopez, Denver, Colorado

"The warning Our Lady calls the moment of silence. And in the moment of silence our internal selves will be revealed. Its purpose is to stir the soul to conversion" (November 11, 1992, delivered in a speech).

Maria Esperanza, Betania, Venezuela

"There is coming the great moment of a great day of light. The conscience of this beloved people must be violently shaken so they may put their own house in order and offer to Jesus the just reparation for the daily infidelities that are committed...."

Details Of The Warning

A visionary in the northeastern United States who is an invalid and seeks anonymity received messages in 1991 and 1992 that provide insights into the nature of the warning that are filled with hope and God's great love. She stated: "Those in My Grace have nothing to fear when the warning comes. When will you learn that there is nothing greater than My love? Don't you feel the warmth of My love? Is there anyone greater than I? Why are you looking anywhere else? Come into My Arms!

"This will be the one time, as never before in the history of mankind, when man will be given the same realization that is given at the hour of his death. This will be My greatest act of mercy! When man is confronted with the sins of his life, the moment belongs to him. I will repair all, but he must ask. I will forgive all, but he must repent. I will take everyone back to My Heart, but they must do the returning.

"...The ignorance that plagued mankind makes it impossible for anyone to grasp the depth [of sin in the world]. As a result, the consequences have to be in proportion. The Divine Majesty is standing alone in anticipation of the glorification of My Passion. **By that, I mean that very soon, the whole human race will witness My Crucifixion once again. At that time, everyone will understand the great offense My Father suffered.**

"The magnitude of it will finally be comprehended. The darkness of everyone's mind will be removed. And, not only that, the capability of restoring the honor that is rightfully His will be made possible for the first time in the history of mankind.

"…The outpouring of My Spirit, after the warning occurs, will be as great as it was on the first Pentecost. Only God can make the world: only He can save it. Can't you see the great love in My Father's Heart? No one desires peace more than My Father.

God, the Father, spoke from the sky: "**My people have forgotten Me. I am going to darken the sun for three hours.**"

"The people will come out of their houses in confusion. It will be impossible to console some of them. The telephone lines will become overloaded. Even the priests will be overcome with grief.

"Tell the people to recite the rosary. This is so important. The people will have to help Me. They will have to do another fast. The people will deprive themselves, reform their lives, and undo all their sins. Cohabitors will separate their lodging, all excesses will come to an end, the addicted will become rehabilitated with the help of My Grace alone.

"**This is about the warning. Let Me tell you about the warning. It will happen at 2 o'clock in the afternoon. You know the date.**

"**The sky will become very, very dark. The earth will shake. The whole world will be in turmoil. The greatest destruction will be in man's heart. People will think the world is coming to an end. The fear will be in proportion to their guilt.**

"**I will give them the time they need. I will hang there patiently. The outpouring of the Holy Spirit will begin at the very moment they see Me. This will be man's moment. He can clear all his sins away or he can bring them to his ruin.**

"My Arms will be outstretched. My Mercy will be overflowing. It's going to be the end. Everybody is going to understand. (He does not mean the end of the world but the end of life as it is now.)

"…I asked if Calvary is going to be accomplished during the warning. He said 'yes'."

"The sins of the world are so enormous that there is nothing that can outweigh them right now. As I was obedient to the Father's Will, so must it be with all of you. The warning *will* happen. Don't have any misgivings. When you least expect it—I have already said it—**you will see the Cross in the sky.** What I have promised, I will carry out. Then all of you will say, 'Truly, this is the Son of God.'

There are twelve points I want to make about the warning:

1. Wherever a person is, I will be there.
2. The whole world will cease activity.
3. The people will say they are sorry.
4. The sinners will want to die.
5. The outpouring of My Grace will raise the sinners up.
6. The Churches will be overflowing with penitents.
7. The pain and confusion will be at its maximum.
8. The priests will have to hear confessions around the clock.
9. There will be no 'life as usual.'
10. Businesses will be closed.
11. People will finally understand the meaning of charity.
12. It is up to the strong to take care of the weak.

Jesus spoke to Blessed Sister Faustina of a cross in the sky in the last days in great detail: **"Before I come as the just judge, I am coming first as the King of Mercy. Before the day of justice arrives, there will be given to people a sign in the heavens of this sort: "All light in the heavens will be extinguished, and there will be great darkness over the whole earth. Then the sign of the cross will be seen in the sky, and from the openings where the hands and the feet of the Savior were nailed will come forth great lights which will light up the earth for a period of time. This will take place shortly before the last day."**[3]

This revelation to Sister Faustina is consistent with the recent revelations from Our Lord to the visionary in the northeastern United States. It appears that there may be two separate periods of darkness. The first will occur during the warning (three hours) and the second during the peak of the chastisement—the three days of darkness.

19

The Miracle,
The Permanent Sign,
And Other Signs

Listen to me, you devout sons of mine, and blossom like a rosebush on a stream bank. Bloom like a sweet-smelling lily, and send your fragrance into the air like incense. Sing the Lord's praise and thank Him for all that He has done.... All that the Lord has done is very good: all that He commands is sooner or later done. No one should ask why things are as they are; these questions will be answered at the right time: whatever He commands is promptly done; there are no limits to His power to save.... He sees the whole of time, from the beginning to end, and nothing takes Him by surprise. No one should ask why things are as they are; everything in creation has its purpose.

Sirach 39:13-21

At Garabandal, Mary has revealed enough about the miracle for us to prepare for this occurrence, which will take place **within one year** of the warning. Its exact date is not known, except by Conchita, one of the visionaries now living in New York. She has been forbidden by the Blessed Virgin to disclose it until eight days before it is to happen. She then will announce it to the whole world. This long waiting-period distinguishes Garabandal from Fatima, where the predicted miracle of the sun was worked during the course of those apparitions. No promise of healing was made at Fatima, but it was made for some of those present for the miracle at Garabandal.

Millions will be able to see it on that day, for Garabandal is perched among hills forming a broad natural amphitheater well able to accommodate the vast multitude which will journey to that remote place. A great assembly will converge on the village from everywhere, and all who manage to reach its hills will behold the same vision of joy that sent Father Luis to Heaven as he witnessed the miracle.

Father Vlasic of Medjugorje, in a letter to Pope John Paul II dated December 2, 1983, wrote of a visible sign. Father Vlasic wrote: "Our Lady has promised to leave a visible sign for all humanity at the site of the apparitions of Medjugorje." The miracle will help to reveal some of what God has planned through these apparitions. Marian visitations convey a message, not only in the verbal communications of the Mother of God, but in the events themselves, the persons involved, the circumstances, and the surroundings.

The Great Sign In Heaven

The message of the Marian Movement of Priests on October 13, 1991, provided detail and clarification on what this great sign in Heaven may be like. It stated: "I am the great sign which appears in Heaven. Today you are calling to mind my last apparition, which took place in Fatima in the Cova da Iria, and which was confirmed by the miracle of the sun. This miracle shows you, in an extraordinary way, that I am the Woman clothed with the sun. **This miracle invites you to look to me as to the great sign which appears in Heaven. I am a great sign of battle between me and my Adversary, between the Woman and the Dragon, between my army and the army guided by the enemy of God. You are entering into the decisive times of the battle. You are preparing to live through the most difficult hours and the greatest of sufferings. It is necessary that all of you come as quickly as possible to form part of my army. For this, I again invite my children to consecrate themselves to my Immaculate Heart and to entrust themselves to me as little children.** Today, I am extending this invitation of mine above all to the little ones, to the poor, to those who are least, to the sick and to the sinners."

Theresa Lopez, Denver, Colorado

In the locutions of Theresa Lopez of Denver, Colorado, considerable information has been given to her about the warning, the miracle, the permanent sign, and the chastisement. The following is from a talk she gave on November 11, 1992: "...will Denver get a permanent sign and is that the same one as in Medjugorje? I don't know if it has do with any apparitions anywhere else. Our Lady has only told me about the significance of her apparitions in Denver. So the permanent sign she speaks about will occur here in Denver. I cannot say it is a link with anything going on anywhere else. But this permanent sign is a sign of conversion, and it's a sign of Our Lady. It is to stir you to conversion and cause the thrust into the Church.

"Once people receive conversion, that spark from the permanent sign, then Our Lady will of course take that sign and take those people to her Son. The second fold of secrets will come in the form of the miracle. And the miracle will be, the miracle of the presence of God. How this will happen, I can't sit here and tell you. Our Lady refers to it as sign in the presence of God. This will be experienced within the Church as is Our Lady's entire plan. It is to spark us and bring us to her Son in the Church, through the sacraments, through receiving the presence of Jesus in the Holy Eucharist.

"The warning, Our Lady calls the moment of silence. And in the moment of silence our internal selves will be revealed. Its purpose is to stir the soul to conversion. The miracle will have two purposes: to reveal the presence of God and the renewal of the Church. Our Lady has said these secrets will come about by proclamation of her last title. Once the miracle occurs the time of grace will end. It has an ending date. Chastisements will follow.

"And there is a great myth that the so-called good people will be taken from the earth and the so-called bad people remain. Everyone will remain. The so-called "good people" will have their focus on Heaven. They will be in what Our Lady calls eternal adoration. And you will have the heavenly gaze as your focus and will no longer be earthly because you will be completely focused on God. You may be aware of your surroundings but you won't have despair or worry, fright, or any of the human emotions. You will be wrapped in a state of eternal adoration. For those who did not choose to convert, they will retain an earthly view because they will be of the earth and they will feel the despair and the agony of the chastisements. Our Lady has said, **those who live a virtuous life have no fear of chastisements.** Even after all these chastisements come to pass, even then, there will be one hour of grace remaining. And in that hour of grace, even the worst of the worst that have undergone the chastisements, will be given the last opportunity for conversion. **The New Jerusalem will then settle upon the earth. All of evil will no longer exist and we will be in perpetual paradise, just as God planned in the beginning."**[1]

The Miracle Is Mercy

The miracle will be a clear revelation of God's mercy. We must prepare ourselves for this, so that when it happens we will fully grasp its significance and absorb its power. Even now we can begin to meditate fruitfully on the information already offered us by Our Lady about the miracle. These hints are for our benefit, so that we will be ready to fully appreciate the miracle when it happens.

One of the messages of Lubbock, Texas, spoke of a cross illuminating the skies: "I give unto ye your sign. Wait on this, for it shall illuminate the [skies]. Be at peace, for thou art My chosen and beloved. Weep for those who weepest and who shall weep. Give hope unto those who have none, as did My Son, Jesus. Be like that of Jesus, My beloved Son. For Jesus is and shall always be the everlasting Light of the World...and life for all mankind" (July 4, 1988).[2]

Saint Louis de Montfort mentioned such a cross in his writings: "Those who follow the cross willingly now, will not fear the last judgement. When the Lord comes to judge, the Sign of the Cross will be in the heavens; then will those servants of the cross, who in their lifetime made themselves one with the Crucified, draw near with great trust to Christ, the judge."[3]

The Miracle Will Be Eucharistic

The miracle will be Eucharistic. The emphasis on devotion to the Most Holy Eucharist is so strong at Garabandal that a Eucharistic theme for the miracle would be in perfect consonance with everything that happened in the village during the apparitions. It has been revealed that the miracle will take place at 8:30 on a Thursday evening; on the day of the miracle, the Church will be celebrating the feast of a young martyr of the Eucharist. We must be ready to receive an unmistakable proof from God, through the miracle, that the Holy Eucharist is the center of our life in the Church and that Jesus is truly present to us in the Eucharist. We are to avail ourselves of this sacrament as frequently as we can.

Mary spoke to "her beloved sons" through Father Gobbi, providing some information on December 8, 1980: "At the hour when all will seem lost, all will be saved through the merciful love of the Father, which will be made visible through the greatest manifestation of the Eucharistic Heart of Jesus."

The miracle will be ecclesial, that is, it will support the truth that through the Body of Christ which is the Church, all graces come, and that all men and women are called not only to follow Jesus personally, but also to enter His Church and to submit to its discipline, teaching, and sacraments. For this reason, the miracle will happen in connection with a great ecclesiastical event. God's timing is the Church's timing, and the Church's authority will be reinforced and authenticated by the fact that the "ecclesiastical event" and the miracle will occur on the same day, perhaps at the very same instant. Also, the Pope will see the miracle from wherever he is.

The Miracle Will Be Marian

The miracle will be Marian. It will assert the glory of the Mother of God, so that all Christians will give up their objections to her role in the Body of Christ and pay her the honor that God Himself gives her. The world will begin to give the Immaculate Heart of Mary the honor and devotion due her. Through this great miracle, many will begin to love, "Holy Mary, Mother of God."

Holy Motherhood

The Blessed Mother told the visionary Mariamante: "The wickedness of men would destroy my plan if possible but my power given to me by God Himself is infinitely greater than all the wickedness in the world. Good always triumphs over evil. Remember this always. It will give you great heart to know and reflect upon this. Satan and his legions cannot prevent my Triumph as hard as they may try, because God Himself has preordained that this should occur in this time. You are fortunate to be living in this time, this era of mercy and love. Not all have been given so great a chance to repent from so much evil. **You will know by the sign in the heavens which is I myself that the time is at hand for the instantaneous conversion of the multitude.** This will be accomplished through a tremendous out-pouring of grace upon the earth given at the hands of God to me for this purpose. This will be the Triumph of my Immaculate Heart of which I spoke at Fatima" (February, 22, 1987).[4]

Power

The miracle is for the conversion of the whole world. This assertion was made by Our Lord Himself to Conchita at Garabandal. The Lord answered her question about Russia's conversion by assuring her that "the miracle was not only for the conversion of Russia," but "for the conversion of the whole world," and that "thus, all will love Our Hearts" [the hearts of Jesus and Mary].

It seems by His words that somehow the miracle will show us all how closely the hearts of Jesus and Mary are united, as a symbol of the peace-giving love that should unite our hearts. The miracle most probably will have great impact on Heaven's lost daughter—Russia.

Perhaps the two hearts on the reverse side of the "Miraculous Medal" were a prophecy as well as a lesson, foretelling an age ahead where all hearts will be reconciled as are the hearts of Jesus and Mary. Reconciliation of hearts is what conversion is all about, and it seems that all the Marian appearances concern themselves with it.

Once the miracle happens, the human race must change or face the most terrible catastrophe the world has ever seen: the punishment. Unless the people heed the message of the miracle, the punishment will surely come. There will be no escape from it. The miracle will have set the fuse. Unless we extinguish its burning by repentance, the punishment will come.

Those who return from the mountain in Garabandal shall have seen the glory of the Lord and be eager to sound His glory to all the world. The glory of Zion, the glory of the New Pentecost prayed for by Pope John XXIII as he opened the Second Vatican Council and again by Pope Paul VI when he drew it to a close, will flow over the whole Church and the entire world. Thus, as Jesus revealed to Conchita, "all will love Our Hearts."

Mary, in a message to Patricia of Cuenca, Ecuador, on March 3, 1990, provided some of the most revealing information about the nature of the miracle: **"Children, I give you the blessing of the all-powerful God, Father, Son and Holy Spirit. Come always to visit me. Never abandon me, little ones, because I love you so much.** *At the end of all the apparitions in the world, I will leave a great sign in this place and in all those where I have been."*

The Permanent Sign

The permanent sign that the Blessed Virgin promised will remain at Garabandal after the miracle at "the pines" (a grove of nine pines outside the village at the top of a rocky lane leading up the hill). Little has been revealed about the nature of this sign. We know the following details: it will remain at the pines until the end of the world; we will be able to see, photograph, and televise it, but not touch it; no one will be able to explain it by scientific analysis.

It will remind us forever of the great miracle, which will center on that very spot. Anyone who wishes will be able to go to Garabandal after the miracle and examine the sign. It will recall to our minds that God summons the world to repentance. Because it will remain there until the world ends, it will also insist by its presence that the world will indeed one day end, and that Jesus will come again on the "clouds of Heaven to make all things new, and to judge the living and the dead."

The sign will focus our attention on the truth that God has visibly intervened on this mountain, just as He did on Mount Sinai, Mount Carmel, Mount Zion, and Calvary, to call His people to Himself. Patriarchs of old set up altars and monuments to commemorate forever their experience of God at a certain place, which became forever sacred by His coming. At Garabandal, for the first time in history, the Lord Himself sets His own sign in the pines for a perpetual memorial of His saving act for today's world.

The sign will call us all to holiness. The Israelites were continually reminded by the fiery cloud called the Shekinah Glory hovering over the Meeting Tent that God was with them, leading them to holiness and to the Holy Land. The sign will be with us like that cloud of God's glory, reminding us that the Lord is leading us to holiness and Heaven and that He will not tolerate idolatry among His people.

Other Signs

In the message of December 31, 1983, to the Marian Movement of Priests, Mary spoke of the signs sent by the Lord that are neither understood nor accepted: "The signs the Lord sends are neither understood nor accepted; the dangers pointed out by 'my Pope' who courageously and anxiously is predicting the storm awaiting you, are not believed. **The messages which I give, through simple and little souls chosen by me in every part of the world, are not taken into consideration. The appearances which I am still making, often in faraway and dangerous places, are ignored. And yet you are only inches from your ruin.** When all will be shouting for peace, a new world war could suddenly fall upon you, spreading death and destruction everywhere. When they will say: 'Tranquillity and security,' then could begin the very greatest overthrow of peoples and individuals. How much blood I see flowing in all the streets of the world! How many of my poor children I see weeping because of the scourge of fire, famine and terrible destruction!"

The Blessed Mother calls herself the prophetess of these last times. She is often obstructed by silence and rejection. She stated on March 5, 1982: "Just as in Jerusalem all the prophets were put to death, just as in this city the very Son of God, the Messiah promised and awaited for so many centuries, was rejected, outraged and condemned, so also today in the Church, the new Israel of God, the salvific action of your Mother, the heavenly prophetess of these last times, is too often obstructed by silence and rejection. In so many ways have I spoken, but my words have not been harkened to. In many ways I have manifested myself, but my signs have been given no credence. My interventions, even the most extraordinary have been contested. O New Jerusalem, Church of Jesus, true Israel of God!"

The New Blood On The Doorpost— The Seal

To be given special protection from Heaven is not a novel or unique occurrence in Scripture. Yahweh singled out those to live and those to die on many occasions. Prophets were told what to do and say. Daniel was favored because of his wisdom and stature. On the other hand, nations and cities were destroyed because of sin; the best known instances are Sodom and Gomorrah. The Scriptures describe many people who met with destruction because of sin. The blood on the door post was a "sign" for the angel of death to pass over that house in the Book of Exodus. However, the book of Ezekiel shows the wrath of God on a sinful generation and the punishment levied because of it. Below is a remarkable passage of which few are aware.

The Cross On The Forehead

"Then as I listened he shouted, 'Come here, you scourges of the city, and bring your weapons of destruction.' Immediately six men advanced from the upper north gate, each holding a deadly weapon. In the middle of them was a man in white, with a scribe's ink horn in his belt. They came in and halted in front of the bronze altar. The glory of the God of Israel rose off the cherubs where it had been and went up to the threshold of the temple. He called the man in white with a scribe's ink horn in his belt and said, **'Go all through the city, all through Jerusalem, and mark a cross on the foreheads of all who deplore and disapprove of all the filth practiced in it.'** I heard him say to the others, **'Follow him through the city, and strike. Show neither pity nor mercy; old men, young men, virgins, women, kill and exterminate them all. But do not touch anyone with a cross on his forehead.** Begin at my sanctuary.'

"So they began with the old men in front of the Temple. He said to them, 'Defile the Temple; fill the courts with corpses, and go.' They went out and hacked their way through the city. While they were hacking them down, I stayed behind; I fell face downwards and exclaimed, 'Ah, Lord Yahweh, are you going to annihilate all that is left of Israel as you turn your anger on Jerusalem?' He said, **'The guilt of the House of Israel and Judah is immense, boundless; the country is full of bloodshed, the city overflows with wickedness, for they say Yahweh has abandoned the country. Yahweh cannot see. Right, then, I too will show no pity, I too will not spare. I mean to call them to account for all their behavior.'** The man in white with the scribe's ink horn in his belt then came back and made his report, **'I have carried out your orders'''** (Ezekiel 9:1-9).

Today's Safety

Presently we are seeing another story unravel for those specially destined for protection. A modern-day "blood on the doorpost" and "the mark of a cross on the forehead of all who deplore and disapprove of filth" is now being given to Mary's cohort. The Marian Movement of Priests' message dated November 12, 1981, said that Heaven is protecting with a seal all of those with God. Nothing will harm those impressed by this image. Below are several messages through 1991 that affirm this remarkable repetition of what happened in the book of Ezekiel.

"You are thus **signed with the seal** of my love, which distinguishes you from those who have allowed themselves to be seduced by the Beast and bear his imprinted blasphemous number. The Dragon and the Beast can do nothing against those who have been signed with my seal.

"The Star of the Abyss will persecute all those who are signed with my seal, but nothing will be able to harm the souls upon whom I myself have impressed my image. By the blood which many of them will have to shed, divine justice will be appeased and the time of my victory will be hastened."

A later message on September 29, 1987, affirmed this: "...The Angels of Light of my Immaculate Heart are now actually gathering from everywhere the elect, called to form part of my victorious cohort. **They are signing you with my seal.** They are reclothing you with sturdy armor for the battle. They are covering you again with my shield. **They are giving you the crucifix and the rosary as the weapons to be used for the great victory.** The time for the decisive struggle has come. For this, the angels of the Lord are intervening in an extraordinary way and placing themselves, each day, at the side of each one of you to guide you, to protect you and to comfort you."

On September 8, 1989, Our Blessed Mother stated: "If my Adversary is signing, with his mark, all his followers, the time has come when **I also, your heavenly leader, am signing, with my heavenly seal, all those who have consecrated themselves to my Immaculate Heart and have formed part of my army. I am imprinting my seal on your foreheads with the most holy sign of the Cross of my Son Jesus.** Thus I am opening the human intellect to receive His divine word.... Against those signed on the forehead with the blasphemous mark, I am opposing my children signed with the Cross of Jesus Christ.... For this, I am imprinting upon your hands my seal which is the sign of the Father, of the Son, and of the Holy Spirit.... Allow yourselves all to be signed on the forehead and on the hand with my motherly seal...."

Turzovka, Czechoslovakia, 1958

Our Lady, appearing to Matous Losuta of Czechoslovakia in 1958, said the following: "All my children will receive and carry the sign of the cross on their foreheads. This sign only my chosen ones will see. These chosen ones will be instructed by my angels how to conduct themselves.

"My faithful will be without any kind of fear during the most difficult hours. They will be protected by the good spirits and will be fed by Heaven from where they will receive further instructions."[5]

For those who may be skeptical of these startling pronouncements, Revelation 7 says exactly the same thing. It is not unusual for God to protect His servants: "Next I saw four angels, standing at the four corners of the earth, holding the four winds of the world back to keep them from blowing over the land or the sea or in the trees. Then I saw another angel rising where the sun rises, carrying the seal of the living God; he called in a powerful voice to the four angels whose duty was to devastate land and sea, "Wait before you do any damage on land or at sea or the trees, until we have put the *seal on the foreheads* of the servants of our God." Then I heard how many were sealed: a hundred and forty-four thousand, out of all the tribes of Israel" (Revelation 7:1-4).

The Children In Medjugorje Speak About The Signs

During a question-and-answer period with Jan Connell, Maria and Mirjana spoke of signs preceding the great sign:[6]

Q. You and the other visionaries have indicated that there will be advanced signs [signs preceding the great sign] in many places in the world to warn the world. When will these advanced signs begin?

A. There are signs in many places in the world now. Many people see preliminary signs. Many experience personal healings, both physical and spiritual, and also psychological. Many have private signs. People have come here from all over the world. Often they have or have had extraordinary signs in their lives.

Q. Will all people on earth believe in God, in the Blessed Mother when the permanent sign occurs?

A. The Blessed Mother has said that those who are still alive when the permanent sign comes will witness many conversions among the people because of the sign, but she also says blessed are those who do not see but who believe.

Q. Mirjana told me that there will still be some unbelievers even when the permanent sign comes.

A. The Blessed Mother has said there will always be Judases.

Q. Vicka told me that there is great urgency in the Blessed Mother's call to immediate conversion. She said that for those who only marginally believe, who choose to wait for the great sign to believe it will be too late. Do you know why it will be too late for them?

A. This is a time of great grace and mercy. Now is the time to listen to these messages and to change our lives. Those who do will never be able to thank God enough."

Dozule, France

Madaleine was born on October 27, 1924, in Normandy, France, and is the mother of five children. Not particularly religious, in 1970 while in church, she said, "something happened which I could not explain...I felt a kind of weakness...I was as though drunk with joy and happiness. I seemed to have discovered another world." On reaching home, she felt transformed with her spirit full of joy. Thus began another story of the supernatural changes experienced by an ordinary person going about her daily life. From 1972 to 1974, she received visions of future events. On March 1, 1974, Jesus said to her: "Tell the Church that she must renew her message of peace to the whole world, because the hour is grave. Satan is directing the world, he seduces minds, makes them capable of destroying humanity in a few moments. If humanity does not resist him, I shall give him leave to act, and it will be a catastrophe, such as has not been since the deluge, and this will be before the end of the century. All those who come to repent at the foot of the Glorious Cross (this apparition is referred to as the Glorious Cross) will be saved. Satan will be destroyed; thereafter it will be only Peace and Joy."[7]

It appears that we may witness a great display of the Cross in the sky as a special grace or preliminary warning before the peak of the chastisement and the occurrence of the darkness. On July 4, 1975, Jesus said to Madaleine, in part: **"Understand this well: In the days which preceded the deluge, people didn't expect anything until the arrival of the flood which carried them off. But today you have been warned, you are living in the times of which I said: 'On this earth there will be disasters of all kinds: Iniquity is the cause of misery and famine, nations will be in anguish, there will be portents and phenomena in Heaven and on the earth.' So, be ready because great tribulation is near, such as has never been seen since the beginning of the world until today, and which will never be again.**

"I tell you, this young generation will not pass before all this happens. But do not be afraid, for behold in the heavens the Sign of the Son of Man which Madaleine saw shining from the East to the West. You, Heads of Churches, in truth I tell you, it is by this Cross set up over the world, that nations shall be saved. My Father has sent Me to save, and the moment has come when I must pour My Mercy into human hearts."

Many of these prophecies and signs also foretell the Second Coming of Christ. Christ said to Madaleine on May 3, 1974: "The Glorious Cross, or the Sign of the Son of Man, is the announcement of the approaching return in glory of the Risen Jesus."

20

The Great Chastisement And The Three Days Of Darkness

The reign of the Father's Mission was complete with the deluge of the flood; the reign of the Son's Mission was complete with the deluge of Blood on the Cross; the reign of the Holy Spirit's Mission will be complete with the deluge of "Fire and Love and Justice" in the latter days.

Saint Louis de Montfort

Exactly where wars and disasters end, and the great chastisement begins, we are not exactly certain. Judging by the readings of Scripture and the Marian Movement of Priests and other mystics, it appears that wars and disasters are merely a prelude to much more significant events. The chastisement, purification, and tribulation have been brought on by man's sins. The Blessed Mother speaks of "fire and blood causing the greatest destruction since the beginning of the world."

The great chastisement will be something greater than normal natural disasters. Readings indicate it is a series of catastrophic events, most likely a comet approaching the earth and causing tidal waves. **The famine that many speak about is not from a dry and**

parched earth but one that is water-soaked. The data do not exist to support one theory over another. Whether it is a comet or an asteroid, as the prophets of old have said, we do know it is something so significant the world has never seen anything like it before. It is at least a continuation of deteriorating events.

Wars, famines, hurricanes, financial and social collapse, earthquakes, nuclear disasters, fire from Heaven, comets, apostasy, three days of darkness, and two thirds or more of humanity being wiped out, are perhaps some or all of the elements of the chastisement.

New Testament

The great chastisement is a catastrophe described by Jesus in Matthew 24, Mark 13, and Luke 21. It is described in 2 Peter 2 and 3, as well as in the Book of Revelation.

In Matthew 24, Jesus tells us the signs of His coming: "You will hear of wars and rumors of wars.... Nation will rise against nation, one kingdom against another. There will be famine, pestilence, and earthquakes in many places. These are the early stages of the birth pangs. They will hand you over to torture and kill you.... Many will falter then, betraying and hating one another. False prophets will arise in great numbers to mislead many. Because of the increase of evil, the love of most will grow cold.... This good news of the kingdom will be proclaimed throughout the world as a witness to all the nations.

"Only after that will the end come. When you see the abominable and destructive thing which the prophet Daniel foretold standing on holy ground (let the reader take note!), those in Judea must flee to the mountains...for these days will be more filled with anguish than any from the beginning of the world until now or in all ages to come. Indeed, if the period had not been shortened, not a human being would be saved.... False messiahs and false prophets will appear, performing signs and wonders so great as to mislead even the chosen if that were possible....

"Immediately after the stress of that period 'the sun will be darkened, the moon will not shed her light, the stars will be shaken loose. Then the sign of the Son of Man will appear in the sky, and all the clans of the earth will strike their breasts' as they see "the Son of Man coming on the clouds of Heaven" with power and great glory.... As for the exact day or hour, no one knows it, neither the angels in

Heaven nor the Son, but the Father only. **The coming of the Son of Man will repeat what happened in Noah's time. In the days before the flood people were eating and drinking, marrying and being married, right up to the day Noah entered the ark. They were totally unconcerned until the flood came and destroyed them."**

Luke 21:20 gives Jesus' words: "When you see Jerusalem encircled by soldiers, know that its devastation is near." In Luke 21:25-27, Jesus says, "There will be signs in the sun, the moon and the stars. On earth, nations will be in anguish, distraught at the roaring of the sea and waves. Men will die of fright in anticipation of what is coming upon the earth. The power in the heavens will be shaken. After that, men will see the Son of Man coming on a cloud with great power and glory."

In 2 Peter 2:4-9 we read: "Did God spare even the angels who sinned? He did not. He held them captive in Tartarus—consigned them to pits of darkness, to be guarded until judgement. Nor did He spare the ancient world—even though He preserved Noah as a preacher of holiness, with seven others, when He brought down the flood on that godless earth. He blanketed the cities of Sodom and Gomorrah in ashes and condemned them to destruction, thereby showing what would happen in the future to the godless. He did deliver Lot, however, a just man oppressed by the conduct of men unprincipled in their lusts.... The Lord, indeed, knows how to rescue devout men from trial, and how to continue the punishment of the wicked up to the day of judgement."

2 Peter 3:3-10 states: "Note this first of all: in the last days, mocking, sneering men who are ruled by their passions will arrive on the scene. They will ask: 'Where is that promised coming of His? Our forefathers have been laid to rest, but everything stays just as it was when the world was created. In believing this, they do not take into account that of old there were heavens and an earth drawn out of the waters and standing between the waters, all brought into being by the word of God. By water that world was then destroyed; it was overwhelmed by the deluge. The present heavens and earth are reserved by God's word for fire; they are kept for the day of judgment, the day when godless men will be destroyed....

"The day of the Lord will come like a thief, and on that day the heavens will vanish with a roar; the elements will be destroyed by fire, and the earth with all its dead will be made manifest. Since everything is to be destroyed in this way, what sort of men must you not be! How holy in your conduct and devotion, looking for the coming of the day of God and trying to hasten it! Because of it, the heavens will be destroyed in flames and the elements will melt away in a blaze. What we await are the new heavens and a new earth, where according to His promise, the Justice of God will reside."

In these scriptural passages we have the events of the great chastisement presented in detail. These events lead to the coming of Jesus, the New Heaven and the New Earth. The Scriptural passages tell of wars, famine, plagues, earthquakes, false prophets, false messiahs, false signs and wonders, the abominable and destructive thing standing on holy ground, the darkening of the sun, the moon failing to shed her light, the stars falling from the sky, the destruction of Babylon (the world) and its wealth by fire within one hour, the coming of Jesus, the casting of the beast and his prophet into the abyss.

Mary, Queen Of Prophets, Apparitions, Messages

God has sent His Mother, the Queen of Prophets, in these last times as Prophetess to warn us to pray, fast, repent, and convert to prevent this great chastisement from destroying mankind. Below are some highlights from several apparitions that speak of these events. Though we have reported on several of these apparitions in earlier chapters, we list them here again to show the powerful, cumulative effect of Our Lady's messages:

LaSalette, 1846

Our Blessed Mother at LaSalette, France, on September 19, 1846, appeared to two children, Melanie and Maximin, who were given secrets to be revealed in 1858, which foretold these days in words that echoed those of Scripture.

Melanie was given the secret "that Lucifer with a large number of demons will be released from hell in 1864. They will put and end to the faith little by little, evil books will be abundant on earth, churches will be built to serve these spirits, Rome will lose the faith and become the seat of the Antichrist, the Church will be in eclipse, the world will be in dismay, wars, earthquakes, fire from Heaven, plagues, infectious diseases, famine and other calamities will strike the earth, the

Antichrist will be born who will perform wonders, the seasons will be altered, the earth will produce nothing but bad fruit, the stars will lose their regular motion, the moon will reflect a faint reddish glow, water and fire will give the earth convulsions, voices will be heard in the air."

Our Blessed Mother said: "Now is the time. The abyss is opening. Here is the king of king of darkness, here is the Beast with his subjects, calling himself the savior of the world. He will rise proudly into the air to go to Heaven. He will be smothered by the breath of the Archangel Saint Michael. He will fall, and the earth, which will have been in a continuous series of evolutions for three days, will open up its fiery bowels; and he will have plunged for eternity with all his followers into the everlasting chasms of hell. And then water and fire will purge the earth and consume all the works of men's pride and all will be renewed. God will be served and glorified."[1]

Fatima, 1917

At Fatima, Portugal, in 1917, Our Blessed Mother predicted the rise of the Red Dragon in Russia before the Bolshevik revolution of November 1917. She asked for the Consecration of Russia to her Immaculate Heart and Communion of Reparation on First Saturdays. If her request were heeded, said Mary, Russia would be converted and there would be peace. If not, Russia would spread her errors throughout the world, promoting wars and persecution of the Church. The good would be martyred, the Holy Father would have to suffer much, and various nations would be annihilated. But in the end her Immaculate Heart would triumph, the Holy Father would consecrate Russia to her, Russia would be converted and some time of peace would be given to the world.

Garabandal, 1961-1965

In 1961, Our Blessed Lady appeared in Garabandal, Spain, where she warned the cup of Divine Justice was filling, that many cardinals, many bishops and many priests were on the path of perdition and would take many souls with them. Our Blessed Mother warned that after Pope John XXIII there would be three more Popes, one of whom would reign only a short time (John Paul I was pontiff for thirty-four days), then it would be the end of times. When Pope Paul VI inherited the Petrine keys, Our Blessed Lady said that only two more Popes would follow him before the end of times.

Our Blessed Mother at Garabandal prophesied a warning for the world and a miracle within a year of the warning. One visionary stated that the warning would be a thousand times worse than earthquakes; it would be like fire but would not burn the flesh. A terrifying event would occur in the sky.

Our Blessed Mother said that a time would come when it would look like the Church was finished, when priests would have difficulty saying Mass and talking about holy things. Daniel speaks about the Mass or "perpetual sacrifice" being eliminated for a period of time.

When asked how this would happen, she answered, "communism." If we do not heed the warning and change after the warning and the miracle, God will send the chastisement.

Akita, 1973-1981

At Akita, Japan on August 3, 1973, Our Blessed Mother told Sister Agnes Sasagawa: **"In order that the world might know His anger, the Heavenly Father is preparing to inflict a great chastisement on all mankind."**

On October 13, 1973, Our Blessed Mother gave Sister Agnes a message which may be the unrevealed third secret of Fatima. In it Our Blessed Mother stated: "As I told you, if men do not repent and better themselves, the Father will inflict a terrible punishment on all humanity. It will be a punishment greater than the deluge, such as one will never have been seen before. Fire will fall from the sky and will wipe out a great part of humanity, the good as well as the bad, sparing neither priests nor faithful. The survivors will find themselves so desolate that they will envy the dead....

"The work of the devil will infiltrate even the Church in such a way that one will see cardinals opposing cardinals, bishops against other bishops, the priests who venerate me will be scorned and opposed by their confreres.... Churches and altars sacked, **the Church will be full of those who accept compromises and the demon will press many priests and consecrated souls to leave the service of the Lord. The demon will be especially implacable against souls consecrated to God."**

Medjugorje, 1981 to present

At Medjugorje, Bosnia-Herzegovina (Yugoslavia), Our Blessed Mother began appearing in 1981 to six visionaries. She also has been giving locutions to two additional young people. She has advised these visionaries that these apparitions are the last apparitions of the Blessed Mother on earth. After each of the visionaries has all ten secrets, humanity will be given three warnings, then a visible sign will appear at the site of the apparitions in Medjugorje as a testimony to the apparitions and in order to call people back to the faith. The ninth and tenth secrets are serious and concern chastisement for the sins of the world. **Our Blessed Mother told Mirjana that punishment is inevitable, but can be diminished by prayer and penance, but cannot be eliminated.**

Our Blessed Mother is still appearing at Medjugorje. Two visionaries have all ten secrets; the others each have nine.

Cuenca, Equador, 1988 to 1990

Our Blessed Mother told Patricia Talbott of Cuenca, Ecuador, January 6, 1990: "Children, there is so much sorrow in my heart, for many natural catastrophes and others created by man are coming. Hard times are already taking place, a short decade filled with suffering. Children the third world war is near.... Children the time is short, very short. Conversion must be faithful.... In these last days in which I will be present, because my leave is near, you must fill your hearts with the light of my Son, so that a desolation of faith will not exist." In February 1990, she said: "We have begun the hard times. It will be ten very sad years. Time is short."

Our Blessed Mother in October 1988 gave Patricia a secret with three parts. Patricia said: "She gave me the secret that there are bad things going to happen in the world, and that what is asked for is conversion." Patricia cannot reveal this at present. The Blessed Mother told her: "One month ahead of time, I'll tell you so you can say." At a later time the Blessed Mother told Patricia that some parts of the secret could be revealed. The great secret contains three parts. Patricia stated that all three parts have something to do with future events which will be chastisements for our world.

Our Lady spoke several times about the possibility of a third world war, of natural disasters and man-made disasters: "Little children, know that all you do benefits the world. Your prayers, penances, and fasts are helping to deter the determination of the third World War. Everything is as I have said before. It is in your hands. It depends on you whether the chastisement be as strong as the sorrow that my Son feels or that it [the chastisement] be appeased with prayer.... Great catastrophes are coming upon humanity; the third World War threatens the world. Catastrophes created by man are coming."

Our Blessed Mother told her some details of the war which she was allowed to share: "The war is near. It will be started with false peace treaties, treaties in which we should not place our trust. Many countries would be involved, among them China, Rumania, Russia, and the United States. Initially Poland will be involved also, but when the Holy Father leaves Rome, going first to France and then to Poland, Poland would be protected." Patricia said that is why conversion now is so important. [2]

Patricia further relayed information the Blessed Mother gave her: "The earth would go out of its orbit for three days. At that time the Second Coming of Jesus will be near. The devil will take over the world. During those days, families should be in continuous prayer. Because of false prophets, who will falsify the words of Christ, we have to be in the state of grace so that we can discern the good from evil. We have to have the flame of Jesus Christ in our soul. We should not open the door of our homes to anybody [during those three days of darkness]. We are simply to keep on praying. The Virgin said it would be better not even to look through the window because we will see the justice of God over the people. It will be so terrible that we will not want to see it."

Our Blessed Mother through Father Gobbi of the Marian Movement of Priests (1973-the present) provided several messages:

On September 15, 1987: **"A chastisement worse than the flood is about to come upon this poor and perverted humanity. Fire will descend from Heaven and this will be a sign that the Justice of God has of now fixed the hour of His great manifestation."**

On December 8, 1987: "You are living the painful times of the chastisement. You are living the dark hour of the victory of my Adversary, who is the Prince of the Night. You are living the most difficult moments of the purification."

On November 15, 1990: **Mary spoke about the great trial coming to the United States and for all humanity. The Blessed Mother specifically mentions that the United States will know the hour of weakness and of poverty as well as "the hour of suffering and defeat." The thunder of God's justice will have arrived:**

"The great trial has arrived for your country [USA].... Sins of impurity have become ever more widespread, and immorality has spread like a sea which has submerged all things. Homosexuality, a sin of impurity which is against nature, has been justified; recourse to the means of preventing life have become commonplace, while abortions—these killings of innocent children, that cry for vengeance before the face of God—have spread and are performed in every part of your homeland. The moment of divine justice and of great mercy has now arrived. You will know the hour of weakness and of poverty; the hour of suffering and defeat; the purifying hour of the great chastisement.

"The great trial has arrived for all humanity. The chastisement, predicted by me at Fatima and contained in that part of the secret which has not yet been revealed, is about to take place. The great moment of divine justice and of mercy has come upon the world. For this reason I have wanted you here. You must be the apostles of these last times...." America will know poverty and defeat! Those are strong statements made by the Blessed Virgin herself. Never before have we known something like this on a national scale.

On November 22, 1992, the Blessed Mother said to Father Gobbi, "In all the land, two-thirds of them will be cut off and perish; and one-third shall be left. I will pass this third through fire; I will refine it as silver is refined, test it as gold is tested."

Mary is saying two-thirds of mankind shall perish!

Dozens of warnings and exhortations have been given to us about the purification through the Marian Movement of Priests. A wealth of information is provided. Secrets have not been kept from us. Each passing year the messages become more specific. Purification of fire and blood, purification through darkness, and coming martyrdom have been constant themes. They are extremely unpleasant and depressing. However, they are true, and we must meet the challenge head-on in truth, for the facts are before us. God the Father, Jesus, Mary, the saints, and Scripture are saying identical things.

On February 8, 1990, Our Lord appeared to Patricia Talbott and told her that one of the signs that would point to the nearness of the chastisement would be a comet which would pass by the earth. He said that His mother was preparing us for His Second Coming.

Messages Of God The Father

Eileen George is the mother of eight children. She is a resident of Worcester, Massachusetts, and has been receiving messages from Our Lord since the very early 1980s. She has a particular ministry to the clergy and has been endorsed by many priests and bishops, including Cardinal O'Connor of New York. She is a woman who has suffered greatly and has had numerous operations relating to cancer. Often when she speaks to priests, it will be only with them in confidence; all others are asked to leave.

Messages of God the Father to Eileen George in 1982:

On February 20, 1982, God the Father told Eileen, "There will be a World War III and it will be started by a man who wears the turban of the faith, a Moslem. He will be an antichrist put on earth by Lucifer. Yet there is a more powerful one to rise in Syria, when this one has accomplished his work. He will cause destruction and pain. He will cause heartbreak and tears, and a great persecution of Christians. The earth will tremble with earthquakes. He will be a great ruler of Satan. After many years of battle." Eileen asked how many years? God the Father answered, "Fifteen. After fifteen years there will be a great peace, a great peace. The land of terror will fall at the knees of Mary. Her blue mantle will overshadow them, and the red will flow into the sea, and covered by the mantle of blue, they will join the free world in peace and harmony. And then there will be a long, long peace, longer than has ever fallen on the earth."

Regarding the Antichrist, Eileen stated "Jesus showed him to me: he has a mustache, black hair and wears a turban."

On February 28, 1982, God the Father told Eileen: "There will be a great famine all over the world. Nothing will grow. The whole world will be hungry. All will be lacking in food. The atmosphere will be changing and cause great disaster upon the earth. A terrible earthquake...." Eileen asked, "Is that San Francisco"? God the Father answered, "It will be opened up and swallowed. You can give warnings to man so they can pray and change things around.... It will be written that God has spoken to His people through one of His little ones, one whom He loved and trusted to reveal His word."

Eileen asked, "What about that bad guy with the turban? Will that be his first act against us?...." 'It will be New York....'

"Wow, we couldn't live under that...Wow, they were intercepted, but that one got through (gasps).... I know you don't punish us, I know you have made a covenant with us, but all this seems like a terrible thing coming to us: the famine, the earthquakes. That will be the end of San Francisco, New York.... There will be nobody left [in those cities].... Father, when will all this start?...."

"Between 1990 and 1999."

In the interview with Eileen about this message she states the famine will have "something to do with the planets changing seasons, a perpetual season of frost and cold. There will be nothing to eat. A great shortage of oil. No heat. The war is not going to come till later, because we are going to be fighting about oil. Then the Antichrist is going to arise from the Mohammedan race, a Moslem. He is going to have a turban. The people will call it, "the eye of Satan." He is young. The famine comes first, sometime between 1990 and 1999. Then he is going to start a great war.

"My Father said he is already planning it. They are building up arms.... He will be connected with the Russians, the communists. He'll be an antichrist.... He wore a long robe. He will be very intelligent and well equipped for nuclear war.... He is going to be worse than Hitler. This Moslem is going to fire rockets at us. Our radar will pick them up, and our rockets will intercept them. But some are going to get through and hit New York City.

" My Father is saying now [about 'the change in the seasons'] the scientists, the astronomers, are going to detect this. They will put the world on an alert, but no one is going to believe them. The earthquakes are horrible. I saw big, big buildings falling down. San Francisco is going to be swallowed up. The earthquake will start on the floor of the ocean. My Father said the floods are going to be terrible. There will be no holding them back. They'll take down buildings and streets and everything. The war will be in progress, which will make it twice as bad.

Note: *These events are conditional.* Their occurrence, extent, and consequences depend upon the prayers and conversion of people. They come from the malice of men, the devil, and natural causes. But a divine miraculous intervention limiting or preventing these disasters depends on us. God is merciful, but He is also just. During these events He will protect and strengthen *those who love Him.*

God the Father on March 3, 1982, told Eileen: "The Church is leaning like the tower of Pisa, and it will topple over unless an apostle comes out of nowhere and speaks the wisdom of God.... There has to be a change in My chosen sons, for the Church is hurtling to nothing. In this coming year, doctrine and tradition will be pulled apart and the Church will start to crumble. There must be this invisible source of faith, holding the pieces together. The priests will turn against each other and build up fortresses against each other and against the Vicar. There will be great darkness and this has now come upon the Church. There will be a great division. There will be warnings, but they will not be heeded...."

Eileen was given a mission to the priests by God the Father. On May 23, 1982, God the Father told Eileen, "It's a very critical time for the Church.... This is the hour of the Father. He's coming to His people to save the Church, for the Evil One himself is walking the earth to devour God's people."[3]

Three Days Of Darkness

The Ninth Plague—The Darkness

"Then Yahweh said to Moses, 'Stretch out your hand towards Heaven, and let darkness, darkness so thick that it can be felt, cover the land of Egypt.' So Moses stretched out his hand towards Heaven, and for three days there was deep darkness over the whole land of Egypt. No one could see anyone else or move about for three days, but where the sons of Israel lived there was light for them" (Exodus 10:21-23).

"Immediately after the distress of those days, the sun will be darkened, the moon will lose its brightness, the stars will fall from the sky, and the powers of Heaven will be shaken" (Matthew 24:29).

"The fifth angel emptied his bowl over the throne of the beast and its whole empire was plunged into darkness. Men were biting their tongues for pain, but instead of repenting for what they had done, they cursed the God of Heaven because of their pains and sores" (Revelation 16:10-11).

Over the last several years, much has been said about the three days of darkness which will purify the earth. The following story is from the vision of Brother David Lopez. His vision is like many others in recent history and conforms to many described in the works of Father Albert Hebert of Louisiana, who until recently was considered by some to be extreme in his thinking. For nearly twenty years, Father Hebert has been writing and speaking on these themes. Today, his books are in great demand. Now as the hour approaches, and with the repetition and the clarity of the messages, the three days of darkness is no longer a theory as far-fetched as it was several years ago.

Brother David lives on the Texas-Mexico border in a hamlet called El Ranchilo, in a hermitage known as Our Lady of Tenderness. Having spent eighteen years as a Franciscan religious, David runs a small retreat house there that assists illegal aliens by giving them generous helpings of food, shelter and prayer. Brother David has cerebral palsy which causes him considerable difficulty in walking and talking, and that much more in taking on such a heavy responsibility as running his little haven. Brother David has made several pilgrimages to Medjugorje and is reluctant even to speak about the three days of darkness, but knows it is a relevant subject in our day. It was made clear to Brother David he should speak about this even though he feels uncomfortable with it. The message given to him by the Blessed Virgin Mary is as follows; this is the account of his vision in its entirety:

The Blessed Virgin Mary's Message
To Brother David Lopez

"Do not be afraid about the three days of darkness that will come over the earth, because those who are living my messages and have a life of interior prayer will be alerted by an interior voice three days to one week before the occurrence. My children must continue with repentance for their sins, and pray more as I have recommended. They should get holy water, and blessed articles, and have special devotion to the Sacred Heart of Jesus, having always a vigil light in front of Him. They must be content with satisfying the basic necessities of life and be less dependent on material goods. The priests must not only take care of their own interior prayer life, but also develop the interior prayer life of all their parishioners. The same way they should avoid anyone who speaks about revolution and rebellion. The ones who speak about revolution and rebellion are the disciples of the Anti-christ. I am sad for the religious of the West who have renounced their signs of consecration. They, especially, will be tempted by Satan and will not be able to resist the spiritual and physical attacks. They must return to a life of sanctity and obedience to Christ, my Son. Do not be afraid of anything or anybody. Be filled with God's love by praying, reading Holy Scripture, and receiving the sacraments. I will be with you during the time of anguish, and my children may call on me for secure refuge.

"Those who are struggling to overcome recurring personal sin should not despair because God will take into account their desires and efforts to conquer their sins. Go in the Peace of God.

"During these three days of darkness, there is not going to be one demon left in hell. All are going to be on earth. Those three days are going to be so dark that we will not be able to see our own hands before our faces.

"In those days, the ones who are not in the state of grace are going to die of fright because of the horrible demons that they will see. The Virgin told me to close all the doors and windows and not to respond to anyone who calls from the outside. The biggest temptation we will have is the devil who is going to imitate the voices of our loved ones. She told me, 'Please do not pay attention because those are not your loved ones; those are demons trying to lure you out of the house.'

"Regarding the places where I reside, at the beginning of those three days, there are going to be people trying to cross the river (the Rio Grande) but they can't do it because they cannot see and will drown. They will be so afraid that they will kill one another; they will die in a state of sin.

"The Virgin told me that God has selected some people who are going to be martyrs at the beginning of the three days of darkness, but they should not be afraid because God will give them perseverance, and, after the martyrdom, the angels are going to take them body and soul into Heaven. She insists that we pray to the Lord that those days will not come in the winter and that there are not pregnant women about to give birth; because if they come in winter, the cold will be intense, there won't be any artificial heat, and the women about to give birth won't have any medical assistance.

"She gave me two graces that I cannot reveal to anybody. She also told me, "The people should not try to look for signs and not waste time trying to figure out the date." She told me this because she said there was a man predicting the exact date of the three days of darkness. When I asked the Virgin about the prophesy, she only said, "Be careful of those who set dates." We should not pay attention to dates. If we knew the date, people would live only waiting for the date and not convert for the love of God.

"She told me that the hours of darkness will be exactly seventy-two, and the only way to count them is with mechanical clocks, because there will not be any electricity. After this purification, there will be spring. Everything will be green, and everything will be clean. The water will be crystal clear, even the water from the faucets in houses. There will be no contamination in the water, nor the air, nor the river.

"The most beautiful thing is that the people are going to live off the land and work not to survive but for love and mutual support.

"The most important way to bring about this change is to come to conversion and live charitably today. Live in a state of grace. It is very important to form communities of fraternal alliances where you can have support from your brothers. The days of darkness are going to be very hard for single people and for the parents of the families that have adult children, because they will hear their voices outside.

"The parents of the family, especially the fathers, must teach their sons and daughters to pray. During the hours of darkness, the children's prayers will be miraculous.

An Added Message To Priests

"I want to add this message for the priests. They have the responsibility to tell these occurrences to all their parishioners, to give them strength and conversion, and to tell the parishioners not to fear. They have the obligation to pass this message on and not to be afraid to communicate it, because the message has been revealed before to many holy saints, and we cannot lose any more time ignoring it. They should put all their emphasis in teaching people to convert, to pray with the Holy Spirit. They should also teach them not to be preoccupied with material goods, money, power, work, etc., because it is not worth it.

"In the same way, they should preach how to prepare for death. It is important to preach about the final things for human beings: death, judgement, Heaven, and hell. Preach expressly on the consciousness for sin, and, especially, mortal sin, with its deadly consequences. The Lord prefers that we convert for love, but if it is necessary, for fear of punishment. Nonetheless, He will accept conversion all ways and will receive us because He loves us and wants our salvation. For love or for fear, the only thing that matters is that we give ourselves to Him. The priests have the obligation to guide the people, especially by example of their lives of absolute dedication to Christ."

The Great Sign

"Before the great tribulation, there is going to be a sign. We will see in the sky one great red cross on a day of blue sky without clouds. The color red signifies the blood of Jesus Who redeemed us and the blood of the martyrs selected by God in the days of darkness. This cross will be seen by everyone: Christians, pagans, atheists, etc., as well as all the prepared ones (understand for prepared ones not only the Christians, because there are people who have never heard the Gospel, but also for those who have the voice of God in their consciences) who will be guided by God in the way of Christ. They will receive grace to interpret the significance of the cross."

How Brother David Finally Came To Write This Message

"I wrote the message of the Virgin on the 11th of September [1987], and for almost a month I resisted doing it. I looked for people who would discourage me about giving this message, but nobody did. So, I went to my spiritual director, and he told me to write it, but I didn't.

"On September 11, I went to San Antonio, Texas. I went a few days early to prepare for the visit of Pope John Paul II. My friends took me to a Shrine of Czestochowa, where I was praying before the Blessed Sacrament exposed in the chapel. About 11:40 a.m., I felt like the Lord was telling me to move from there and go to the main church (the chapel for the Blessed Sacrament is at the side of the main part of the church). So, I went and started praying the rosary before the statue of the Virgin of Guadalupe. It was 11:45 a.m., when, for no reason at all, I raised my eyes and perceived the statue coming alive. The statue then revealed some private things about my friends and called my attention to the fact that I had not yet done what she had asked me to do. Then she told me, 'I want you to write the message I gave you in Medjugorje before you forget, and I want you to take it to the Bishop to have it confirmed.' So, I thought, 'If what she told me about my friends is true, I will write the message, if not, no, I will remain silent.' I talked to my friends about what the Virgin had revealed to me about them and everything was true. So, I didn't have any more excuses; I decided to write.

"Two weeks later, I went to Bishop Fitzpatrick, [Bishop of Brownsville, Texas, now retired] and I showed what I had written with the hope that he would not believe and disapprove. But that didn't happen. He told me, 'David, these words are not new. This message is not yours and is not to keep. It is for the whole world, and I am not going to stop you from publishing these words, but be prudent because not everyone wants to accept nor understand. Certainly, there is no doctrinal, spiritual, nor moral error. (Brother David expressly asks for us to understand that Bishop Fitzpatrick has not given his official endorsement to this message).'"[4]

Culmination Of The Chastisement

Are the three days of darkness the peak or culmination of the chastisement? For several years the world has been going through the purification, and with each new year will come further destruction if mystics world-wide are correct. In most parts of the world there are wars, famines, economic and social hardship, with a continuing list of problems. The great chastisement is when chaos is all around us due to calamities on a world-wide scale. Purification brings us back to God. One example is the Philippines. Over the last five years, it has had severe floods, a large earthquake, the eruption of Mount Pinatubo, and several other catastrophic events. Today, in the Philippines, once again the churches are full.

The present situation in the Balkans is an indicator of what will become more widespread. Many seers believe immediately after the three days of darkness, the reign of Jesus Christ in all of His glory will be established. Whether this will be the Eucharistic or the Physical Reign is unclear at this point. Voices from the past speak of these events. As the bishop mentioned to Brother Lopez, "these words are not new." Below we list some other saints and seers who have spoken about these events.

Wisdom from the Ages About the Chastisement

The Blessed Mother's words to **Sister Elena Aiello**, a Calabrian stigmatist nun and foundress of a religious order: "Clouds with lightning rays of fire and a tempest of fire will pass over the whole world and the punishment will be the most terrible ever known in the history of mankind. It will last seventy hours. The wicked will be crushed and eliminated. Many will be lost because they will have stubbornly remained in their sins. Then they will feel the force of light over darkness. The hours of darkness are near."

The Blessed Mother told **Mother Elena Leonardi:** "An unforeseen fire will descend over the whole earth, and a great part of humanity will be destroyed. This will be a time of despair for the impious: with shouts and satanic blasphemy, they will beg to be covered by the mountains, and they will try to seek refuge in caverns, but to no avail. Those who remain will find God's mercy in my power and protection, while all who refuse to repent of their sins will perish in a sea of fire!"

Blessed Gaspar Del Bufalo (Nineteenth Century): "The death of the impenitent persecutors of the Church will take place during the three days of darkness. He who outlives the darkness and the fear of these three days will think that he is alone on earth because the whole world will be covered by carcasses."

"During a darkness lasting three days the people given to evil will perish so that only one fourth of mankind will survive." **Sister Mary of Jesus Crucified, of Pau, the "Little Arab"** (d.1878), beatified in 1983, by Pope John Paul II, Foundress of a Carmelite convent at Bethlehem. [5]

Blessed Anna Maria Taigi knew with certainty the fate of the dead. Her gaze traveled to the ends of the earth and discovered there people on whom she had never set eyes, reading them to the depth of their souls. One glance sufficed; upon whatever she focused her thoughts, it was revealed to her and her understanding. She saw the whole world as we see the front of a building. It was the same with nations as with individuals; she saw the cause of their distresses and the remedies that would heal them.

By means of this permanent and prodigious miracle, the poor wife of Domenico Taigi became a theologian, a teacher, and a prophet. The miracle lasted forty-seven years. The poor, the great of the world, and the princes of the Church came to her for advice or help. They found her in the midst of her household cares and often suffering from illness. She refused neither her last crust of bread nor the most precious moment of her time, yet she would accept neither presents nor praise.

Her most powerful friends could not induce her to allow them to favor her children beyond the conditions in which they were born. When she was at the end of her resources, she told God about it, and God sent what was necessary. She thought it good to live from day to day, like the birds. A refugee queen in Rome wished to give her money. "Madame," she said, "how simple you are! I serve God, and He is richer than you."

"She touched the sick, and they were cured; she warned others of their approaching end, and they died holy deaths. She endured great austerities for the souls of purgatory, and the souls, once set free, came to thank her.... She suffered in body and soul.... She realized that her role was to expiate the sins of others, that Jesus was associating her with His Sacrifice. We list some of her prophecies:

"God will send two punishments; one will be in the form of wars, revolutions and other evils; it shall originate on earth. The other will be sent from Heaven. There shall come over the whole earth an intense darkness lasting three days and three nights. Nothing can be seen, and the air will be laden with pestilence which will claim mainly, but not only, the enemies of religion. It will be impossible to use any man–made lighting during this darkness, except blessed candles. He, who out of curiosity, opens his window to look out, or leaves his home, will fall dead on the spot. During these three days, people should remain in their homes, pray the rosary and beg God for mercy....

"All the enemies of the Church, whether known or unknown, will perish over the whole earth during that universal darkness with the exception of a few whom God will soon convert. The air shall be infected by demons who will appear under all sorts of hideous forms. Religion shall be persecuted, and priests massacred. Churches shall be closed, but only for a short time. The Holy Father shall be obliged to leave Rome...

"After the three days of darkness, Saint Peter and Saint Paul, having come down from Heaven, shall preach in the whole world and designate a new Pope. A great light will flash from their bodies and will settle upon the cardinal who is to become Pope. Christianity, then, will spread throughout the world. He is the Holy Pontiff, chosen by God to withstand the storm. At the end, he will have the gift of miracles, and his name shall be praised over the whole earth. Whole nations will come back to the Church and the face of the earth will be renewed. Russia, England, and China will come into the Church."

Marie de la Fraudais (Nineteenth Century): "There will come three days of complete darkness. Only blessed candles made of wax will give some light during this horrible darkness. One candle will last for three days, but they will not give light in the houses of the godless. Lightning will penetrate your houses, but it will not put out the blessed candles. Neither wind, nor storm, nor earthquake will put out the blessed candles. Red clouds, like blood, will cross the sky, and the crash of thunder will shake the earth to its very core. The ocean will cast its foaming waves over the land, and the earth will be turned into a huge graveyard. The bodies of the wicked and of the righteous will cover the face of the earth. The famine that follows will be severe. All plant-life will be destroyed as well as three-fourths of the human race. This crisis will be sudden and the punishment will be world-wide."[7]

Julka, Zagreb, former Yugoslavia: "...But after the darkness the earth remained waste. The beautiful warm sun rose to shine upon the earth and all living things upon it, but only here and there was any human being still alive. Nature, created by God, remained empty— without human beings."[8]

Our Lord gave this message to Julka: "The darkness, which I caused you to see, has this meaning, too: The sins of man are so black that they will poison everything upon the earth, and the whole pure atmosphere, even My Teaching which I preach through My servants. Sin will obscure everything. The sun which warms the earth symbolizes Me, its Creator. The unbelievers say that I do not exist, and deny Me, since I cannot be seen anywhere. As you have seen, so it will be. I shall come quickly and in splendor. All My creatures who survive the Great Tribulation will see Me. No one will then be able to say that

I do not exist, because I shall be near the earth; and all the creatures of the earth will hear My Voice. They will see Me present then, and, for the second time, at the Final Judgment.

"This will be the Little Flock and I shall hover over it. In those days there will be one Shepherd and one Faith, that of the Roman Catholic Church, which I established when I walked visibly on the earth. After the distresses, which I am now permitting to come upon My obstinate people on earth, there will arise a fair and pure race and the earth will abound with My gifts. My sons and My daughters will keep My Commandments, thus everything will live and grow with My Blessing for thirty years. Later on My people will again tend to evil and to sin. I shall then send My Messengers, Elijah and Enoch, from Heaven to instruct the people in the true Faith.

"A strong warm wind will come from the south. It will seize upon the whole globe and cause dreadful storms. After this, about ten claps of thunder at once will strike the earth with such force that it will shudder throughout. **This is a sign that the great tribulation and the black darkness are beginning. These will last three days and three nights.** On this account people should go into their houses, close them up well, darken the windows, bless themselves and the house with holy water, and light blessed candles. Outside such dreadful things will be happening, that those who venture to look will die. All the devils will be let loose on earth, so that they can destroy their prey themselves.

"The demons will howl upon the earth and call many, in order to destroy them. What? They will imitate the voices of relations and acquaintances, who have not reached a safer place. Once the horror commences, do not open your door to anyone at all!

"In many places, several people will gather together in fear. From the same group, some will perish, others remain alive for this Day and moment, and for that darkness, many will have prepared the blessed candles, but they will not burn, if the people have not lived in accordance with My Commandments; others will even be unable to light them for fear. But, for those who believe, although they have but a stub of the blessed candle, it will burn for these three days and nights without going out. Some people will fall into a deep sleep granted by Me, so as not to see what is happening on the earth."

For many years the Blessed Mother has shed tears in her apparitions and through statues as a sign of her sorrow over the sins of mankind. In recent years, visionaries (or victim souls) have wept blood as have many statues. Julka was told the significance of these blood tears means the chastisement is imminent. "The tears of blood which have been flowing from my eyes foretell that the Great Chastisement will befall the whole world."

Christina Gallagher: Christina quotes Jeremiah, when he says in the Scriptures: "The Lord enters into judgement with the nations...of all flesh...the Lord of Hosts says: 'Behold evil shall go forth from nation to nation, and a great whirlwind shall go forth... and the slain of the Lord shall... from one end of the earth to the other...**in the latter days, you shall understand these things.**"

Jesus said to Christina Gallagher: "**My little one, tonight I invite you to write. Be not afraid. My peace I freely give you. Tell all humanity to prepare themselves; the time has come for the cleansing of all humanity. A great darkness will come upon the world. The heavens will shake. The only light will be through the Son of God and Man. The lightning bolts will flash like nothing the world has ever seen. My hand will come over the world more swiftly than the wind. Be not afraid. Many tried to make you stumble. I tell you, My little one, always unite yourselves with Me, your Lord and Redeemer. I am your shield. I thirst for souls out of love. The demons rage upon the earth. They are loosened from their pit. Tell all humanity of the Seven Seals of God**" (January 30, 1991).

Nothing To Fear

Despite the terror she felt during and after that awesome vision on August 20, 1991, Mrs. Gallagher stresses that the serious messages she has received are not meant to cause panic or upset for anyone, and she points out that Our Lady and Jesus have promised that those who do as the Blessed Mother has asked have nothing to fear."

In a message on July 23, 1988, she was told: "My child, the purification will come. Those who have served God in His Light need not fear...."

Lubbock

The Blessed Mother also spoke of chastisement. "For lo, seest the winds do stir and violently they shall toss to and fro by the commands of My mighty hands. I say unto ye, old and young alike: No one knows the day nor hour. For it is in My divine Will that thou shalt taste the bitterness of My chastisements. Ye, though I say unto ye. Though there are many who have [forsaken] Me those of the beloved few who remain true unto Me shall find shelter in My mighty shadow. For My right arm shall strike at the sinful who have not turned from their sins. Theirs are the afflictions upon My Heart. Theirs are the coals cast upon My anger" (May 30, 1988).

"Yea, I say unto ye: Though many shall perish, those who are worthy of My new world shall therefore flourish in it. And bring forth a new life which shall rekindle that which has been lost. The chastisements are just. Rejoice in My "Fire of Love." For it is in being that those who remain faithful unto Me shall have everlasting life" (June 13, 1988).

"For lo, the Lord God is angered by the nations; and the Lord God will have His day of chastisements. The Lord God will have His day of vengeance; for His mighty sword shall be with blood. Woe unto the inhabitants of the earth; for their afflictions shall surely come, and they shall know therefore, prophets were [among] them and they heeded not their warnings" (July 18, 1988).[9]

The times will not be comfortable for any on earth. The messages of Mary are given in graphic detail with little room for interpretation. Phrases like "the great trial has arrived for all humanity...the chastisement is about to take place...America will know poverty and defeat... Blessed candles which will be your only source of light...the living will envy the dead," all conjure up images which make us feel very insecure about the future. For these reasons there is no security other than the safety of being in union with God. The Blessed Mother speaks of "our safety in the frail cord of the rosary and the Eucharist, and being consecrated to her Immaculate Heart." Jesus, Our Blessed Mother, prophets, saints, and mystics are saying what is contained in Sacred Scripture.

As the prophet Daniel has said, "These words are to remain secret and sealed until the time of the end. Many will be cleansed, made white and purged, but the wicked ones will go on doing wrong. No one who is wicked will ever understand these things; the wise one will understand them." (Daniel 12:9-10)

Book V
The New Era—
The Triumph Of The
Two Hearts

21

The Second Pentecost
And The Era Of Peace

You are entering into the last decade of this century of yours, when the events of which I have foretold you will come to completion and when my secrets will be revealed to you. You are entering into the time of the triumph of my Immaculate Heart. You are now close to the Second Pentecost. The Second Pentecost will come like a river of grace and of mercy which will purify the Church and make her poor and chaste, humble and strong, without a spot or wrinkle, all beautiful, in imitation of your heavenly Mother. You are here to be molded by me in order to become the new heart of this Church, completely renewed by the Spirit.

Our Lady to Father Gobbi
June 28, 1990

Saint Louis de Montfort (1673-1716) wrote about our times, the spirit of the age, the events of the Second Coming, and the era of peace.

"In the Second Coming of the Lord, Mary will be made known in a special way by the Holy Spirit so that through her, Jesus may be better known and served.... Mary will shine forth higher than ever in these latter days to bring back poor sinners who have strayed from the Family of God.... However, souls hardened by impiety will provoke a terrible rebellion against God, attempting to lead all souls astray (even those who oppose their revolt) and they will cause many to fall by their threats, snares and alluring promises.... Satan, knowing that he has little time left, will redouble his efforts and his combats. He will conjure up cruel persecutions and put terrible snares in the path of the faithful.... Mary will raise up apostles of the latter times to make war against the evil one.... They shall be little and poor in the world's esteem and will even be persecuted by other members of the Body of Christ."[1]

On December 24, 1978, the Blessed Mother spoke to the Marian Movement of Priests. The words of Saint Louis de Montfort and the Queen of Heaven are similar: "...His Second Coming, beloved children, will be like the first. As was His birth on this night, so also will be the return of Jesus in glory, before His final coming for the last judgment, the hour of which, however, is still hidden in the secrets of the Father. The world will be completely covered in the darkness of the denial of God, of its obstinate rejection of Him and of rebellion against His law of love. The coldness of hatred will still cause the roadways of this world to be deserted. *Almost no one will be ready to receive Him.*

"The great ones will not even remember Him, the rich will close their doors on Him, while His own will be too busy with seeking and affirming themselves. 'When the Son of Man comes, will He still find faith on the earth?' He will come suddenly and the world will not be ready for His coming. He will come for a judgment for which man will find himself unprepared. He will come to establish His kingdom in the world, after having defeated and annihilated His enemies.

"Even in this Second Coming, the Son will come to you through His Mother."

Chosen By The Holy Trinity: A Mystery

The Blessed Mother's words to Father Gobbi on December 8, 1990, spoke of the very unusual role she had been given by the Most Holy Trinity: "I was chosen by the Most Holy Trinity to become the Mother of the Word, who became incarnate in my virginal womb, and thus I have given you my Son Jesus. His first coming among you took place in poverty, in humility and in suffering, because Jesus wanted to assume the limitations, the misery and the weakness of our human nature. And so my motherly action was carried out in silence, in prayer, in hiddenness and in humility.

"I was chosen by the Most Holy Trinity to become the Mother of the Second Advent, and thus my motherly task is that of preparing the Church and all humanity to receive Jesus, who is returning to you in glory."

Mary's words to Father Gobbi on August 15, 1991, as she spoke about a New Era were clear. She stated: "The new era, which awaits you, corresponds to a particular encounter of love, of light and of life between paradise. Where I am in perfect blessedness with the angels and the saints, and earth, where you, my children, live in the midst of many dangers and innumerable tribulations. This is the heavenly Jerusalem, which comes down from Heaven upon earth, to transform it completely and to thus shape the new Heavens and the new earth. The new era, toward which you are journeying, is bringing all creation to the perfect glorification of the Most Holy Trinity. The Father receives His greatest glory from every creature which reflects His light, His love, and His divine splendor. The Son restores His reign of grace and of holiness, setting free every creature from the slavery of evil and of sin. The Holy Spirit pours out in fullness His holy gifts, leads to the understanding of the whole truth, and renews the face of the earth.

"The new era, which I am preparing for you, coincides with the defeat of Satan and of his universal reign. All his power is destroyed. He is bound, with all the wicked spirits, and shut up in hell from which he will not be able to get out to do harm in the world. Herein, Christ reigns in the splendor of His glorified body, and the Immaculate Heart of your heavenly Mother triumphs in the light of her body, assumed into the glory of paradise."

Several mystics and modern-day visionaries speak about the times in which we live and the New Era which awaits us:

Julka, Zagreb, Yugoslavia

"But they will be so few, that all the survivors of one region will gather in one place."[2]

"A terrible black darkness arose in the northeast. It filled the whole sky. Above this thick darkness a wonderful new Moon appeared which was separated from the darkness. Our Lord Jesus spoke as follows: "The terrible black darkness represents deadly sins committed by people. The glorious new moon signifies the Little Flock, the people who will survive the great catastrophe. It will be a beautiful race which will shine with purity of soul and body."

"The Earth was transformed into a most beautiful garden full of flowers. It was soaked in bright sun-beams and veiled in gleaming purity. Everything seemed transparent, orderly and pure. No more mountains were to be seen, only plains and hills" (October, 21, 1974).

"...In this time, the people live far from Me, according to their own cleverness. My Wisdom and My Humility are derided on the Earth. Therefore I will transform the Earth and it will be new, according to My Law. The people whose lives I spare will revere My Holy Name. Their hearts will be shaken by My Voice, which they will hear after the Great Trial...."

It seemed to one priest that many prophecies, particularly that of the warning and the great miracle of Garabandal, should have been long-since fulfilled. Our Lord Jesus answered as follows: "As it has been foretold, so it will be. But one cannot postpone one incident without postponing all other events. If I have extended one happening there, I have also extended the others, and have shortened [the duration and intensity of punishment]." There are many victim souls on the earth. Through their prayers and sacrifices, and especially through the intercession of Mary, the Mother of God, many postponements have been granted. Through this the whole purification process has been significantly extended, but because of this, the great catastrophe will not be as severe as prophesied.

"After a certain amount of time, Our Lord Jesus commanded the great trial to cease. Thereupon the terrible darkness receded from the earth and, along with all the demons, disappeared into the horrible abyss. The Earth's surface was rent asunder and filled with craters. It was as if it had experienced a dreadful bombardment. Only here and there some small areas were preserved.

"Our Lord Jesus and His Heavenly Mother descended to their previous position. Our Lord said: 'I have removed the living earth from the dead earth. To the living earth I have given the Grace of My Wisdom that it may live in My Spirit.' God the Father and the Holy Spirit commanded that the sun should shine with renewed strength upon the Earth. The air became crystal clear and the earth appeared new-born.'

"I shall fashion and renew it, and it will be more beautiful than it is now. My laws will be different from what they are now, because My Divinity will be present in everything. I shall go amongst My creatures so that many will see Me and countless numbers will hear Me and they will recognize that I am the Living God from Heaven. I shall descend visibly amongst the Communities of the Little Flock which will be the Kingdom of My Most Holy Mother." (May 31, 1976).

An Angel came from Heaven inviting the seeress: "Come with Me!" And they flew above the earth for a long time in a southerly direction.

When they landed on the ground, the Angel left and the Lord Jesus appeared. He wore a white robe and a blue cloak. The Lord said: "Julka, I shall measure the Earth with My Yardstick and shall arrange it according to My Plan as I intended it." The seeress remarked: "My Lord Jesus Christ, but the Earth is a wilderness!" One could see neither a house nor a hut. The Lord replied: "We are in a region after the great chastisement.... The chastisement is over!" The seeress: "O Lord, I cannot see any people!" The Lord Jesus only smiled.

"Then Julka noticed an old man in the south. He came closer with heavy steps. When he suddenly saw living people, he was surprised and stopped. He recognized the Lord Jesus, came closer to Him and said: "I adore You, Lord Jesus Christ, My God! I thank you that You found it worthy to be here! I am alone and exhausted. I do not know where to go to find anyone, and You Yourself have come to make me happy!

"Lord Jesus came very close to him, caressed and comforted him: "You will find people who are still alive. However, before you meet, you must walk a distance of one hundred or even two hundred kilometers. Be reassured you will find them! I warn you through My chosen ones and prophets, yet I have but few zealous priests and monks, who call dead souls, with a strong voice, to awake from their deadly sleep before My Second Coming. Those who do not believe that I Am, will see Me on the Day of Judgment, when I come in Glory as God of Heaven and earth, and all creation. To the good I shall then be all joy, but to the wicked, fear and affliction. Loud crying will come from the earth and there will be no more time for anything. The way you are at that moment you will remain. Some will die, others will survive, in accordance with God's will. It will be terrible! **That is why I appeared with Tears of Blood as a sign of the arrival of the chastisement in the world.**

"Praised and honored be the Holiest and Indivisible Trinity, One God in Us for all Eternity and in the God-fearing souls which seek refuge in Him and live according to His Laws. In that hour you will be in My Protection.... However, the Lord adds, that the time is coming, when the face of the Earth will be renewed. After the great catastrophe, all regions of the world will be transformed" (October, 1975).

Sister Natalia

Sister Natalia is a Hungarian nun born in 1901 and is alive at the time of this writing. She was chosen by Jesus to suffer as a victim soul for the priesthood and to be a messenger to the world. Her most important task was to communicate to the world Jesus' desire that the whole world recognize His Mother as the "Victorious Queen of the World." Based partly on the messages that Sister Natalia received, Pope Pius XII consecrated the world to Mary in 1954, and designated May 31 as "Feast of Mary, Queen of the World." Like many of the saintly ones of God, she has led a life of suffering after living under the communist system in Hungary. She started receiving apparitions from Our Lady at a very early age. The following are messages from several apparitions concerning an era of peace.

"Jesus showed me in a vision that after the cleansing, mankind will live an angelic and clean life. There will be an end to sins against the sixth commandment, adultery, and an end to lies. The Savior showed me that unceasing love, happiness, and divine joy will signify this future clean world. I saw the blessing of God abundantly poured out upon the earth. Satan and sin were completely defeated and took leave."[3]

Sister Natalia is like most of the other apocalyptic mystics concerning this subject, that before this victory of peace, great confusion and terror would reign in the Church primarily due to the penetration of godlessness in the sanctuaries of the Church. She never knew a time frame, or how these events would happen. However, after these events she knew there would be a different Church.

The Renewed Church

Sister Natalia speaks about the renewed Church: "Jesus also told me that the Church, cleansed and renewed by great sufferings, will again be clothed in humility and simplicity, and will be poor as at her beginning. As we get closer to the end of the world, this simplicity and poverty will have wider and wider acceptance. After the chastisement, there will be no means of building great palaces and wearing ornate clothing. Everyone will know his duties, thus titles won't be needed.

"I saw that when the glorious peace arrives and love reigns, there will be only 'one fold and one shepherd.' Mary, the mother of all believers, will guide the life of souls, appearing under various forms. She will be the Queen of the Coming Age."

Jesus explains further: "**My Immaculate Mother will be victorious over sin with her power as Queen. The lily represents the cleansing of the world, the coming age of Paradise, when humanity will live as** if without sin. This will be a new world and a new age. This will be the age when mankind will get back what it lost in Paradise. When My Immaculate Mother will step on the neck of the serpent, the gates of hell will be closed. The hosts of angels will be part of this flight. I have sealed My own with My seal that they shall not be lost in this flight.[4]

Brother David Lopez, Texas

"She told me that the hours of darkness will be exactly seventy-two, and the only way to count them is with mechanical clocks, because there will not be any electricity. After this purification, there will be spring. Everything will be green, and everything will be clean. The water will be crystal clear, even the water from the faucets in houses. There will be no contamination in the water, nor the air, nor the river."[5]

Theresa Lopez, Denver, Colorado

"Even after all these chastisements come to pass, even then, there will be one hour of grace remaining. And in that hour of grace, even the worst of the worst that have undergone the chastisements will be given the last opportunity for conversion. The New Jerusalem will settle upon the earth. All of evil will no longer exist and we will be in perpetual paradise, just as God planned in the beginning."[6]

The message of the Blessed Virgin to Father Gobbi on December 31, 1986, has the themes of purification, a second Pentecost, chastisement, and the Triumph of the Immaculate Heart. Mary stated: "Pray in order to invoke the Holy Spirit, that He may be able to accomplish as quickly as possible the prodigy of a Second Pentecost of holiness and of Grace, which may truly change the face of the earth. Pray and do penance. Recite the holy rosary with love and with confidence. With this prayer, made by you together with me, you are able to influence all human events, and even the future events which are awaiting you. With this prayer, you can possess the grace of a change of hearts and you can obtain the much-desired gift of peace."

The Blessed Mother shed further light on these events in a message to Father Gobbi, January 1, 1991: "...The great suffering which awaits you is to prepare you for the birth of the new era, which is coming upon the world. Live this new year in my Immaculate Heart: it is the refuge which I have prepared for you for these times, burdened with sufferings for individuals and for nations. And so, you will not be afraid. Your suffering will increase with the increase of the trial which has already begun .... I am the announcement of the new era. In the deep darkness of this, your time, if you live with me, you can already glimpse the glimmer of the new times which are awaiting you."

As the years have passed, Mary has become less cryptic and more explicit in her explanations about this new era. Pain and suffering surely precede it, and the remnant of which Scripture speaks will inherit this new era so vividly promised.

Saint Louis de Montfort wrote of the Second Coming and Mary's role in that time: **"When my sweet Jesus comes a second time on earth in His glory, as it is most certain He will do, to reign there, He will choose no other way for His journey than Mary, by whom He came the first time, so surely and so perfectly. But there will be a difference between His first and last coming. The first time He came secretly and hiddenly; the second time He will have come perfectly, because both times He will have come by Mary. Alas! Here is a mystery which is not understood. Here let all tongues be mute."[7]**

The Era Of Peace

"If people do as I ask, there will be peace." These words of hope spoken by Our Lady of Fatima preceded a long litany of the misfortunes that she predicted would come upon the world if her requests were not taken seriously. It is imperative to realize that her assertion still holds true today: there definitely will be peace, if people do as she asks. If even now, during the "last warnings," we respond with repentance, letting our hearts be cleansed of sin by God's forgiving grace, there will indeed be peace: peace first in each person's heart, then throughout the whole world in society, initiating an era of peace, which Mary prophesied would inevitably arrive.

Had we listened to her at the beginning, or at any time over the years she was speaking with us, we could have averted "wars, famine, persecution of the Church and of the Holy Father." Many good people would have been spared martyrdom, hunger would not have ravaged nations, Russia would have already been converted and would not be able to "spread her errors throughout the world." World War II would never have happened.

The New Era

The permanent sign will guard the "era of peace." The period of peace that Our Lady promised at Fatima will come. The duration of that peace is indefinite; she assures us that we will be given a "certain period" of peace. The peace can be squandered by sin.

As children are born who have never known the previous age and its degradation, nor the warning, the miracle, or the punishment, they like all others before them will be tempted by sin. The permanent sign will instruct them, reinforcing the teaching of their parents that they must never sin as their forebears did. Otherwise, the peace they have inherited will be lost again, and then surely people will destroy one another and bring a final end to the world.

"These children and their children in turn will be able to go to Garabandal to gaze on the sign—a testimony against the sins of past generations, an explanation of why the old world had to end and why there is now peace and unity, and a warning for the future, that never again must men and women offend our Lord so much. The children of today's generation will return home chastened by the sight of the permanent sign and by its power, for somehow it will enlighten their minds and fire their hearts to know their own sinfulness, and call them to repentance too, purifying them as they come near its glory.

As events unfold in the world and the pace of life picks up, those who are moving in the Spirit will be given the light to understand the Gospel and its messages to know how to prepare. The secrets will be unraveled for us, and the Lord will reveal what is necessary to prepare us for the days ahead.

The Marian Movement of Priests confirmed this in a message dated May 19, 1991: "...**The task of the Spirit is to prepare humanity for its complete change, to renew the face of creation, to form the new heavens and the new earth. For this reason, I ask you to persevere with fidelity in the cenacles which I have requested of you.**"

Lubbock, Texas

"I did not come here to prepare you for the Feast of my Assumption but to prepare you for the coming of my Son...for the final judgement. My dear little children, listen to me, your Mother" (July 11, 1988).

"I, the Lord God, shall make anew...a new moon...a new dawning and so forth. A new Sabbath. The old shall pass away as [will] their offenses against Me. Again the peoples will call Me their God and I shall have them as My people. It is in this that praise and glory shall be given unto Me again...and worship, once more." (August 1, 1988)

Marian Movement Of Priests

There is consolation and hope for the future in the locution to Father Gobbi and the message of November 1, 1989, about the New Jerusalem. The environment and all things are changed back in the image of God as He intended it for Adam and Eve. Sin is taken away and purged from the earth. Here is our hope for the future when all things become new: "**...And you are forming the dwelling place of God among men, that all may become His people, where every tear will be wiped from their eyes and there will no longer be any death, or strife, or mourning, or anguish, because the former things have passed away.**"

Second Pentecost

On November 22, 1992, Our Blessed Mother told Father Gobbi on the Feast of Christ the King: "Jesus Christ is King, because it pertains to His divine mission to bring the created universe back to the perfect glorification of the Father, purifying it with the burning fire of the Holy Spirit, in such a way that it may become completely freed of every spirit of evil, of every shadow of sin, and thus be able to open itself to the enchantment of a new earthly paradise....In this creation, renewed by a perfect communion of life with the Father, Jesus Christ will restore His reign of glory, so that the work of His divine redemption may attain its perfect fulfillment."

On December 8, 1992, the Blessed Mother through Father Gobbi stated: "**The Holy City shall in the end gather together that humanity which has been redeemed and saved, once it will have been set completely free from the slavery of Satan, sin and evil, by means of the purification, the great tribulation, and the terrible chastisement. The sinful city will now have vanished, and thus all creation will open itself with joy to receive the Holy City, the new Jerusalem, come down out of Heaven....**

"**I saw a new Heaven and a new earth, because the former Heaven and earth passed away, and the sea was no more. I saw the Holy City, the new Jerusalem...prepared as a bride adorned to meet her husband...allow yourselves to be drawn by the enchantment of your heavenly Mother and follow me, in the wake of my sweet fragrance, in order to go down with me to meet the Holy City, which will come down out of Heaven, at the end of the painful purification and of the great tribulation in which you are living in these last times.**"

A Time To Assess

On June 14, 1979, in Garabandal, Spain, on the Feast of Corpus Christi, Mary through Father Gobbi stated: "His glorious reign will shine forth above all in the triumph of His Eucharistic Person, because the Eucharist will once again be the heart and center of the whole life of the Church."

And so the Mystical Body of Christ continues to forge new paths. Our habits and theology should be assessed carefully if we are to move with the flow of the Spirit in our age. As Mary carried out her motherly action in silence, in prayer, in hiddenness, and in humility, so must we. She points the way to Jesus. There appears to be no room for negotiation with Heaven. We are in uncharted waters. As the Blessed Mother said to the servants at the wedding feast at Cana, "Do whatever He tells you."

22

Apostles Of The
Last Times

"This is what the Lord asks of you: only this,
to act justly,
to love tenderly,
and to walk humbly with your God."

Micah 6:8

If what is written from the Gospels, the Magisterium of the Church, and past and present prophets is true, then our lives will change dramatically in the next several years. Heaven has spoken loudly, and the apparition sites have allowed us unique opportunities for further enhancing our spiritual formation. We are all being called to tasks according to our states in life, and Heaven has given us some guidelines to follow. In the passage below, Jesus gives His disciples some instructions:

"After this the Lord appointed seventy-two others and sent them out ahead of Him, in pairs, to all the towns and places He Himself was to visit. He said to them, 'The harvest is rich but the laborers are few, so ask the Lord of the harvest to send laborers to His harvest..Start off now, but remember, I am sending you out like lambs among wolves. Carry no purse, no haversack, no sandals. Salute no one on the road. Whatever house you go into, let your first words be "Peace to this house!" And if a man of peace lives there your peace will go and rest on him; if not it will come back to you. Stay in the same house, taking what food and drink they have to offer, for the laborer deserves his wages; do not move from house to house. Whenever you go into a town where they make you welcome, eat what is set before you. Cure those in it who are sick, and say, "The kingdom of God is very near to you." But whenever you enter a town and they do not make you welcome, go out into its streets and say, "We wipe off the very dust of your town that clings to our feet, and leave it with you. Yet be sure of this: the kingdom of God is very near." I tell you, on that day it will not go as hard with Sodom as with that town" (Luke 10:1-12).

On June 8, 1991, through Father Gobbi, Mary encouraged us to be resolute in our role as "Apostles of the Last Times." There is no difference in the message of the Gospels or Mary's locutions to the Marian Movement of Priests as it relates to our faith. Mary said: "As apostles of the last times, you must announce with courage the truths of the Catholic faith; proclaim the Gospel with force; and resolutely unmask the dangerous heresies which disguise themselves with truth in order to better deceive minds and thus lead astray from the true faith a great number of my children.

"As apostles of the last times, you must withstand with the strength of little ones the proud force of the great and the learned, who, seduced by a false science and by vainglory, have torn to pieces the Gospel of Jesus, by propounding an interpretation of it which is rationalistic, humanistic, and entirely erroneous."

The role of an apostle is to preach the Gospel with whatever means and talents he or she has been given. Some are prophets, teachers, pastors, and evangelists. The days of a casual observance of our faith are like the days of unlocked doors—things of the past. In these times we need to know our faith or we will be buffeted like a small boat on a stormy night. The wheat and chaff is being winnowed and the seal of Heaven is being placed on the forehead of those who are with God (Revelation 7:3-4). The messages of the Gospel and the mystics are the same. The fires of justice are now upon us and the severity and urgency of the pleas of Heaven are on a scale never known before.

The Call Of The Prophets

The calling of a prophet proclaiming the news of God is an unusual one. It knows no race, gender, or class distinction. The Scriptures tell us Isaiah was an aristocrat, Moses was reared and favored in Pharaoh's court, and David was the youngest in a large family, a shepherd boy who had no apparent leadership qualities. God looked to the heart. Elijah feared no man and thus was called to battle. He never considered the odds against him as God plus one is always a majority. Saint Francis of Assisi was born into the family of a wealthy merchant and was schooled in the arts and languages. Don Bosco was a playful youth born into abject poverty and unable to attend school because of a lack of funds, yet he rose to form a religious order (the Salesians) with world-wide prominence, even though the political climate of his day was alien to capturing young hearts for Christ. Catherine of Siena was the youngest of twenty-two children, illiterate at a late age, and today a Seraphic Doctor of the Catholic Church whose writings have inspired generations. Popes and kings sought her advice and counsel. Many of these people had nothing in common other than Heaven had ordained them to preach the Gospel without reservation or compromise. Friends were made and lost in the process, but these prophets and saints were not respecters of the wisdom of men. In almost every instance they operated on little knowledge and went on faith. Only with hindsight do we see that they were right. They were often unsure themselves while in the midst of the call, but they obeyed. It is no different for us today.

Saint Louis de Montfort spoke of the days in which we are now living: **"I have said that this would come to pass, particularly at the end of the world and indeed presently, because the Most High and His most holy Mother has to form for Himself great saints who shall surpass most of the other saints in sanctity as much as the cedars of Lebanon outgrow the little shrubs. These great souls, full of grace and zeal, shall be chosen to match themselves against the enemies of God, who shall rage on all sides; and they shall be singularly devout to our Blessed Lady, illuminated by her light, strengthened by her nourishment, led by her spirit, supported by her arm and sheltered under her protection, so that they shall fight with one hand and build with the other. With the one hand they shall fight, overthrow and crush the heretics with their heresies, the schismatics with their schisms, the idolaters with their idolatries and the sinners with their impieties...by their words and examples they shall draw the whole world to true devotion to Mary. This shall bring upon them many enemies, but** shall also bring many victories and much glory for God alone."[1]

The Call Of Isaiah

One of the greatest biblical prophets was Isaiah, a man who was well schooled and highly educated. He was aware of his sin ("What a wretched state I am in! I am lost, for I am a man of unclean lips"). His humility was probably a reason for his being so exalted. As the Seraph brought the coal to touch his lips, his iniquity was purged. Isaiah then agreed to be an intercessor. Isaiah wrote:

"Then I heard the voice of the Lord saying:
'Whom shall I send? Who will be our messenger?'
I answered, 'Here I am, send me'. He said:
'Go, and say to this people,
"Hear and hear again, but do not understand;
see and see again, but do not perceive."
Make the heart of this people gross,
its ears dull;
shut its eyes,
so that it will not see with its eyes,
hear with its ears,
understand with its heart,
and be converted and healed.'
Then I said, 'Until when, Lord?' He answered:
'Until towns have been laid waste and deserted,
houses left untenanted,
countryside made desolate,
and Yahweh drives the people out.
There will be a great emptiness in the country
and, though a tenth of the people remain,
it will be stripped like a terebinth
of which, once felled, only the stock remains.
The stock is a holy seed' (Isaiah 6:1-13)."

Similar circumstances surrounded Jeremiah. He feels unworthy, is appointed a prophet for the nations, and he is told as was Moses that the words will be put in his mouth, and kingdoms will rise and fall. He then becomes God's man for his age. Jeremiah speaks:

"The word of Yahweh was addressed to me, saying,

Before I formed you in the womb I knew you;
Before you came to birth I consecrated you;
I have appointed you as a prophet to the nations.
I said, "Ah, Lord Yahweh; Look, I do not know how to speak:
I am a child!"
But Yahweh replied, "Do not say, 'I am a child,'
Go now to those to whom I send you
and say whatever I command you.
Do not be afraid of them,
for I am with you to protect you—
It is Yahweh who speaks!"
Then Yahweh put out His hand and touched my mouth
 and said to me:
"There! I am putting my words into your mouth.
Look, today I am setting you over nations and over kingdoms,
to tear up and to knock down,
to destroy and to overthrow,
to build and plant" (Jeremiah 1:4-10).

If John the Baptist, Francis of Assisi, or one of the Biblical prophets were to walk into our church on a Sunday morning, what would we think? Quite probably we would find their personal conduct and their strident views a bit strange and forthright. Probably over one-half to three-quarters of the congregation would get up and walk out as the views would be considered too extreme. Those whom God calls are given the grace to proclaim His word. John the Baptist minced no words, and when he said to the authority of the day, "Herod, you are sleeping with your brother's wife," it cost him his head. The life in Christ is contrary to the ways of the world and will always require a commitment against the *status quo*. The establishment will never endorse change, as it has too much to lose. A prophet will always be outside of mainstream thinking. This is the call.

The lives of the people who have found God and proclaimed His messages have been similar throughout the ages—each of them had the courage to speak the truth. That is the virtue Heaven is asking of its apostles in the end times. To speak the truth without a blush and fear of man is, and will always be, the call of a prophet.

Maria Pavlovic, one of the young visionaries of Medjugorje, points us in the right direction. She reminded us that the Blessed

Mother said "nothing is new" in all that we are hearing: "We discovered a new life with the Blessed Mother. For example, in the beginning she permitted us to fall in love with her. And then through her messages she permitted us to go deeper and deeper into living what is written in Holy Scriptures. The Blessed Mother said, '**All those messages I'm giving you now are nothing new.**' For that reason, she has invited us to put the Holy Bible in a visible place in our home. She has invited us to walk the right path. When we were fully in love with the Blessed Mother, she put like a veil over herself and she said, '**I am not important. The important one is Jesus.**'"

Mystical Body Of Christ

The Church, beginning with Saint Paul, refers to itself as the Mystical Body of Christ. It is important to understand that this is more than an honorary title. The phrase, when understood correctly, places an almost unbearable importance on us weak and fallible human beings.

The doctrine of the Mystical Body of Christ means simply this: that from after His Ascension and until His return in glory to usher in the new heavens and new earth, **the Church is the only Body Jesus has to perform His work in the world.** In His profound humility and inexhaustible love for humanity, the Lord has willed to continue His salvific ministry primarily through the men and women who acknowledge His Lordship and constitute His Church.

The doctrine of the Mystical Body shows the extraordinary humility of Our Lord, who did not deem equality with God something to be grasped at. In associating humans with His continuing work of salvation, Jesus in a sense continues the abandoning of His omnipotence, begun with His Incarnation. Because we are Christ's Mystical Body, we really can disrupt the Lord's plans; frustrating them with our lukewarmness and slowing them with our sluggishness.

The converse of this is also true, however; we participate in the redemption of the world when we unite to the Lord's sacrifice our loves and our labors, our sufferings and our prayers. In his letter to the Colossians, Saint Paul writes that he actually rejoices in the sufferings he is undergoing for the infant Church, since "I help to pay off the debt which the afflictions of Christ leave still to be paid" (Colossians 1:24). Of course, Saint Paul is not telling us that the sacrifice of Christ is incomplete—all that God meant it to accomplish, it did. But part of what Christ's sacrifice accomplished was the empowering of men and women to work with Jesus in His redemptive mission. Saint Paul's sufferings—and ours—have a share in redeeming the world.

Our role as God's instruments in the world is stressed repeatedly by Our Lord and Our Lady in their messages. In her January 25, 1987, message at Medjugorje, Our Lady stressed that the witnessing of her messages is a mission by which we can save the world. "**God has chosen each one of you in order to use you in a great plan for the salvation of mankind,**" Mary said. Her words underscore those of Saint Paul to the Corinthians: "It was God Who reconciled Himself to us through Christ and gave us the work of handing on this reconciliation. In other words, God in Christ was reconciling the world to Himself, not holding men's faults against them, and He has entrusted to us the news that they are reconciled. **So we are ambassadors for Christ**; it is as though God were appealing through us, and the appeal that we make in Christ's name is: be reconciled with God" (2 Corinthians 5: 18-21).

In her January 2, 1989, message, Our Lady again said we are to collaborate with her to fulfill God's plan: "**My dear children, for this year I want to tell you: pray! Your mother loves you. I want to collaborate with you, for I need your collaboration. I want you to become, dear children, my announcers and my Son's, who will bring peace, love, conversion...I want you to be a sign for others.**"

In the message of July 24, 1988, Our Lady said we must have peace in our own hearts before we can give it to others. She asked for our cooperation in helping to fulfill her divinely-ordained plan: "Dear children...live love. I want to give you peace so you can carry it to others. You cannot give peace to others if you do not have this peace within yourselves. **I need you, dear children, to cooperate with me, because there are many plans that I cannot fulfill without you. I need your cooperation.** Pray, pray, pray!" Less than two weeks later, on August 4, 1988, Our Lady reiterated this point: "Dear children...I **want your cooperation. I want to work with you. Your cooperation is necessary to me. I cannot do anything without you.**"

Perhaps Our Lady's most powerful words on this subject were reserved for the Medjugorje locutionist Jelena on July 30, 1987: "Dear children, to be chosen by God is really something great, but it is also a responsibility for you to pray more, for you, the chosen ones, to encourage others, so you can be a light for people in darkness.... Dear children, this is the reason for my presence among you for such a long time: to lead you on the path of Jesus. **I want to save you and, through you, to save the whole world.**"

As we have already seen, Our Lord's July 22, 1993, message to Australian visionary Josefina-Maria is very much in line with Our Lady's messages at Medjugorje: "Remain in peace and be constant in love, leading my people in peace; but always reminding them of My love. Make sacrifices, my children, and be my co-redeemers in helping in my Father's plan."

Christina Gallagher

Similar messages from several apparition sites give us counsel on what our role should be in these latter days:

Christina Gallagher had this to say about the Blessed Mother's message: "Also striking is her constant emphasis on the value of suffering, and how those who suffer can do great good, and help save many other souls "in darkness" by accepting whatever cross God permits. When people recognize the true value of the Cross, they really recognize the love of God which alone heals souls and hearts."

Be Prepared

"People should not be waiting for a purification or a chastisement or anything else. They should be prepared every day of their lives, because none of us, young or old, knows when we are going to be taken, when God wants us. He can pluck us like a flower any day, and our purification could be today or tomorrow. Anyone of us can be taken at any time, and we should always be prepared, and not be too concerned about when this or that is going to happen," she emphasized.

"People are being warned of what lies ahead in order to help them to turn back to God, and to ask for His mercy. Those who are praying and living the messages, and following the Word of God have nothing to be afraid of, whatever may lie ahead, and whether their lives are taken out or they are left."

Consecrated Souls

Mrs. Gallagher lays great stress on the sacredness of the priesthood. She says that people should not criticize priests, or find fault with them, but should instead offer more and more prayers for them. She explains: "We need constantly to pray for consecrated souls, priests, and religious, bishops, cardinals, asking God to give them the graces they need."

Our Lady had told her how these consecrated souls are being attacked much more than lay people: "They are the ones who are over His flock, and they have such an influence on believers, and we must always pray that they will be surrounded by the Light of God and protected, because they are so important to us. If we think a priest has failed, or fallen, what we have to realize is that we have failed that priest, because if we had prayed more for him, he would have been helped to be stronger, and to resist the attacks upon him."

The Value of the rosary

"Through all the messages, the Virgin Mary stressed the power of the rosary, and constantly asks that the rosary be prayed. She also asks that it be prayed from the heart, and in one of the first messages, Our Lady advised people who found it difficult to "accept my message and those of my Son; pray the rosary from your heart, all three mysteries, for nine days. Offer up these prayers to my Son's Heart and to the Holy Spirit for enlightenment. If you can do that, you will understand. Our Lady has said to me to tell people to arm themselves with her rosary, and never to let it be out of their hearts." It will protect them during the times of trial and suffering.

Listen To All That She Tells You

Jesus has some amazing things to say to Mariamante, the visionary whose messages have inspired His Apostolate of Holy Motherhood.

Christ Child: **"My Mother wishes to continue speaking to you. Listen carefully to everything she tells you. She will employ many of her faithful followers in accomplishing this wonderful task. You must be prepared to give completely of yourselves now especially, as the time is so crucial. Hold back nothing for yourselves in service to her and the cause for which she inspires you, that is the Triumph of her Immaculate Heart. This will facilitate the reign of My Sacred Heart. As Mary was a fore-shadow of My glory when I came to earth, so she will again be the precursor to My age of love and peace which she foretold at Fatima.**

Lubbock, Texas

Other modern-day mystics provide substantive material concerning what our daily activities should be for the days ahead.

"My dear children, I wish you knew the power of prayers...the power of fasting. For when you pray and fast, my Son and our Father in Heaven hears your prayers. Be persistent, my children, in your prayers. You must pray constantly. Make every action—all your works, all you do—a prayer. For when you pray with your heart, the angels and saints in Heaven join in with your prayers. Again, my children, I must remind you of the importance of frequent reception of the sacraments. You need the many graces given when you receive the sacraments of Confession and Holy Communion. The whole world needs the graces that are given when you receive the sacraments" (June 20, 1988).

"My dear children, Satan is prowling this earth, seeking the destruction of marriages and the family. My dear children, you must pray as families. You must teach your children, you must teach your families. You must teach your children to pray with you at a very early age. But, if your children are older, its never too late to start. Pray as a family. For I remind you again, my dear children, your prayers will blind the eyes of Satan" (September 26, 1988).

"My children, do not be so involved in your world that you cannot take time to pray, to love. Remember, my children, the Kingdom of God should be your first concern. Meditate on the Scripture of Matthew, where [Jesus] urges you to seek after God's Kingdom first" (October 24, 1988).

"My little ones, my graces are poured out to you constantly as I pray for you, but special times of graces and blessings are in the Sacrifice of the Mass, at the time of the Benediction and at the times of prayer time for families I have specified for your parish. I also will not forget the times of intercessory group prayer to shed my love on you. The heavenly angels will always be in your midst, praising and glorifying the King." (December 25, 1988).

Gladys Of Argentina

"My daughter, my messages must be read slowly for them to be digested as I wish. I want each child to start living in God's grace, loving Him as He should be loved. **The weakness of human beings** becomes greater, the further they are from God; that is why in present times the enemy would seem to be winning. If my children were to understand everything the mother says, everything would change. May they surrender body and soul to the Lord, in the certainty that the Lord will save them" (January 24, 1986).

"My daughter, because of a few good people, many bad people will be saved. I mean that with prayer, with the continual prayer of true Christians, many will reach salvation. Here, I explain the reason for my presence and the meaning of my messages, that are in final instance, the Lord's word. There must be conversion for the salvation of the soul to be possible" (December 15, 1986).

"The one who hopes in God will be greatly rewarded. You are in all my thoughts, that is why I say to you: Fill yourselves with virtues, withdraw from defects. The Lord asks this of you, do not doubt, follow Him" (February 14, 1985).

"All creation is the work of God. To Him belongs divine justice and His greatness surpasses all human understanding. Let man fly from pride. There is nothing more beautiful than heartfelt humility, as this is the humility that the Lord asks for insistently. What is material passes, what is spiritual remains, What is earthly wilts and dies; what is heavenly lasts" (May 15, 1987).

Julia Kim Of Naju, Korea

"Pray constantly for the Pope and for the bishops and priests of the Church. Priests just now are like lanterns trying to continue giving light in spite of strong winds hitting them on every side. Priests nowadays need more and more victim souls who will pray, fast and offer up sacrifices to God for their sanctification, and for the success of their ministry" (August 11, 1985).

Evangelization

The role of an apostle has and will always be to preach the Gospel. For twenty years, in detailed messages to the Marian Movement of Priests, the Blessed Mother has been warning, exhorting, teaching, encouraging, and in general watching out for her children. The messages of 1992 are striking in their specific call for evangelization. In the United States alone, there are over 200 Marian Centers, Peace Centers, Medjugorje Centers (or others with a similar mandate) as listed in the National Catholic Register—Mary's People. The secular media have steadily refused to report what is happening throughout the world, so the Blessed Mother has created a new cottage industry of those who will tell the story. The two messages below, dated on separate occasions, of the Marian Movement of Priests reveal where the heart of Mary now lies concerning apostolic work.

"I Am the Mother Of The Second Evangelization"

"I am guiding you as a star along the bright way of fidelity in the Gospel of Jesus. You must announce it to all in the strength of its integrity. Preach it with the same clarity with which my Son Jesus announced it to you. My motherly task is that of forming you into apostles of the second evangelization" (February 27, 1992).

"The moment of your public witness has come. Show yourselves to all as my little sons, as the apostles formed by me for the great task of the new evangelization which is awaiting you...go and evangelize" (March 27, 1992).

Angels And Their Role In Protecting Man

One of the great impoverishments of the Catholic faith today is the sharp decline in belief in and reliance on angels. Most Catholics regard devotion to the angels as a relic from a more superstitious past or as a practice that was done away with by the reforms of the Second Vatican Council.

Nothing could be further from the truth. In recent years the Popes have spoken out strongly and at length on the need for Catholics to seek and acknowledge the protection of the guardian angels. They have presented to the faithful the powerful teachings on angels found in the Bible and solemn Church teaching, extending from the earliest days of the faith to today. Leading their flocks by example, the modern Popes have all been known for cultivating a warm relationship with their guardian angels.

The stress on the angels by Popes and theologians has a parallel in the messages of today's seers and mystics. For virtually all of them, now is a special "hour of the angels," in which we on earth must particularly rely on the strength and protection of our heavenly guardians during the troubled days that loom ahead.

As the future Pope Paul I said when he was Bishop of Venato: "The angels are the great strangers in this time. It is necessary to speak much more about them as ministers of providence in the government of the world and of men...[and to] develop an intimate relationship with them."[2]

Church Teaching And Scripture

The Bible is teeming with references to angels and to their special activities on earth. Angels are present throughout the Old and New Testament, helping humans in a variety of ways. The angels proclaim God's will (Luke 1:5-19 and 26-38); lead and assist God's people (Exodus 14:19 and Acts 12:5-11); counsel and teach right conduct (Tobias 36:10-21 and 12:7-12); heal and deliver people from sickness and evil spirits (Tobias 3:24, 6:7-9, 8:1-3, and 12:14-15); and enact God's justice (Genesis 19:12-13, Acts 12:18-22, as well as throughout the Book of Revelation).

The Catholic Church has also given strong teaching on the subject. In 1215 the Fourth Lateran Council declared that God, at the same time He created the corporal, visible world, also created a vast universe of the spirit—the angels and their heavenly realm. The teaching was reaffirmed by the First Vatican Council in 1869.[3] The Second Vatican Council spoke on angels again, reminding the faithful strongly in the *Dogmatic Constitution of the Church* that the Church has always venerated the angels—along with the Blessed Virgin and the saints—with a holy and special love.[4]

The Church has taught so strongly and consistently on angels that in 1968 Pope Paul VI issued a solemn statement declaring belief in angels to be an essential part of the Catholic faith.[5] Father Karl Rahner, one of the greatest theologians of modern times, wrote in the *Encyclopedia of Theology* that the " existence of the angels cannot be disputed by a sincere Christian."[6] All of the modern Popes—from Pope Pius XI to John Paul II— have been known for developing a relationship to their guardian angels and urging the faithful to do the same with their own.

John Paul II is perhaps most outstanding in his catechesis on the angels.[7] In 1986 the Holy Father gave six teachings on the subject— a powerful sign of the importance he places upon angels in this decisive epoch of Church history. John Paul II spoke of our time being one of "conflict between the dark powers of evil and the powers of redemption."[8]

Seer and Mystics

Padre Pio

This modern emphasis by Church leaders on the angels is echoed by today's seers and mystics. With virtually one voice, they insist that angels are present to help, guide, protect, and comfort us—and that their aid is especially needed in the present hour.

Padre Pio, the famous Italian priest and stigmatist, was a strong advocate for devotion to the angels. He was able to see and talk with his own heavenly guardian. Padre Pio frequently prayed for people to realize the great love God has shown them because of His bequeathing all of us our own guardian angels. Pio thought this was a truth with special relevance for our time, saying repeatedly that "I am convinced this is the hour of the angels."[9]

Mariamante

Mariamante, the seer whose messages have inspired the *Apostolate of Holy Motherhood*, has received several messages on the importance of the angels. She received this message from the Blessed Mother: "I wish to employ the power of the legions of the Holy Angels to help and instruct you in all these way which are God's, for I am the Queen of the Angels. They will be highly instrumental in procuring my Triumph. They continue to do battle for your souls daily. When they speak to you, often through your conscience, listen to them. They will help you to obey the laws of God, and grow in holiness. Pray to the Holy Angels often for guidance and wisdom to do God's will in your daily duties, and they will help you to follow His will."

Mariamante received a similar message from the Christ Child: "My most Holy Mother is a cause for joy to all the Heavenly Angels and Blessed Spirits. They wait upon her word to do her will, which is at all times the will of God. They are her legions of Blessed Spirits called upon to wage this battle for your souls. Be attentive to the working of the Holy Angels in your lives. They will help you to accomplish what God has planned for you in your life."

Eileen George

Eileen George is a reported mystic who, besides having gifts of healing and teaching, is said to be able to see her guardian angel. In the book *Eileen George: Beacon of God's Love*, she tells of twice receiving communion from angels. She also writes that two of her children were saved from being struck by a speeding car by the miraculous intervention of their guardian angels. Eileen stresses that the care and solicitude she receives from her guardian angel is not unique to her alone: All people are gifted by God with such heavenly protectors. Eileen urges everyone to communicate with, depend upon, and love his guardian angel.[10]

Marian Movement of Priests

Angels are a constant theme in Our Lady's messages to Father Gobbi. Throughout the messages, Mary tells us that the angels are constantly with us, fighting on our behalf in a great spiritual battle now moving to its peak. The message of September 29, 1981, gives a good sense of the power and urgency of Mary's teaching: "In the struggle to which I am calling you, beloved sons, you are being especially helped and defended by the angels of light. *I am the Queen of the Angels*. At my orders, they are bringing together, from every part of the world, those who I am calling into my great victorious cohort. In the struggle between the Woman clothed with the sun and the Red Dragon, the angels have a most important part to play. For this reason, you must let yourself be guided docilely by them.

"The angels, the archangels, and all the heavenly cohorts are united with you in the terrible battle against the Dragon and his followers. They are defending you against the terrible snares of Satan and the many demons who have now been unleashed with furious and destructive frenzy upon every part of the world.

"This is why I call upon you to entrust yourselves more and more to the angels of the Lord. Have an affectionate intimacy with them, because they are closer to you than your friends and dear ones. Walk in the light of their invisible, but certain and precious presence. They pray for you, walk at your side, sustain you in your weariness, console you in your sorrow, keep guard over your repose, take you by the hand and lead you gently along the road I have pointed out for you.

"Pray to your guardian angels and live out with trust and serenity the painful hours of the purification. Indeed, in these moments Heaven and earth are united in an extraordinary communion of prayer, of love and of action, at the orders of your heavenly Leader."

On October 2, 1992, the Blessed Mother spoke to Father Gobbi on the Feast of the Holy Guardian Angels about the active role of the angels as messengers in the end days. Mary said, "This final period of the purification and the great tribulation corresponds with a particular and powerful manifestation of the angels of the Lord.

"You have entered into the most painful and difficult phase of the battle between the Spirits of Good and the Spirits of Evil, between the angels and the demons. It is a terrible struggle which is taking place around you and above you. And so these are the times when the action of your guardian angels must become still stronger and continuous. Pray to them often, listen to them with docility, follow them at every moment. *To the first angel* there befalls the task of making this announcement to all: "Give to God glory and obedience; praise Him because the moment has come when He will judge the world.... All the power of Satan will be destroyed. *To the second angel* there befalls the task of making this announcement: 'Fallen, fallen is Babylon the great, she who made all the nations drink of the intoxicating wine of her prostitution.' *To the third angel* there befalls the task of announcing the great chastisement: 'Anyone who worships the beast and its image, and accepts the mark on forehead or hand, will drink the wine of God's wrath....'"

Mary then stated on October 7, 1992, to Father Gobbi that, "An '*angel*' is a spirit who is sent by God to carry out a particular mission. *I am the Queen of the Angels*, because it is of the very nature of my role to be sent by the Lord to accomplish the very great and important mission of conquering Satan."

The message is somber in its depiction of these times as one of great crisis. We are in a fierce battle; the forces of Hell are in the midst of a great assault. But the essence of the messages are quite hopeful. For in the midst of this battle we are surrounded by a vast army, with the brightness and splendor of the heavenly Host. Under the banner of Jesus and with the leadership of Mary—and with the aid of our fellow prayer-warriors, the angels—we are assured of their help and our ultimate victory.

Act Of Consecration To The Sacred Heart Of Jesus

O Sacred Heart of Jesus, filled with infinite love, broken by my ingratitude, pierced by my sins, yet loving me still—accept the consecration that I make to You of all that I am and all that I have. Take every faculty of my soul and body. Draw me, day by day, nearer and nearer to your Sacred Heart, and there, as I can bear the lesson, teach me Your blessed ways. Amen.

23

The Remedy

I am calling you to pray with your whole heart and day by day to change your life....I am calling that by your prayers and sacrifices you begin to live in holiness....daily change your life to become holy.

Our Lady of Medjugorje
November 13, 1986

The Spirit Of The World

In this concluding chapter, we have gleaned from the Marian messages the central points of her requests. We humbly offer them to our readers as the only remedy for bringing the world back to Christ and to offer expiation for all of our sins, for His mercy is boundless. We have attempted to weave a positive thread throughout, in that those who pray and live the messages and follow the Word of God have nothing to fear, whatever may lie ahead, and whether their lives are taken or they are left behind when His Thunder of Justice comes crashing around us.

We have often sought the answers in the wrong places and not found them. The solutions to our ills have not been found in beguiling philosophies, existentialism, the nihilism of the East, politics, secular humanism, or the strength of our own wisdom. Jesus Christ specifically came into the world to die for the expiation of sin. He is the only person to say, "I am the Way, the Truth, and the Light, and there is no way to the Father but by Me." He is God, "When the Word became flesh and dwelt among us."

In the pursuit of answers, we often ask what is missing? What have we lost? We have blindly pursued remedies, foolishly usurping the role of God. We have been unsuccessful, and the depth of our failure has reached a point where we are a mass of contradictions on a personal and societal level. The Voltaires ("Ecrasez l'infame!— crush the infamous thing—that is, the Catholic Church") and the Nietzsches went to the grave with their own pride and remain there, after vilifying and giving the world nothing. No other man rose from the dead after prophesying it in advance.

The genius in God the Father is His simplicity. If the messages world-wide were to be summed up in two words, they would be "peace" and "love." The Ten Commandments were given to us in the space of seventeen verses in the twentieth chapter of Exodus. The simplest of minds are able to comprehend what is written. The *Federal Register* of the United States takes up several large rooms and at this point essentially contradicts itself with overlapping law. The United Nations acting as the world enforcement agency is unable to execute the simplest of agreements and have them last. It is mired in layer after layer of bureaucracy. We have left our first love, the God who made us—and we are no longer able to govern ourselves in a civil manner. *The Bonfire of the Vanities* is played out in every jurisdiction across the land. The main character, Sherman McCoy, is a neighbor or friend, and we know him all too well. The system is broken, and we know it.

The spirit of antichrist spoken of in Scripture and the Marian Movement of Priests is the spirit of the world, or those things not of God. These things we see each day. They may be avarice, hatred, negativity, corporate sin, and in general, those things which God is not. The Antichrist (with a capital A) will be a manifestation of a real person who, according to many, will appear on the scene before the year 2000. As the world sinks further into recession, likely soon to be a global depression, it is easier to see how this could happen.

As the pace of world events quickens, we will no longer be able to process in our minds the outcome. The complexity is beyond our intellectual ability so we must rely on what Heaven is teaching in so many places. The basics of Scripture have never been difficult to understand; we complicate them to appear intellectual and erudite. Apparition sites principally say the same thing, often with a different emphasis of the Gospel message. The Apostle Paul spoke a message of purity at Corinth, (a port city) and then spoke to the intellect at Mars Hill in Athens, as this is where the city rulers congregated. Each audience needs to hear something different for its edification. For this reason we cannot dismiss other apparition sites. We simply do not know. This is why we must wait for the judgment of the Magisterium of the Church.

Once we know this message, we must move on to the essence of the Gospel— obedience. We have heard the messages of Medjugorje, the major component of which is fasting and prayer. When was the last time we fasted on Wednesdays and Fridays as called for? When was the last time we spent an hour in front of the Blessed Sacrament in prayer? We desire year after year to be dazzled by the more sensational aspects of the Marian messages but continue to ignore the factors which are the cure for our personal, family, and national sins.

The Displacement Of Divinity

The last several decades in Western culture have been character-ized by the relentless pursuit of pleasure and comfort. With each new year we have acquired more "things," and the discontentment and lack of joy continue to invade our homes. Our conversations have been reduced to the trite and the mundane and there seems no escape. We are a civilization drowning in materialism, attempting to find the answers to our existence in all the wrong places. If financial security, faster and sleeker cars, larger homes, better restaurants, a lower golf handicap, and a more fit body are the keys to our worries, then why are we not happier?

The answer lies in the perception of our values. The most volatile issue during the time of Jesus was that of Roman occupation of Jewish territory. The Praetorian Guard and its legions enslaved the people of Israel, and the Jews expected a Messiah to ride in majestically and win battles as in the days of the patriarchs. This political and social issue was foremost in the minds of the Jews. Jesus did not ever address this issue until asked. When the outcry was, "What should we give to Caesar," Jesus responded, "Give to Caesar what is Caesar's, and give to God what is God's." The issues of the heart were far more important to Jesus than any political agenda. He was aware that until there is a conversion of the heart, no good can come from man. The roots of His law were in the Ten Commandments which need no commentary for understanding.

The Commandment forbidding false idols has so many shapes and forms in our daily lives. If anything is taking a dominant position over honoring God, then this is a false idol. This is a place where we see many of the root causes of our problems. It is the commandment of "Keeping the Sabbath Holy." In the Old Testament, not honoring this day was only one of several sins punishable by death. Although we are not living under the law of the Old Testament, there is widespread abuse all throughout the Christian culture concerning the Sabbath. In the West, we have lost God through our affluence, and in the East, God has been lost through communism and suffering. Both have lost sight of a Sabbath, and thus our problems have become so large we no longer even know where to start to find the solutions to our ills.

God's intention for the Sabbath was a day of rest honoring God through worship, conversation, teaching, and praise. Today if someone even bothers to go to church at all, Sunday will be an endless litany of recreation, television, athletic events, shopping, and errands all crammed together. Family time has become something of the preceding generations. The idols pile up before the altar displacing the supremacy of God in our lives. The abdication of spiritual responsibility has led us to a place where peace has eluded us. When the Scriptures were adhered to as a beacon and a guideline for living, the world was a better place. Doors were not locked, there was prayer in the classroom, and there was a sense of civil obedience. Nothing was ever perfect, but society was a safer place. The more the standard of God has been stripped from our lives, the more people have lost a sense of goodness. Our elected leaders merely reflect the will of the people. Sin has been given a sophisticated, psychiatric language.

Happiness And Contentment

This book of the law shall not depart out of your mouth; but you shall meditate on it day and night, that you may observe to do according to all that is written in it: for then you shall make your way prosperous, and then you shall have good success (Joshua 1:8).

If pleasure is pursued inordinately, it will finally cause death of soul or body. Recreation, sports, and hobbies are wonderful things that must be cultivated for a balanced outlook, but we must put them in proper perspective for a healthy mind and body. They will never provide happiness, but they may offer a sense of fulfillment and enjoyment. If we constantly pursue the "greater thrill," the inordinate pursuit of pleasure will destroy peace of soul. If we continue to seek a greater thrill than the one before it, we become like a spent bullet.

Anything in excess soon becomes its opposite. The more we indulge ourselves to fill the spiritual void which exists, the more the sales have rung up on the psychiatrist's couch. After Ernest Hemingway fulfilled his passions with marlin fishing in the Florida Keys and Cuba, running with the bulls in Pamplona, hunting the big game of Africa, trout-fishing in Idaho, the Spanish Riviera, and the nightly conviviality at the Cafe Vendome in Paris, walking with the jet set of Hollywood, he walked into a bathroom, pulled the trigger, and his wife picked up his brains from the floor. For all of his pleasure-seeking, he still was not happy.

As Our Lady told young Bernadette Soubirous at Lourdes, "I cannot guarantee you happiness in this life, but I can in the next." The best that we can hope to achieve will be some peace, joy, content-ment, and love in our life. There will always be a void because our souls will never be totally fulfilled until we reach Heaven. Here we can enjoy only the sparks of goodness, beauty, and love. But in the hereafter, we will be in the eternal presence of that flame from which those sparks come. Where our restless hearts will find peace and contentment is in the loving and Merciful Heart of Christ. Saint Augustine said, "Our hearts are restless until they rest in Thee."

The Heart Of The Movement:
The Apostolate Of Holy Motherhood

In February through August of 1987, in the first part of the Marian year declared by Pope John Paul II, visions were given to a mother with three children in the midwestern United States. The visions were those of Jesus and the Blessed Virgin Mary. To protect the mother's privacy and to avoid the inconveniences that accompany such a state of responsibility, the mother has sought and been granted anonymity and was assured this by the Blessed Virgin. The children, being seven, three, and one at the time of the visions, would have been at hazard by the exposure that usually comes with a vision. The woman has adopted the name "Mariamante" which in Latin means "Lover of Mary." She was instructed in a vision by the Christ Child on March 25th, 1987, "to name it [the movement] after My Mother, the Queen of Heaven" and call it, *"The Apostolate of Holy Motherhood in*

Catholic Families." According to the prophecy, this Apostolate will be approved by the Holy Father and will be known in the four corners of the earth and will do great good and help much in stemming the tide of evil ravaging so many families today.

The single best resource of inspiration to remedy the ills of our families and society as a whole is to adhere to the basics we have extracted from these messages. The two main targets of Satan today are the clergy and the family. One does not need to have a great deal of discernment to understand the repercussions of the breakdown of these institutions. The following material is meant to serve as a guideline to achieve peace and understanding in the days ahead.

The Major Points Of The Apostolate Of Holy Motherhood

1. "...They must devote all their time, energy, and resources, including their very selves, to the greater glory of God and the pursuit of the divine Will in their lives;

2. "They must be consecrated to My Most Holy Mother under the title of 'Mother of God';

3. "They must seek to fulfill their daily duties, that is, as mothers and wives, in an exemplary manner of holiness by pursuing the contemplative life in their homes...."[1]

The messages contain all the most necessary aspects of the interior life comprising a virtual catechism of the spiritual life. Particular emphasis on the virtue of purity is given, referred to by Our Lady as "evangelical purity." By extolling the virtues of the Blessed Mother and communicating by Grace these same virtues to the members of her Apostolate, the Christ Child also speaks. This movement is meant to play an important role in the Triumph of her Immaculate Heart foretold at Fatima and of God's renewing the face of the earth.

This is a spiritual movement rather than an organization, whose major fruit will be renewed appreciation of and esteem for children and the person of Christ in children, brought about particularly through devotion to the Christ Child. The Holy Family is to be the model for these families. The graces won by the members of this Apostolate will aid in the mitigation of the suffering of innocent children throughout the world, many of whom are now suffering from spiritual and physical neglect. Children are being impoverished spiritually in the developed world by the materialism and spiritual neglect of their parents. They are not receiving the faith from their parents. This is the most severe neglect, the one which robs the children of eternal life with God in Heaven. God in His goodness loves in an unfathomable way each one of these precious little ones and wishes for them to be loved by their parents as "precious jewels," which they truly are.

Some of the major points of this movement (along with similar messages from other sources) are listed below:

Adoration Of The Eucharist

The Blessed Mother: "The Eucharist must be adored. Adore the Eucharist. The Eucharistic Heart of Jesus is the greatest gift God has given to men. Sadly, it is not appreciated. This is a grave tragedy. My Son shed His blood for your sins. The least you can do is adore His Eucharistic Heart in the tabernacle. The churches are locked. This is another tragedy. People should be praying in front of the tabernacle day and night for the salvation of the world, and especially for purity in the West."

On August 21, 1987, through the Marian Movement of Priests, Mary exhorts us to go before the tabernacle to establish a relationship with Jesus. "Go before the tabernacle to establish with Jesus a simple and daily rapport of life. With the same naturalness with which you seek out a friend, or entrust yourself to persons who are dear to you, or feel the need of friends who assist you, in that same way go before the tabernacle to seek out Jesus. Make of Jesus your dearest friend, the most trusted person, the most desired and the most loved."

In addition, on February 26, 1991, Mary spoke to Father Gobbi of Jesus present in the Eucharist as our spiritual nourishment so we may hunger and thirst no longer: "I ask you to give with abundance this spiritual food, and above all, to you my beloved ones and sons consecrated to me, I ask a still greater effort in communicating to all the light of the Gospel. Preach the Gospel with courage and without fear; present it with the clarity of its completeness; announce it with the same vigor with which my Son Jesus preached it to you. Thus you will help all to walk along the way of the true faith, in the greatest obedience to the Magisterium of the Pope and of the bishops united with him.... The Eucharistic Jesus is the Living Bread come down from Heaven, the food to eat that one may hunger no longer, the water to drink that one may thirst no longer. The Eucharistic Jesus wants to become today the Good Samaritan for your Church, so divided and suffering, and for your fatherland, so ill and threatened." Mother Teresa has said, "If people spent one hour per week in Eucharistic Adoration, abortion would be ended."

Priests

The Blessed Mother: "The priests who neglect their flock are likewise in error. Recreation is not an important aspect of the Christian life and indeed is not in accord with the way of perfection of which I want all my children to trod. They must renounce the selfishness that causes them to waste great amounts of time when souls go unattended in need of the sacraments, particularly Confession. Many of my children are unable to confess their sins due to this. They cannot find a priest who is willing to spend his time in administering this most holy sacrament.

"How sad this is for me to see. The purpose of the priesthood is the administering of the sacraments. Why have they forgotten this? They need to rearrange their priorities and tend to their flock entrusted to them by my Son Himself. Follow His example while on earth. Did He spend needless hours in recreation? Of course not. Then why should you, if you profess to follow Him, and are called in perfection which is His will for you? The administering of the sacraments of the Holy Eucharist and Penance should be of the foremost importance in their lives. Nothing else should take precedence over this ever."

Frequent Confession

The Blessed Mother: "I wish all my children would make use of this sacrament and go to Confession frequently, not sporadically or seldom. Frequent, regular Confession, will make them grow in holiness in a way in which nothing else can. Pray for those who neglect or fear the confessional. They must overcome this in order to grow closer to my divine Son. May He be praised now and for eternity. I will protect you in all circumstances."

Seek Only To Love Me: The Blessed Sacrament

(Vision of the Christ Child): "**Again I state to you: the best preparation you can have is to be prepared through long hours in prayer, penance done out of love for Me and more time spent with**

Me in the Blessed Sacrament. This will not only prepare you for any occurrence in this world, but also in the next."

The Sacraments: The Answer To All Modern Day Woes

(Vision of the Christ Child): "They must seek Me in the sacraments of Holy Mother Church who is their supreme guide to holiness on earth. The Church I have founded is their answer. The answer to all modern day woes is in the sacraments of My Church. It is an everlasting gift of My love to you, the path is so clear and yet so often unchosen. It need not be unchosen for you, if you turn to Me in the holy Sacrament of Penance. I will give you the strength to be all that I wish you would be, if you turn to Me and be cleansed of your sins in this way."

Prayer Is The Answer

(Vision of the Christ Child): "Turn to Me rather than each other in times of crisis. Persons spend hours talking about their problems to each other when if they spent half that time with Me in the Blessed Sacrament, all their problems would be solved. I say solved in the sense of them having strength to carry their crosses or, in some cases, even removed if it is not for the betterment of their soul that they carry it. Many carry needless burdens because they do not come to Me. They seek human solutions when there are none.

"...As you know, prayer is the prerequisite that God has set forth for all that is to be granted to you in the spiritual realm. "Ask and it shall be given to you, seek and you shall find, knock and it shall be opened to you. Do this and you shall receive, nay even in abundance. Ask for the virtues of My mother, the seven gifts of the Holy Spirit and they will be granted to you. Amen I say to you, the Kingdom of Heaven belongs to those who pray. Pray and you shall attain it. Pray and you shall obtain more than your hearts now imagine in their smallness. I bless you all from My Heart."

The Blessed Mother spoke through Father Gobbi about children being brought up with no faith: "Hundreds of millions of my poor children have thus been educated from childhood to do without God. And often they are good and generous children, though deprived of the true light which alone can give joy and hope to their lives. Think of all the great suffering that covers this immense land. I assure you that what I already foretold you at Fatima has truly come to pass: Russia has spread its errors throughout the whole world. The Lord has made use of godless nations to chastise the Christian peoples who have left the path marked out by my Son Jesus. Now that you are living through those events of which I have foretold you, what must you do, my poor children, to run for shelter? First of all, have recourse to prayer. Pray more, pray with greater confidence, pray with humility and absolute self-abandonment. Especially, recite the holy rosary every day. By your prayer, you prevent error from becoming even more widespread; you hold in check the action of the Evil One; you move to the counter-attack and you limit, more and more, his capacity to act."

Daily Rosary

The Blessed Mother: "My Son suffered horribly for your sins. You must make atonement for them. Do not neglect your duties. They are most important. Say a fifteen decade rosary daily. This is most pleasing to God. It is important."

Humility And Purity

The Blessed Mother: "I wish to continue my teaching on humility. Humility and purity are what is needed now in the world. Without them there can be no true love. Say many Rosaries for this purpose. I will give you great humility personally, so that it will be clear that this message is from me and not from you.... Love your neighbor. Charity must prevail. There is no time for pettiness. Be forgiving towards one another. I am preparing many souls to do great things for God."

Silence And Obscurity

The Blessed Mother: "Silence and obscurity. This is what I ask of you. Let the light of the Lord shine through you in your daily duties. Many misunderstand this and think that they must be in the public eye to do great things for God. It is often quite the contrary. Silence and obscurity as I was in Bethlehem and Nazareth. So many of my priest sons wish to leave their mark in the world rather than preaching the

Gospel of my Son. This is an error. My Son has revealed everything. There is nothing new. They should be following in His footsteps rather than forging their own path. They are leading many astray through their errors. Tell them Jesus is the light, not the human mind. They worship the human intellect rather than God Himself.

"Mothers, teach your children to be kind to one another. The important lessons are learned at home. Do not expect others to teach your children. This is your responsibility and should be your joy. The world has taken the joy out of parenting. This is an error. Discipline is necessary, but so is joy. Love your children. Many children are suffering from lack of love. This is a tragedy. They are made to feel as burdens. Their parents should beg God for forgiveness, for he who leads the little ones astray will be held to account for it. Love and only cherish your children."

The Scapular

The Blessed Mother: "Do not worry, my children who are living the sign of my protection. Wear it always. It will help you to do good because it is a sign of my love and will remind you of me often. This is the purpose of all sacramentals, to remind you of the person behind them and to help you to imitate their virtues. The scapular and the rosary are the greatest of these and will afford you the most protection. I want all my children to wear one. It will help them to love Jesus more. This is a simple means by which God helps His children. Wear it always."

Children

The Blessed Mother: "Cherish your children and give them the stable environment they deserve. Cast off the mentality of the world which says you must indulge your own whims, and sacrifice for your families. This is true love, when manifested in sacrifice. Luxuries are not important; they could be your ruin. Do not seek material wealth. It is of no importance and can often be detrimental to your coming to my Son. Forget the things of earth and seek the things of Heaven, that which is everlasting, so that when you are to account for all, you can rejoice that you have done well with your time on earth. You need not be scrupulous in every detail, just live a good life, as the teachings of the Church dictate."

Widen The Circle Of Prayer

Vision of the Christ Child: "I am disturbed by the number of My followers who do nothing to offer reparation for sin for pure love of Me, but spend most of their prayer time in petition for favors and conversion of only family members. You must widen your circle of prayer to include now the whole human race if you wish to fulfill My will. I am the sole judge as to when a person's heart is prepared to receive graces of conversion, and many stand waiting to receive, yet there is no one who will make the effort to ask of this for them. Prayer is the prerequisite to spiritual favors and gifts and must be asked for by someone."

Human Life Is Sacred

Vision of the Christ Child: "The Lord deals out vengeance with a two-edged sword and vengeance is Mine say the Lord. Those who have mutilated their bodies in the never-ending attempt to prevent life are in need of repentance. They have sinned in a grievous manner and should remain chaste in atonement for their sin. Behold the sorrow which this aberration of today's society has caused, particularly to the children who are victims of it, victims in the sense of having all in the material realm but deficient in love due to having no brother and sisters.

"The parents who have opted to destroy life even before it has begun have created a void for the few who have survived the stipulations of the modern world's thinking. They suffer from loneliness, lack of affection, and in all manner that is manifested directly from this aberration. To deny human life because of the whimsical and precarious excuses of today's person is an outrage against the Divine Order, and is directly responsible for much of the sin and tragedy that you witness today."

The Sacred Heart

Christ Child: "My children are suffering so from these rampant errors in thought and practice, I wish to intervene for them. They must honor Me in the image of the Sacred Heart and I will help them to overcome the insidious plagues which are creeping into homes. I speak of plagues in a sense of sin from immorality and immodesty. You will enjoy peace in your homes from this tyranny if you honor Me in this fashion. Protect your homes and your children with the image of Me and My Sacred Heart. Wear the Sacred Heart badge and place My image in a prominent place in your homes, and I will bless you in abundance. Few know or truly understand the power that I have given to this devotion of honoring Me in this fashion. If they knew, they would indeed practice it. I have come to tell you again to use the practices which I have revealed in the past for your salvation and protection. The myriad of devotions which have been handed down through the ages, approved by My Church, should be put into practice and their use widespread to curb the evil which lurks today waiting to devour like a hungry lion any who fall prey. Arm yourselves with holiness and that which is holy, My sacramentals and devotions, so that you will not fall prey. My Mother's rosary and scapular and the Sacred Heart devotion will offer you the most protection and aid in your holiness to a great degree."

Saint Margaret Mary in the Seventeenth Century said of the devotion to the Sacred Heart: "I understand that the devotion of the Sacred Heart is a last effort of His Love towards the Christians of these latter days, by offering to them an object and means so calculated to persuade them to love Him."

Age Of The Two Hearts

Jesus: "The Sacred and Immaculate Hearts are to be the constant source of your inspiration and the focus of your prayer. This is the age of the Two Hearts and the way in which We wish to be venerated and honored. The depth of this devotion escapes many who are looking to relate to their God in what they blindly perceive to be some modern form, which is none other than a lessening of the degree of holiness to which men are to aspire. They seek to relate in only human terms when My command to them is to be perfect even as My Heavenly Father is perfect. This requires a form of supernatural love which is made available to you in abundance through the devotion to the Two Hearts. It is through this means that you are able to love in a similar fashion in which My mother and I love and glorify the Father. My mother's rosary and scapular and the Sacred Heart's devotion will offer you the most protection and aid in your holiness to a great degree. I want all My children to practice the Nine First Fridays in reparation for sins and the Five First Saturdays in honor of My mother, so that the tide of evil sweeping across the world will end in defeat. These two monthly devotions, if practiced faithfully by My followers, would alone win this battle, so great are their powers in the appeasement of divine justice and the eradication of sin and evil.

Respond Now With Your Fiat

Vision of Our Blessed Mother and the Christ Child: "My Mother's intercession will aid you in all your needs. You need not fear anything. Call on her in all circumstances and she will aid you, even to bringing many of you to great heights of holiness which is so necessary right now. I say to all who read this: Respond now with your fiat and let it be whole hearted so that you will aid in the Triumph of My Mother, which will be the salvation of the world in this generation and the era of peace of which she spoke at Fatima. Now is the time. Do not delay. Tomorrow is no more. I wish all My children to understand the importance of this immediate response to My Mother and My requests. They are simple and easily accomplished by My grace. They need not fear any extraordinary burdens who call upon My Name. I will give them all the graces necessary to accomplish all things, even easily if you have faith. Faith can change the world. Have faith in Me and My Mother's intercession and let the world be changed."

Love My Mother And You Will Love Me

Vision of the Christ Child: "When a soul is united to My Mother and firmly ensconced in her Heart, I can refuse them nothing, they are so pleasing to Me. They are made pleasing by her intercession which purifies them of this world and fashions them after Me, even as I was fashioned in her womb by the power of the Holy Spirit. But again, she was necessary for the plan of the Incarnation to be fulfilled, so she is necessary for your personal redemption, or coming to Me. She is the Gate of Heaven by which I have come to you and you will come to Me. The protestantism that has crept into my Church, that is the one I founded, the Catholic Church, is just that—protestantism. It is not Catholic truth. It is an error to diminish the importance of My Mother's role in your salvation and the salvation of the world. She was and is most important in all facets of redemption because I chose to come to you by this means and I choose for you to come to Me by the same means, that is the Blessed Virgin Mary, My Mother and your Mother. She is Queen of all Saints, Queen of Angels, and Queen of Heaven and Earth. She will lead you to Heaven if you allow her."

The Remedy—Seek Holiness

Seek the refuge of the Immaculate Heart of Mary and pray for the graces that come through her heart to protect you and your loved ones. Pray for the graces to lead you to holiness.

As Moses led the Jews out of Egypt, Our Blessed Mother is leading her remnant through the tribulation. Do not have any fear because fear comes from the evil one, but trust in Jesus and the Blessed Mother to send the Holy Spirit to lead us to holiness and ultimately to heaven.

The messages of Medjugorje summarize for us the ways to holiness: **prayer, fasting, faith, conversion, and peace.** These messages lead us to the holiness which is the heavenly remedy for the ills of our age.

The spiritual teaching of Mother Teresa of Calcutta beautifully instructs each of us:

The fruit of silence is prayer.
The fruit of prayer is faith.
The fruit of faith is love.
The fruit of love is service.
The fruit of service is peace.

and:

May the Merciful Heart of Jesus and the Immaculate Heart of His Beloved Mother, Mary, bring each of us to the fulfillment of our heavenly hopes, joys, and aspirations.

Prayer To The Holy Spirit

Oh, Holy Spirit, beloved of my soul...I adore you. Enlighten me, guide me, strengthen me, console me. Tell me what I should do...give me Your orders. I promise to submit myself to all that You desire of me and to accept all that You permit to happen to me. Let me only know Your will.

Consecration To The Hearts Of Jesus And Mary
With Saint Joseph As Our Model

Hail, most loving Hearts of Jesus and Mary! We venerate You. We love and honor You. We give and consecrate ourselves to You forever. Receive us and possess us entirely.

Purify, enlighten, and sanctify us so that we may love You, Jesus, with the Heart of Mary, and love you, Mary, with the Heart of Jesus. O Heart of Jesus living in Mary and by Mary! O Heart of Mary living in Jesus and for Jesus!

O Heart of Jesus pierced for our sins and giving us Your Mother on Calvary! O Heart of Mary pierced by sorrow and sharing in the sufferings of your divine Son for our redemption! O sacred union of these Two Hearts! Praised be the God of Love Who united Them together!

May He unite our hearts and every heart so that all hearts may live in unity in imitation of that sacred unity which exists in these Two Hearts. Triumph, O Sorrowful and Immaculate Heart of Mary! Reign, O Most Sacred Heart of Jesus! In our hearts, in our homes and families, in the hearts of those who as yet know You not and in all the nations of the world. Establish in the hearts of all mankind the sovereign triumph and reign of Your Two Hearts so that the earth may resound from pole to pole with one cry: Blessed forever be the Most Sacred Heart of Jesus and the Sorrowful and Immaculate Heart of Mary!

O dearest Saint Joseph, I consecrate and give myself to you that you may always be my father, protector, and guide in the way of salvation. Obtain for me a greater purity of heart and a fervent love of the interior life. After your example, may I do all my actions for the greater glory of God in union with the divine Heart of Jesus and the Immaculate Heart of Mary.

O Blessed Saint Joseph, pray for me that I may share the peace and joy of your holy death. Amen.

Appendix I
Selected Scriptures

Matthew 24: 1-44
The Last Days Of Jesus

In the daytime he would be in the Temple teaching, but would spend the night on the hill called the Mount of Olives. And from early morning the people would gather round him in the Temple to listen to him.

Jesus left the Temple, and as he was going away his disciples came up to draw his attention to the Temple buildings. He said to them in reply, "You see all these? I tell you solemnly, not a single stone here will be left on another: everything will be destroyed." And when he was sitting on the Mount of Olives the disciples came and asked him privately, "Tell us, when is this going to happen and what will be the sign of your coming and of the end of the world?"

The Beginning of Sorrows

And Jesus answered them, "Take care that no one deceives you; because many will come using my name and saying, I am the Christ, and they will deceive many. You will hear of wars and rumors of wars; do not be alarmed, for this is something that must happen, but the end will not be yet. For nation will fight against nation, and kingdom against kingdom. There will be famines and earthquakes here and there. All this is only the beginning of the birthpangs. Then they will hand you over to be tortured and put to death; and you will be hated by all the nations on account of my name. And then many will fall away; men will betray one another and hate one another. Many false prophets will arise; they will deceive many, and with the increase of lawlessness, love in most men will grow cold; but the man who stands firm to the end will be saved. This Good News of the kingdom will be proclaimed to the whole world as a witness to all the nations. And then the end will come.

The Great Tribulation of Jerusalem

"So when you see the disastrous abomination, of which the prophet Daniel spoke, set up in the Holy Place (let the reader understand), then those in Judea must escape to the mountains; if a man is on the housetop, he must not come down to collect his belongings; if a man is in the fields, he must not turn back to fetch his cloak. Alas for those with child, or with babies at the breast, when those days come! Pray that you will not have to escape in winter or on a sabbath. For then there will be great distress such as, until now, since the world began, there never has been, nor ever will be again. And if that time had not been shortened, no one would have survived; but shortened that time shall be, for the sake of those who are chosen. If anyone says to you then, "Look, here is the Christ" or, "He is there," do not believe it; for false Christs and false prophets will arise and produce great signs and portents, enough to deceive even the chosen, if that were possible. There; I have forewarned you.

The Coming of the Son of Man will be Evident

"If, then, they say to you, Look, he is in the desert, do not go there; Look, he is in some hiding place, do not believe it; because the coming of the Son of Man will be like lightning striking in the east and flashing far into the west. Wherever the corpse is, there will the vultures gather.

The Universal Significance of this Coming

"Immediately after the distress of those days the sun will be darkened, the moon will lose its brightness, the stars will fall from the sky and the powers of heaven will be shaken. And then the sign of the Son of Man will appear in heaven; then too all the peoples of the earth will beat their breasts; and they will see the Son of Man coming on the clouds of heaven with power and great glory. And he will send his angels with a loud trumpet to gather his chosen from the four winds, from one end of heaven to the other.

The Time of this Coming

"Take the fig tree as a parable: as soon as its twigs grow supple and its leaves come out, you know that summer is near. So with you when you see all these things: know that he is near, at the very gates. . I tell you solemnly, before this generation has passed away all these things will have taken place. Heaven and earth will pass away, but my words will never pass away. But as for that day and hour, nobody knows it, neither the angels of heaven, nor the Son, no one but the Father only.

Be on the Alert

"As it was in Noah's day, so will it be when the Son of Man comes. For in those days before the Flood people were eating, drinking, taking wives, taking husbands, right up to the day Noah went into the ark, and they suspected nothing till the Flood came and swept all away. It will be like this when the Son of Man comes. Then of two men in the fields one is taken, one left; of two women at the millstone grinding, one is taken, one left. So stay awake, because you do not know the day when your master is coming. You may be quite sure of this that if the householder had known at what time of the night the burglar would come, he would have stayed awake and would not have allowed anyone to break through the wall of his house. Therefore, you too must stand ready because the Son of Man is coming at an hour you do not expect."

Matthew 25:1-13
Parable Of The Ten Bridesmaids

"Then the kingdom of heaven will be like this: Ten bridesmaids took their lamps and went to meet the bridegroom. Five of them were foolish and five were sensible: the foolish ones did take their lamps, but they brought no oil whereas the sensible ones took flasks of oil as well as their lamps. The bridegroom was late, and they all grew drowsy and fell asleep. But at midnight there was a cry, The bridegroom is here! Go out and meet him. At this, all those bridesmaids woke up and trimmed their lamps, and the foolish ones said to the sensible ones, Give us some of your oil: our lamps are going out. But they replied, There may not be enough for us and for you; you had better go to those who sell it and buy some for yourselves. They had gone off to buy it when the bridegroom arrived. Those who were ready went in with him to the wedding hall and the door was closed. The other bridesmaids arrived later. Lord, Lord, they said open the door for us. But he replied, "I tell you solemnly, I do not know you." So stay awake, because you do not know either the day or the hour."

Matthew 25:31-46
The Last Judgement

"When the Son of Man comes in his glory, escorted by all the angels, then he will take his seat on his throne of glory. All the nations will be assembled before him and he will separate men one from another as the shepherd separates sheep from goats. He will place the sheep on his right hand and the goats on his left. Then the King will say to those on his right hand, Come, you whom my Father has blessed, take for your heritage the kingdom prepared for you since the foundation of the world. For I was hungry and you gave me food; I was thirsty and you gave me drink; I was a stranger and you made me welcome; naked and you clothed me, sick and you visited me, in prison and you came to see me. Then the virtuous will say to him in reply, Lord, when did we see you hungry and feed you; or thirsty and give you drink? When did we see you a stranger and make you welcome; naked and clothe you; sick or in prison and go to see you? And the King will answer, I tell you solemnly, in so far as you did this to one of the least of these brothers of mine, you did it to me.

"Next he will say to those on his left hand, Go away from me, with your curse upon you, to the eternal fire prepared for the devil and his angels. For I was hungry and you never gave me food; I was thirsty and you never gave me anything to drink; I was a stranger and you never made me welcome, naked and you never clothed me, sick and in prison and you never visited me. When it will be their turn to ask, Lord, when did we see you hungry or thirsty, a stranger or naked, sick or in prison, and did not come to your help? Then he will answer, I tell you solemnly, in so far as you neglected to do this to one of the least of these, you neglected to do it to me. And they will go away to eternal punishment, and the virtuous to eternal life."

2 Timothy 3:1-7
The Dangers Of The Last Days

But understand this; there will be terrifying times in the last days. People will be self-centered and lovers of money, proud, haughty, abusive, disobedient to their parents, ungrateful, irreligious, callous, implacable, slanderous, licentious, brutal, hating what is good, traitors, reckless, conceited, lovers of pleasure rather than lovers of God, as they make a pretense of religion but deny its power. Reject them.

Romans 1:24-32
Homosexuality

The words of Saint Paul to the Romans rings as true as it did nearly 2,000 years ago. The times may change, but the heart of man does not. "Therefore, God handed them over to impurity through the lusts of their hearts for the mutual degradation of their bodies. They exchanged the truth of God for a lie and revered and worshipped the creature rather than the Creator, who is blessed forever, Amen. Therefore, God handed them over to degrading passions. Their females exchanged natural relations for unnatural, and the males likewise gave up natural relations with females and burned with lust for one another. Males did shameful things with males and thus received in their own persons the due penalty for their perversity. And since they did not see fit to acknowledge God, God handed them over to their undiscerning mind to do what is improper. They are filled with every form of wickedness, evil, greed, and malice; full of envy, murder, rivalry, treachery, and spite. They are gossips and scandalmongers and they hate God. They are insolent, haughty, boastful, ingenious in their wickedness, and rebellious towards their parents. They are senseless, faithless, heartless, ruthless. Although they know the just decree of God that all who practice such things deserve death, they not only do them but give approval to those who practice them."

Hosea 4:1-11
The Crimes And Punishment Of Israel

General Corruption

Sons of Israel, listen to the word of Yahweh,
for Yahweh indicts the inhabitants of the country:
there is no fidelity, no tenderness,
no knowledge of God in the country,
only perjury and lies, slaughter, theft,
adultery and violence, murder after murder.
This is why the country is in mourning, and all who live
 in it pineaway, even the wild animals
and the birds of heaven;
the fish of the sea themselves are perishing.

Against the priests

> But let no man denounce, no man rebuke;
> it is you, priest that I denounce.
> Day and night you stumble along,
> the prophet stumbling with you,
> and you are the ruin of your people.
> My people perish for want of knowledge.
> As you have rejected knowledge
> so do I reject you from my priesthood;
> you have forgotten the teaching of your God,
> I in my turn will forget your children.
> Many as they are, all of them have sinned against me,
> they have bartered their glory for shame.
> They feed on the sin of my people,
> they are all greedy for their iniquity.
> But as with the people, so let it be with the priest:
> I will make them pay for their conduct,
> I will pay them out for their deeds.
> They will eat but never be satisfied,
> they will play the whore but still be sterile,
> because they have deserted Yahweh
> to give themselves up to whoring.

Hosea 5:15-16
Yahweh Abandons His People

Yes, I am going to return to my dwelling place
until they confess their guilt and seek my face;
they will search for me in their misery.

Isaiah 13:9-11

Lo, the day of the Lord comes, cruel, with wrath and burning anger; to lay waste the land, destroy the sinners within it! The stars and the constellations of the heavens send forth no light; the sun is dark when it rises, and the light of the moon does not shine. Thus will I punish the world for its evil and the wicked for their guilt. I will put an end to the pride of the arrogant, the insolence of tyrants I will humble.

Notes

Important Notice

Every effort possible was made by the author's to verify facts. Due to the nature of the material, this is not always easy, as heresay and personal interpretations often cloud the facts. Where an error was made, please *write* us so we may clear up any ambiguities for updated versions.

Material has been gathered from sources over many years. The authors are more scribes compiling information on many apparitions. We try to present an understandable picture of what Mary has been weaving for centuries through her intervention in history. The Bibliography and Resource section at the end of the book provides a great deal of information about the books used in compiling this text. Several of the chapters in this book are from newsletters or magazines that we have produced quarterly over the last five years. For those who wish to know more about the books used for compilation, the information is provided in detail. Many of the books quoted throughout are carried by **Signs Of The Times,** 6 Pidgeon Hill Drive, Suite 260, Sterling, Virginia, 20165. Telephone (703) 450-7766. FAX 450-7796. Signs of the Times is a Catholic Resource Center writing and distributing Catholic literature throughout the world. Newsletters/magazines on Marian Apparitions and similar topics have been printed quarterly. Back orders may be obtained from using the Order Form in the back of this book.

This book quotes many visionaries. Frequently the material is from a pamphlet, notebook, or book published by the visionary. In many instances we will give information once and not continue to make a note on every occasion we quote from the source.

There are quotes from the **Marian Movement of Priests** in many chapters. From 1973 to the present, Father Stefano Gobbi of Milan, Italy, has been receiving locutions from the Blessed Mother. The authors have quoted the messages communicated by Our Blessed Mother to Father Stefano Gobbi from the book *To the Priests, Our Lady's Beloved Sons.* The interpretation, selection, and application of these messages are the sole responsibility of the authors and in no way imply implicit or explicit agreement of the Marian Movement of Priests.

It should be noted that reading the messages quoted herein in no way constitutes an acceptable alternative to reading all the messages in their entirety. Our Lady repeatedly asks us not to be concerned about future events as she calls us to live in the present. She continues to warn and enlighten us with her words of exhortation and encouragement as she prepares us for the trials ahead. The full intent of the messages of Mary is to spiritually form us and bring us closer to Jesus.

The reader should not be misled by the title *To The Priests, Our Lady's Beloved Sons* into thinking that this book is meant only for priests. The messages contained in the book are for everyone. Therefore, the reader is strongly urged to obtain the book at the following address: The Marian Movement of Priests, Rev. Albert G. Roux, P.O. Box 8, St. Francis, Maine, 04774-0008.

The distinguished Dr. and Mrs. Francis B. Henessey, Endwell, New York, helped the authors compile and make sense of the blending of this information for this book. The scholarly Dr. Hennessey has a mind like a steel trap. Some say like a scalpel. The jury is still out on this one. He is wise as a serpent and gentle as a dove. There are only a handful of people who see the large picture as do Dr. and Mrs. Hennessey. It has been agreed by all that Jim O'Rourke, who had a heavy hand in this material, has a mind like a razor. This we are sure as the jury is in.

Chapter 1.—The Wake-Up Call. 1. R. Vincent, *Please Come Back To Me And My Son,* Ireland's Eye, Ireland, 1992, p. 7. 2. *Ibid.,* p. 10. 3. Jean Guitton, *The Private Life of Pope Paul VI*, p. 152. 4. Apostolate for Family Consecration, Bloomingdale, Ohio, July 21, 1993. 5. Material on Interior Locutions is from *Our Lady Speaks to Her Beloved Sons,* introduction.

Chapter 2—The Grand Finale. 1. R. Vincent, *Please Come Back To Me And My Son,* Ireland's Eye, Ireland, 1992, p. 15. 2. *Ibid.* 3. Father Lambert Terstroet, SMM, a Montfortian priest living in Iceland, divided Marian apparitions into four major periods. We have used his outline with permission. The framework from the narrative was provided by him, but nearly all the information came from different sources, most notably *Signs of the Times* newsletters and personal interviews over a five-year period. Other information came from personal visits or friends who have known visionaries. 4. *Our Lady of All Nations* is from a *Signs of the Times* newsletter. 5. All quotes from Gladys of San Nicolas, Argentina are from *San Nicolas, Argentina,* edited and published by Faith Publishing, Milford, Ohio, 45150. 6. Patricia of England is from a *Signs of the Times* newsletter. There is some controversy around her with her local bishop, the Bishop of Southwark, England. Material was obtained from *Mother of the Hidden Wounds.* 7. Apparitions in the Ukraine is from *Witness* by Josyp Terelya and Michael H. Brown, page 211-213.

Information on Seredne or Ukraine in general is from this source. 8. Information on Cuenca, Ecuador, is from *I Am the Guardian of the Faith*, Sister Isabel Bettwy, Franciscan University Press, p. 90-95. 9. *Litmanova* material is from the Pittsburgh Center for Peace, Tom Petrisco, 6111 Steubenville Pike, McKees Rocks Pike, PA., 15136. The gaps were filled in from the chart in *Signs, Wonders, and Response*, by Father Albert Hebert, S.M., P.O. Box 309, Paulina, LA, and Dr. Rosalie Turton of the 101 Foundation, NJ. There are hundreds more unmentioned and were not included only because of space.

Chapter 3—Prophetess For Our Times. 1. Material is from Ellen Commerce, Herndon, VA. 2. St. Louis de Montfort quotes are both from, *True Devotion to Mary*. 3. Ellen Commerce, Herndon, VA. 4. *Ibid.* 5. *Ibid.* 6. Gerhard Kittel and Gerhard Friedrich, *Theological Dictionary of the New Testament:* Abridged Volume, Michigan, 1985, p.782-3; Scheeben, Mariology, v.II, p.262. 7. St. Irenaeus in J.H. Newman, *Letter to Pusey, Anglican Difficulties*, London, 1866, p.37; St. John Damascence, Serm. Dorm. II, PG 96, 733D; O'Carroll, Advocate, Theotokos, p.6. 8. M.J. Scheeben, tr. Geukers, *Mariology*, v.II, p.262. 9. Cf. Chapter II of this work, i.e. *Mary: Coredemptrix, Mediatrix , Advocate* section, The Holy Spirit and the Mediatrix of All Graces. 10. St. Maximilian Kolbe, Notes, 1938, ed. Manteau-Bonamy, tr. Armandez, *The Immaculate Conception and the Holy Spirit*, Marian Writings of Fr. Kolbe, 1977, Franciscan Marytown Press, p.39. 11. Manteau-Bonamy, *The Immaculate Conception and the Holy Spirit*, Marian Writings of St. Maximilian Kolbe, 1977, p.39-40. 12. Pope John Paul II, *Redemptoris Mater*, n. 24; Vatican Council II, *Lumen Gentium*, n. 59. 13. ibid, n. 48. 14. St. Louis Marie Grignion de Montfort, tr. F. Faber, *True Devotion to Mary*, ns. 20,35; cf. also 21, 25. 15. Pope John Paul II, *Redemptoris Mater*, n. 41. 16. For example, cf. Pope John Paul II, *Redemptor Hominis*, 1978, ns. 15-17; Encylical Letter, *Dives in Misericordia*, 1980, n. 15; Apostolic Exhortation, *Christifideles Laici*, ns. 3-7. 17. Pope John Paul II, *Dives in Misericordia*, 1980, n. 15. Material in footnotes 6-17 is from *Mary: Co-Redemptrix, Mediatrix, Advocate*, pgs. 66-70, by Dr. Mark Miravalle, Franciscan University of Steubenville, Ohio., used with permission. 18. *Lumen Gentium*, para. 60. 19. *Lumen Gentium*, para. 62. 20. *Inter Sodalica*, letter of May 22, 1918. 21. *Signs of the Times* magazine issue on Our Lady of All Nations. 22. *Redemptoris Mater*, para., 3. 23. Quote is originally from Father Rene Laurentin, France, although this is quoted from Janice T. Connell, *Visions of the Children*, St. Martins Press, 1992.

Chapter 4—Prophets In Our Midst. 1. AAS, 59, 1186. 2. The small amount of introductory material is from the books on said topic cited throughout the book. 3. Maria Esperanza is from Stan Karminski and *The Apparitions in Betania, Venezula*, by Sister Margaret Catherine Sims,

Framingham, MA. 4. Mirna of Damascus is from the Pittsburgh Center for Peace, Tom Petrisco, Pittsburgh, PA. 5. Julia Kim of Naju, Korea, and the life of Luz Amparo Cuevas was partially excerpted from Father Liam O'Glannor in a compiled pamphlet called, *Warnings and Messages from Mater Dolorosa* on what the Blessed Mother is doing in the world today at several apparition sites. Published by Dolas, P.O. Box 148, Allaagash, ME, 04774. There is some from the same author in the section on Ukrainian apparitions. 6. All messages from Jim Singer are from *The Messages of Our Lord*, by Jim Singer, 4082 Stephanie Street, Burlington, Ontario, Canada, L7L 1X1. Material was sent to the authors by Jim Singer in a xerox copy of a pamplet. 7. Information on Estela Ruiz is from a newsletter by *Signs of the Times*, Vol., 5. 8. Theresa Lopez of Colorado, *The Denver Apparitions Return Focus to Fatima*, Signs of the Times newsletter. 9. Josefina material provided by Kevin Morley of Melbourne, Australia, Chestnut Hill Marian Lodge. 10. Anything on the apparitions of Joseph Januszkiewicz is from personal interviews. His apparition messages as of the time of this writing are not available for the public.

Chapter 5—Our Lady's Role In The Salvation Of Mankind. 1. Saint Louis de Montfort, *True Devotion to Mary*, Montfort Publications, Bayshore, NY. 2. Ida of Amsterdam and Our Lady of All Nations was from a newsletter by *Signs of the Times*. There is renewed interest by Rome and the new release by Dr. Mark Miravalle called *Mary-Coredemptrix, Mediatrix, Advocate*, published by Queenship Publishing, California. 3. The sections, Given a Unique Role, The Universal Church, Mary and Her Protestant Children, Teaching Authority of the Church, and The Incarnation were primarily written by Monk Joseph, of Mount Tabor Monastery in Redwood Valley, CA, 95470.

Chapter 6—Apocalypse. 1. All Marian Movement of Priests quotes are from Father Gobbi of Milan, Italy. Messages are presented on a date basis for each ascending year with all pertinent information in Chapter One notes. 2. *The New World Order* by Pat Robertson, Thomas Nelson, Inc., Word Publishing, p. 95, 1991. 3. Turzovka-*Pittsburgh Center for Peace*, Tom Petrisco.

Chapter 7—Weeping. 1. All quotes from Christina Gallagher are from *Please Come Back to Me and My Son*, R. Vincent, Ireland's Eye, Published in Ireland. 2. Rosa Mystica, *Signs of the Times* newsletter, Rosa Mystica: Mary the Mystical Rose, Vo., #4, July 1989. 3. Father James Bruse, personal interview, newsletter, and friend of Signs of the Times.

Chapter 8—Satan In the World; LaSalette. 1. Messages from Medjugorje are from *Words From Heaven*, by St. James Publishing Company, Birmingham, Alabama. 2. St. Louis de Montfort quotes are from *True Devotion to Mary*, from Montfort publications in Bayshore, New York. 3. The message of LaSalette is from the original translation. See Resources: LaSalette. 4. Patricia of Cuenca Ecuador, See Resources. 5. Christina Gallagher, R. Vincent, published by Ireland's Eye. 6. *Focus on the Family*, newsletter, April 1993, p. 1. 7. Father Lucia Martin, *Perpetual Adoration*. 8. Quotes in this section on abortion are from *Abortion, What Heaven Has to Say*, a compilation of messages from the Pittsburgh Center for Peace, Tom Petrisco, PA. 9. Guadalupe is from a *Signs of the Times* newsletter that wrote of this apparition and its continuing role in ending abortion.

Chapter 9—Fatima. 1. *Fatima Family Messenger*, July-September, 1992. 2. *Ibid.* 3. *Ibid.* 4. Apparition of the Blessed Virgin on the mountain of LaSalette the 19th of September 1846, original edition of Lecce. 5. Information about the apparition itself is from the newsletter by *Signs of the Times*. 6. *Fatima Family Messenger*, July-September, 1992. 7. *The Final Hour*, Michael H. Brown, Faith Publishing Company, Milford, Ohio. 8. All remaining points above are from the *Fatima Family Messenger*, July 1992. 9. The information about Fatima originates from the work by Brother Michel de la Sainte Trinite, four volumes, *The Third Secret of Fatima*, Augustine Publishing, Chulmleigh, Devon EXIS 7HL, 1986. 10. *Ibid.* 11. *Ibid.* 12. *Ibid.* 13. *Ibid.* 14. *Ibid.* 15. *Ibid.* 16. *Ibid.* 17. *Garabandal* Magazine, July-September, 1993, Lindenhurst, NY. 18. op. cit.-Michel. 19. *Ibid.* 20. *Ibid.* 21. *Ibid.* 22. *Ibid.* 23. *Ibid.* 24. *Ibid.* All material in this section for the "Third Secret," "Was The Secret To Be Revealed?" and "Danger to a Nation" is from the work by Brother Michel with the exception of the point on scholars disagreeing on whether the secret was for the public or the pontiffs only. 25. *Stimme des Glaubens*, Fulda, Germany meeting 1980. There is considerable disagreement on whether or not this conversation ever took place. Many credible people on both sides of this issue disagree, and therefore we present the two points of view. Whether John Paul II would ever say "the Church cannot be reformed" is the critical point. The opposing argument is, does he know the destiny of the Church, therefore he did say it?

The Fulda meeting is a *possible* example of heresay that becomes accepted truth over the years. 26. *The Keys of This Blood*, Father Malachi Martin, p., 680-695, Simon and Schuster, 1990, N.Y. 27. *Ibid.* 28. *Ibid.* 29. *The Final Hour*, Michael Brown. 30. *The Third Secret* of Fatima, Brother Michel. 31. Material in Controversy 2 is from the *Fatima Family Messenger*, July-September, 1992. 32. *Ibid.* 33. Synopsis of *New Lies for Old* by Analtoliy Golitsyn, Dodd Publishers, 1984, 412 pgs. 34. Francis Johnston, *Fatima: The Great Sign*, TAN Books, 1980, Rockford, IL, quote on back cover.

Chapter 10—Garabandal. 1. This chapter is a newsletter that was done for Signs of the Times written by Stan Karminski of Wayne, PA. Mr. Karminski was one of the early supporters of Garabandal and one of the first Americans to promote the messages of Medjugorje. Some sources of information are, *O Children Listen to Me*, by Robert Francois, *Star on the Mountain*, by Fr. Materne Laffineur and M.T. le Pelletier. The best resource for information that we know for Garabandal is The Workers of Our Lady of Mount Carmel de Garabandal, in Lindenhurst, New York. For more texts on the subject see Resources. 2. *The Warnings of Garabandal* is quoted by Father Joseph A. Pelletier, A.A., who wrote on Marian apparitions for many years—See Resources. 3. The material from Garabandal and the Synogogue is from a speech that was delivered by the French Dominican, Father Francois Turner, in a barn near the pines on August 8, 1988. It has been used with permission and changed only in grammar and style for readability from his French translation. The Book of Exodus speaks of the pillar of smoke by day and the fire by night guiding the Jews into the promised land. Father Turner is considered to be a very credible witness to Garabandal.

Chapter 11—Akita. 1. Information from Akita is from a newsletter from Signs of the Times. Resources were *Akita—The Tears and Message of Mary*, by Teiji Yasuda, O.S.V., with the English version by John Haffert, and the *The Meaning of Akita*, both from the 101 Foundation, Asbury, NJ. See Resources.

Chapter 12—Medjugorje. 1. Medjugorje Network for the United Kingdom, January 12, 1992. 2. Medjugorje is truly the "Mother" of them all. *Signs of the Times* has published a newsletter on this, but it focused mostly on the story and personalities. This material is from *Medjugorje: Its Background and Messages* by Mary Joan Wallace of Follow Me Communications, Inc., Huntington Beach Calif. We were granted permission. This is an excellent work. 3. *The Queen of Peace Visits Medjugorje*, by Father Joseph Pelletier, A.A., Assumption Publications, Worcester, Mass. 4. Marian Workers in Canada, issue devoted to Father Peyton.

Chapter 13—Smoke Enters the Church. 1. Messages of LaSalette are quoted from *The Apparitions of the Blessed Virgin on the Mountain in 1846*. Reproduction without commentary, 12th Ave. of grain d'or, 49600, Beaupreau, France. 2. *Syllabus of Errors* and *Humanum Genus*, (Tan Publishers) and Quod Apostolici Muneris are reprinted by The Remnant, 2539 Morrison Ave., Saint Paul, Minnesota, and available from Servants of Jesus and Mary, Nazareth Homestead, R.D. I, Box 258, Constable, NY 12926. Also see Resources for information on encyclicals of the Roman Catholic Church. 3. *Our Sunday's Visitor Catholic Encyclopedia*, 1991, Our Sunday Visitor Publishing Division, 200 Noll Plaza, Huntington, Indiana. 4. *Ibid.* 5. *The Electronic Encyclopedia*, (TM) (c) 1990, Groiler Electronic Publishing, Inc. 6. *Ibid.* 7. *Divini Redemptoris.* 8. *A Catechism of Modernism*, The Rev. J.B. Lemius, O.M.I., TAN Books and Publishers, Rockford, Illinois, 1981. 9. *Ibid.* 10. *Ibid.* 11. *Ibid.* 12. The encyclical *Quanta Cura* and the *Syllabus of Errors* issued by Pope Pius IX in 1864 and The Syllabus condemning the errors of the Modernists (Lamentabili Sane) and *Divini Redemptoris* reprinted by the Remnant. 13. *The Antichrist,* Vincent P. Miceli., S.J., Roman Catholic Books, P.O. Box 255, Harrison, NY, 1981. 14. *Ibid.* 15. *Ibid.* 16. *Ibid.* 17. *Ibid.*—all above this is from the same source. 18. *AA-1025, The Memoirs of an Anti-Apostle,* Marie Carre, TAN Books, P.O. Box 424, Rockford, Illinois, 61105, 1991.

Chapter 14—The Great Apostasy. 1. Material from LaSalette and Akita are from *Signs of the Times* newsletters. Quote from Father St. Marie is from a friend of his living in Annandale, Virginia, who wishes anonymity. 2. *Inside the New Age Nightmare,* Randall Baer, Huntington House, Inc., Lafayette, La., 1989. 3. *Ibid.,* p. 78-79. 4. *Ibid.,* p. 84. 5. *Ibid.,* p. 85-87. 6. *Ibid.,* p. 88. 7. *Ibid.,* p. 89. 8. *Ibid.,* p. 91. 9. *Ibid.,* p. 94. 10. *Ibid.* 168.

Chapter 15—The 100 Years of Satan. 1. Quito, Ecuador, Our Lady of Good Fortune, leaflet printed by Gregorian Press, Holy Family Monastery, 261 Cross Keys Road, Berlin, NJ. 2. *The Keys of This Blood,* by Malachi Martin, 1990, pgs., 677-685, Simon and Schuster, 1990. 3. *The Problems With the New Mass,* p. 24, Rama P. Coomaraswamy, M.D., TAN Books, Rockford, Illinois, 1990. 4. *Ibid.,* p. 25. 5. *The Ottaviani Intervention, A Short Critical Study of the New Order of the Mass,* Cardinal Ottaviani and Cardinal Bacci, pgs. 4-25, TAN Books and Publishers, Rockford, Il. 1992. 6. *The Problems with the New Mass.* 7. *Ibid.,* p. 15. 8. Ottaviani Intervention, p. 4. 9. All *Divine Appeal* is from Newborne Enterprises Ltd., Ibadan, Nigeria, 1992. 10. All quotes throughout the book from *Anne Catherine Emmerick* are from Reverend Carl Schmoger CSSR, Volume 1 and 2, 1976 edition, TAN Books, Rockford, Illinois. 11. Richard Langley, *The Signs of the Times,* June 24, 1992, publisher unlisted. 12. Reverend Gerald Cullerton, *The Reign of Antichrist,* TAN Books, Rockford, Il. 13. Yves DuPont, *Catholic Prophecy,* p. 28, TAN Books. 14. *Ibid.,* p. 45. 15. *Ibid.,* p. 73. 16. *Ibid.* 17. *Ibid.* 18. *Our Lady at Garabandal,* Judith M. Albright, Faith Publishing Company, p. 28, Milford, Ohio, 1992. 19. Cullerton, *The Reign of Antichrist,* TAN Books. 20-28, *Ibid.* 29. Eileen George, *Conversations in Heaven,* Meet the Father Ministry, Millbury, MA. 30. *Toward a New World Order,* Donald McAlvaney, p. 336, Western Publishing Company, 1992, Phoenix, AZ. 31. *Forbes* Magazine, ASAP Issue, April 1993, An interview with Tom Peters, author of *In Search of Excellence* and *Liberation Management.* 32. *En Route to Global Occupation,* Gary Kah, Huntington House Publishers, p. 193-195, 1992. 33. *Ibid.* 34. *Ibid.* 35. *Ibid.*

Chapter 16—Wars and Disasters. 1. Message from Tony Fernwalt sent by fax to authors. 2. *The Washington Post,* George Will, March 28, 1993, p. C 7. 3. *The International Herald Tribune,* article by David Broder, "The Loss of Two Parent Families," March 25, 1993. 4. *Apostasy Within,* Father Paul

Trinchard, Christopher Publishing House, Hanover, MA, 1989. 5. "Banking on the Brink," *The Washington Post*, Business Section, October 6, 1992. 6. *AIDS: Rage and Reality, Why Silence is Deadly*, Gene Antonio, Anchor Books, Dallas, Texas, p. x. 7. *Ibid.* 8. *Ibid.* 9. *Ibid.*, p. 2. 10. *Ibid.* xv. 11. Material from Chernobyl is from five trips by the author near the reactor site and surrounding Republics, for a combined time of nearly four months. 12. Mr. Terelya received his vision while in prayer in Marmora, Ontario, and material was sent to Signs of the Times. 13. *I Am the Guardian of the Faith*, Sister Isabel Bettwy, Franciscan University Press, Steubenville, Ohio. 14. *The Apparitions at Oliveto Citra—Mary Among Us—The Apparitions at Oliveto Citra*, by Robert Faricy, S.J., and Luciana Pecoraio, Franciscan University Press, Steubenville, Ohio, 1989.

Chapter 17—Where Mercy and Justice Meet. 1. Francis Johnston, *Fatima: The Great Sign*, TAN Books, 1980. 2. *Ibid.* 3. Messages from Blessed Sister Faustina Kowalska's are from her personal diary called *Divine Mercy in My Soul*, Messages are numbered, Marian Press, Stockbridge, MA, 1987. The certain place is thought to be Warsaw, Poland, which was leveled by the Germans in World War II. 4. Faustina Diary. 5. *Please Come Back to My Son*, R. Vincent, published by Ireland's Eye, Ireland, 1992.

Chapter 18—The Warning. The original framework for this chapter was a pamphlet called *The Warning*, by Father Philip Bebie. The material was from his personal diary while he was in the last stages of terminal cancer. He had a deep Marian devotion and because Garabandal has not been recognized to date by the Holy See, the order of which he was a member at this time is not able to endorse this diary. *The Warning* was written in 1981, and Father Philip died in 1987. The Provincial of his order has given us permission to use his material as long as we put the above quoted disclaimer. The pamphlet does not have a copyright and says it has been printed with ecclesiastical permission. Material from *The Warning* is quoted throughout in the above mentioned sections as well as the Permanent Sign. 1. Information on Blessed Anna Maria Taigi is from *The Warning*. 2. *Divine Mercy in My Soul*, the personal diary of Sister Faustina. 3. *Ibid.*, Message 83.

Chapter 19—The Miracle. 1. Theresa Lopez was provided by Scott White of the Denver, Colorado, group in the form of a video tape. A talk was given in November of 1992 and this material was taken from this talk. 2. Lubbock, Texas, are from *The Lubbock Rosary Messages—Queen of Mercy*, published by Queen of Mercy Center, P.O. Box 683, Earth, Texas. 3. *Total Consecration*, St. Louis de Montfort, Montfort Publications, p. 75, Bayshore, New York. 4. *Apostolate of Holy Motherhood* messages are from Mariamante (at an unknown address in the United States), by Dr. Mark Miraville, Riehle Foundation, Milford, Ohio. 5. Tom Petrisco, The Pittsburgh Center for Peace,

Steubenville Pike, Pittsburgh, PA. Janice T. Connell, *Visions of the Children*, St. Martins' Press, 1992, New York, p.123-129. 7. Dozule', France, is from *The Glorious Cross*, by Les Amis de la Croix Glorieuse, 171, rue de l'Universite', Paris, France. The English edition is from the same source.

Chapter 20—The Great Chastisement. 1. LaSalette, See Resources. 2. Bettwy, p., 57-58, See Resources. 3. Eileen George, *Beacon of God's Love: Her Teaching, Meet The Father Ministry*, Millbury, MA, 01527. 4. The several pages of "Three Days of Darkness" and the Blessed Virgin Mary's Message to Brother David Lopez were written by Wayne Weible and are used with permission. The material is from the Weible Columns, August 1992, Myrtle Beach, SC. 5. Quotes from Yves DuPont, See Resources, *Catholic Prophecy*. 6. *The Warning*, Bebie. 7. The Messages of Fraudais, See Resources. 8. Julka of Zagreb, is from Volume 3 of *Jesus Calls Us*, 1975-1976. Published in 1988, from In Wahrheit Und Treue, Postfach 279, 8401 Winterthur, Switzerland. 9. Lubbock, *Queen of Mercy*, See Resources.

Chapter 21—Second Pentecost. 1. Saint Louis de Montfort, *True Devotion to Mary*, Montfort Publications, Bayshore, New York. 2. Julka messages are from source quoted in previous chapter. 3. Sister Natalia of Hungary is from her diary called *Victorious Queen of the World*, published by Two Hearts Books and Publishers, second edition 1992. 4. *Ibid*. 5. Brother Lopez quote from The Great Chastisement chapter from the Weible Columns. 6. Theresa Lopez from the November 1992 video tape sent to the authors by Scott White. 7. Quote from Saint Louis de Montfort, *True Devotion to Mary*.

Chapter 22—Our Role: Apostles Of The Last Times. 1. Montfort, *True Devotion to Mary*, Montfort Publications, Bayshore, NY. 2. *Our Guardian Angels*, Reverend Alfred Boedecker, O.F.M., World Apostolate of Fatima, Washington, NJ. 3. *Ibid*. 4. *The Angels are Waiting*, Reverend Randall Paine, O.R.C., p. 44, The Leaflet Missal Company, 418 W. Minnehaha Ave., St. Paul, MN 1988. 5. *Ibid.*, p. 5. 6. *Our Guardian Angels*, Boedecker. 7. *The Angels are Waiting*, p. 45. 8. *Ibid.*, p. 61. 9. *Ibid.*, p. 46. 10. *Eileen George: Beacon of God's Love: Her Teaching*, Meet The Father Ministry, Inc., 363 Greenwood St., Millbury, MA, 01527, 1990.

Chapter 23—The Remedy. 1. Messages from the Apostolate of Holy Motherhood are from the Riehle Foundation, Dr. Mark Miravalle, Milford, Ohio. The Act of Consecration is from the Alliance of the Two Hearts.

Bibliography

A Call to Peace, Published by Mir-A-Call Center, 6 Bentley Lane, Bella Vista, AR.

Abortion, What Heaven Has to Say, Messages from Our Lord and the Blessed Virgin Mary Concerning Abortion to Prophets of Today, a compilation of messages, Pittsburgh Center for Peace, Pittsburgh, PA, 1992.

Agreda, Mary of, *Mystical City of God*, 4 vols., AMI Press, Washington, NJ.

Antonio, Gene, *AIDS: Rage and Reality—Why Silence is Deadly*, Anchor Books, Dallas TX 1992.

Aquinas, St. Thomas, *Summa Theologica*, 5 Vols., Westminister, MD, Classics, 1981.

Baer, Randall N., *Inside the New Age Nightmare*, Lafayette, LA, Huntington House, Inc., 1989.

Bander, Peter, *The Prophecies of St. Malachy*, Tan Books, Rockford, IL, 1973.

Bebie, Father Philip, C.P., *The Warning*, Printed in 1986 with ecclesiastical permission.

Bessiers, S.J., Albert, *Wife, Mother and Mystic, Blessed Anna Maria Taigi*, Tan Books, 1970.

Bettwy, Sister Isabel,. *I am the Guardian of the Faith*, Patricia of Ecuador, Franciscan University Press, Steubenville, OH.

Borelli-Spann, Antonio A. & John R, *Our Lady at Fatima, Prophecies of Tragedy of Hope for America and the World*, Am, TFP, Box 823 Carmel, NY, 1985.

Brown, Michael H., *The Final Hour*, Faith Publishing, Milford, OH, 1992.

Carre', Marie, *AA-1025, The Memoirs of an Anti-Apostle*, Tan Books and Publishers, Rockford, IL.

Carter, Michelle, and Christensen, Michael, *The Children of Chernobyl—Hope from the Ashes*, Augsburg Fortress, Minneapolis, MN, 1993.

The Catholic World Report, November 1992, Ignatius Press, 2515 McAllister Street, San Francisco, CA.

Connell, Janice T., *The Visions of the Children*, St. Martin's Press, NY, 1992.

Connor, Edward, *Prophecy for Today*, Tan Books, 1984.

Coomaraswamy, Rama, MD., *The Problems With the New Mass*, Tan Books and Publishers, Rockford, IL, 1990.

Culleton, Rev. R. Gerald, *The Prophets and Our Times*, Tan Books, 1974.

Dale, Algina Stone, *The Outline of Sanity, The Life of G.K. Chesterton*, Williams Eerdmons Publishing Co., 1982.

Delaney, John J., *A Woman Clothed With the Sun*, Image Books, 1960.

De Marchi, I.M.C., John, *The Immaculate Heart, The True Story of Fatima*, Farrar, Strauss and Young, NY, 1952.

De Montfort, St. Louis Marie Grignion, *The Secret of the Rosary*, T.O.P., Montfort Publications, Bayshore, NY, 1965. Also, True *Devotion to Mary, and Letter to His Missionaries*, same source.

Devotion to Divine Innocence, Patricia of England, Signs of the Time, 6 Pidgeon Hill Drive, Suite 260, Sterling, VA, Newsletter Volume 1, 1990.

Dozule', *The Messages of Christ, The Glorious Cross in 1972*, Les Amis de la Glorious Cross, 171 rue de l'universite', 75007, Paris, France.

Dupont, Yves, *Catholic Prophecy*, Tan Books, Rockford, IL, 1970.

Dupont, Yves, *Prophecies and Portent*, Tenet Books, Hawthorn, Australia.

Dupont, Yves, *The Prophecies of La Fraudais*, Parts I, II, III, Tenet Books.

Faricy, Robert, S.J. and Pecoraio Luciana, *Mary Among Us, The Apparitions at Oliveto Citra*, 1989, Franciscan University Press, Steubenville, OH.

Farrell, Gerald, M.M., and Kosicki, George, C.S.B., *The Spirit and the Bride Say Come*, AMI Press, Asbury, NJ.

Fatima Family Messenger, October-December, 1992, Fatima Family Department, New Hope, KY.

Fatima in Lucia's Own Words, Postulation Center, Fatima, Portugal.

Flame of Love of the Immaculate Heart of Mary, Diary of a Third Order Carmelite, and The Victorious Queen of the World, Sister Natalia of Hungary, second edition, Two Hearts Books, Mountain View, CA, 1991.

Foglein, Stephen A., *The Age of One Fold and One Shepherd is Coming*, Atlas Books, Box 844, Mountain View, CA, 1981.

Francois, Robert, *O Children Listen to Me, Our Lady Teaches at Garabandal*, The Workers of Our Lady of Mount Carmel, PO Box 606, Lindenhurst, NY.

Freemasonry, Humanun Genus, Encyclical Letter by Pope Leo XIII, April 20, 1834, Servants of Jesus and Mary, Box 258, Constable, NY.

Garabandal, *The Warning and the Miracle, A Summary of Events, 1961-1965*, The Workers of Our Lady of Mount Carmel, P.O. Box 606, Lindenhurst, NY.

Gobbi, Don Stefano, *Our Lady Speaks to Her Beloved Priests, Marian Movement of Priests*, P.O. Box 8, St. Francis, ME, 1991 edition.

Golitsyn, Anatoli, *New Lies for Old*, 1984.

Gouin Abbe, *Sister Mary of the Cross, Sherpherdess of LaSalette*, Melanie Calvat, Marian Centre for Unitas, Catolica, 31, Parkdale, Wolverhampton, WVI 4TE, England.

Groiler Electronic Publishing, Inc., *The Electronic Encyclopedia*, 1990.

Haffert, John M, *Explosion of the Supernatural*, AMI Press, Washington, NJ, 1975.

Haffert, John M., *The Meaning of Akita*, 101 Foundation, P.O. Box 151, Asbury, NJ.

Hebert, Father Albert, S.M., *Prophecies! The Chastisement and the Purification*, P.O. Box 309, Paulina, LA.

Hebert, Father Albert, S.M., *Three Days of Darkness*, P.O. Box 309, Paulina, LA.

Jesus, King of All Nations, written and released by *Signs of the Time*, 6 Pidgeon Hill Drive, Suite 260, Sterling, VA, 20165, Volume 3, 1992.

Jesus and Mary Speak in Ireland, Messages to Christina Gallagher.

Johnston, Francis, Alexandrina, *The Agony and the Glory*, Veritas Pubs., Dublin, 1979, Tan Books, 1982.

Johnston, Francis, *Fatima: The Great Sign*, AMI Press, Washington, NJ, 1980. Published Under Agreement by Tan Books, Rockford, IL.

Johnston, Francis, *When Millions Saw Mary*, Augustin Pub. Co., Chulmleigh, Devon, United Kingdom, 1980.

Jongen, S.M.M., H., *Look—The Madonna is Weeping*, Montfort Pubs., Bayshore, NY, 1959.

Julka of Yugoslavia, *Jesus Calls Us, Volumes 1 and 3, Messages from 1945 to 1976*, Vol 1 Published 1990, Vol 3 published 1988 by In Wahrheit Und Treve, Postfach 279, CH-8401 Winterthur, Switzerland.

Kah, Gary H., *En Route to Global Occupation*, Huntington House Publishers, 1992.

Karminski, Stanley J, *Our Lady at Garabandal, Signs of the Times*, 6 Pidgeon Hill Drive, Suite 260, Sterling, VA, Volume 3, July 1991.

The Kingship of Christ, Quas Primas, Encyclical Letter of Pope Pius XI, December 11, 1925, Servants of Mary and Jesus, Box 258, Constable, NY.

Kosicki. George W., C.S.B., *Special Urgency of Mercy, Why Sister Faustina*? Franciscan University Press, Steubenville, OH, 1990.

Kowalska, Sister Faustina, Apostle of Divine Mercy, Marian Fathers, Stockbridge, MA.

Kowalska, Sister Faustina, *Divine Mercy in My Soul, The Diary of Sister Faustina*, Marian Press, Stockbridge, MA, 1987.

Laffineur, Fr. Materne, and Pelletier, M.T., *Star on the Mountain*, Our Lady of Mount Carmel de Garabandal, Inc., Lindenhurst, NJ, 1969.

Langley, Richard, *The Signs of the Time*, June 24, 1992.

The Language of Silence, Apparitions in Shoubra and Zeitun, Signs of the Times, Sterling, VA, Newsletter Volume 1, 1989.

LaSalette, the Apparitions of the Blessed Virgin on the Mountain in 1846, reproduction without commentary, 12th Ave. of Grain d'or, 49600, Beaupreau, France.

Laurentin, Father Rene, *The Apparitions of the Blessed Virgin Mary Today*, (Revised Edition) 1991, Veritas Pubs.

Lemius, J. B., Reverend, *A Catechism of Modernism*, Founded on the Encyclical Pascendi Dominici Gregis, by Pope Pius X, Tan Books and Publishers, Rockford, IL, 1981.

Leonardi, Mother Elena Patricia, House of the Kingdom of God and Reconciliation of Souls, *Mary's Triumph, Years of Revelation*, Via dei Gracchi, 29 B. Roma, Italia.

Lopez, Theresa, *Denver Apparitions Return Focus to Fatima, Signs of the Times*, 6 Pidgeon Hill Drive, Suite 260, Sterling, VA, Volume 4, 1992.

Lubbock Rosary Messages, Queen of Mercy, 1992, The Queen of Mercy Center, Lubbock, TX.

Mariamante, *The Apostolate of Holy Motherhood*, Compiled and Edited by Mark I. Miravalle, S.T.D., Published by the Riehle Foundation, Milford, Ohio, 1991.

Martin, Malachi, *The Keys of This Blood*, 1990, Simon and Schuster, New York, NY.

Mbukanma, Jude, Dominican, edited by, *On the Eucharist: A Divine Appeal, Revelations to Sister Anna Ali*, D.O.J.G.S., published by Newborne Enterprises Ltd., P.O. Box 21006, U.I. PO Ibadan, Nigeria, 1992.

McAlvany, Donald, S., *Toward a New World Order*, 192, Western Pacific Publishing, P.O. Box, Phoenix, AZ, 85071.

Menendez, Sister Josefa, *The Way of Divine Love*, Tan Books, 1973.

Miceli, Vincent, P, S.J., *The Antichrist*, Roman Catholic Books, P.O. Box 255, Harrison, NY.

Michel, Frere, *The Whole Truth About Fatima*: Volume I: Science and the Facts, 1989 Volume 2: The Secret and the Church, 1989 Volume 3: The Third Secret, 1990 Volume 4: In the End My Immaculate Heart Will Triumph-In Preparation, Immaculate Heart Publications, Box 1028, Buffalo, NY.

Mother of the Hidden Wounds, Messages to Patricia of England, Divine Innocence Trust, 9 Broomfield Road, Surbiton, Surrey, KT5, 9AZ, England.

Newman, Cardinal John Henry, *Apologia Pro Vita Sua*, Doubleday & Company, 1956.

Odell, Catherine M., *Those Who Saw Her*, Our Sunday Visitor Publishing Division, 1986, Huntington, IN.

Our Holy Mother of Virtues, Messages for the Harvest, Volume I, 1992, Apparitions at the Mother Cabrini Shrine, Denver, CO.

Our Lady of America, first printed February 2, 1960, notes from a personal diary, author anonymous.

Our Lady of Fatima's Peace Plan From Heaven, Tan Books, P.O. Box 424, Rockford, Illinois.

Our Lady of Kibeho, Produced by the Marian Guadalupe Press, 6 Whitestrand Park, Galway, Ireland.

Our Lady of Lourdes Shrine in Mellary Grotto, County Waterford, Ireland, Signs of the Times, 6 Pidgeon Hill Drive, Suite 260, Sterling, VA.

Our Lady of the Rosary, The Messages of Fatima, Signs of the Time, 6 Pidgeon Hill Drive, Suite 260, Sterling, VA, May 1989.

Our Lady's Wounds and Eucharist, Purification to Mankind, Patricia of England, Newsletter Volume 3, April 1991, *Signs of the Time*, 6 Pidgeon Hill Drive, Suite 260, Sterling, VA.

O'Reilly, Father James P, *The Story of LaSalette*, J.S. Paluch Co. Inc., 1953.

Our Sunday's Visitor Catholic Encyclopedia, 1991, 220 Noll Plaza, Huntington, IN.

Ottaviani, Cardinal Alfredo, and Bacci, Cardinal Antonio, *The Ottaviani Intervention*, A Short Critical Study of the Mass, Tan Books, Rockford, IL.

Pascual, P. Sanchez-Ventura, *Garabandal, The Apparitions*, St. Michael's Garabandal Center, 889 Palo Verde Ave., Pasadena, CA, 1966.

Pelletier, A.A., Joseph A., *Our Lady Comes to Garabandal*, Assumption Pubs., Worcester, MA, 1971, and *God Speaks at Garabandal*, 1970.

Pelletier, Joseph, A.A., *The Warning of Garabandal*, An interview, The Workers of Our Lady of Mount Carmel, P.O. Box 606, Lindenhurst, NY.

Perleman, Ida of Amsterda, *Our Lady of All Nations and the Links Between Akita, Signs of the Times*, 6 Pidgeon Hill Drive, Suite 260, Sterling, VA.

Perleman, Ida, *Visionary of Amsterdam, The Hour of The Lady of All Peoples*, Earl Massecar translated from the French, L'Armee de Marie, P.O Box 95, Limoilou, Quebec, Canada, G1L, 4TB., 1978.

Ratzinger, Cardinal Joseph, Messori Vittorio, *The Ratzinger Report*, Ignatius Press, San Francisco, CA, 1985.

Quito, Ecuador, *Our Lady of Good Fortune in Quito, Ecuador, 1634*, leaflet by Gregorian Press, Holy Family Monastery, 261 Cross Keys Road, Berlin, NJ.

Roberdel, Pierre, *Prophecies of La Fraudais*, 53150 Montsours, France.

Robertson, Pat, *The New World Order*, Thomas Nelson, Inc. Publishing, 1991.

Rosa Mystica Speaks to the World, Signs of the Time, 6 Pidgeon Hill Drive, Suite 260, Sterling, VA.

San Nicolas, Argentina, Messages edited and published by Faith Publishing, PO Box 237, Milford, Ohio.

Schmoger, Reverend Carl, CSSR., *Emmerich, Anne Catherine,* Volume 1 and 2, Tan Books, Rockford, IL.

The Secret Letter of Fatima, Two Hearts Books and Publishers, P.O. Box 844, Mountain View, CA.

Shamon, Rev. Albert, *Apocalypse, The Book for Our Times,* Faith Publishing Company, PO Box 237, Milford, OH.

Signs of the Times, 6 Pidgeon Hill Drive, Suite 260, Sterling, VA, 20165. Publications are quarterly in the form of a magazine reporting on Marian apparitions and spiritual issues of our day. Address and phone are in the order form in the back of this book. Many of the topics in this book have been reported in the form of an article, newsletter, or story/magazine.

Sims, Sister Margaret Catherin, CSJ, *The Apparitions in Betania, Venezuela,* Medjugorje Messengers, 85 Bethany Road, Framingham, MA.

Stimme Des Glaubens, *The Pope on the Secret Letter of Fatima,* a speech delivered in Fulda, Germany.

The Syllabus of Errors, The Encyclical of Quanta Cura, issued by Pope Pius IX in 1864, and a *Syllabus Condemning Modernism (Lamentabili Sane),* issued by Pope Pius X in 1907, The Remnant, 2539 Morrison Ave., St. Paul, MN, 55117.

Terelya, Josyp, and Michael Brown, *Witness,* Faith Publishing Company, Milford, OH, 1991. The vision of Terelya at Marmora, Ontario, Canada, was sent to the authors by Michael Brown, coauthor of *Witness* and author of *The Final Hour,* 1992.

Vincent, R., *Please Come Back to Me and My Son,* 1992, Ireland's Eye Publication, Mullingar, Co., Westmeath, Ireland.

Wallace, Mary Joan, *Medjugorje-Its Backround and Messages,* Follow Me Communications, 18600 Main Street, Suite 210, Huntington, Beach, CA, 1991.

To the Priests, Our Lady's Beloved Sons, Marian Movement of Priests, P.O. Box 8, St. Francis, ME, 1991.

Yasuda, Teiji, OSV., Akita: *The Tears and Messages,* 101 Foundation, P.O. Box 151, Asbury, NJ.

Index

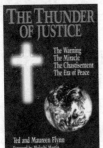

The Thunder of Justice
by Ted & Maureen Flynn

Order Form

"This book has changed my life."

That's been the response of readers of **The Thunder of Justice.** Nearly all are profoundly changed by reading the words of warning and hope given today by Our Lady. Now you can bring these same powerful words to your friends and loved ones. Share Heaven's urgent warnings and ultimate promise of victory—by sending them their own copy of **The Thunder of Justice.** Use the convenient order form below!

Now let it change your friends.

Order today! Send your mail orders to **MaxKol Communications, 109 Executive Drive * Suite D * Sterling, VA 20166.** Phone orders: 703-709-0200. Fax orders: 703-709-1499

❏ Yes, I want to order a copy of Thunder of Justice for $15.95 plus shipping and handling. I have included an additional $15.95 plus $1.00 shipping and handling per book to cover the cost of sending more than one to the same address. (Spanish available—$15.95 plus S&H)

My Name _____

Address _____

City, State, Zip _____

Phone (h)_____(o) _____

Recipient of book (if different from sender above)

My Name _____

Address _____

City, State, Zip _____

Phone (h)_____(o) _____

MASTERCARD/VISA/CHECK

From the Publishers of *The Thunder of Justice. . .*

Order Form

❏ Yes, I want to be kept up-to-date on all of Our Lady's appearances around the world. I've enclosed $24 to subscribe to *Signs of Our Times* magazine. I understand I will receive four issues per year, plus special updates and reports (Canadian subscriptions $35 per year, other foreign subscriptions $40).

❏ Yes, please send me both **SOT Binders, Volumes I** and **II,** containing all issues of *Signs of Our Times* from April 1989 through December 1993 ($54.95 includes shipping and handling).

❏ Yes, please send me the **SOT Binder Volume I** containing all issues of the **SOT** newsletters from April 1989 through December 1992 ($34.95 includes S&H.)

❏ Yes, please send me the **SOT Binder Volume II** containing all issues of the **SOT** magazine from January 1993 through December 1993 ($20 includes S&H)

❏ Yes, please send me the **SOT Binder Volume III** containing all issues of the **SOT** magazine from January 1994 through December 1994 ($20 includes S&H)

❏ Yes, please send me the **SOT** magazine from January 1995 through December 1995 ($30 includes S&H)

Donations

❏ Yes, l want to help spread Our Lady's messages of peace and conversion throughout the world. I wish to donate $_____ per month to become a **Monthly Partner for Our Lady's Peace Plan.**

❏ Yes, I want to help spread Our Lady's messages of peace and conversion throughout the world. I've enclosed a one-time donation of $_____ to help your apostolate.

My Name _____

Address _____

City, State, Zip _____

Phone (h)_____ (o)_____

Recipient of Subscription (if different from above)

My Name _____

Address _____

City, State, Zip _____

Phone (h)_____ (o)_____

Payment is by

❏ Check

❏ MasterCard _____Exp. _____

❏ Visa_____Exp. _____

Signature for credit card orders

Order today! Send your mail orders to:

Signs of the Times Apostolate
109 Executive Drive * Suite D * Sterling, VA 20166
Phone orders: 703-742-3939. Fax orders: 703-742-0808

NOTES

NOTES

Ted Flynn is President of **MaxKol Communications,** a publishing and International Management Consulting firm. He has degrees from the University of Massachusetts and American University, and he has attended the University of Fribourg, Switzerland, and the London School of Economics. He has travelled in over forty-five countries and has a Master's Degree in Economics.

Maureen Flynn is the President of ***Signs of the Times***, a nonprofit lay apostolate distributing Catholic literature and information on Marian apparitions worldwide. She has earned degrees from Boston College and Catholic University. She has a Master's Degree in Social Work.